By the 1920s and 30s, French Impressionism was firmly woven into the art of all but the most recalcitrant Realist artists, art critics and bureaucrats. In truth, even though the old masters, Raphael, Reni, the Carracci and Rubens were acknowledged, these artists only affected art education and training. More influential, and probably through the Moscow art institute named after him, was the resurgence in interest (or rehabilitation) in the plebeian Realism of Vasilii Ivanovich Surikov (1848-1916). Once the Soviet artists began professional careers, the French rural Realists like Leon L'hermitte, Julien Dupre and Jules Bastien-Lepage really held sway.[20] In fact, the Pushkin Museum's Lepage painting was a particular favorite of a number of Social Realists. The art of the Proto-Impressionists and early Impressionists, particularly figurative painters, such as Edouard Manet, Edgar Degas, Henri Fantin-LaTour, Frédéric Bazille and Gustave Caillebotte, also dominated discourse.

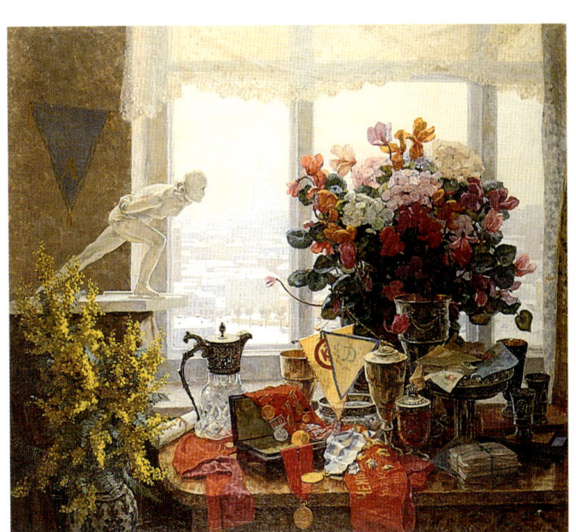

8. ***Still-life with the Medals of M. Isaakova*** 1951
Anatoli Yurevich Nikich-Krilichevski
58 x 65 inches
Oil on canvas
private collection

It should be remembered that Impressionism is essentially a Realist art form and after its initial radicalism, eventually evolved into an acceptable, even conservative addition to world art. Some say a major break came with the formal distortions and subjectivism of the Post-Impressionists. The Post-Impressionist tree had many stylistic branches, out of Cezanne grew the Formalist branch, from Van Gogh came the Expressionists. Symbolism grew out of Paul Gauguin's work, and from Toulouse-Lautrec came the Decadents. These were the despised "French Impressionists" that led directly to "Modern" art, claimed Russian officials.

The Classical response by *AKhRR* and the Art Unions to these perceived aggressions should not be interpreted in the same manner as "Salon" art of western Europe, which was rejected as being bourgeois. While violently opposing Post-Impressionism and the avant-garde, it promoted academic art training and was accepting of traditional, yet modified Impressionist modes. As the years passed, this amalgam of Academicism and Impressionism began to assert itself in a uniquely Soviet manner.

The need to communicate with a mass audience in Soviet society spawned the emphasis on relevance of motif and intelligibility. This in turn led to numerous themes relating directly to the people: the portrait, domestic genre, collective farms (*kolkhoz*), major events, sports and the industrial/urban subject. Though painted later, Andrei Korotkov's ***Soccer Football Match*** (PLATE 111) is a perfect example of a populace pictorial statement combining Classical with Impressionist techniques. A technique evolved allowing the artist to engage his audiences most effectively—a loosely painted Realism which was both non-academic and non-modernist. Other elements included obligatory optimism, Party spirit, typicality and concrete reality. By the late 1930s, such a broad-based style began to emerge.

Like other arts organizations, *AKhRR* was dismantled in 1932. It should be remembered that, although it did defer to the Party line, it was an independent group of artists, and not an official government or Party organ. As such, it was dissolved and became the model for the later art unions of the Socialist Realist era.[21] In fact, many members were quickly elevated to prominent positions in the new art unions founded during the 1930s.

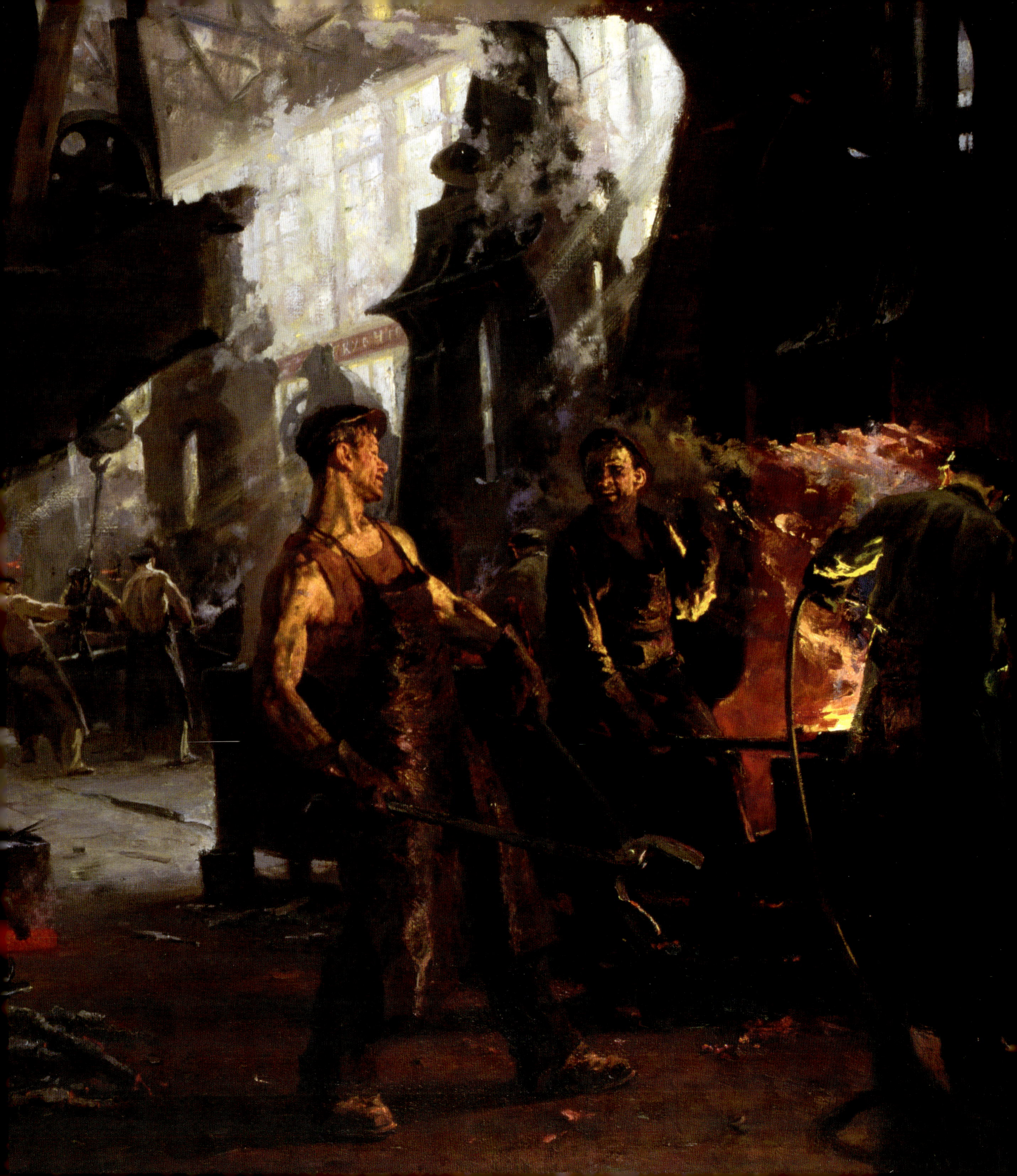

PROTO-SOCIALIST REALISM: AKHRR

The problem of culture cannot be resolved as quickly as political and military objectives ...

Lenin, 1921

The years just preceding the October Revolution of 1917 featured the emergence of a number of Modernist art movements including Primitivism, Rayonism, Cubo-Futurism, Suprematism and Constructivism. Once the Bolsheviks overthrew the Duma, the radical Modernist artists gained greater prestige. Avant-garde groups, such as the *Proletkults*, attempted to wrestle control over the artistic organs of the country. Each group vied with the other for the leading role of building the new socialist man. Now the new dialectic in art was between the Futurists and the Realists. A middle group called *OST* or Society of Easel Painters attempted to bond avant-garde and traditional elements of Russian art into a Revolutionary Development.

Anatoli V. Lunacharski, Commissar of Education for *Izo NarKomPros* (People's Commissariat for Education), fired the first volley in the Realists' assault on Russian Futurism. Though generally even-handed, it was his responsibility to find a philosophy of cultural development for the new Socialist experiment. He understood from experience that Modernist aesthetics were irrelevant to Bolshevism and a Proletarian state. Addressing the Communist International in 1921 he declared:

> "The Proletariat will also continue the art of the past, but will begin from some healthy stage, like the Renaissance... If we are talking of the masses, the natural form of their art will be the traditional and classical one, clear to the point of transparency, resting...on healthy, convincing Realism and on eloquent, transparent Symbolism in decorative and monumental forms."[15]

Certainly the most important development in Russian art leading directly toward Socialist Realism was the organizing of the Moscow-based group *AKhRR*, the Association of Arts of Revolutionary Russia, in May of 1922. First called Association of Artists Studying Revolutionary Life, its declared goal was to depict the Red Army, workers, peasants, revolutionary activities and heroes of labor. Their acknowledged goal was to base their works on a contemporary world view. They sought to depict their own times, though in a decidedly traditional manner.

7. ***Still-life with the Medals of M. Isaakova*** 1951
Anatoli Yurevich Nikich-Krilichevski
Detail of plate 8

AKhRR was by far the largest and most powerful of the arts organizations formed during the 1920s. It stood in stark contrast to the rampant avant-gardism of the day. Members criticized as decadent late pre-revolutionary artists such as the Fauvists, Cubists and Futurists. This attitude was forcefully declared:

> "The Great October Revolution, in liberating the creative forces of the people, has aroused the consciousness of the masses and the artists—the spokesmen of the people's spiritual life. . . We will provide a true picture of events and not abstract concoctions discrediting our Revolution in the face of the international Proletariat."[16]

They believed, at that time, that foreign influences were detrimental to the development of a pure and truly Soviet style of painting. They felt that French art of a Modernist sort was particularly dissolute. Art after Cezanne was considered corrupt. *AKhRR* rejected apolitical stances as being rootless. Instead, members preferred art patriotic in origin, Realistic in style and devoted to the cause of the Revolution.[17]

It attempted to establish a continuity in art of the Russian tradition, especially linked with the *Peredvizhniki* because of their social concern and the masterly quality of their paintings. A number of former Itinerants joined the ranks of *AKhRR* as the best position to hold in the new social order of Revolutionary Russia. They could not induce Ilya Repin to return to Moscow from his home in Finland, so they settled on the more academic Isaak Brodski as their exemplar for the period.[18]

AKhRR held a number of exhibitions, published catalogues and a journal, *Iskusstvo v massy* (Art for the Masses), from 1929 until it was dissolved in 1932. *AKhRR* was the major source for inspiration for the future Socialist Realist art movement. Some of its more noted artists were N.A. Kasatkin, Abram E. Arkhipov, Sergei Malyutin, Konstantin Yuon, Alexander Grigoriev, Pavel Radimov, Georgi Ryazhski, Evgeni Katsman, M. Grekov, Serafima Ryangina, Igor Grabar, Aleksandr Gerasimov, F. Bogorodski and Boris Ioganson.

It should be noted that a substantial number of these artists had distinctly Impressionist, though conservative, tendencies. The general condemnation of Impressionism by *AKhRR* was not so much directly against the 1874 Impressionism of Monet, Renoir and Degas, as it was toward what we called Post-Impressionism and French Modernism in general. Artists like Cezanne, Matisse and Picasso were objects of heated ridicule. Some contemporary critics, like Matthew C. Bown and Brandon Taylor, understand that it was not French Impressionism itself, but the later mechanisms secured from it that the official circles abhorred:

> By the end of the 1930s, the official critical and historical definition of Realism had narrowed to exclude even stylistic devices derived from French Impressionism, a movement much loved by Russian artists...[18]

Development of Socialist Realism

The interplay of several factors summoned Soviet art from an avant-garde future. Some of these developments would infuse Socialist Realism with an Impressionist twist. The foremost influence was the fact that both V.I. Lenin and Joseph Stalin enjoyed conservative Realistic paintings — they disliked the avant-garde and suffered a xenophobia alien to Western culture. Modernist obscurities and Decadence were an anathema to the Soviet need for a powerful art which could move the masses. According to Alan Bird:

> Stalin had his finger on the common pulse and sensed the innate conservatism of the workers, not least in their attitudes to the arts. He saw all aspects of avant-garde culture, including painting, as subversive infiltrations of the purity of Soviet life. [22]

The Communist functionaries now resolutely rejected the Marxist avant-garde artists such as El Lissitsky, Kazimir Malevich, Alexander Rodchenko, M. Larionov and Vladimir Tatlin, et al. Those who wished to be independent revolutionaries or wished privilege because of past service to the Party were persecuted. Stalin's aesthetico-political coup was particularly ruthless with those who had previously been the Party's most ardent supporters. If the avant-garde had remained purely formal and not political it might have continued, but once it was accused, even its formality galled. R.C. Williams perhaps overstates the situation:

> The Russian avant-garde was born as a protest against bourgeois pre-revolutionary Russian society. It died of old age in the new revolutionary Russia it helped invent. [23]

The factional fighting between the different artistic groups, each seeking dominance in a hoped for coalition or cooperative of the arts, finally forced the Communist Party's hand. Their independence was compromised by a decree from the Central Committee in April of 1932 — "On the Reorganization of Literary and Artistic Organizations." All artistic groups, such as the avant-garde *Proletkults* and the Realist *AKhRR* were to form a single platform. It was declared that all "creative workers" would soon be organized into professional unions of artists, architects, writers, etc. The declaration was intended to end factional strife and subsumed all cultural activity under Party leadership (*partiinost*).

9. ***In the Stalin Factory*** 1949
Mikhail A. Kostin
Detail of plate 10

The 1932 decree was well received by most artistic groups, who saw for themselves a preeminent role in the future culture of the Soviet Union. The functions of these artistic groups were assumed for the most part by the Moscow Section of the Union of Soviet Artists, *MOSSKh*. Now the Party could directly implement ideological control, provide minimal subsistence, workspace and art supplies, and certain avenues for commissions.

However, Stalin had a more practical vision for the arts, which followed Lenin's phrase, "part of the common cause of the Party."[24] This subordination would further give "power to the Soviets" to build "Socialism in one country."[25] In explaining the crossfire, Boris Groys maintains "that the aestheticization of politics was merely the Party's reaction to the avant-garde's politicization of aesthetics."[26]

A consequential development occurred during the first All Union Congress of Soviet Writers held in Moscow during the summer of 1934. Since literature was the most articulate of the arts, it was felt that what was decided at this conference would apply to the arts throughout Soviet culture. There it was proclaimed by Secretary of the Communist Party, Andrei A. Zhdanov and others, that Socialist Realism was the approved creative method for Soviet artists to engineer an image of the ideal socialist man. Zhdanov helped with the writers' constitution which states that Socialist Realism "demands from the artist a true and historically concrete depiction of reality in its revolutionary development...combined with the task of educating workers in the spirit of Communism." [27]

While Stalin himself was not present at the conference, he insisted that the arts should include "cultures, national in form and Socialist in content." The only visual artist to speak at the Congress was Igor E. Grabar, an Impressionist painter and *AKhRR* member who fully endorsed Socialist Realism. A former member of the *Peredvizhniki* and Union of Russian Artists, he was highly respected in several camps. Like Zhdanov, he espoused the concept of an "ideological transformation and education of the working people in the spirit of Socialism."[28] As much as anyone, his corrected Impressionism served as a basis for the quintessential Socialist Realist style.

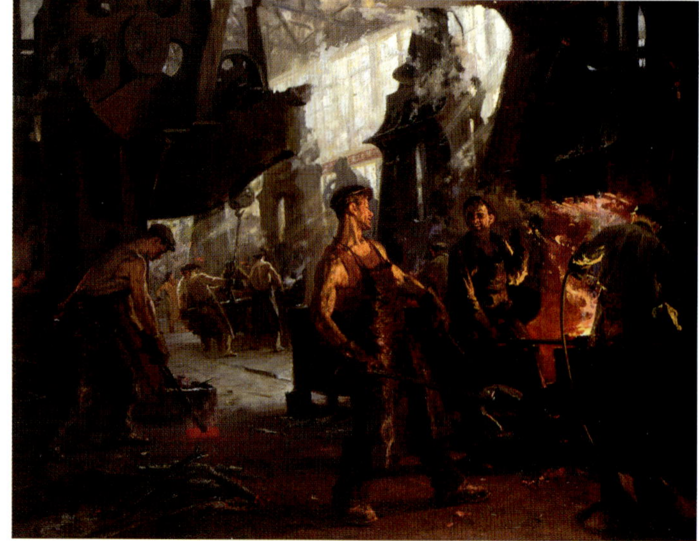

A large number of artists were soon galvanized who also believed that they were agents of social change. Unlike Nazi art, which was decreed from above by the will of the dictator, Soviet art grew more naturally from the ferment of the times. Alan Bird proposes:

> Far from being a doctrine imposed on the country there is ample proof that Socialist Realism originated among the older intelligentsia with socialist sympathies and that it was a natural and logical evolution of the Proletarian articles of faith. [29]

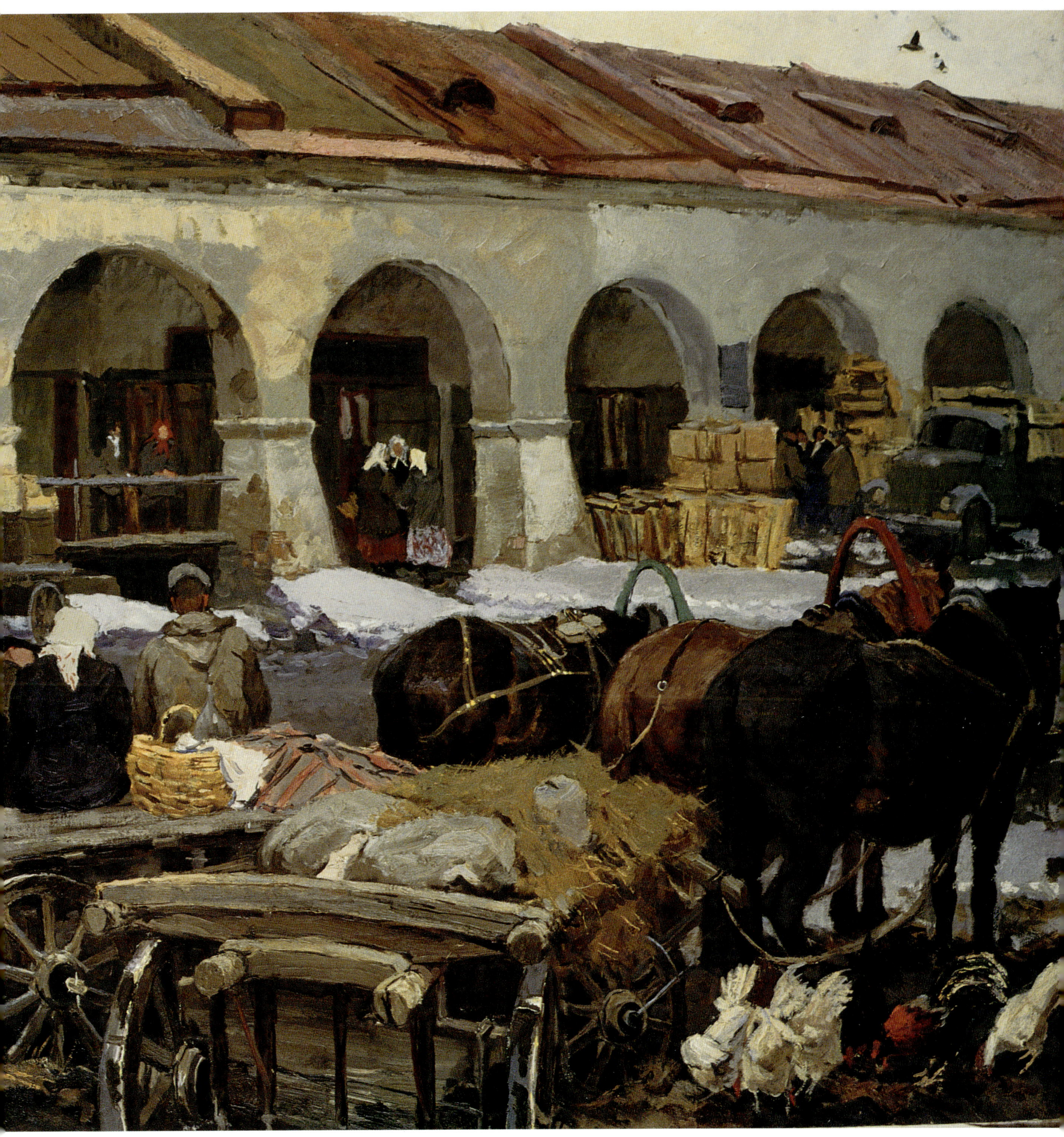

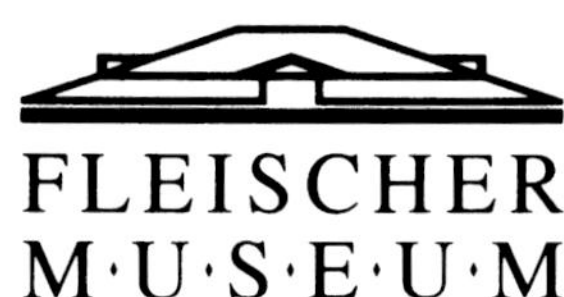

FRONT COVER: ***Young Pioneer at the Door*** 1955
Fedor V. Shapaev
58-1/2 x 27 inches, oil on canvas
private collection

FRONTISPIECE: ***The Gingerbread Arcade*** 1956
Vladimir F. Stozharov
41 x 83 inches, oil on canvas
private collection

BACK COVER: ***Azov Steel*** 1957
Konstantin A. Shurupov
35 x 44-3/4 inches, oil on canvas mounted
private collection

Published on the occasion of the exhibition:

HIDDEN TREASURES:
RUSSIAN AND SOVIET IMPRESSIONISM
1930-1970s

January 15 - April 30, 1994

Sponsored by

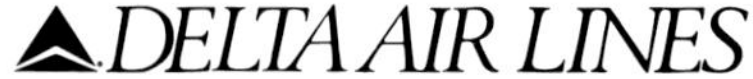

exclusive U.S. airline serving Moscow and St. Petersburg

ISBN: 0-9617882-5-9
FFCA Publishing Company

TABLE OF CONTENTS

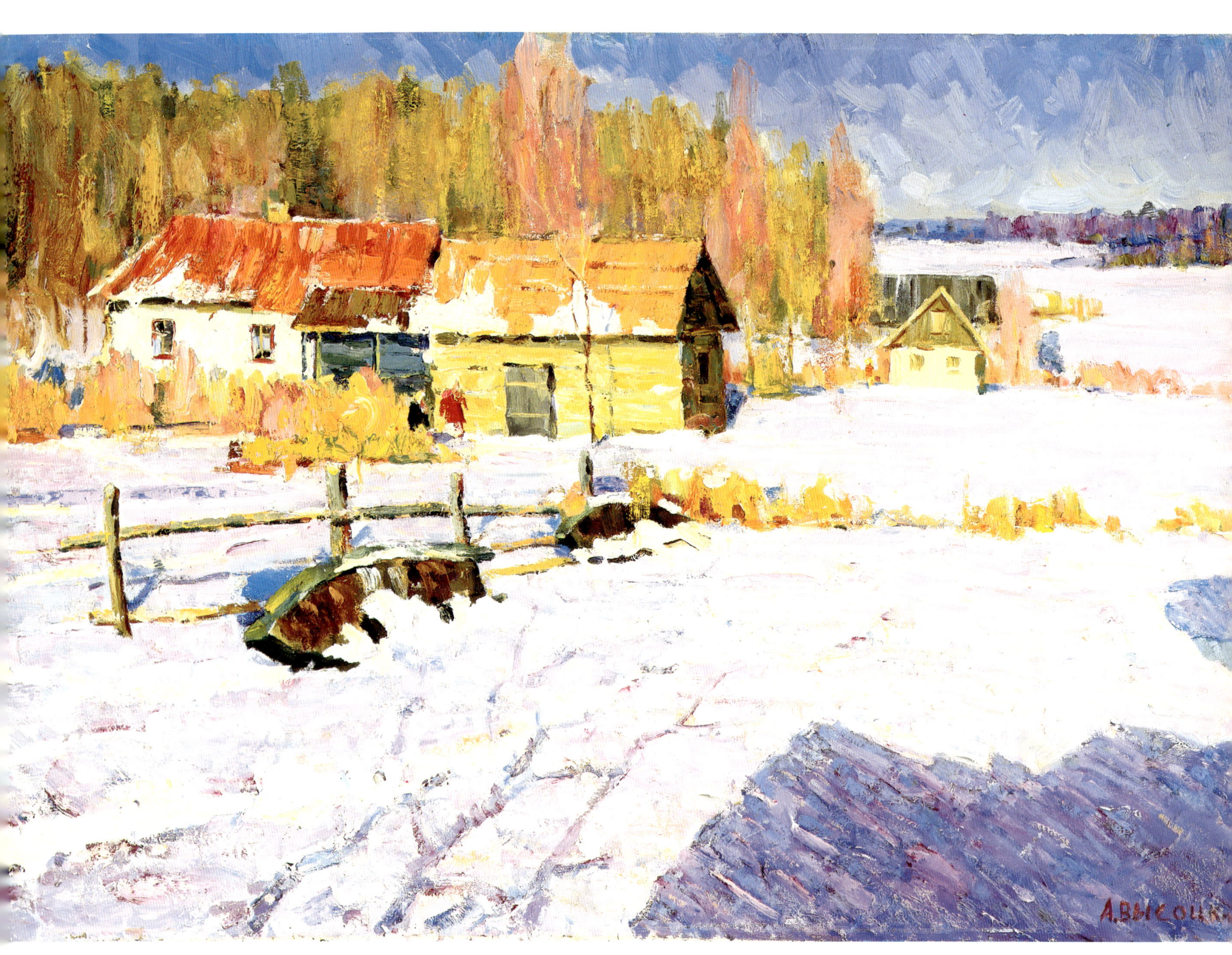
А.ВЫСОЦК

Preface

The Fleischer Museum opened its doors in the summer of 1990 as the first museum dedicated to the California School of American Impressionism. Its goals are first and foremost to preserve these works of art and to give these artists and this period the recognition we believe they truly deserve. The Museum also seeks to create a scholarly forum for education. To this end we have created, and continue to create, a comprehensive art library and slide repository of this period. Finally, the Museum continues its commitment to assist in enhancing the cultural aspects of our community. To accomplish this goal, we have provided a permanent home for our collection and offer the viewing of these masterworks and other exhibitions to the public free of charge.

My husband, Mort, and I began collecting the California School of American Impressionism as we were influenced by and loved the French Impressionists, but were interested in developing a collection of art with American origins. Upon being introduced to the California School, which had been long overlooked, we fell in love with the work and began collecting paintings by the artists who comprised this period. The works in our collection, many of which were painted plein air (outdoors), include landscapes, architectural and figurative subjects, as well as still lifes. They are steeped with light and bright colors, and we believe they are beautiful and uplifting to the spirit.

While our focus for the Fleischer Collection remains on California Impressionism, we have begun to broaden our perspective as we were introduced to still another period of exciting art that has been inaccessible to the West for a period of over fifty years. The work is of Russian origin and is referred to as Russian and Soviet Realism depicted in an Impressionistic style. As with the instant love we felt for the California paintings, this art work struck a similar chord. From the late 1930s, the Soviets commissioned its preeminent artists to create on canvas the Utopia they believed Communism would achieve for the Soviet Union. For more than 40 years, these artists painted with passion, creating their contribution to furthering the cause. For this reason, this art has an inherent honesty that confirms its unique historical importance. The artistic quality of the works clearly shows the mastery the artists attained. The works are not only historical, but are bold, beautiful, steeped in light and dramatically appealing.

1. ***March*** 1970
Anatoli Ivanovich Vysotski
Oil on canvas
25-5/8 x 39-7/8 inches
Fleischer Museum Collection

During the period between 1930 and 1980, much of the cultural life in the Communist Soviet Union was denied Western exposure. The demise of Communism, the lifting of the Iron Curtain and the movement towards freedom and democracy of the newly formed Commonwealth of Independent States has allowed the world the opportunity to experience a unique and important historical past through the art work.

The Soviet paintings, the window to this world, cover a range of subject matter that include bucolic vistas and industrialized scenes along with sensitive portraits and still lifes. Many of the works glorify the common laborer: steel workers, farmers, milkmaids, builders and loggers. Others depict landscapes, family and social life and a few portray political figures, although any political message is obscured or lost altogether.

We are grateful to Ray E. Johnson of Overland Galleries who has spent many dedicated years acquiring the work and who introduced us to these treasures, thus giving rise to our museum collection expansion and this exhibition. Our appreciation is extended to those private individuals who so willingly contributed their works for this exhibit. Further, we wish to recognize Vern G. Swanson, of the Springville Museum of Art, for writing the comprehensive editorial that follows and Kathy Verplank, of the Fleischer Museum, for compiling the information to produce this book.

The exceptional quality of Russian and Soviet Impressionism astounds and overpowers us, consequently, as a small private Museum with flexible agendas, there was minimal discussion between my husband and myself about the idea of an exhibition of Russian Impressionism. You will find these artists masters of artistic creations, whether it is portrait genre, still lifes or historical subjects. Their canvases exude an inherent, truthful spirit of strength, courage and pride of the common man.

Donna Fleischer
Executive Director
Fleischer Museum
Scottsdale, Arizona

Hidden Treasures:

Russian and Soviet Impressionism

— 1930 - 1970s —

Vern Grosvenor Swanson

Preface by
Donna Fleischer

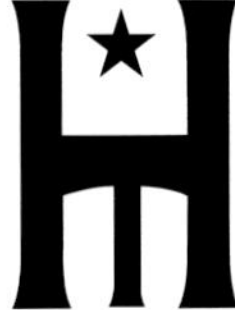

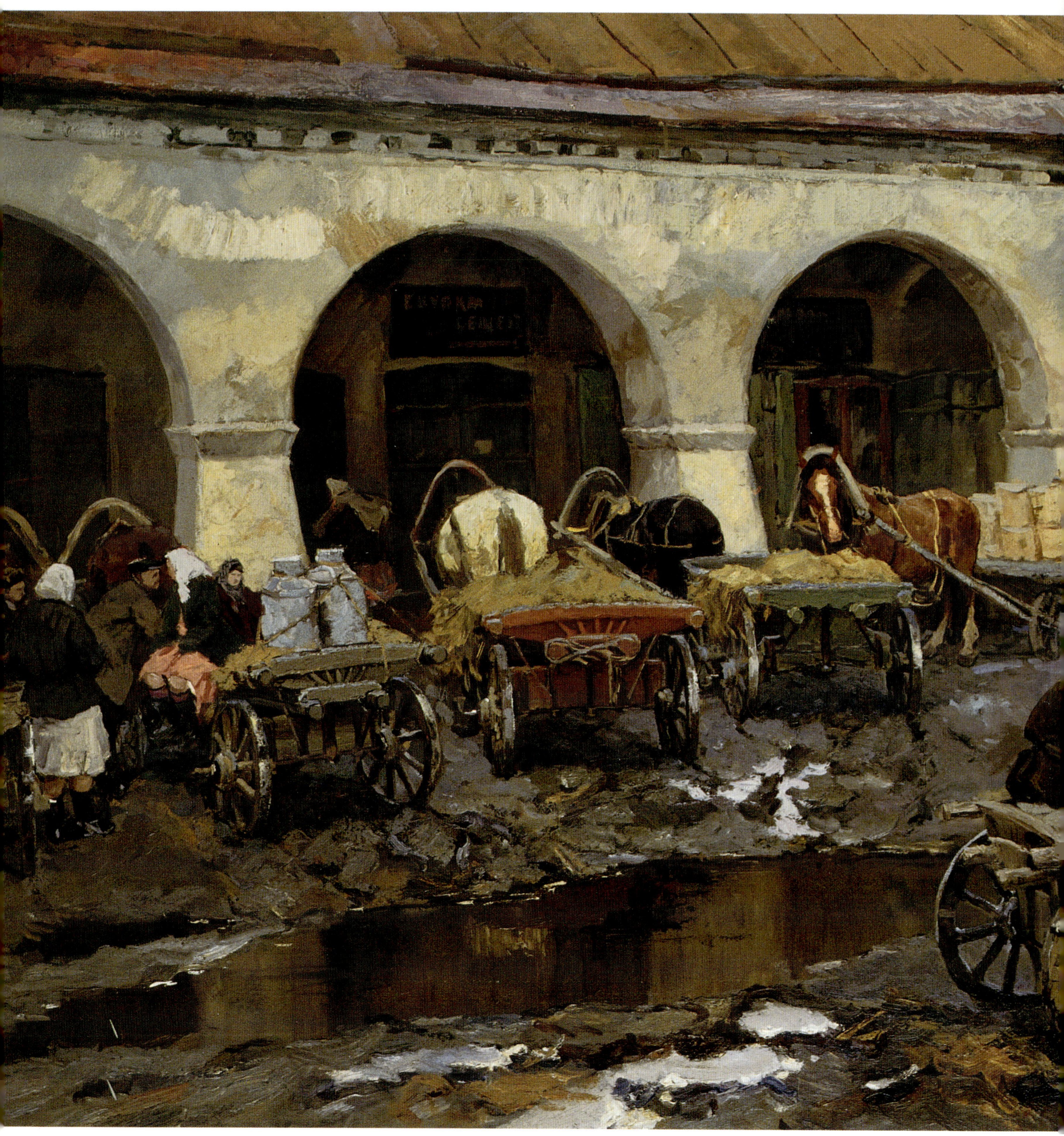

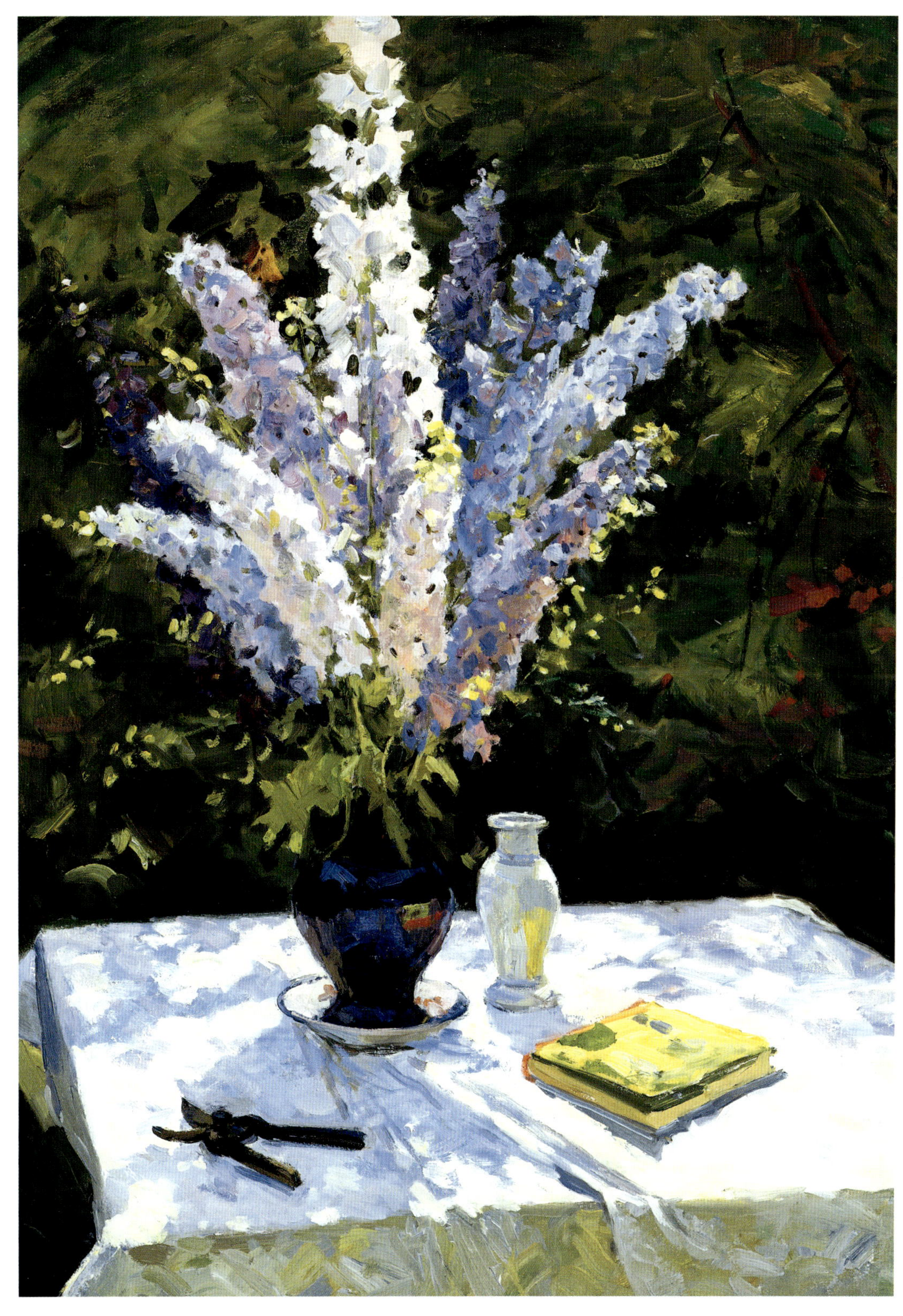

2. ***In the Garden: Delphiniums*** 1950s
Pavel Georgievich Markov
Oil on canvas
48-7/8 x 35-5/16 inches
Fleischer Museum Collection

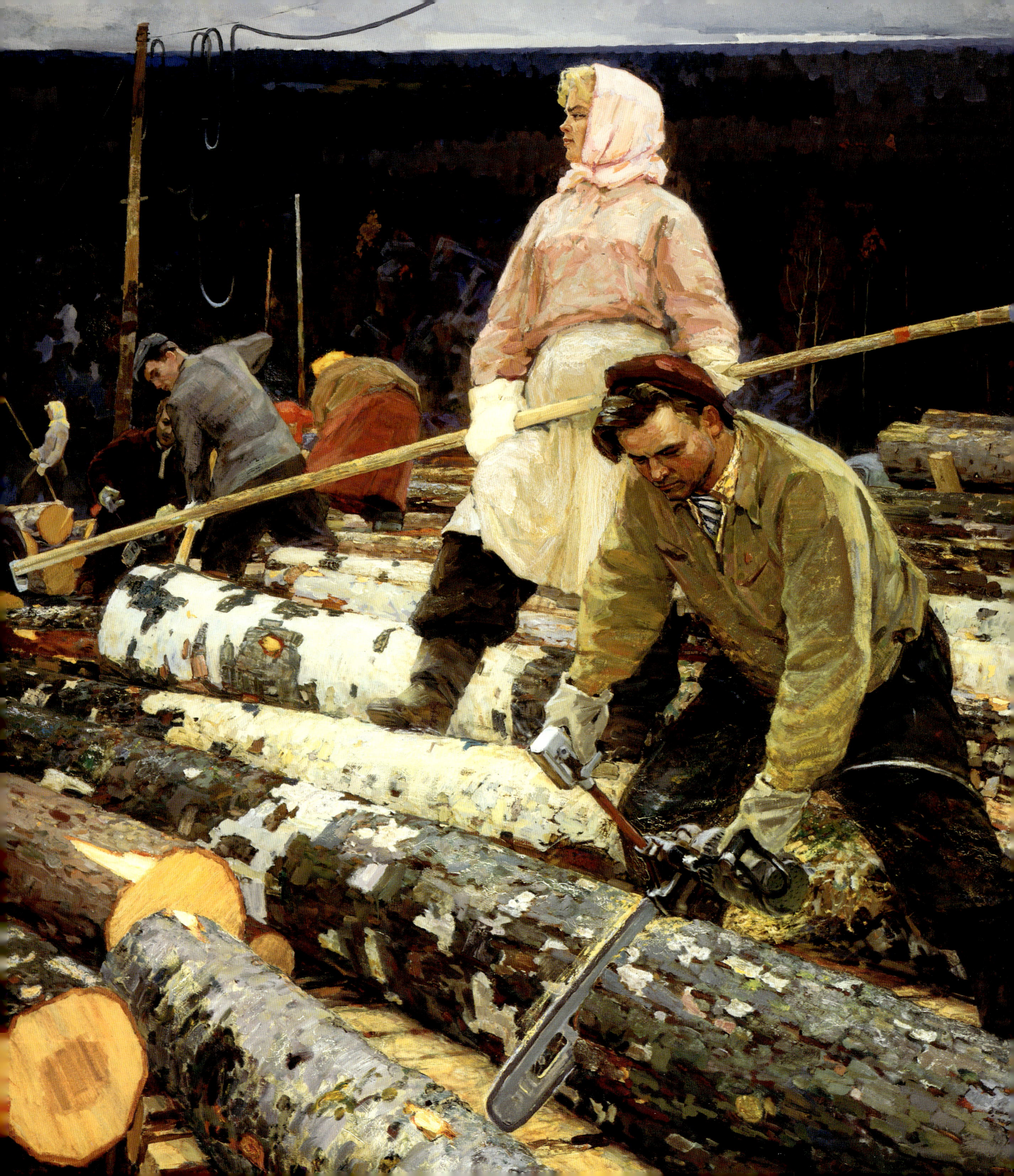

SOVIET IMPRESSIONISM

The disarming title of this volume may evoke visions of Giverny at Gorki, La Grenouillère in Leningrad or Monet in Moscow. But such is not the case for art during the Soviet period. The Soviets had their own brand of Impressionism. Its pedigree stretches back to seventeenth century Dutch art, through the Englishmen, Turner and Constable, to the Barbizon School, Rural-Impressionism, Proto-Impressionism of Eugene Boudin and Edouard Manet to French Impressionism itself.

Soviet Impressionism is not French Impressionism. It is Russian in several unique ways. Essentially, it is masculine whereas French Impressionism is quite feminine. French Impressionism was basically bourgeois, while Soviet Impressionism was proletarian. French Impressionism was primarily an aesthetic movement and did not carry the moral or social force of Soviet Socialist Realist art, which was more of a method and mind set than a definite style. The Russianization of Impressionism might be called "Working-Class Impressionism." It was built upon an entirely different *raisonne d'etre* from its Western Impressionistic models. It is the examination of this aspect of Soviet art with which this study is concerned.

Not all Socialist Realist painting was Impressionistic, but there was such a component. The illustrations in this publication will not focus just on the technical or chromatic aspects of Impressionism in Soviet painting. Rather it will explore the gamut of trends of fifty years of art in the Soviet Union with a special emphasis on Impressionism.

In the tree of Official Soviet Socialist Realist painting there are three primary stylistic branches: **Classical** - Most literature characterizes this painting mode as Soviet academy art.[1] This smooth and low-keyed manner is what we generally believe Soviet art to be like, but in fact this aspect of it might be the least significant. This method produced the smallest number of paintings, though several important artists worked in this style, which held greater influence before the 1950s. **Working-Class Impressionism -** This gestural manner was typical for most Soviet painters. As it was positive and accessible to the masses, it tended to be the most effective Socialist Realist mode. It reached its zenith during the 1950s and 60s.

3. ***Young Timber Cutters*** 1961-68
Alexei Pavelovich Belykh
Detail of plate 4

Rough or Severe Style[2] - Sometimes called ugly or schematic realism, in a sense it was a revival of Modernist elements melded into a generally Realist format imbued with a socialist statement. This umbrella term includes several quite diverse stylistic strategies: Cubo-Realism, Primitivism, Mannerist elongation, and Nativism from the republics, etc. These official, Modernist styles flourished mostly from the 1960s onward, and were more strident in their propagandistic tendencies.

In its broadest sense, Working-Class Impressionism in Soviet painting was somewhat conservative and based on academic training. The two stylistic terms, Impressionism and Academicism, are not entirely opposed.[3] Examination reveals that most of the painters during the period superimposed Impressionist devices over essentially academic works.[4] Academicism may be described as the rigorous training in and the application of sophisticated painting techniques and rhetoric. It was employed mostly during the student and early professional years of most Soviet artists. Working-Class Impressionism, and later the Rough-Style strategies, represented the aesthetic approaches used by most official artists during their mature professional careers. Far from attempting to reject the training they received, Soviet artists used it as a spring-board toward personal stylistic expressions.

Throughout my years as an art historian at both the student and professional levels, I was assured that "official" Soviet painting was mechanically, rhetorically and didactically Realistic. I was told by my professors that it was hopelessly propagandistic and stylistically retardataire. Of course, none of these professors had ever seen any original pictures by Soviet Realists, but mostly relied upon dissident Russian emigreé artists for their opinion.

Notions of the quality and significance of Soviet art were formulated for us by Western critics who damned it more on ideological grounds than upon critical judgment. "In the West," writes Matthew Cullerne Bown, "ideological antagonism and the impossibility of reconciling Socialist Realism with Modernism have led to its being virtually ignored."[5] Interestingly, these critics were saying equally condescending things about the European academic realists of the late nineteenth century, whose work I have favored in my research.[6]

Never having viewed any Soviet paintings in person, and with hardly a glimpse of reproductions, I could then venture no opinion. But, after visiting the Soviet Union in 1989, I viewed first-hand what had been purported to be the worst painting of the twentieth century!

Immediately it became apparent that I had been misled by some members of the American art establishment. What I was privileged to view were works of unsurpassed quality, equaling the best Realist painting in the West during the same period! My initial reaction has since been confirmed by the opinions of hundreds of connoisseurs, collectors and contemporary artists. My own appreciation of art from the Soviet period continues to grow as I slowly become more expert in a school of art too long hidden from the West.[7]

The Springville Museum of Art began to exhibit Soviet Realism in 1990, much to the delight of Utah audiences. Thousands of people visited the Museum and gained a personal appreciation as they viewed the exhibition. We trained our docents to deal with the art as expressions of the Soviet experiment and the Slavic soul.

We taught that the art style was Realism, pure and simple. But in every tour, at least one person would ask, "Wouldn't you say that the style of these paintings is Impressionistic?"

Puckishly, I responded, "No, it only looks Impressionistic!" However, we began to notice outright Impressionist properties in most of the paintings. We even coined the term "Working-Class Impressionism" to describe the paintings on loan to the Museum. Knowing that none of the literature dealt with the paintings of the Soviet mid-century as being Impressionistic, I backed off from committing myself in print to this observation.[8]

Finally, the full merits of this newly advanced position became apparent when Mort and Donna Fleischer of Scottsdale acquired Anatoli Vysotski's bold landscape ***March*** (PLATE 1) and suggested that I write about Soviet art in Impressionist terms. I realized that the term Socialist Realism, was an umbrella term for all official Soviet painting of the period, and in truth, spanned a broad range of styles. Of the three major branches of the Soviet tree of art, this book reflects the author's opinion that the middle branch, Working-Class Impressionism, best epitomizes the unique qualities of Soviet painting.

I dedicate this book in loving memory to my mother, Mildred Grosvenor Swanson.

Vern G. Swanson
Director
Springville Museum of Art
Springville, Utah

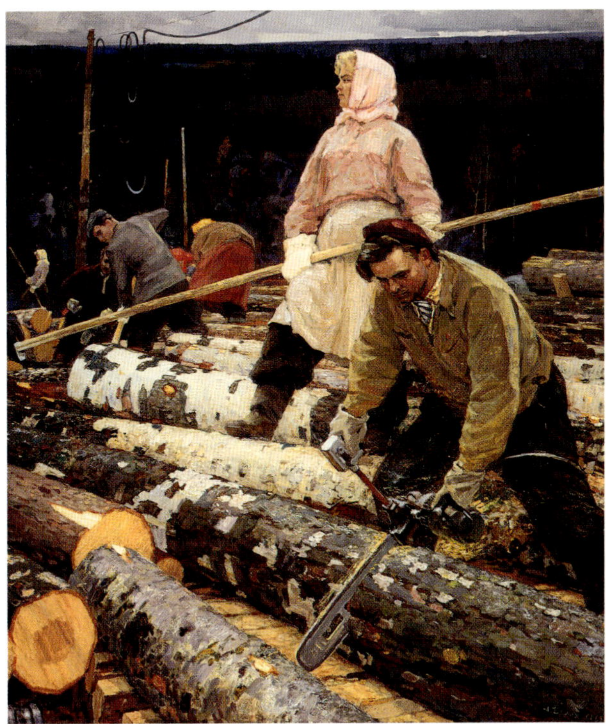

4. ***Young Timber Cutters*** 1961-68
Alexei Pavelovich Belykh
Oil on canvas
82-3/4 x 72-1/4 inches
private collection

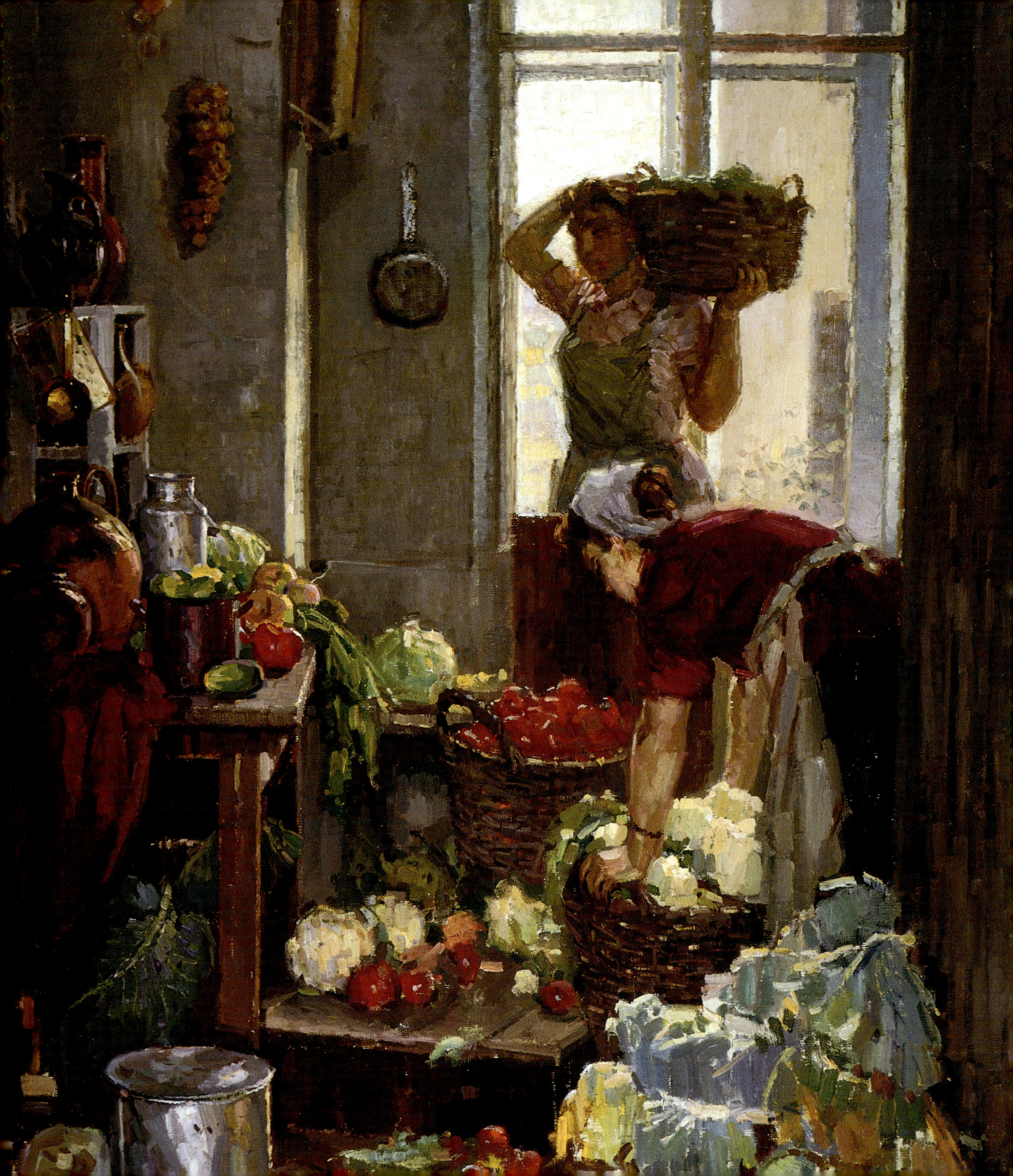

CHAPTER ONE

THE LOWLIFE TRADITION

Few words in the art world carry the magic that Impressionism does. The workings of fine art technique became more and more sophisticated and enigmatic throughout the nineteenth century. But with full-bodied Impressionism, we witnessed a reaction against the grimy pigments signifying the industrial revolution as well as the calculated precision of the academic painters. Art once again reverted back to the people with Impressionism. Now, instead of being amazed by some labored method of painting, the viewer had greater access into the artist's soul and sensibilities.

Though highly admired by the commoner, the polished academic paintings of the nineteenth century were not geared toward the working class, but to the upper-classes, including the nouveau riche and bourgeoisie. First of all, they were too expensive for commoners because of the excessive time the artist spent on each painting. Secondly, these paintings often expressed the patrician classes' display of wealth and privilege. Academic Realism and Impressionism thus became the major polemics surrounding late nineteenth century art. Both deserve a place of honor in art history, but while one survived the last century, the other seems to have been largely ignored.

Discourse between what is now termed Impressionism and Academic/Classical Realism was not just a nineteenth century phenomena. For centuries both poles have interplayed throughout the course of world art. In the past, they might have been called "high-life" and "low-life," referring to both genre and technique. For example, in seventeenth century Rome, there existed the "high art" of the Classicists, versus the loosely-brushed "low art" of the genre paintings by the *Bambichanni*, artists who depicted peasant life.

Seventeenth century Holland offers a poignant archetype. There were high-life artists such as Gerald TerBorch, Jan Vermeer, Jacob Octervelt and Frans Van Mieres. These masters painted with incredible skill and marvelous observation, the silk and silver of the wealthy merchants. On the other hand, low-life genre painters such as Frans Hals, late Rembrandt, Adrian and Isaac Van Ostade, David Tenniers the elder and Adrian Brouwer depicted the workers and the common folk.[9] Among other influences, the lowlife genre served as models for Soviet Realists to follow.

5. ***September*** 1957
Konstantin Gavrilovich Dorokhov
Detail of plate 6

The differences displayed were not just in subject, or in technique, but also in style and aesthetics. The important issue became, not so much the subject, but the method and manner of observation the artist employed. The high-life artist painted a multitude of detail with unbelieveable verisimilitude. The more Impressionistic low-life artists tended to paint with a gestural sense and not necessarily from detail to detail. Their quicker metre allowed them a greater sensitivity to the transience of light, weather conditions and mood.

In the early nineteenth century, the Hegelian dialectic was championed by the Classicists versus the Romanticists. Then their successors, the Juste-Milieu artists, contrasted with the Barbizon painters. Later it was the Salon artists versus the Realists, the Hague Impressionists and Proto-Impressionists. Depicting the laboring peasantry since the 1840s, the artist Francois Millet and Social Realist Gustave Courbet were critical to the development of Soviet painting.[10] Later the Proto-Impressionism of Eugene Boudin and, more importantly, Edouard Manet were at least as powerful in their influence on Soviet art as later manifestations of Impressionism.[11]

With the advent of the French Impressionist movement, highlighted by Pierre Auguste Renoir, Claude Monet, Alfred Sisley and Camille Pissaro, Impressionism finally broke free of its low-life connotation. Three things changed at this crucial juncture. First, with the induction of coal-tar pigments, the artists began to employ more vibrant hues. Secondly, with the advancement of new color theories based upon visual perception, the Impressionists greatly lightened their palettes and utilized complementary juxtapositions of color. Finally, the subject matter changed from depictions of lower classes to the burgeoning middle class of Paris. Thus, an uplifting tone permeated French Impressionist canvases from the 1870s on.

French Impressionism had tremendous reverberations worldwide throughout the late nineteenth and early twentieth centuries. The earlier *Macchiaioli* in Italy seemed to both influence and be influenced by the French. Great Britain, with the New English Art Club, Camden Town and Scottish Impressionists, quickly absorbed the lessons of French art. Then came the Munich school of Liebermann, Corinth and Menzel. American Impressionism, commencing with Winslow Homer, Theodore Robinson, William M. Chase, Childe Hassam, Mary Cassatt, Daniel Garber and John Twachtman, began assimilating the New Painting of France, embuing it with localized and authentic pictorial equivalents. In the twentieth century, a native brand of Impressionism from California anticipated many of the strengths of Soviet Working-Class Impressionism.[12]

During the Post-Impressionist period and the rise of the *avant garde* at the turn of the century, Academic Realism and its off-shoots began to fade in importance. The early twentieth century saw an endless parade of manifestos, many of which penetrated deeply into the Russian Empire. In the West by the 1950s, Abstract art in its Formal and Expressionist branches became the triumphant opposition to Realism, which was now championed by illustrators.

In examining the art climate of nineteenth century Russia, we see critical Realism assuming the interests of the suffering peasant class. Vasili Perov (1833-82) was

6. ***September*** 1957
Konstantin Gavrilovich Dorokhov
Oil on canvas
79 x 51 inches
private collection

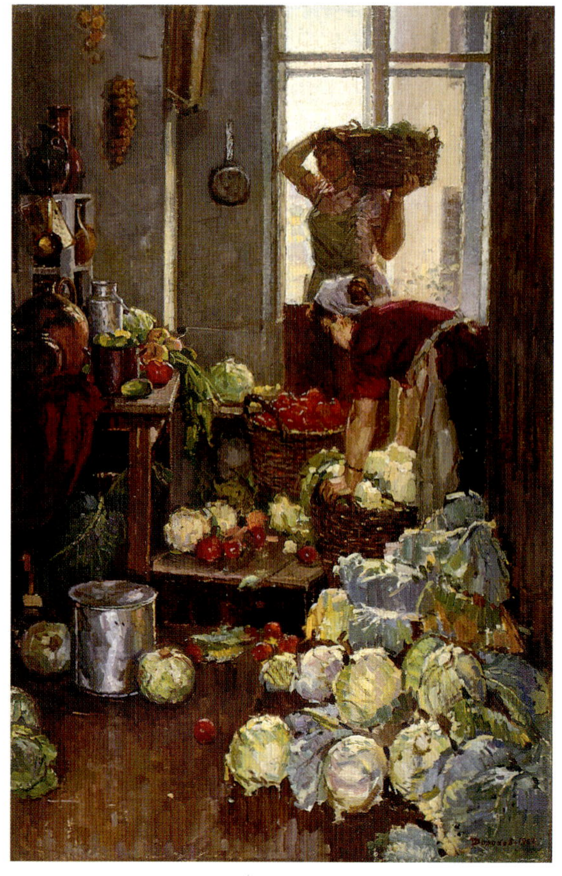

not an Impressionist but rather a socially conscious painter who challenged the ruling powers, especially the clergy. By the 1870s and 1880s, younger artists sympathizing with the plight of the downtrodden embarked upon an extensive program of education and enlightenment through the length and breadth of Russia.[13] These *Peredvizhniki* (Wanderers or Itinerants), as they were called, helped create an approach called Social Genre.

Among the masters of this stylistic precursor to Soviet Socialist Realism are included Ivan N. Kramskoi, Nikolai A. Yaroshenko, Alexei K. Savrasov, Konstantin Savitski, Ivan I. Shishkin, Isaak I. Levitan, and most importantly, Ilya Repin (1844-1930). Literature of writers like Leo Tolstoy served as other models for Socialist Realism, which attempted to expose the ills of society. A contrast exists in the work of German *Biedermeyer* artists, where the workers were depicted as overly idealized and sentimentalized.

So influential were the xenophobic *Peredvizhniki* artists that Czarist Russia came late to Impressionism. But by the late 1880s, Levitan, Valintin Serov and Konstantin Korovin, among others, helped bring the Impressionist palette and spontaneity of brushwork to Russia. Also, not only did Russian painters have the opportunity to visit Paris, but art collectors and patrons like Sergei Shchukin and Ivan Morozov purchased contemporary French works and brought them to Russia. Altogether they brought to Moscow more than 350 Impressionist and Post-Impressionist pictures! Exhibitions of modern foreign paintings began in 1888 and numerous art journals also promoted newer forms of art. This created an educative ambiance, heavily indebted to France, in a country deeply entrenched in the tradition of religious icons, folk art and Classical-Academic painting.

These worldwide developments played out against Russia's own artistic progress. In 1903, the Moscow Union of Russian Artists was founded under the direction of Leonid Pasternak at the Stroganov School. A number of artists such as Sergei A. Vinogradov, Igor E. Grabar, S.V. Malyutin and Konstantin Yuon exercised an Impressionist style. The strain of Impressionism, which would later predominate in Soviet Socialist painting, had its roots through these artists. The Union of Russian Artists and other Moscow-based societies likely created the figuratively-based Impressionist mode which would inform Soviet painting from the 1930s to the 1970s.

Meanwhile, Russian artists like Mikhail Vrubel, Viktor Borisov-Musatov and Alexander N. Benois absorbed the innovations of the other western European art movements; principally the Nabis, Fauves and the Symbolists. Many were deeply influenced by Post-Impressionist styles as well as later convulsions of French Modernism, such as hard-edged or the faceted qualities in Cubism and Futurism. It may be said that Russia engaged in a greater creative synergism with the Modernist movements of France than any other country. Foreign influences were internalized and adapted, often tending toward Primitivism or Abstraction, as in the work of Aleksei Jawlensky, Kazimir Malevich, Vasily Kandinsky, Marc Chagall and many others.

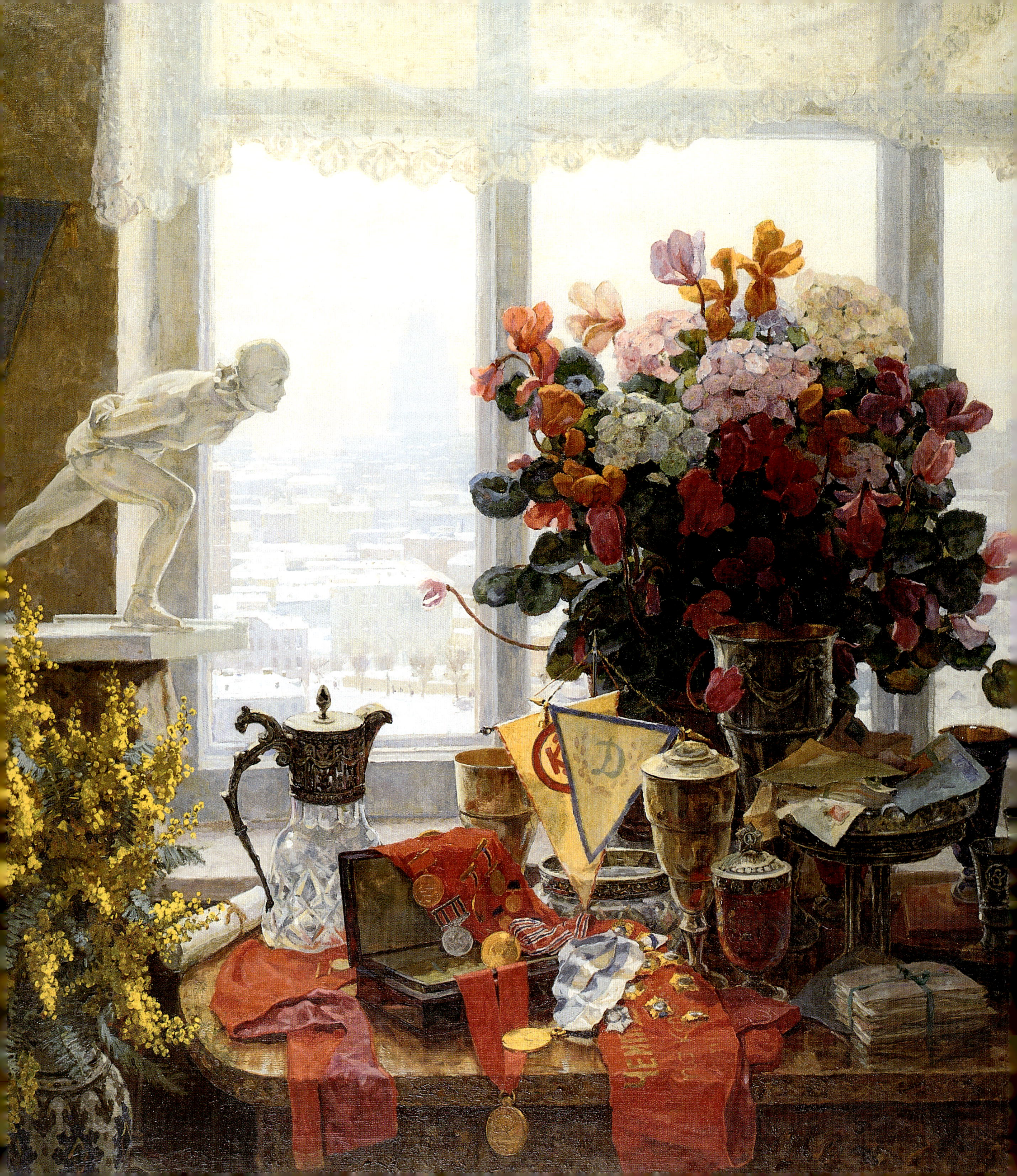

CHAPTER THREE

In an atheistic society, the worker became the mythic hero of the perfected state. Soviet artists rallied to the cause, to what Gorki espoused, "that labor should be the true hero of literature (and art)." That the artist should be the representative servant of the society was an old idea which found a home in the Soviet Union of the twentieth century. The earlier credo of the favored Association of Artists of Revolutionary Russia (*AKhRR*) helped define the mission of Soviet Realism:

> "Our civic duty before mankind is to set down artistically and documentarily the revolutionary impulse of this great moment of history. We will depict the present day: Red Army, the workers, the peasants, the revolutionaries and the heroes of labor." [30]

While no particular artistic future was delineated, this subordination initiated the beginning of the Stalinist phase in Soviet culture. No specific style was forwarded as being unequivocally appropriate for the cause. There seem to have been several elements posited, however, as representing Socialist Realism: It must be easily understood, discerned and accessible by the people (the masses). It needed to be popular with the masses. They needed to appreciate it for its value, message and agreeability. It worked best if it could be story-telling or narrative. For the purposes of the Party it needed to illustrate the history, mission and achievements of the Soviet regime. It must have a tendentious function to inspire, educate and motivate the Soviet citizen to greater loyalty and effort. It must remain in step with the ever changing needs of the Communist Party and be ready to serve.

Beyond the above mentioned propagandistic purposes, what was the nature of the art? The predominant manifestation of Socialist Realism was firmly in a Working- Class Impressionist camp. In doing so, our narrow understanding of Soviet art will broaden to offer an amplified appreciation of its quality and unique place in art history. At the same time, our restricted view of the term Impressionism should expand as well.

Contrary to literature which states that Socialist Realism had a well-defined aesthetic with which each artist needed to be conversant, it seems as though no precise manifesto dominated their ideology. Artists working within the general guidelines and conditions mentioned above were assisted by an enormous wealth of material inherited from Russian history, the revolution, socialism, science and technology and the working classes. They found a vast reservoir from both the past and present from which to draw inspiration.

10. ***In the Stalin Factory*** 1949
Mikhail A. Kostin
52 x 68 inches
Oil on canvas
private collection

The traditional Realists, who were opposed to the Communist Revolution in the first place, now found themselves, albeit with changed attitudes, empowered again. Stalin changed things in favor of the new official Party art, Socialist Realism, which style was just beginning to take shape. Stalin explained to Isaak Brodski that he wanted art that was comprehensible to the masses, pictures that contained "living people."[31] It is true that the school would often be epitomized by an easy optimism and facile pictorialism, attributes which some critics disdain, but which gives Soviet Impressionism its peculiar charm.

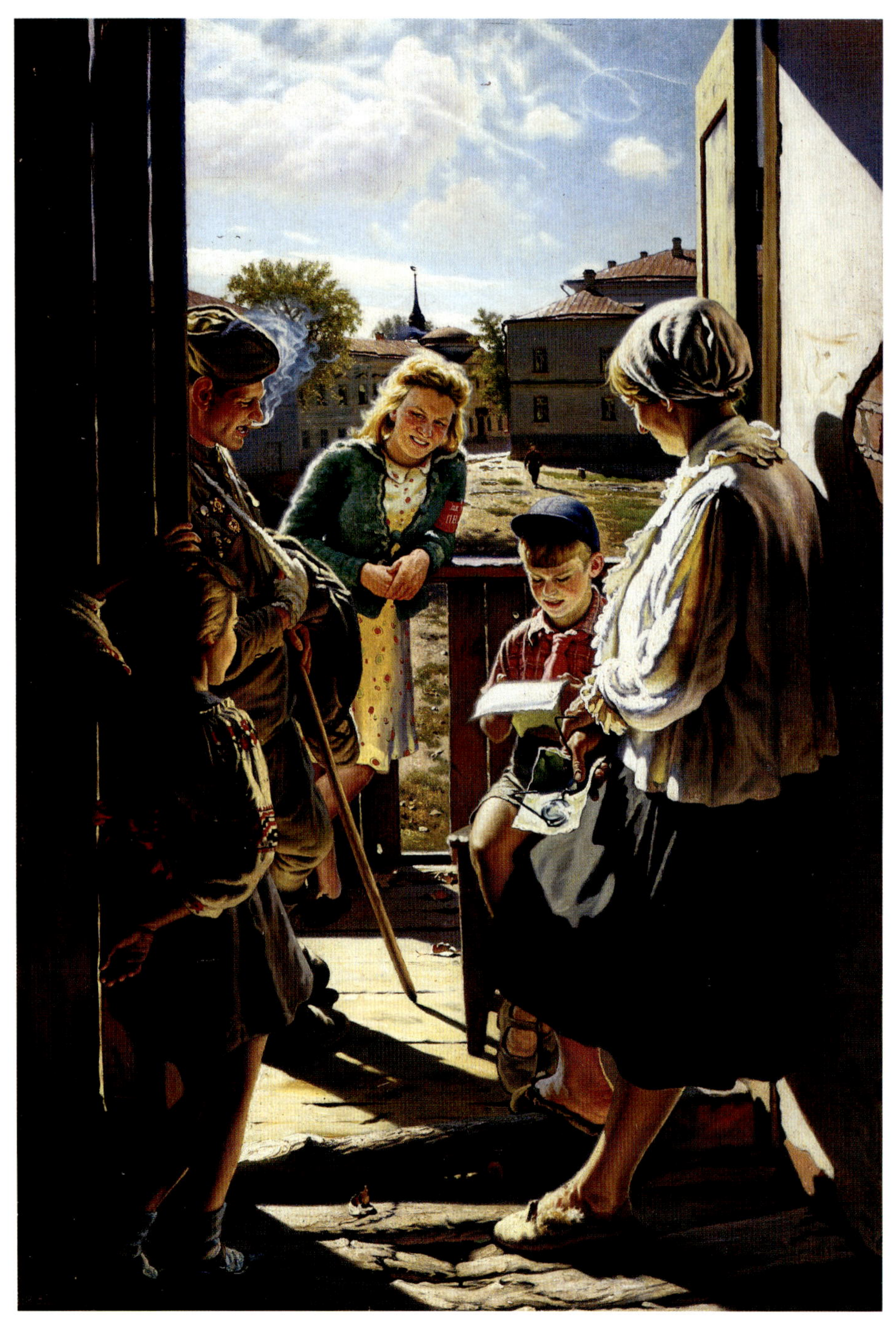

11. ***A Letter from the Front*** 1950-52
Alexander Ivanovich Laktionov
66-3/4 x 45-3/4 inch
Oil on canvas
private collection

CHAPTER THREE

Although the official artists themselves invoked the special name of the Wanderers for their own benefit, their technical means and expressive thrust were very different. The Stalinist critic Zhdanov noted:

> "The Party has completely resurrected the inheritance of Repin, Bryullov, Vereshchagin, Vasnetsov, Surikov. Did we do right in preserving the treasury of classical painting and smashing the liquidators of paintings?"[32] The answer from the gallery was a resounding "Yes!"

Much has been written about the Classical or Academic predilection of the Socialist Realists. The school, when taken as a whole, was expressly non-academic in the "cabinet" or Salon sense of the word. It actually was a gloss to establish pedigree and outline curricula in the art institutes, but certainly not to impress upon the working union artist or professor. There were a number of artists who eschewed Impressionism in favor of *zakonchennost* or Academic finish. Yet only in the Classical works of Isaak Brodski, Vasili Yakovlev, Dmitri Nalbandyan, Alexander Laktionov, Boris Scherbakov, Sokolov-Skalia, Pyotr Belousov and others did smooth Academic methods find any followers.

It is known that Brodski and Evgeni Katsman relied upon photographs instead of first hand observation, much to the detriment of their art. Laktionov's photographic look possibly stems from the same use of the camera. Rather than working directly from nature, en plein-air, these artists relied upon the packaged two-dimensional image and upon the studio model for inspiration. But Laktionov's two versions of ***A Letter from the Front*** (PLATE 11) were certainly the most captivating images of the post-war years, striking deep into the national ethos.

A Social Realist balance between Classicism and Impressionism was hesitantly struck by the official and ceremonious propaganda painters: Aleksandr Gerasimov, Boris Ioganson, Vladimir Serov, Fyodor Shurpin and early Vasili Efanov. Gerasimov, who had been a founding member of *AKhRR,* found it easy to switch over to the new art unions now being formed. Bird states that even Gerasimov, the most official of all Soviet artists, had an Impressionist streak and his work was "basically Realistic in its concentration on significant visual details but made use of certain features of Impressionism."[33]

These were the painters of big theme subjects or *kartina* pictures.[34] They were not painted in a particularly Academic fashion but rather modified to complement the Proletarian subject matter of its motifs. Academicism did not work so well when portraying peasants working in the fields or factories. In this respect, Mikhail A. Kostin's ***In the Stalin Factory*** (PLATE 9, 10) and Nikolai Obrynba's ***Before the Storm*** (PLATE 12) effectively blend sound draftsmanship with "two-fisted Impressionism."

Gerasimov became the court painter to the Kremlin and head of the USSR Academy in 1948. His ***A Russian Communal Bath (study)*** (PLATE 13) is certainly more relaxed than the determined Realism of his official paintings of Stalin and other Party leaders. Bown finds the case of Gerasimov indicative of the rest of the Soviet school:

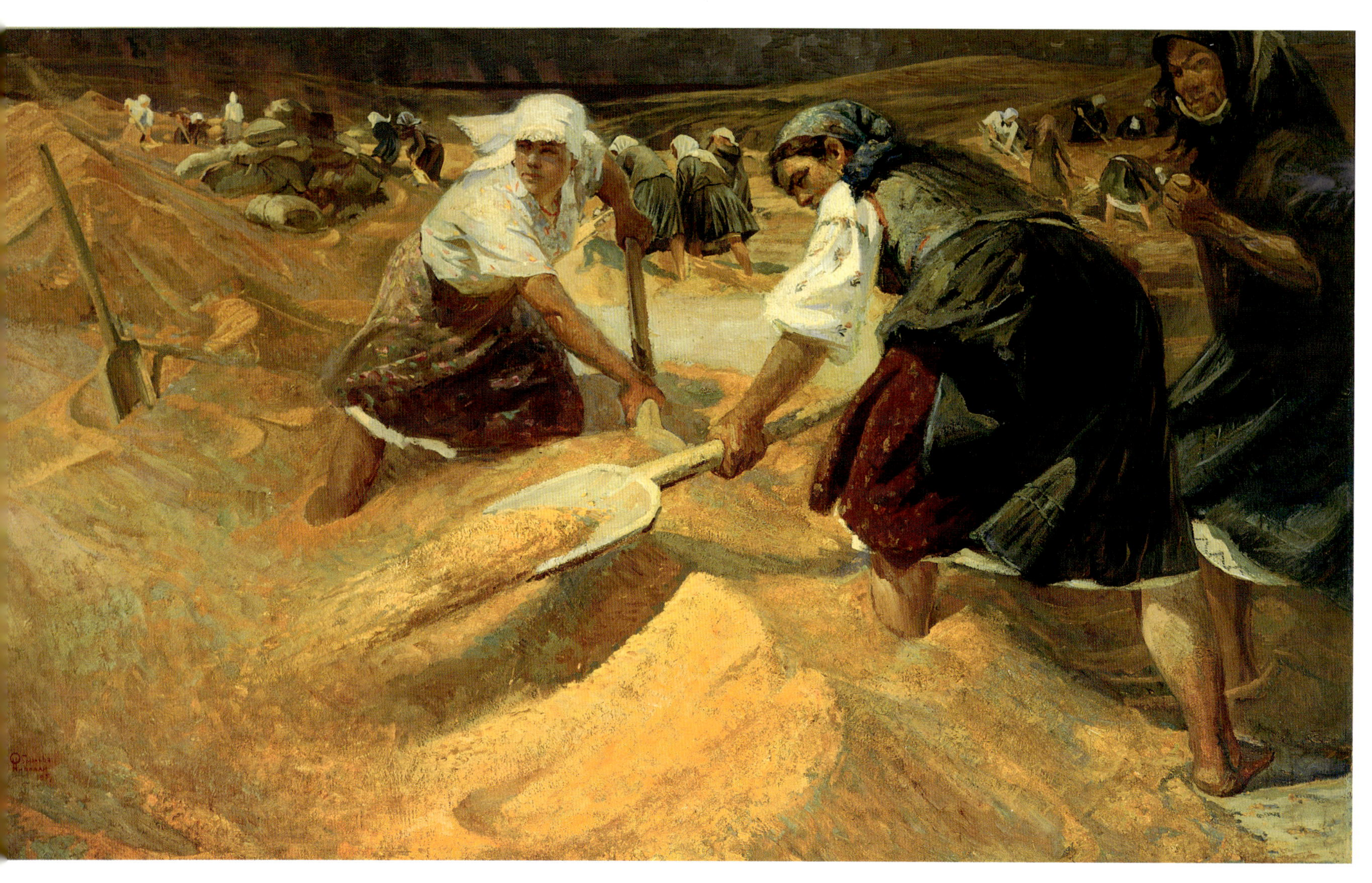

12. ***Before the Storm*** 1955-57
Nikolai Ippolitovich Obrynba
59 x 102-1/2 inches
Oil on canvas
private collection

CHAPTER THREE

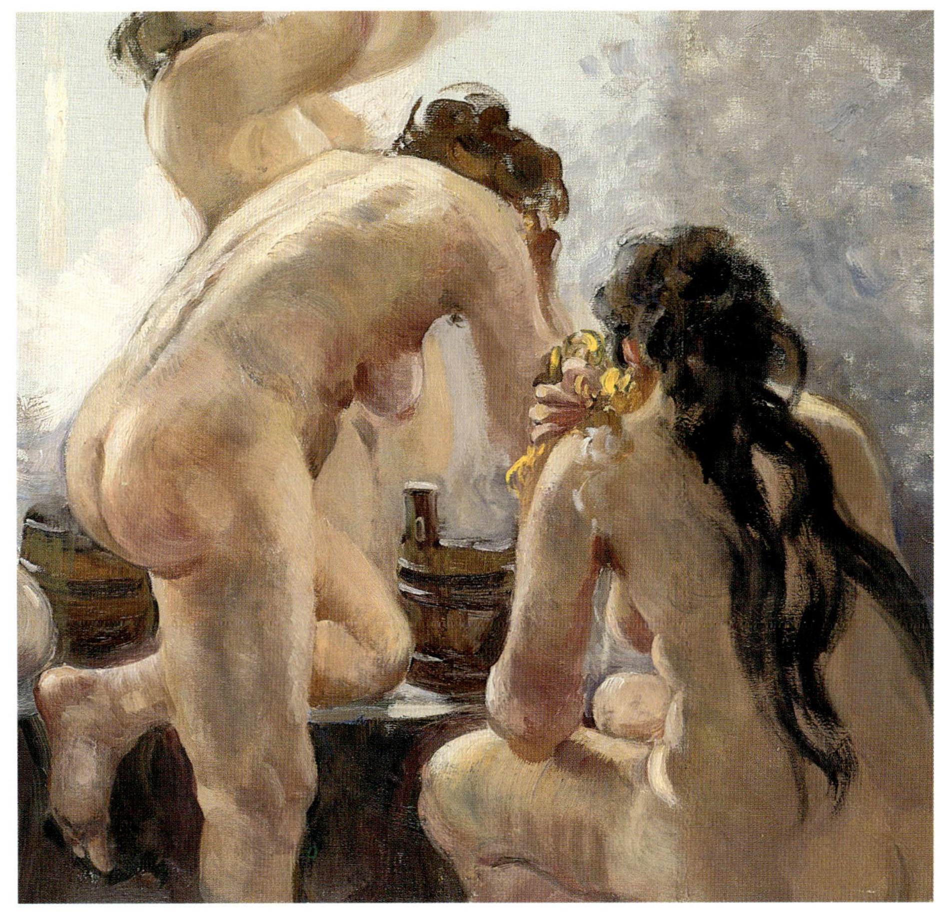

13. ***A Russian Communal Bath* (study)** 1946
Aleksandr Mikhailovich Gerasimov
31 x 34 inches
Oil on canvas
private collection

> Aleksandr Gerasimov epitomizes the plight of the Soviet artist in the late 1940s. He loved and was profoundly influenced by Impressionism, but felt constrained by official pressure to criticize it publicly. He betrayed his own principles. Gerasimov is an extreme case, but the same dilemma to a lesser extent, was faced by many painters in the forties.[35]

Vasilii Surikov's work was a major example of what correct painting should be. His paintings were a little brown, a little smooth and not too Academic but thoroughly Russian. By the later 1940s when Impressionism was being challenged, Surikov was cleared of his taint and classified as a true Realist. As the feeble official statement went, "Impressionism is a denial of the tradition of Realist art."[36] In three areas was Impressionism vilified: first, it was seen as a "slippery slope" into the excesses of Modernism. Secondly, it was seen as a corrupting Western influence, a French concoction. And finally, it was seen as lacking moral purpose, class consciousness and was decidedly bourgeois.

Many artists succeeded in avoiding these pitfalls while incorporating the technical elements of Impressionism into their art. Three highly important paintings, Zinaida Kovalevskaya's ***Tomato Picking*** (PLATE 14), Antonina Sofronova's ***In a Country Garden*** (PLATE 15) and Sergei V. Gerasimov's ***Evening*** (PLATE 16) may be seen as courageous Impressionist evocations broached in Socialist Realist terms. All were painted ahead of the acceptance curve.

Through the forties and early fifties, art did tighten up a bit in terms of color, brushwork and surface, but not totally and not for long.[37] A prime example of this reassertion of traditional training in art union artists is Gregori S. Galkin's oil, ***Kharkov Railway Station: Stalin is Peace*** (PLATE 19). At a glance the work has Salon written all over it, but upon closer examination, one sees that its details were more suggested than closely mimicked. Sergei F. Babkov's ***Girl Radio Operator*** (PLATE18) was somewhat Classical in style, but once the lid was removed by 1953, he was right back painting in the "dab and spot school." Even supposedly hard focused paintings such as Alexander Laktionov's ***Letter from the Front*** (PLATE 11) cannot be considered very linear and meticulously detailed, even though they give the impression of being so.

In a sense, the above was a rear-garde rather than an avant-garde movement. Critics such as John Bowlt see this as the period's weakness. "The post-war period until the mid 1950s was the most static in the history of Soviet art, haunted as it was by the severe and conservative (Andrei) Zhdanov administration."[38] Yet, in truth, the *Zhdanovshchina* (period of dictatorial artistic conservatism) had only sporadic and tenuous effect on Soviet art.[38] The *Zhdanovshchina* was jettisoned after 1951-53, bringing back a freer painting style.

All the while, common people appreciated the direction which painting was taking, toward a mass art. In 1946, the All-Union Art Exhibition in Moscow was visited by 800,000 people testifying to the interest the populace had in the art of the day. Aleksandr Gerasimov noted how appreciated Soviet art was becoming, "works saturated with ideas and formally complete, answering to the needs of the people, educating the Soviet person in the spirit of cheerfulness..."[40]

CHAPTER THREE

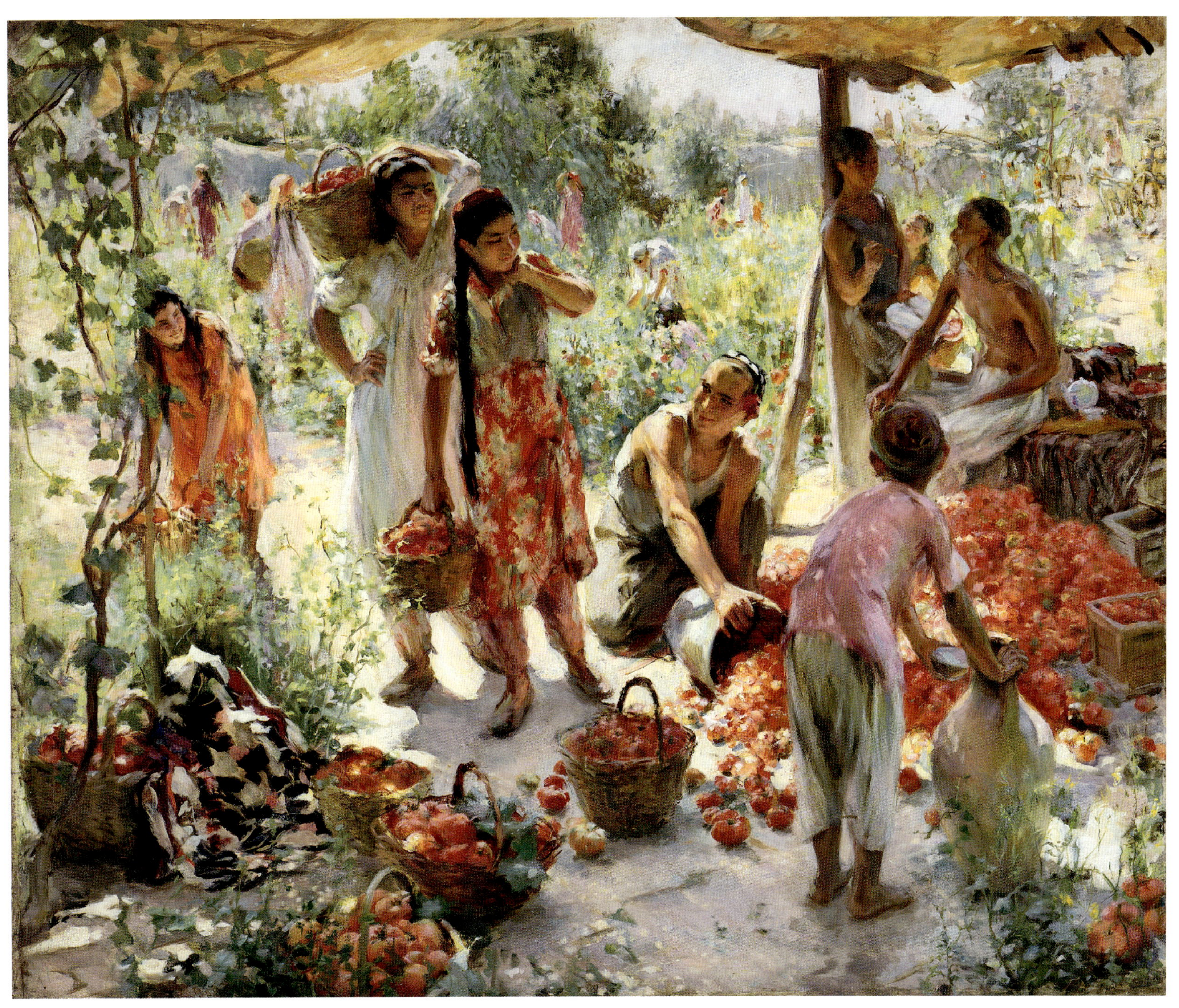

14. ***Tomato Picking*** 1949
Zinaida Kovalevskaya
59 x 71 inches
Oil on canvas
private collection

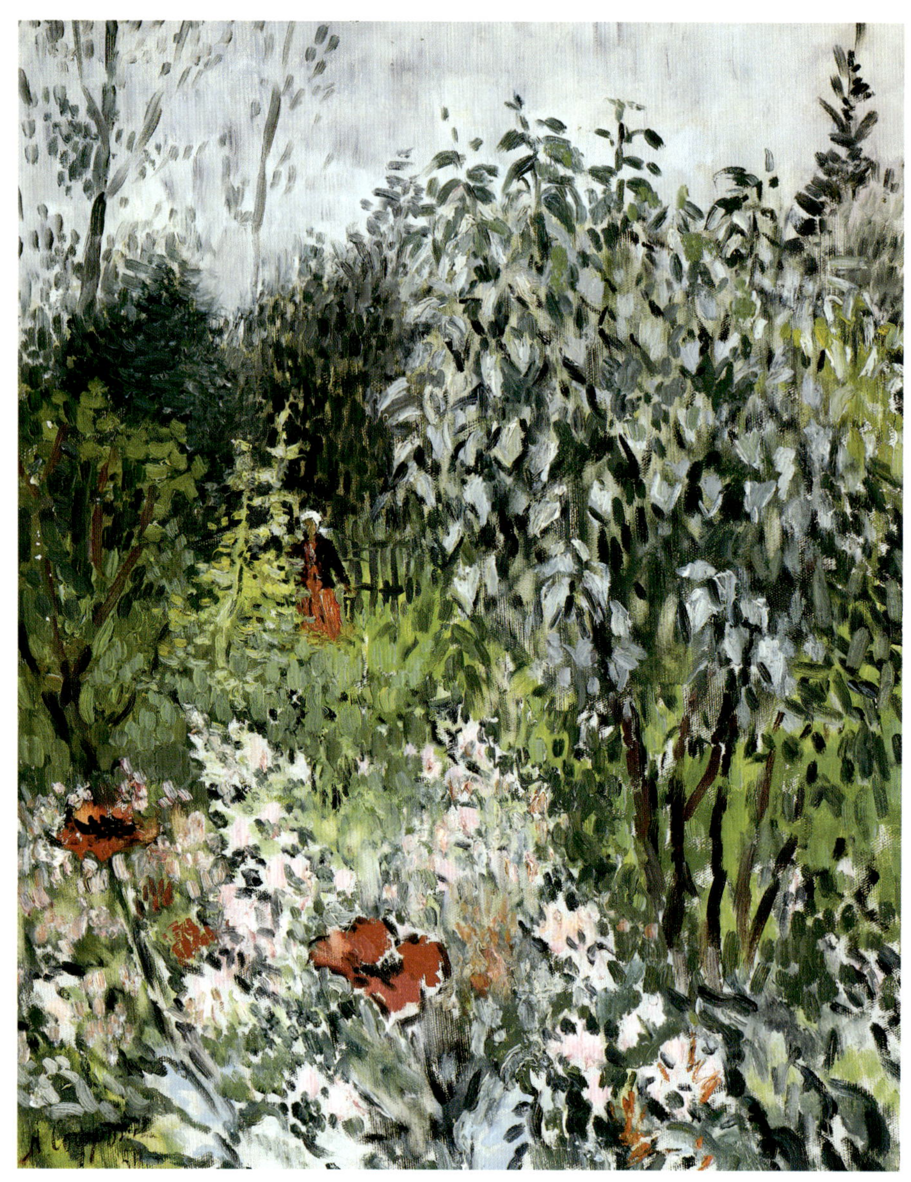

15. ***In a Country Garden*** 1950
Antonina Sofronova
26 x 22 inches
Oil on canvas
private collection

16. ***Evening*** 1950
Sergei Vasilyevich Gerasimov
31 x 39 inches
Oil on canvas
private collection

CHAPTER THREE

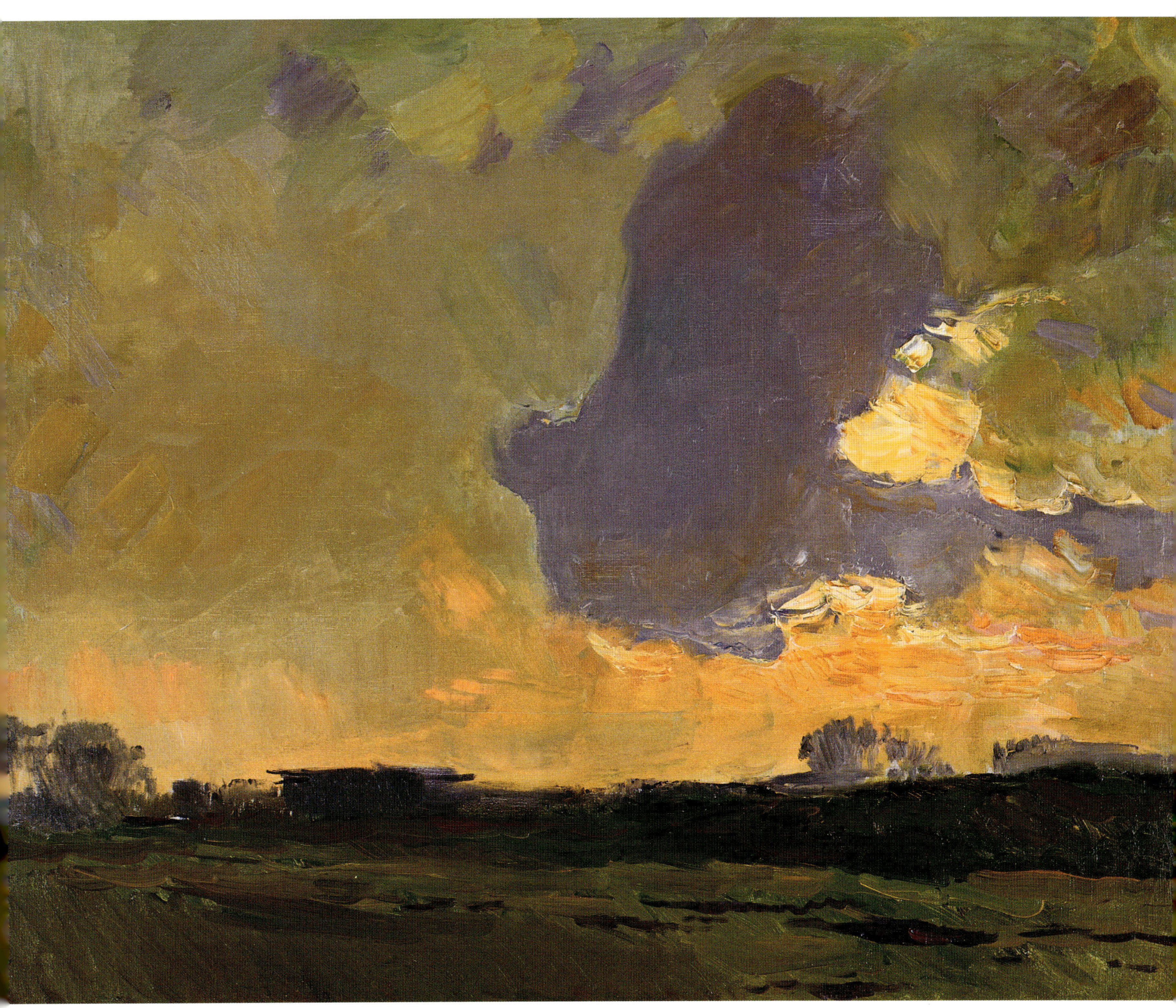

When Stalin died in 1953, it opened the Party to greater diversity which trickled down in its own way to the union artist. In January of 1954, an exhibition by young Moscow artists organized by Alexander Kamenski echoed the shift in Party policy away from the ceremonious splendor and the cult of personality to Stalin. In a sense, this opened the path to painting the people more than when Stalin's *KPDI* (Committee of Art Affairs) controlled the scene.

Although the local unions in Moscow and Leningrad had been organized for some time, the *Soyuz Khudozhnikov SSSR,* or Union of Artists of the USSR, was not established until 1957. It functioned as the All-Union had before and eventually numbered over 13,000 artists. It was responsible for the implementation of Party orthodoxy, though not for artistic orthodoxy which was liberalizing fairly rapidly. The Leningrad Union was a self-running organization which felt it was a waste of time to deal with the national union.

Most artists painted what they wanted, but would paint acceptable subjects for the major exhibitions. These exhibitions had grandiose titles such as "50 Years of Soviet Power" or "60 Years of the Great October Socialist Revolution." What many of the artists wanted to paint was Socialist Realism with an Impressionist bent, not the "School of Mud" preached by retardataire art critics. For example, the Leningrad painter Semon A. Rotnitski's ***Seryogo*** (PLATE 17) combines traditional subject and Party work-ethic with a quintessential Impressionist technique. Its scintillating strokes and harmonious chords of color proferred a renewal for Soviet art.

By the 1960s, Socialist Realist art had developed into a nonhackneyed combination of pictures with monumentality and contemporaneity in a tough Impressionist style. Whereas before we saw Working-Class Impressionism mitigating Classical tendencies, now it moderated the severity of Rough style painting. ***A Sunny Day*** (PLATE 20) by Mai V. Dantsig is an emblem of the total Soviet woman, the clothespins around her neck might as well be a bullet-belt. Nikolai A. Abramov's ***April in the Motherland of V.I. Lenin*** (PLATE 21) is a huge painting telling of the encroachment of Stalinist Towers (high-rise apartments) and is painted with a powerfully Impressionist brush. In 1967, Nikolai N. Baskakov painted the controlled style ***Easter Picnic*** (PLATE 23) which includes emblems of modern times, i.e., its portable radio and plastic over the food on the table. Georgian artist Mikhail D. Gabuniya painted a powerfully Impressionistic/Rough-style painting with his ***Tea Pickers Festival*** (PLATE 22). Though traditional in subject, the dresses worn by the village girls are all trendy and the brushwork is audacious.

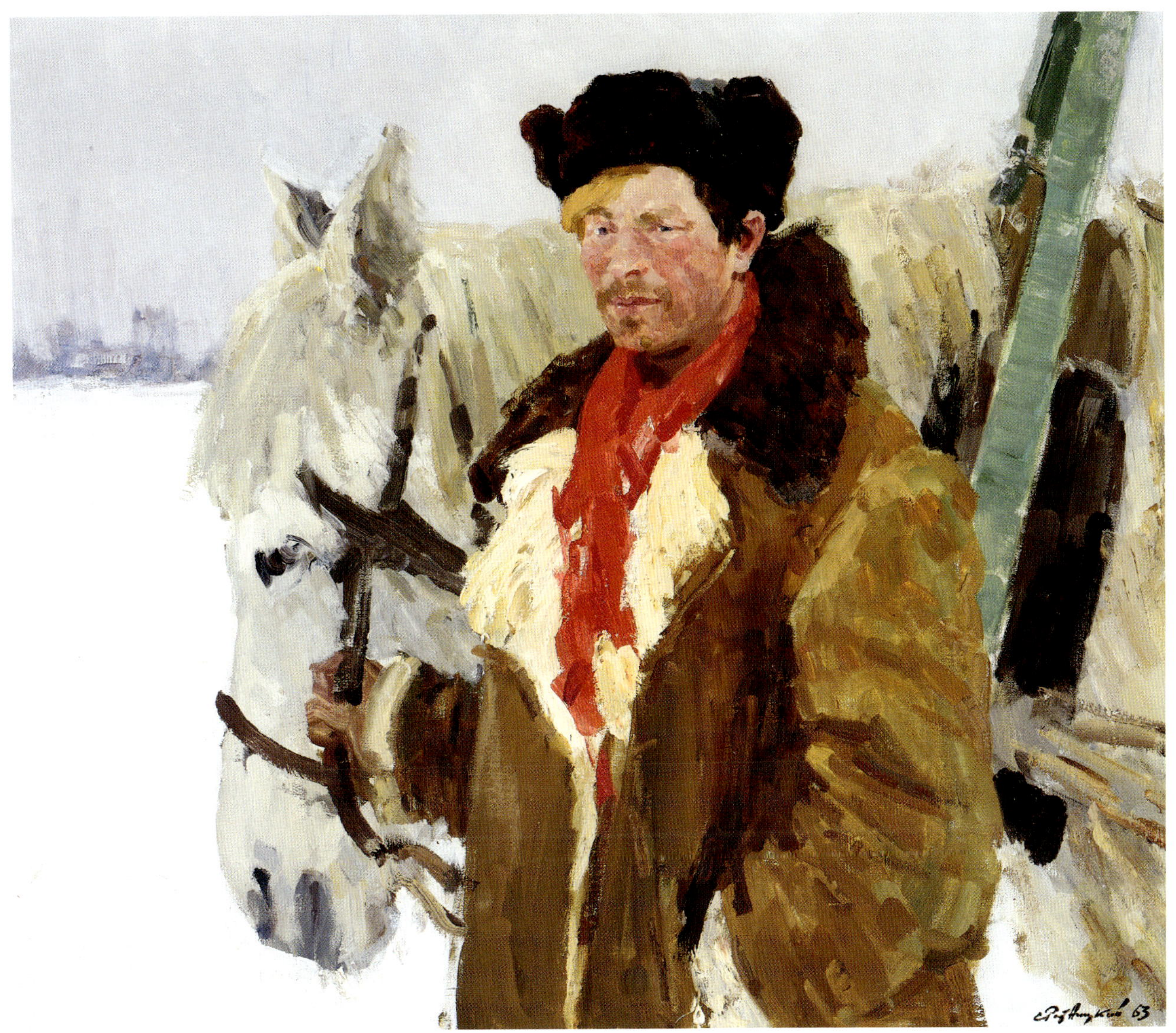

17. ***Seryogo*** 1963
Semon Aronovich Rotnitski
34-1/8 x 39-1/4 inches
Oil on canvas
Fleischer Museum Collection

Russian artists considered it their civic duty to mankind to portray this great moment in history, to artistically document the workers, the peasants, the heroes of labor.

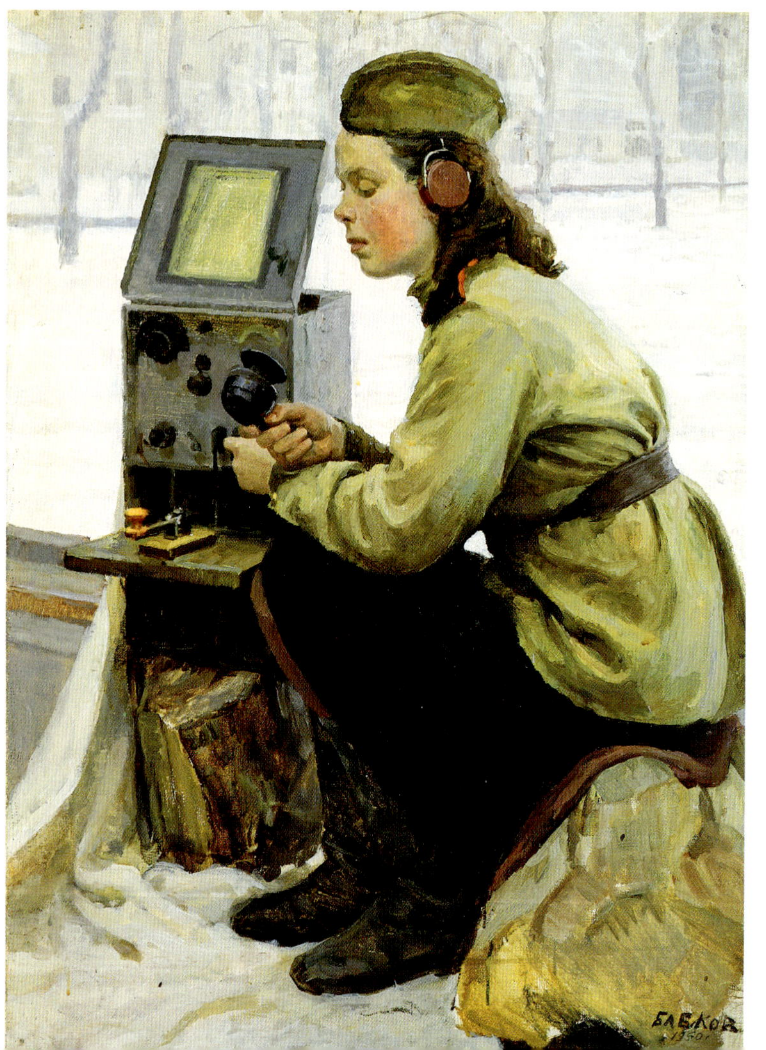

18. ***Girl Radio Operator*** 1950
Sergei Fedorovich Babkov
34 x 25-1/2 inches
Oil on canvas
private collection

CHAPTER THREE

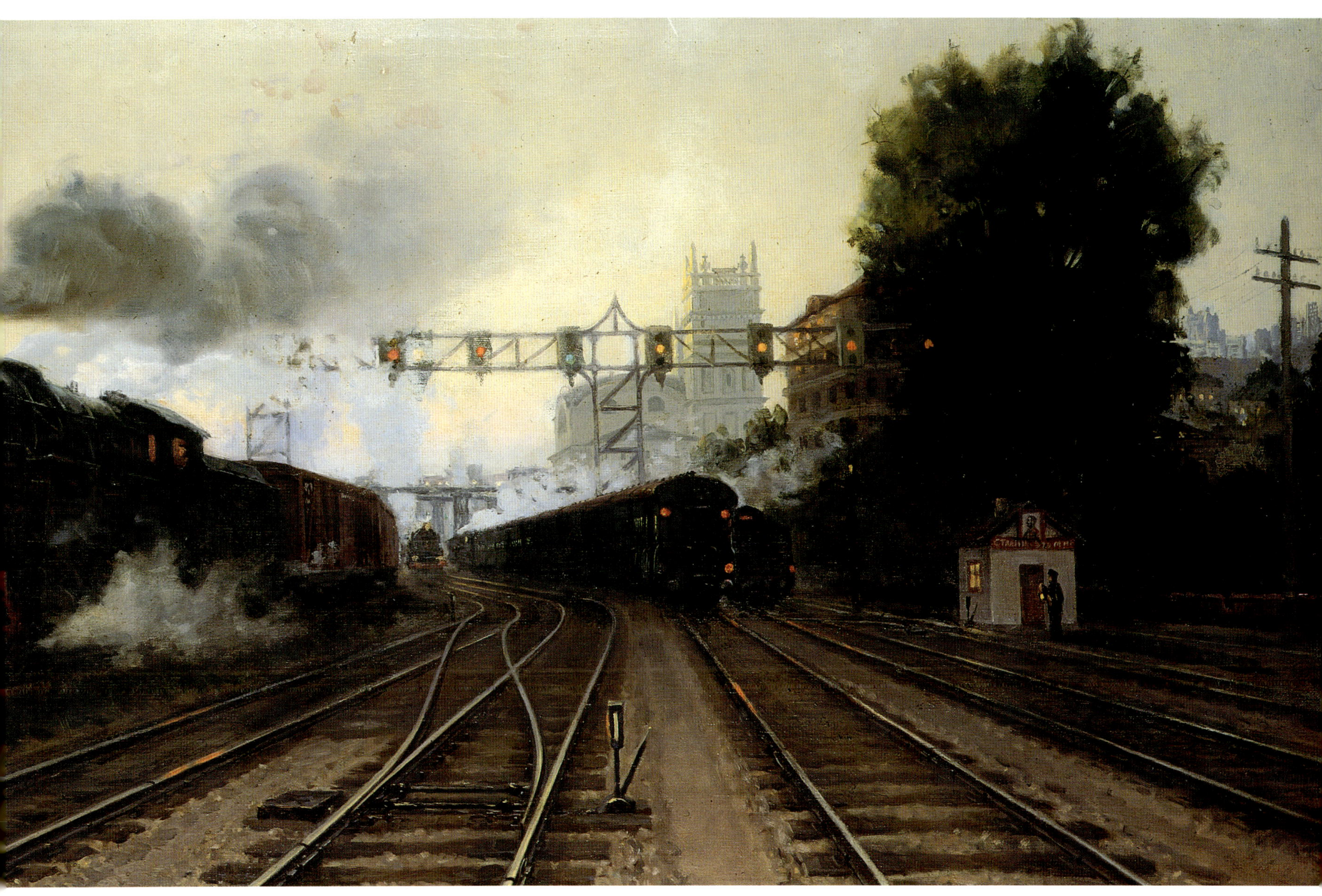

19. ***Kharkov Railway Station: Stalin is Peace*** 1952
Gregori Sergeevich Galkin
29-3/4 x 61-1/4 inches
Oil on canvas
private collection

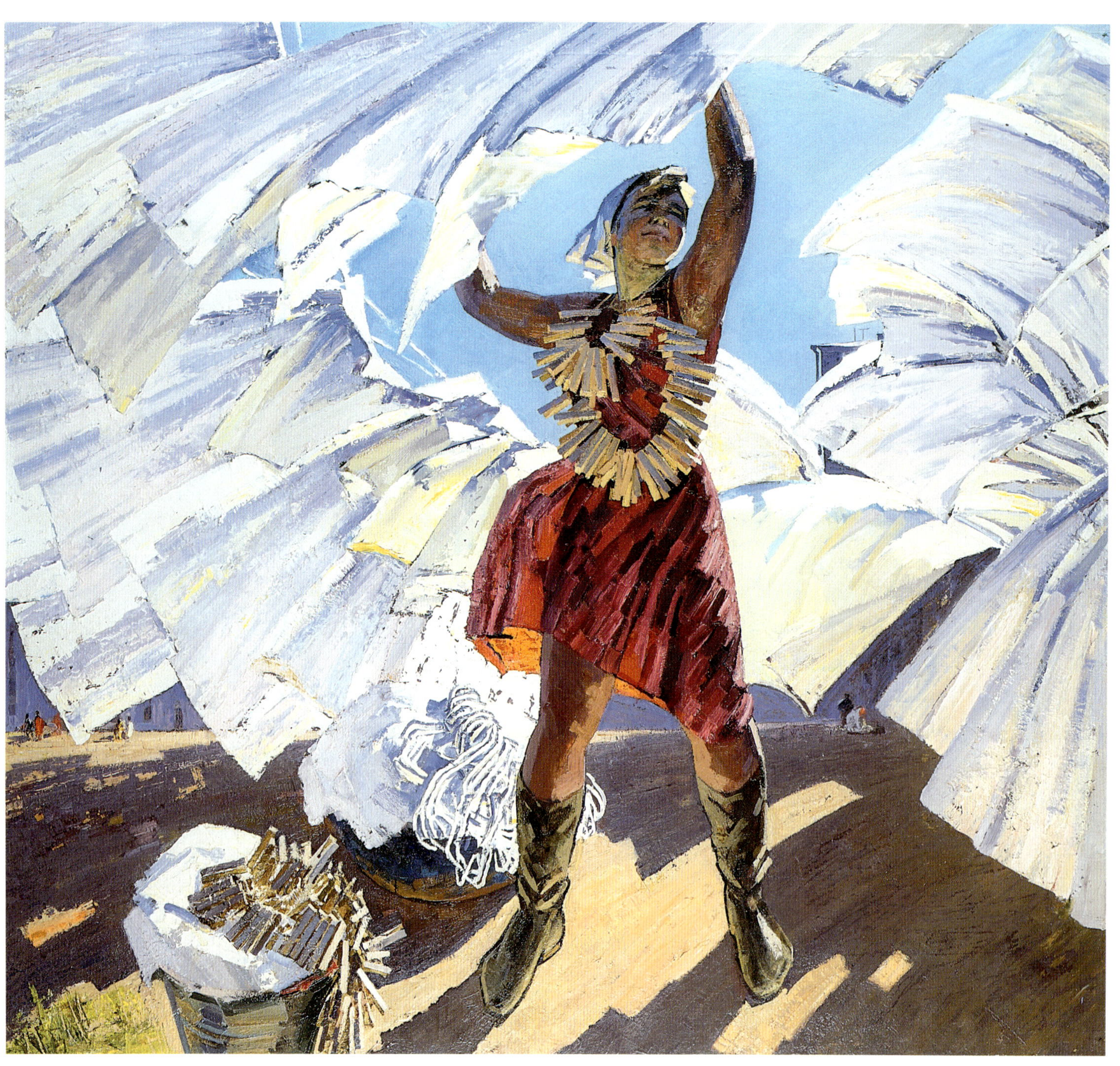

20. ***A Sunny Day*** 1965
Mai Volphovich Dantsig
74 x 82 inches
Oil on canvas
private collection

21. ***April in the Motherland of V.I. Lenin*** 1969
Nikolai A. Abramov
93-3/4 x 77-5/8 inches
Oil on canvas
private collection

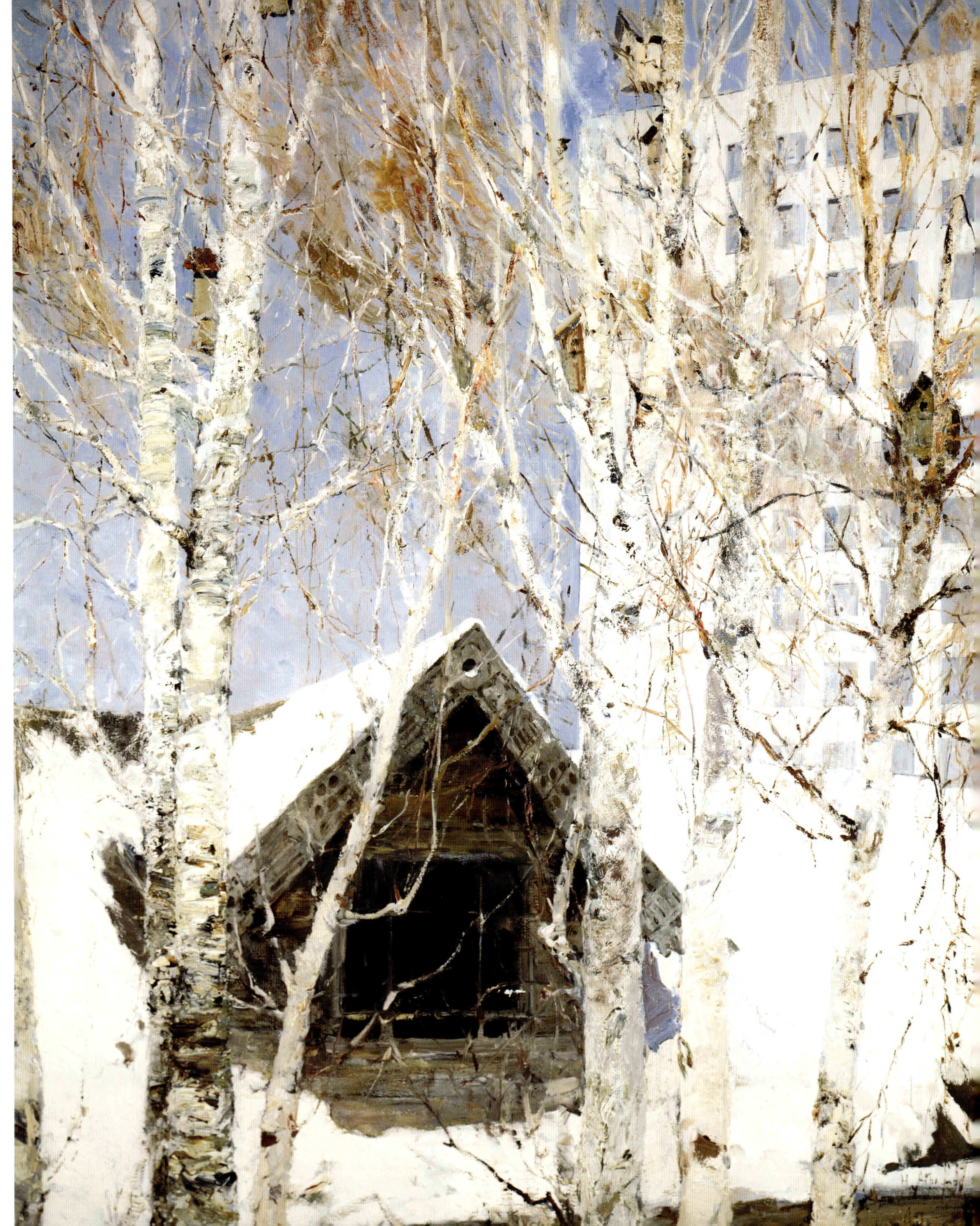

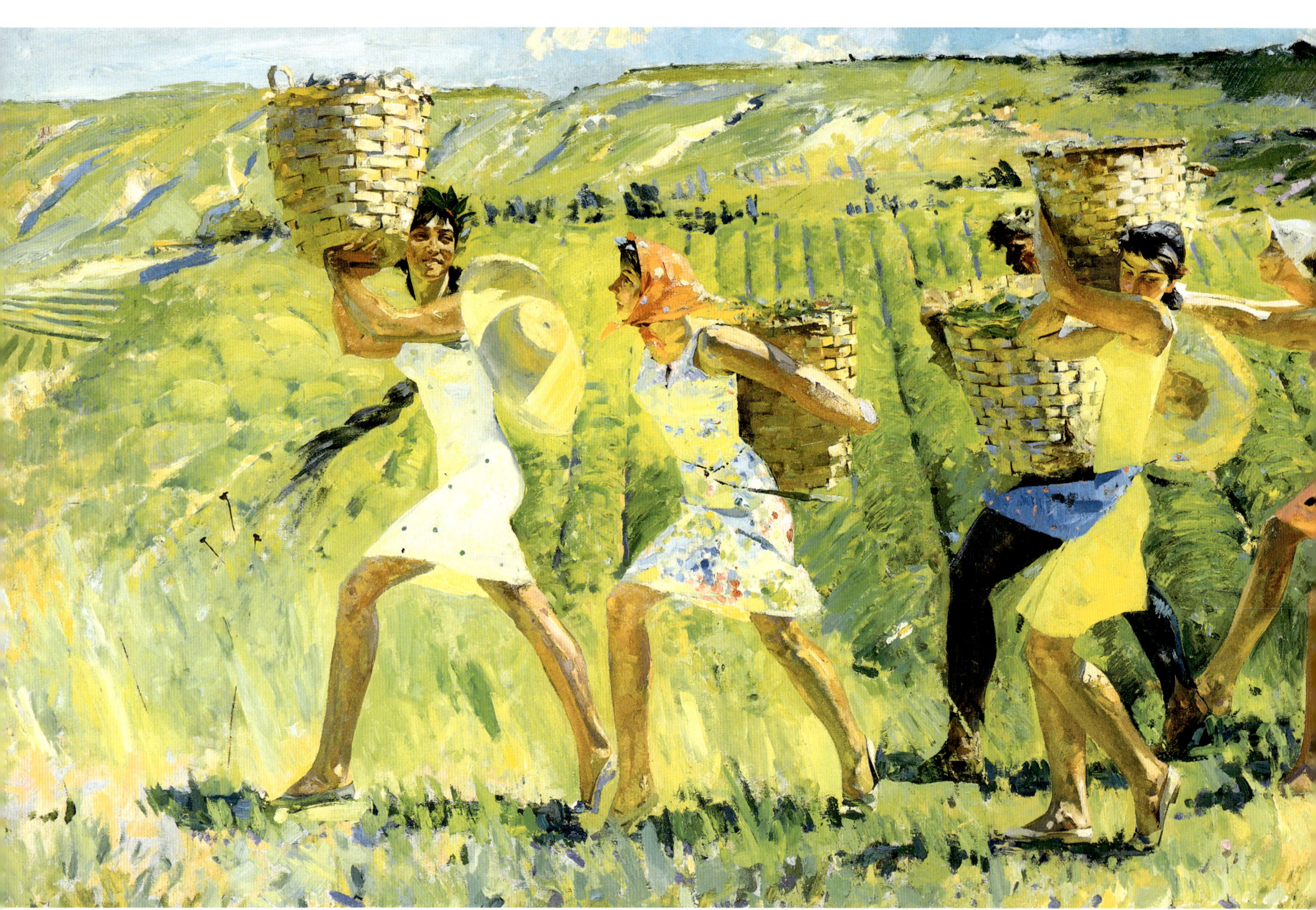

CHAPTER THREE

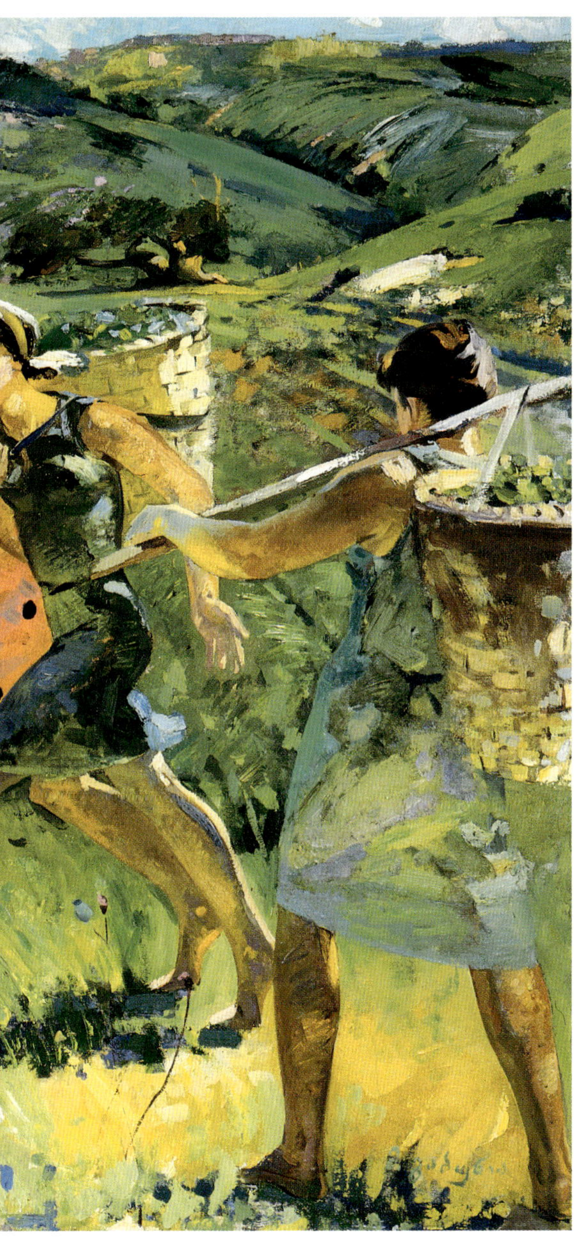

22. ***Tea Pickers Festival*** 1971
Mikhail D. Gabuniya
60-1/4 x 122 inches
Oil on canvas
private collection

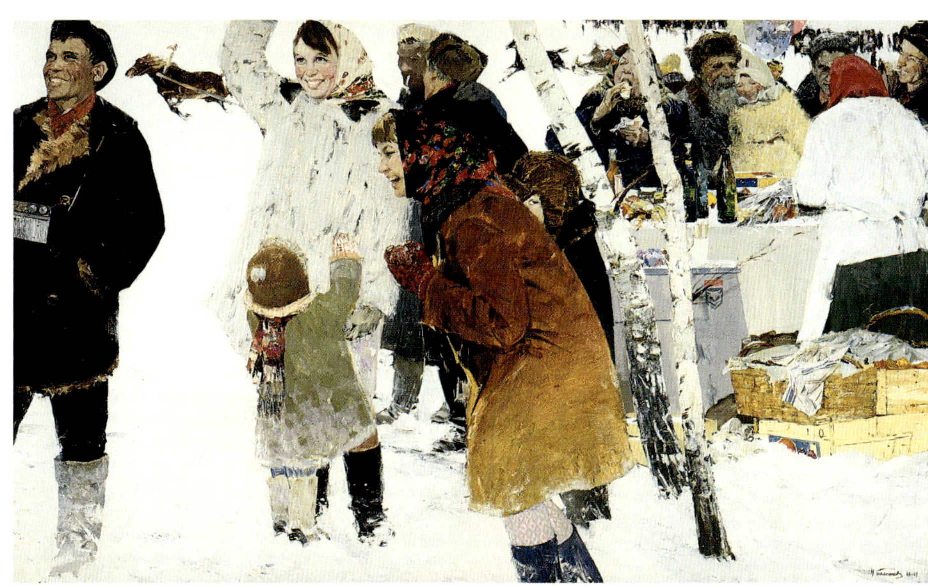

23. ***Easter Picnic*** 1967-69
Nikolai Nikolayevich Baskakov
58-1/2 x 98 inches
Oil on canvas
private collection

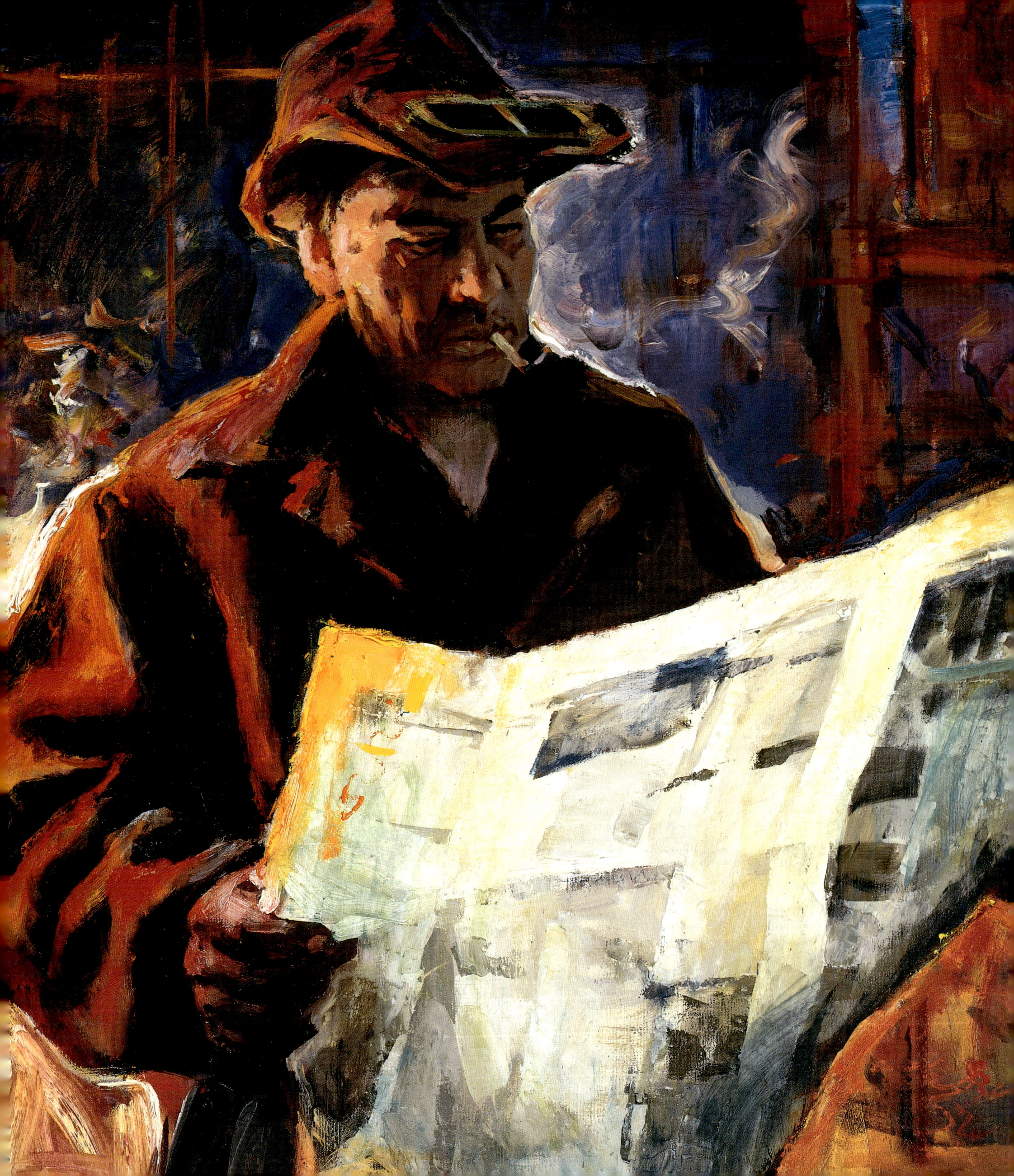

CHAPTER FOUR

Soviet Working-Class Impressionism

The generalization which links Impressionism with Socialist Realism has both perils and legitimacy. Not since Ilya Repin, Konstantin Savitski, Abram Arkhipov and the Wanderers had form and content so melded into a single purpose. A few critics of our time have acknowledged the admixture of these seemingly disparate elements. John Bowlt conceded about an exhibition of contemporary official artists: "Still, a few works which we see at this exhibition have more in common with a latter day Impressionism than with Realism..."[41]

Soviet art exhibited many crosscurrents throughout the Stalinist period and the line of demarcation between the official and non-official artists was not always clear. There was a gamut of variations which allowed the natural proclivities of each artist to be unleashed. While calling the painterly Impressionist approach of the majority of Socialist Realism conservative, this does not imply that it was insipid or maudlin. On the contrary, it offered a nationalist style which unified the artistic diversity of the Soviet Union in a common cause, for more years than one could rightly expect. During that time, essentially Realist pictures, extolling humanity more than anything, were painted with courage, innovation, sensitivity and passion.

Impressionist-style paintings depicting daily life and the charms of the Russian countryside captured the hearts of the masses. The Impressionist branch of the Socialist Realist tree was the most artistically satisfying. Its prime period extended from the beginning of Khrushchev's Virgin Land experiment in 1954 to the 1970s. This was a time of perfecting the middle path of Socialist Realism, though it was not known for aggressive excursions on the frontiers of art innovation.

Painters during the 1950s through the 1970s, such as Fyodor Reshetnikov, Aleksei Gritsai, Mikhail Samkov and Nikolai I. Barchenkov, should be remembered for their rich chromatic range. Anatoli P. Levitin captured exquisite harmonies and tonal brilliance of white on grey in his oil ***Warm Day*** (***study***) (PLATE 25). It depicts a washer-woman sitting on a window sill overflowing with sunlight. Alexei P. Belykh's oil ***Spring—Beyond the Volga*** (PLATE 26) has the delicately colored pigments and surface of the American Impressionist Willard Metcalf. The broadly brushed canvases by Oleg L. Lomakin in such paintings as ***Returning from the Front*** (PLATE 69) and ***Steel Worker Reading Pravda*** (PLATE 24) exude raw power.

24. ***Steel Worker Reading Pravda*** 1965
Oleg Leonidovich Lomakin
49-5/8 x 39-3/8 inches, detail
Oil on canvas
Fleischer Museum Collection

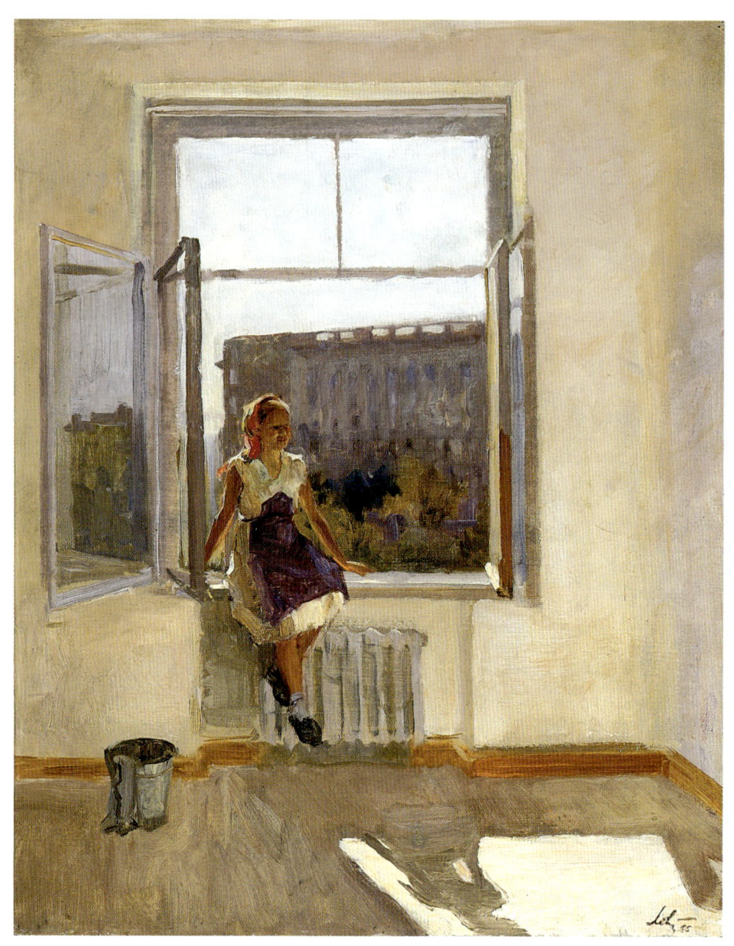

25. ***Warm Day (study)*** 1955
Anatoli Paviovich Levitin
25 x 20 inches
Oil on canvas
private collection

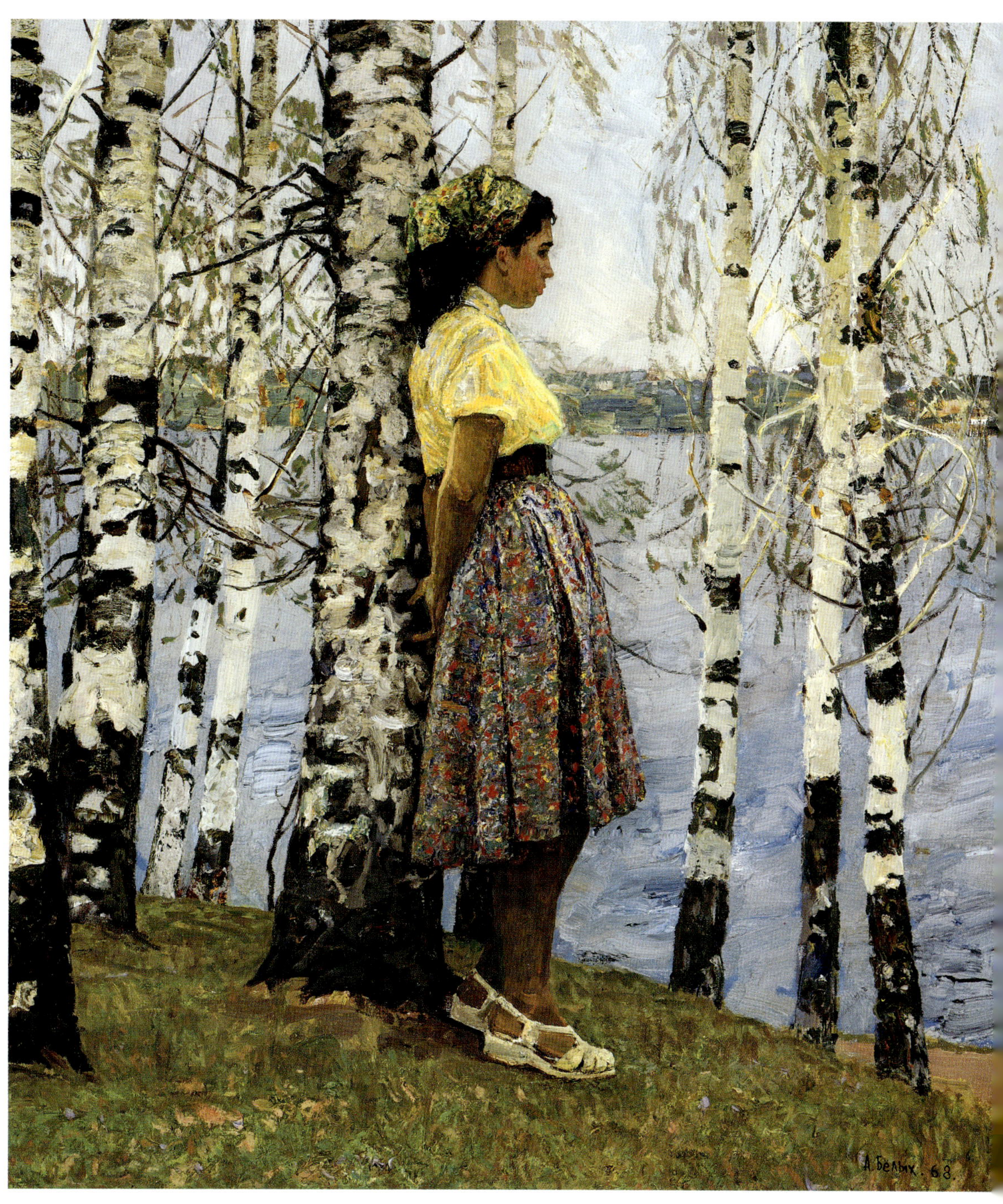

26. ***Spring – Beyond the Volga*** 1968
Alexei Pavelovich Belykh
39-1/4 x 35-1/4 inches
Oil on canvas
Fleischer Museum Collection

What had developed was not Impressionism as prescribed from Paris, but rather it was a working class, muscular Impressionism more in keeping with that of Jules Bastien-Lepage, Georges Laugée, John S. Sargent and their Russian counterparts, Valintin Serov, K. Korovin and S.A. Vinogradov. Unlike the detached objectivity of the French, the Soviet artist thoroughly engaged the subject, the viewer and most of all himself, in the work at hand. There was nothing casual in his intentions.

The work sometimes married the lyrical and intimate, while at the same time keeping sentimentalism and compromise at bay. Fedor Shapaev's compelling ***Young Pioneer at the Door*** (PLATE 112) is a prime example of how the artist could use industrial strength technique while expressing a heart warming incident. It depicts a young girl who expects a reprimand from her mother because she has dawdled, picking lilacs, while walking home from school.

Yuri S. Podlyaski's ***Portrait of Masha Surtukova, Reading*** (PLATE 27) also captures the heart without becoming melodramatically sweet. The youngster has dressed herself with colors that clash. Her yellow socks particularly stand out. The artist now has an excuse to paint radical juxtapositions of colors which would have been aesthetically unacceptable under any other pretext.

The Ukrainian artist Tamara A. Khitrova was somewhat out of her time when she painted the multi-colored ***Geese Farm*** (PLATE 58) right in the middle of the art purges. Her compatriot, Konstantin A. Shurupov utilized licks of color in his radiant oils, ***Lilacs*** (PLATE 89) and ***Azov Steel*** (PLATE 43) through layering of light and tinted pigment. Nikolai E.Timkov's oils ***Evening: The Lavender Hour*** (PLATE 99) uses a single dominant hue while his ***Leningrad: The Petrograd Side*** (PLATE 28) is a pageant of color. They captured the national psyche in ways that the history painters could not.

A sense of *zeitgeist* animated the Russian artist's need to portray the farm and the factory—they were participants in creating a new society. This was somewhat like the spirit of social conscience that moved the American Great Depression artists such as Thomas Hart Benton, Grant Wood and John Stewart Curry to paint along similar lines. In Russia, these subjects and ideas were expressed profoundly by non-sentimental and forceful artistic means for nearly fifty years, whereas, in America, a like movement lasted but a decade. The times themselves gave the artist powerful aesthetic motivation in which to help build a new society. Artists, forever the utopians, responded with creative and productive dedication. Or, as Maksim Gorki put it, the artist was both the "midwife and gravedigger" to society.[42]

Certain constraints, while making Russian and Soviet Realism more insular, also gave it its own definition. Occasionally, if an artist became too influenced by foreign art, he would be accused of rootless *cosmopolitanism*. Being charged as a *zapadnik*, or devotee of Western culture, could lead to ostracism or worse. While rejecting the senseless and inhumane treatment by the art unions and *KPDI* of even compliant Formalist artists, Bown adds this perspective:

27. ***Portrait of Masha Surtukova, Reading*** 1953
Yuri Stanislavovich Podlyaski
31-1/4 x 19-5/8 inches
Oil on canvas mounted
private collection

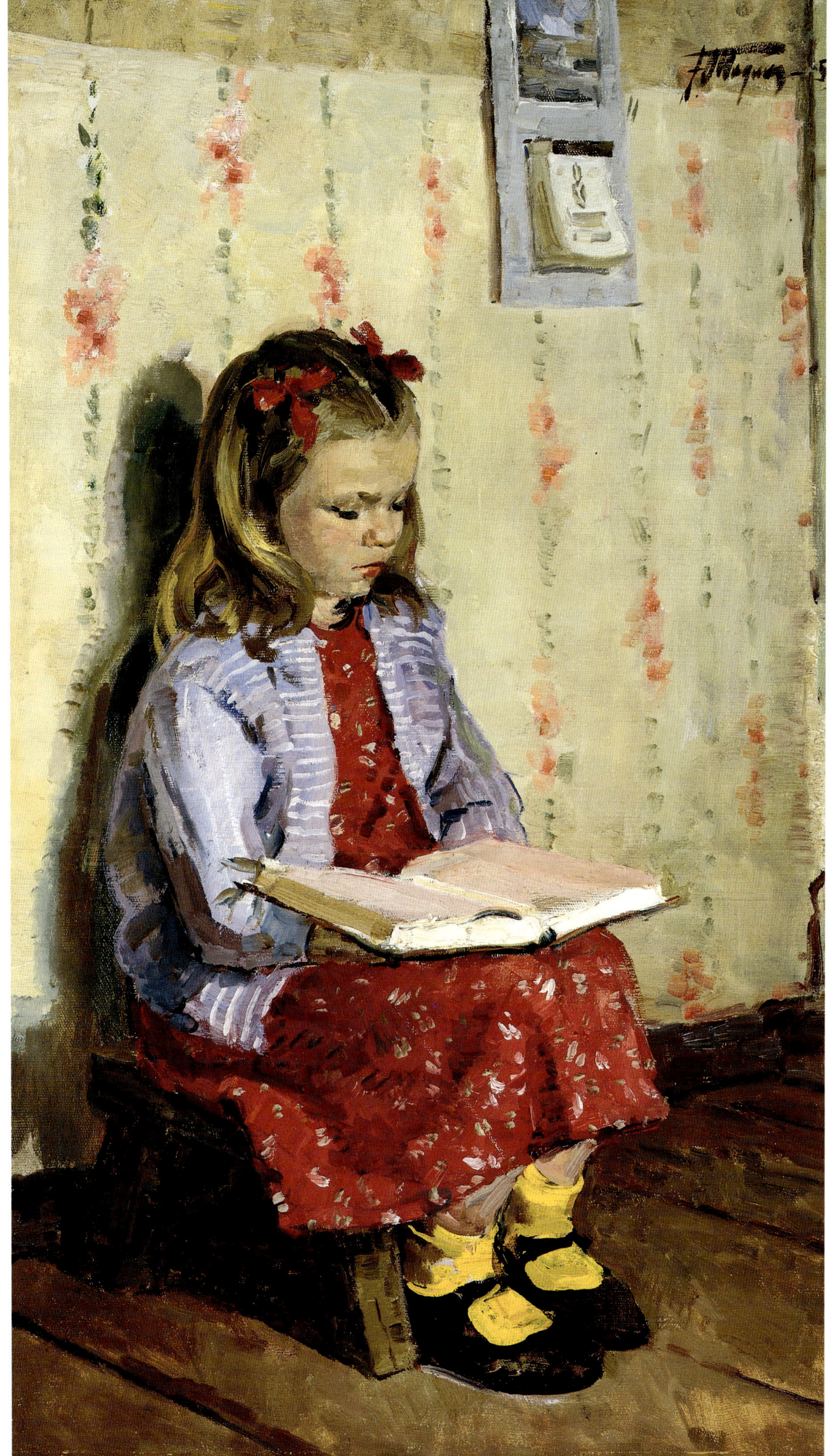

> If the Soviet art establishment had not been so rabid in rejection of foreign influence, so intent on the native heritage, Socialist Realism would not have been the unique phenomenon in twentieth-century art that it (was)...from the vantage point of the western liberal tradition, and with the hindsight provided by history, the conditions of cultural life under Stalin may seen reprehensible. For Soviet artists at the time, these conditions merely represented the bald facts of life...The notion that they might have had moral scruples about doing so would have been incomprehensible to nearly all artists.[43]

There was no doubt in the minds of Soviet artists that the Russian model for art was superior to the trivial Western dalliances. Gerasimov's enthusiasm was typical: "Soviet art opens a new era in world art; its strength and brilliance—and this cannot be doubted—will eclipse even the most outstanding epoches of art's flowering in the past."[44] Of course it did not achieve this lofty position. Compared to the Russian avant-garde of the first third of the century, Socialist Realism took a back seat. It was, however, more characteristic of the ethos of the Soviet state and people and remains ultimately the world's most significant twentieth century Realist school of art.

The breadth of Russian and Soviet Realism seems qualitatively, though not politically, better than its American counterpart during the same period. While heartily rejecting the message of the more overtly political manifestations of the tree of Soviet art, across the board, it seems to master American Realism in at least six ways: 1. It was Fine Arts rather than illustrator (graphic design) oriented. This usually showed in the richness of pigmentation and expressiveness of style. 2. It was more "process" rather than "product" driven. It relied more on first-hand studies rather than shortcuts made through the overuse of photography. 3. It dealt mostly with contemporary life rather than the nostalgic past. Artists sought recent developments in science, technology, industry and society to represent on canvas. 4. It was based on the actual human condition rather than on mere things or appearances. It was figurative rather than landscape based. 5. Realism was taken more seriously in Soviet art during this period than it was in America, where experimentation drew most of the best talent. 6. There was a national agenda with substantive funding behind it. This was a catalyst for giving a more powerful direction to the creative talents of the artists.

A major characteristic of Soviet painting was its concentration on painting en plein-air. In order to do this in the temperamental weather conditions pervasive to most of the USSR, artists would paint innumerable oil sketches out-of-doors. One artist, Sergei F. Babkov, called them "inspirational pieces."[45] As color photography was not readily available to the artist and black and white photography was barely adequate, Russian artists tended to rely on first-hand observation rather than detached sensations gleaned from photographs. Because of this, Soviet artists were spared the numbing influence of working off shallow stimuli.

CHAPTER FOUR

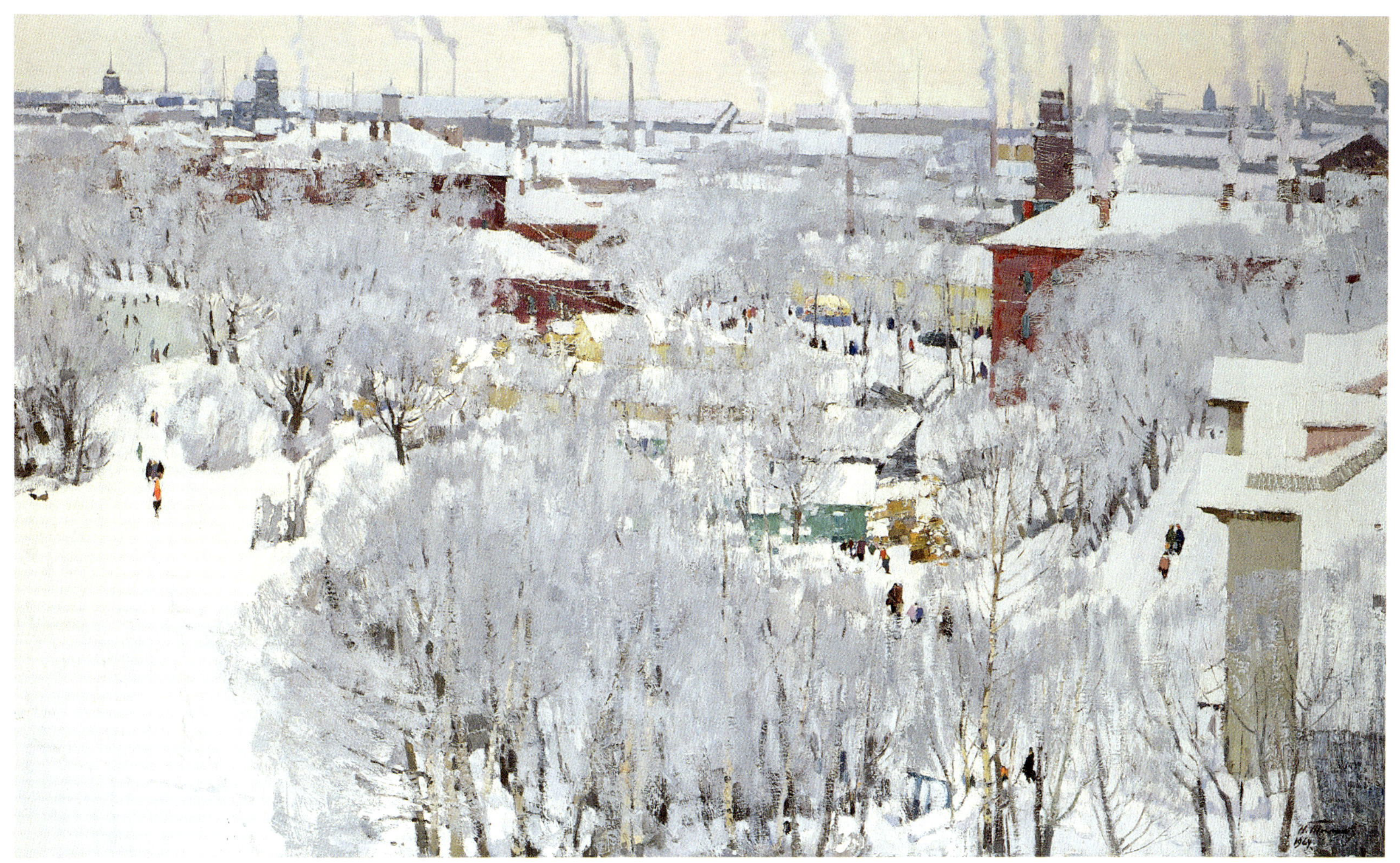

28. ***Leningrad: The Petrograd Side*** 1964
Nikolai Efimovich Timkov
40 x 67 inches
Oil on canvas
private collection

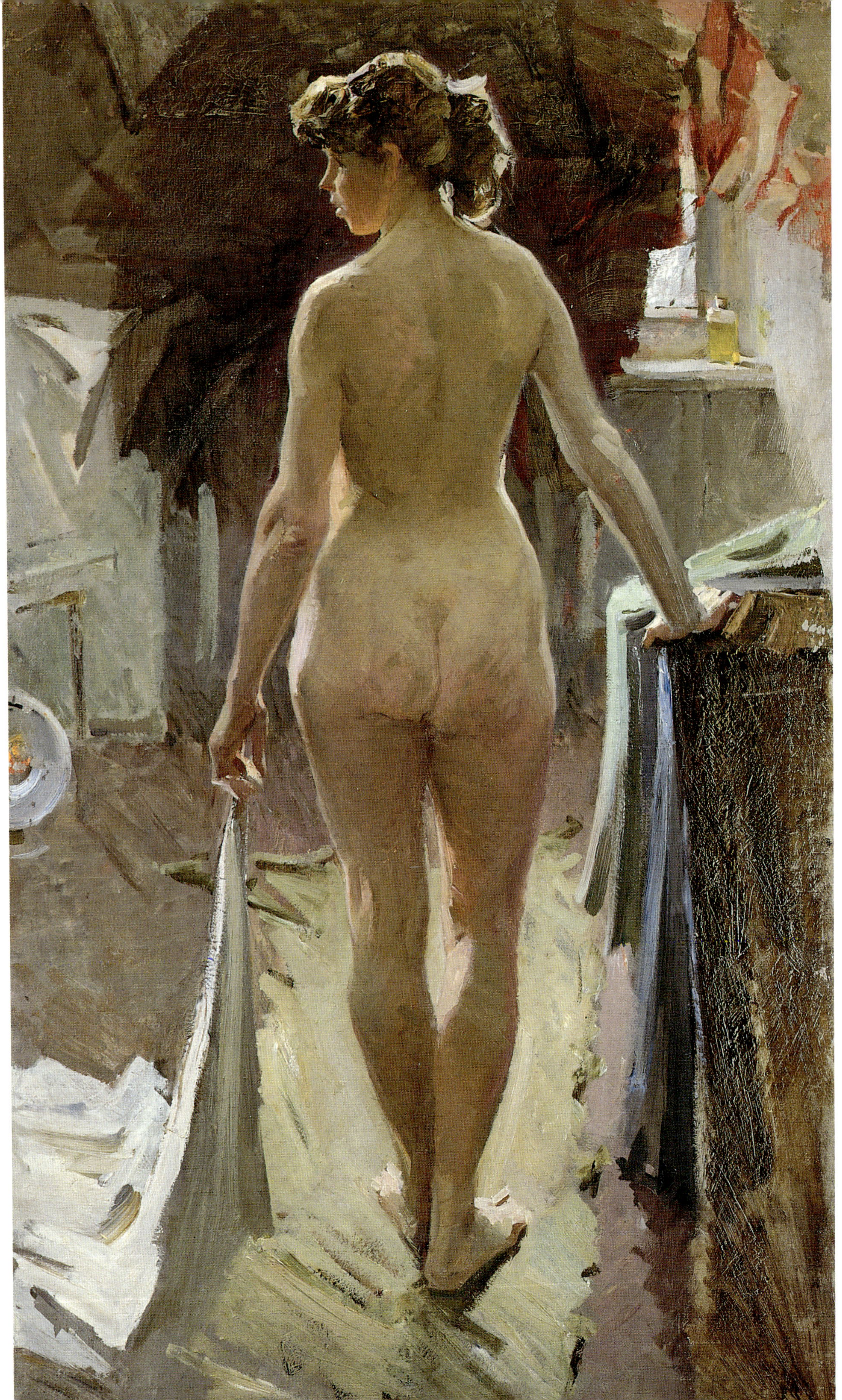

CHAPTER FOUR

In late twentieth century America, most Realist artists have been trained in graphic design or illustration departments at universities or other schools. In the Soviet Union, almost all Realist artists go to fine art institutes, such as the Repin in Leningrad or the Surikov in Moscow to receive training. Mai V. Dantsig's ***Nude*** (PLATE 29) vouches for the strength of the academic training students received from these environments. Because of this, Russian Realism differs vastly from its American counterpart. Whereas we are more product-driven, the Soviet artist is, or at least was, more process-driven.

In the West, the triumph of Abstract Expressionism and a myriad of other "isms," seemed to extoll a cult of originality and to promote alienation of the artist from common society. Soviet Realism drew strength from the society it glorified—not rejected. Russian art, which had been dominated by the avant-garde during the first third of the century, moved inexorably to a more populist and neo-regionalist content. This course of art was a consistent progression from the earlier Itinerant movement. It drew power from within the Russian national ideals and its new, but ultimately tragic, social experiment - Communism.

In the broad course of Russian art, the momentary explosion of Cubism, Suprematism and Constructivism, though significant in art historical terms, were only some of the many strains running through Slavic art. The Realism of Soviet painting related more closely to the central tradition of Russian culture than did these Modernist schools. This artistic tradition was so strongly rooted in Mother Russia that a Working-Class Impressionism more appropriately evolved from the national symbiosis of aesthetics and technology. It was both the highest and the lowest common denominator.

When Western critics ventured written opinions, they found little value in the movement. "In such settings," writes Bird, "the pictures of the traditional Socialist Realist school looked uncomfortable, downright shoddy and, sometimes, laughably absurd."[46] Now with the opening of the Iron Curtain and the importing of significant representations of Soviet Realism, a reevaluation is underway. What was thought to be tired and worn out, now seems fresh, alive and potent when seen from the better examples, first-hand and in new contexts.

In the face of this reevaluation, it is being acknowledged that a powerful new genre had been forged by outstanding Soviet Impressionist artists during the high Socialist Realist period and the subsequent 'thaw.' Unjaundiced by many of the fragmenting tenets of Western Modernism, Soviet art represented its own cultural aspirations as effectively as any school of art in history.

29. ***Nude*** 1957
Mai Volphovich Dantsig
59 x 35 inches
Oil on canvas
private collection

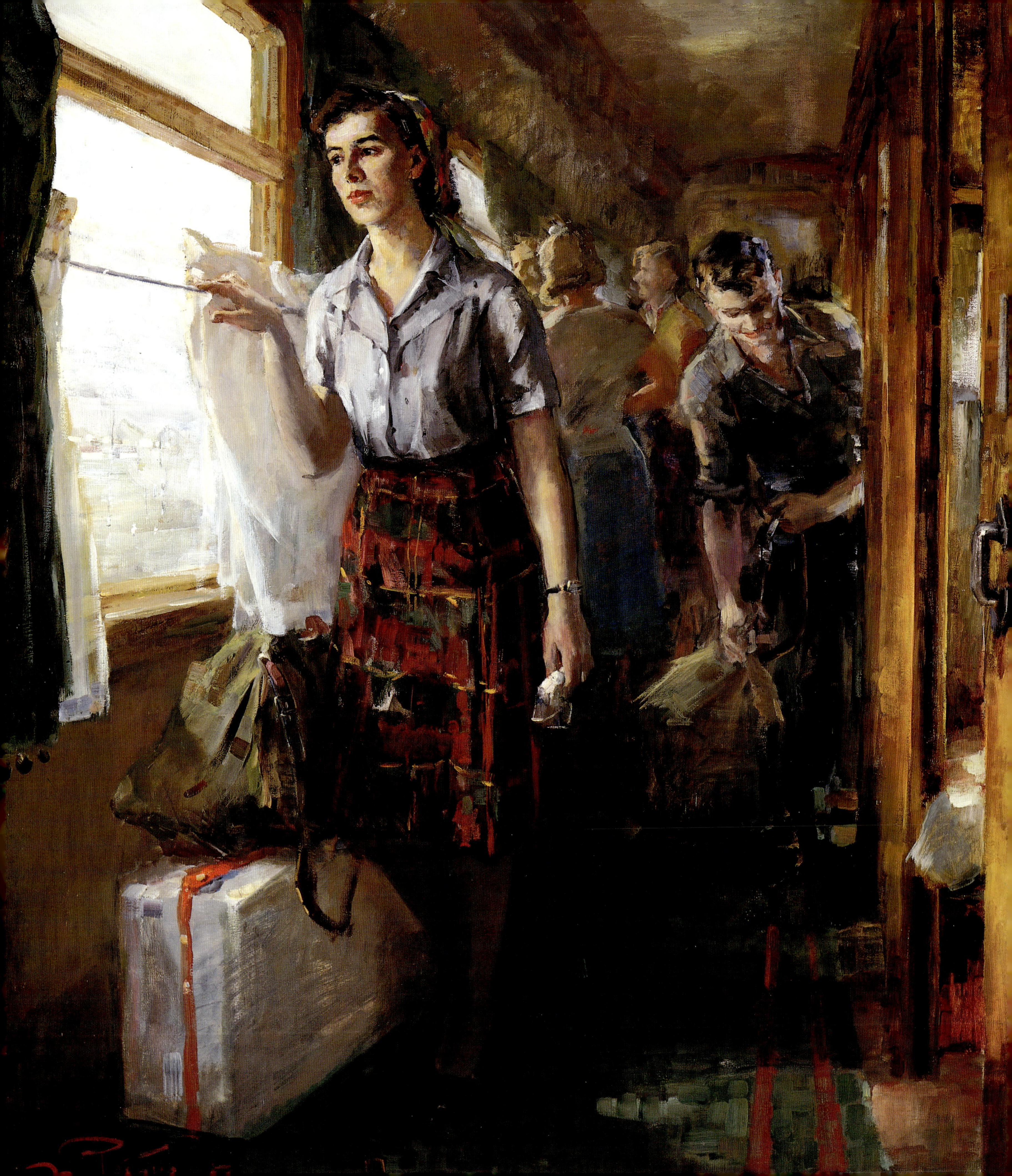

Art of the Virgin Lands

When Agriculture Minister Nikita Khrushchev began his leadership of the Communist Party in 1953, one of the Party's first decrees was to open up central Asia to cultivation. It was called the Virgin Lands because no plow had ever tilled its fertile soil. The agricultural-political experiment in the Republic of Kazakhstan, western Siberia (Altai territory) and in the Urals was begun in the spring of 1954. Along with the successes in outer-space, it became the most significant national theme in the decade of the 1950s.

Thousands of *KomSoMol* (Young Communists) volunteers, farmers and even artists were "called" to the service of the Motherland in the vast steppes of the Soviet Union. In June of 1954, the Surikov Institute of Art in Moscow sent a number of students to the Lomonosovsky *Sovkhoz* (settlements) to work and paint the pioneers and patriots of Soviet labor for a season. Other artists too felt the lure of the southeastern steppe whose psychological pull made it the place to be. Hundreds of *Sovkhoz* with adobe houses, white tents, radio masks and tractors quickly dotted the region.

Throughout the mid to late 1950s, this movement became the single most emphatic motif for official Soviet artists. A great epic, not dissimilar to the sod-busting on the American prairie in the late nineteenth century, the Virgin Lands captured the national imagination. These long fallow lands were to be the source of inspiration for hundreds of artists; their credo announced their intentions:

> "To reflect in Realistic, artistic forms the beauty and grandeur of the labors of the Soviet Patriots in the Virgin Land and to help them gain victory in their new pursuit is one of the important objectives of Soviet art at the present stage." [47]

To this end, young artists were sent to chronicle this great epic, with unerring accuracy, from its inception. They lived side by side with caterpillar operators, agronomists, geologists and other workers who voluntarily answered the call of the Party and *KomSoMol*. Close proximity to the difficult life of the Virgin Landers helped the artists capture the essence of these patriotic times. Those artists who went to the steppes were able to see and paint the heartbeat of the Virgin Lands, a profound national theme.

30. ***Into a New Life: Virgin Lands*** 1959
Erik I. Rebane
63-3/8 x 53-5/8 inches, detail
Oil on canvas
Fleischer Museum Collection

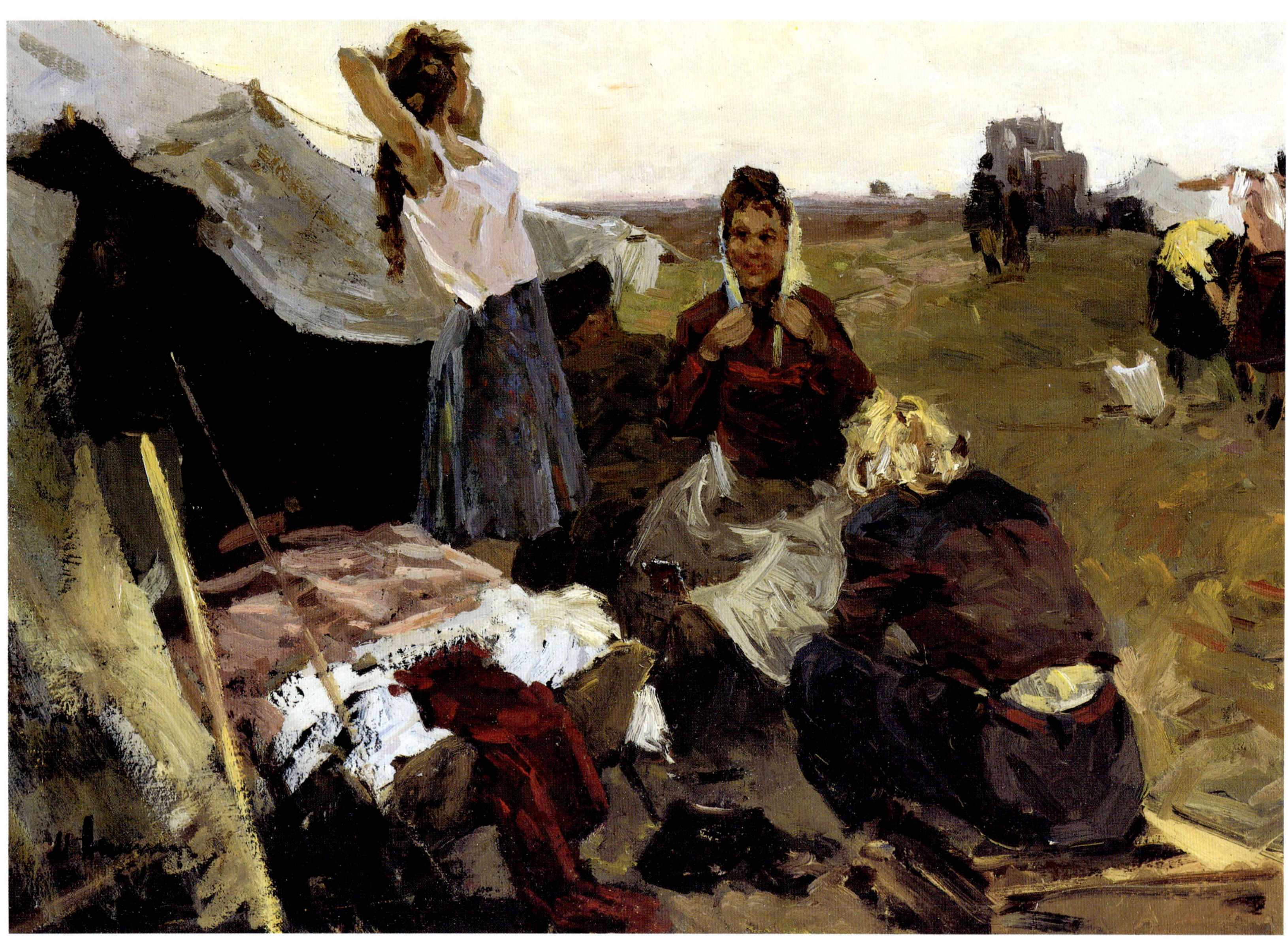

31. ***Morning in the Virgin Lands*** 1954-55
Mikhail Korneevich Anikeev
20-1/4 x 28-3/4 inches
Oil on canvas
Fleischer Museum Collection

32. ***On Kuban Virgin Land*** 1958
Vasili Kirillovich Nechitailo
31-1/2 x 59-1/8 inches
Oil on canvas
private collection

CHAPTER FIVE

The movement was like the spirit of social conscience that inspired the American Great Depression artists. The ideas were expressed profoundly by non-sentimental and forceful artistic means for nearly fifty years, whereas in America the movement lasted but a decade.

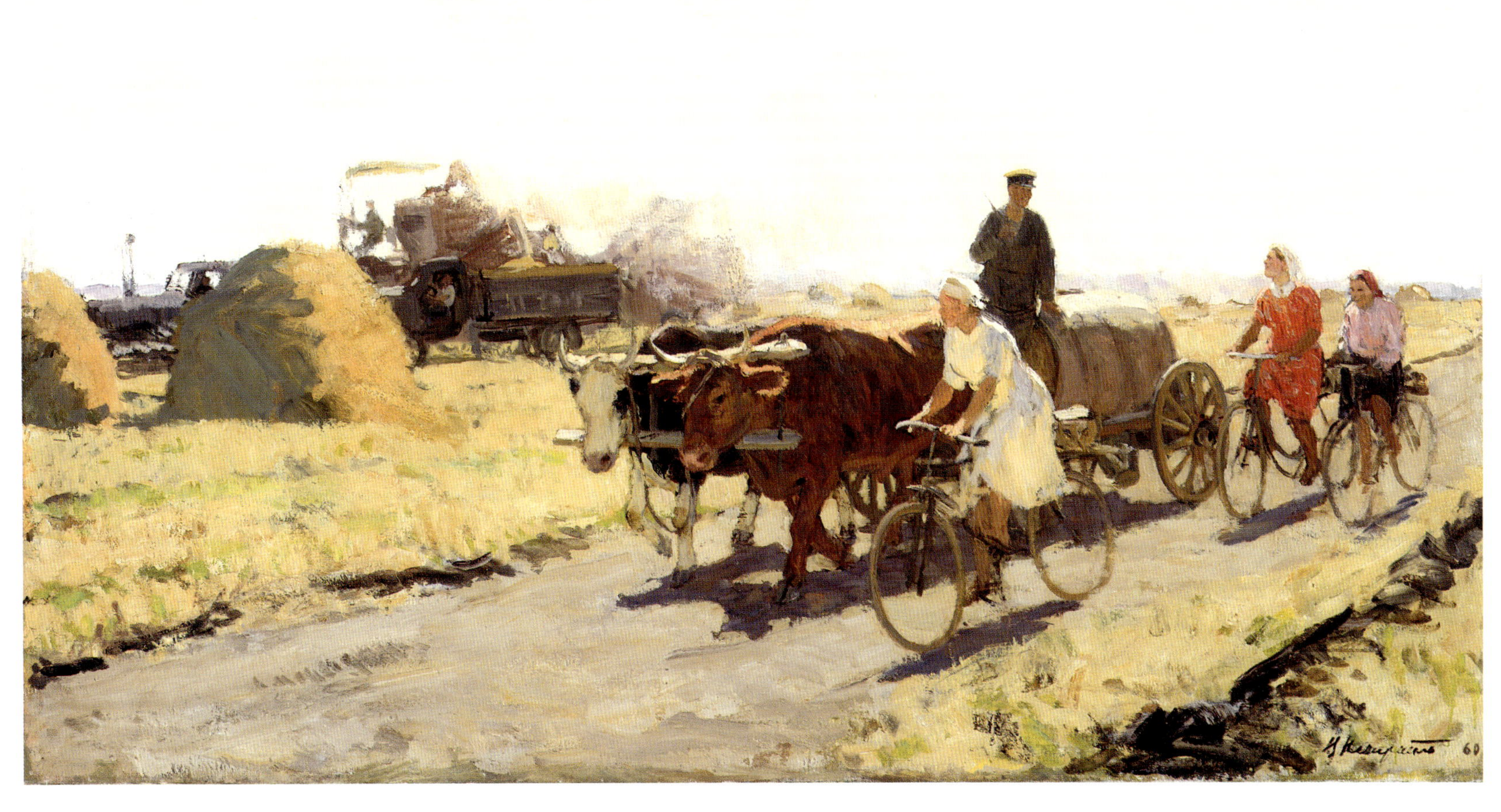

Soviet Impressionism/Realism, especially at this time, was characterized by its portrayal of contemporary life. This is not new, for it has traditionally been the pattern for successful art movements throughout history. Except for a number of pieces painted in honor of the October Revolution, the Great War and the cults of Lenin and Stalin, almost all content and subject matter depicts life as lived in the Soviet Union at the time the artist created his work. Dmitri Mochalski notes that "The lifestyle in the Virgin Lands is peculiar, distinctive and somehow reminiscent of life in the front line. Life here is full of difficulties, but also of romantic appeal and big bright prospects."[48]

These new Itinerant artists painted life where it was being lived–en plein-air. In the oil sketches done of the Virgin Lands, there was an air of authenticity which was remarkably lacking in late twentieth century American representations of cowboys and Indians. The Soviet Realists painted "today, today" not waiting until tomorrow to represent it. In this sense, it became an invaluable historical account, as well as a nourishing artistic experience for those painters who went to the Soviet outback.

The first artists of the initial season had a special section at the All Union Exhibit in 1954 and an exhibition at the Palace of Culture in Moscow. Included in the exhibitions were Mikhail K. Anikeev, Vladimir F. Stozharov and Mikhail E. Tkachev among many others. ***Morning in the Virgin Lands*** (PLATE 31) by Anikeev is a plein-air painting of young women arising early from their tents to ready themselves for the arduous labor of conquering the steppes. A masterpiece of Impressionistic observation, Anikeev has at once captured the sense of difficult camp life in Kazakhstan and the lack of amenities common to civilized Russian women. Vasili K. Nechitailo visited the village of Peredovaya in the summer of 1954 and later created the vigorously rendered oil ***On Kuban Virgin Land*** (PLATE 32). Nikolai Sokolov in Kazakhstan and Semon A. Rotnitski in Altai were also among the first wave of artists.

Artists of the stature of Vladimir I. Nekrasov, Alexander G. Gulyayev and Dmitri I. Shemelyov arrived the next season, June of 1955. Nekrasov painted ***Just Married, Virgin Lands*** (PLATE 33) depicting a newlywed couple who met and married while fighting the battle for bread on the Kazakhskaya steppe. Even today, his oil sketches made in the Virgin Lands reverberate with new interpretations on old themes. Shmelyov painted in the lower intensity of the chromatic scale in his marvelous ***Kazakhstan's Virgin Land: Tents on the Frontier*** (PLATE 34) which shows what tent life was like.

Alexander Gulyayev went to Altai territory in western Siberia to paint his masterpiece, ***Waiting for the Mail in the Virgin Lands*** (PLATE 35). Each of these paintings blend a powerful and sensitive use of color of the best Impressionist work of Monet, Sisley and Pissarro. Using a figurative base and moral purpose, the Soviet works become living documents to the intense inspiration each artist brought back from the Kuludinskaya and Altaian steppes.

CHAPTER FIVE

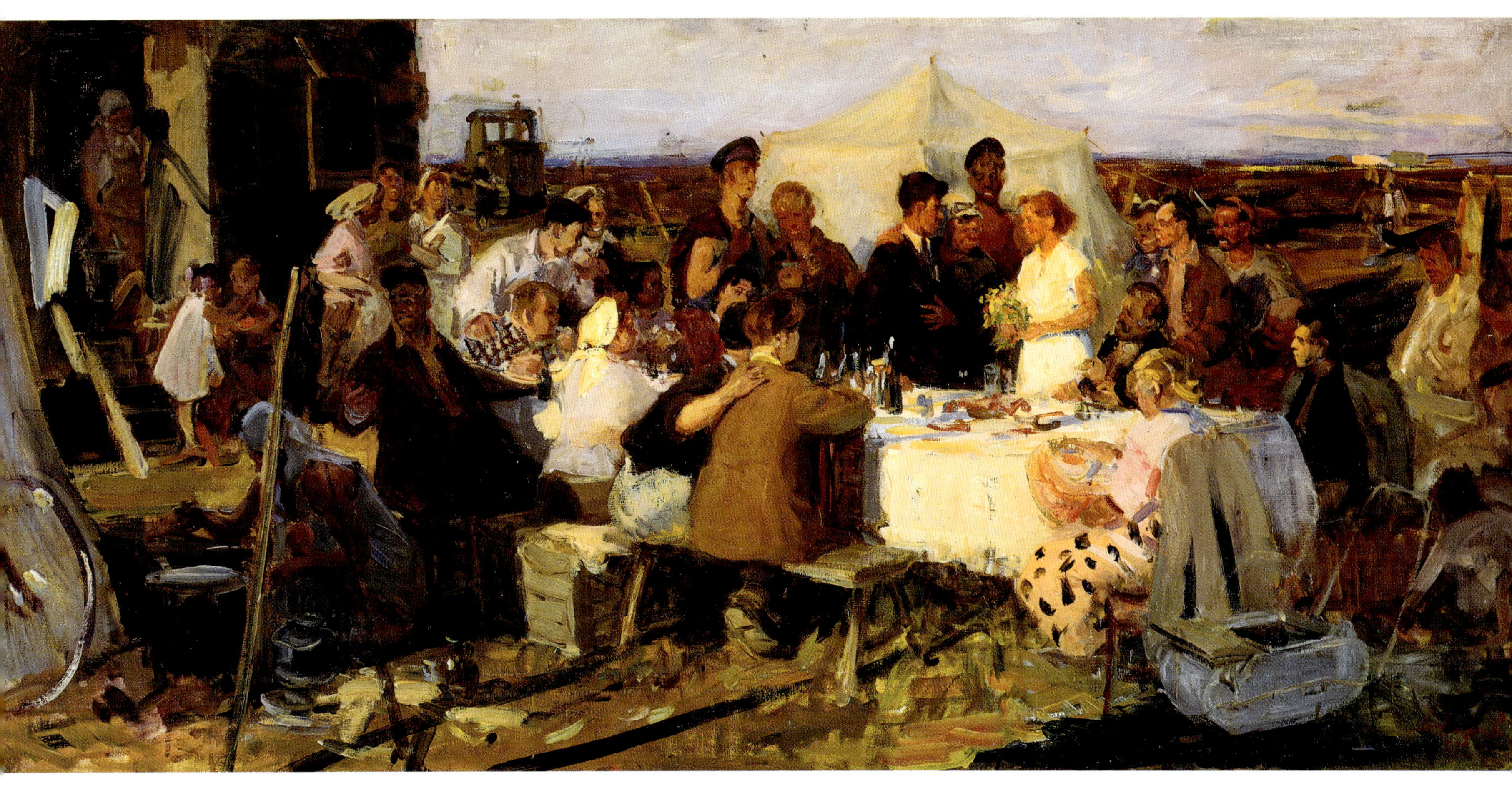

33. ***Just Married, Virgin Lands*** 1956
Vladimir Ilych Nekrasov
23-1/2 x 38 inches
Oil on canvas
private collection

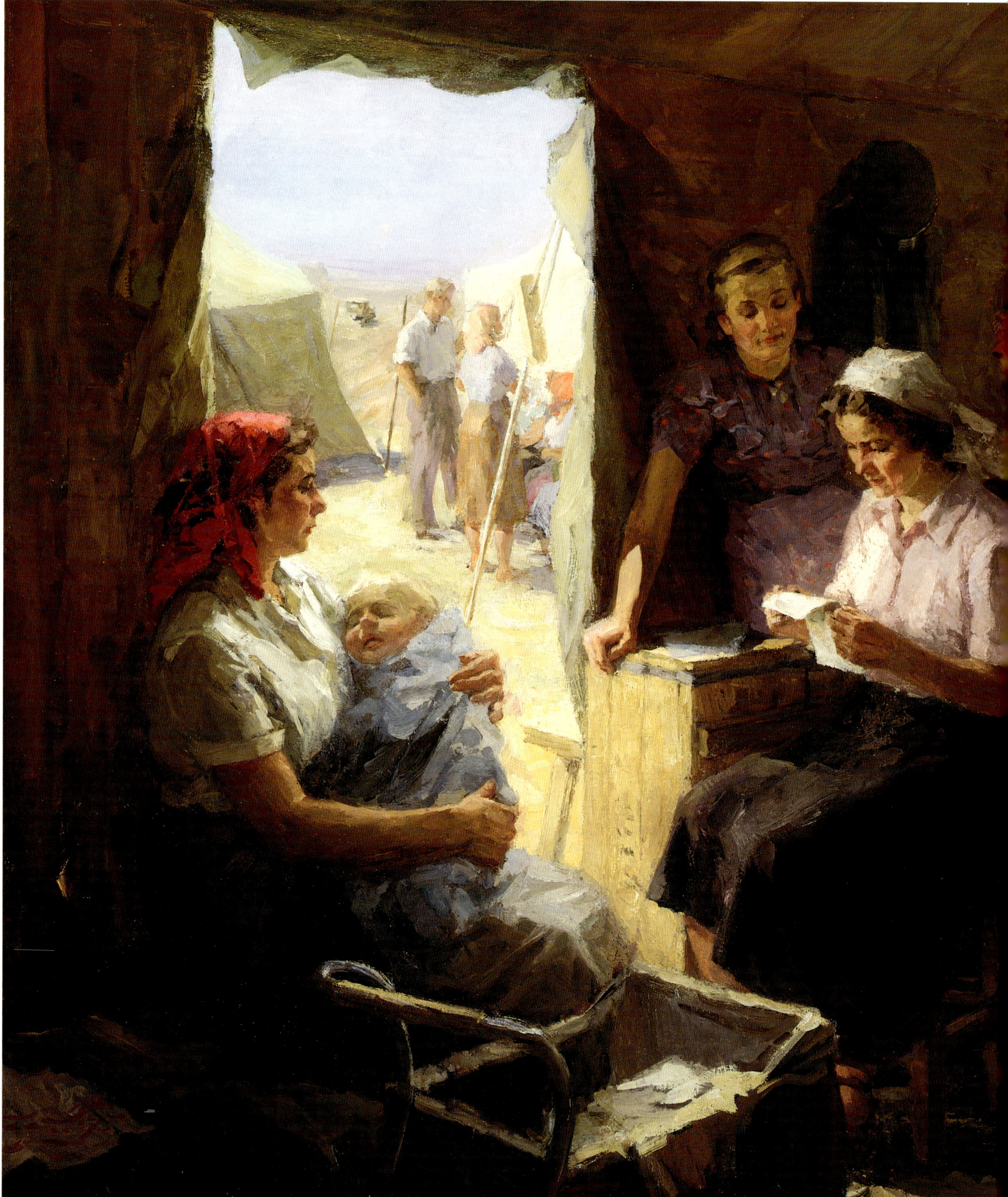

CHAPTER FIVE

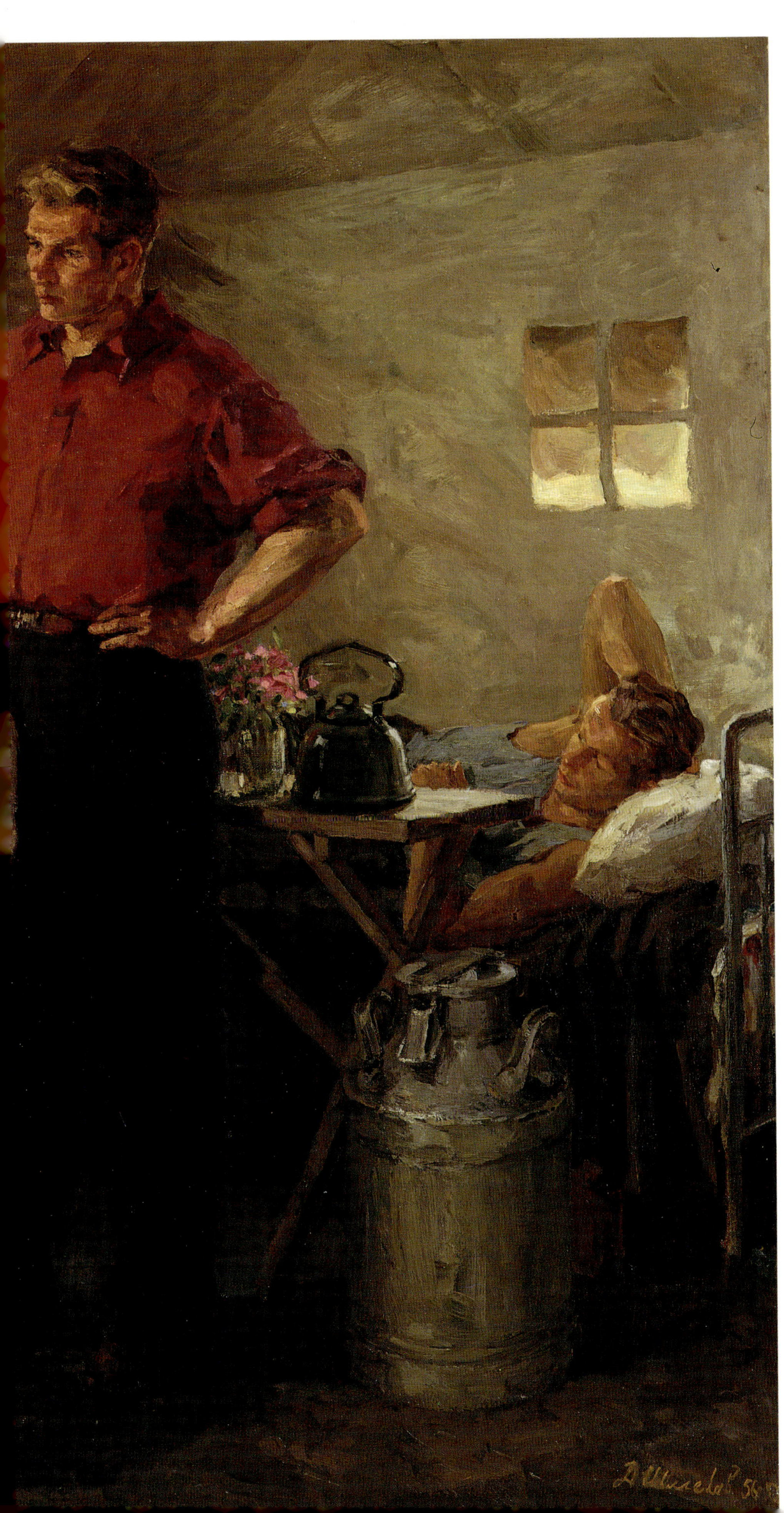

34. ***Kazakhstan's Virgin Land: Tents on the Frontier*** 1955-56
Dmitri Ivanovich Shmelyov
46 X 65 inches
Oil on canvas
private collection

The emblems of sacrifice for the greater good are typified by the field kitchen, white tent, trailer, the caterpillar-tractor and the endless black furrows plowed into the low horizon. In America, some may grin at the idea of big Russian women driving tractors. Yet in Alexei V. Fedorov's ***Virgin Land Tractor Driver*** (PLATE 36), the rough but friendly attitude of the female tractorist commands our respect. One caterpillar-tractor operator, the colorful Dasha Tereshova, became famous and was much written about.

From sketches and drafts made in the wake of the Virgin Land experience, Erik I. Rebane painted ***Into a New Life: Virgin Lands*** (PLATE 30). It depicts a young *KomSoMol* who has volunteered to be a pioneer thousands of miles from her home. Her tears are symbolized by the raindrops on the train window. The work poignantly represents the tremendous national outpouring of interest in the topic.

Almost every painting on the Virgin Lands theme during the decade of its prominence was painted boldly in the Working-Class Impressionist style. Delicate Academicism would have been unbefitting. Of these paintings it was said, "Virgin Land (art) witnessed that the artists strove to capture life in its diversity and to leave an impression of the character of the Soviet people in the origin of their labors and way of life."[49]

A Muscovite once said, "We Russians love to suffer. Show us something to endure and we'll suffer for it!" There is something about the Slavic soul that is given to melancholia. Perhaps it is the weather in the northern latitudes that stimulates this mood; in sunnier climates elsewhere in the vast Russian steppes, such dreariness is dispelled. There has always been a certain somber quality to the color and light of northern Russian paintings.

The Virgin Lands experience created an antidote for this stereotype of ongoing suffering. In a sense, the Soviet art unions joined together to collectively ban pessimism from their depictions of contemporary life and landscape themes. To dispel negativism and to express positive qualities in art became crucial to the efforts of official artists. Vasili Yakovlev, one of Stalin's court painters, said it best:

> "A landscape is a picture, skillfully drawn, enlivened with things of interest today, depicting all the new things that contemporary society offers. A landscape full of movement, life and the work of the Soviet people – such a landscape will be both lively and life-affirming." [50]

It was the art mission to the Virgin Lands which caused, to a great extent, the lightening of the Russian palette. Once artists ventured into the vast steppes of central Asia, bathed in sunlight and bereft of humidity, they were never the same. It wasn't so much the color, but the light which affected them. Stronger color had already begun to be reintroduced after the post-Stalin thaw. Now, combined with the experience in the Virgin Lands, Soviet painting began to take on a more Impressionist look. In a sense, Virgin Land Impressionism was the remedy to the dank Northern Impressionism previously characteristic of Soviet art.

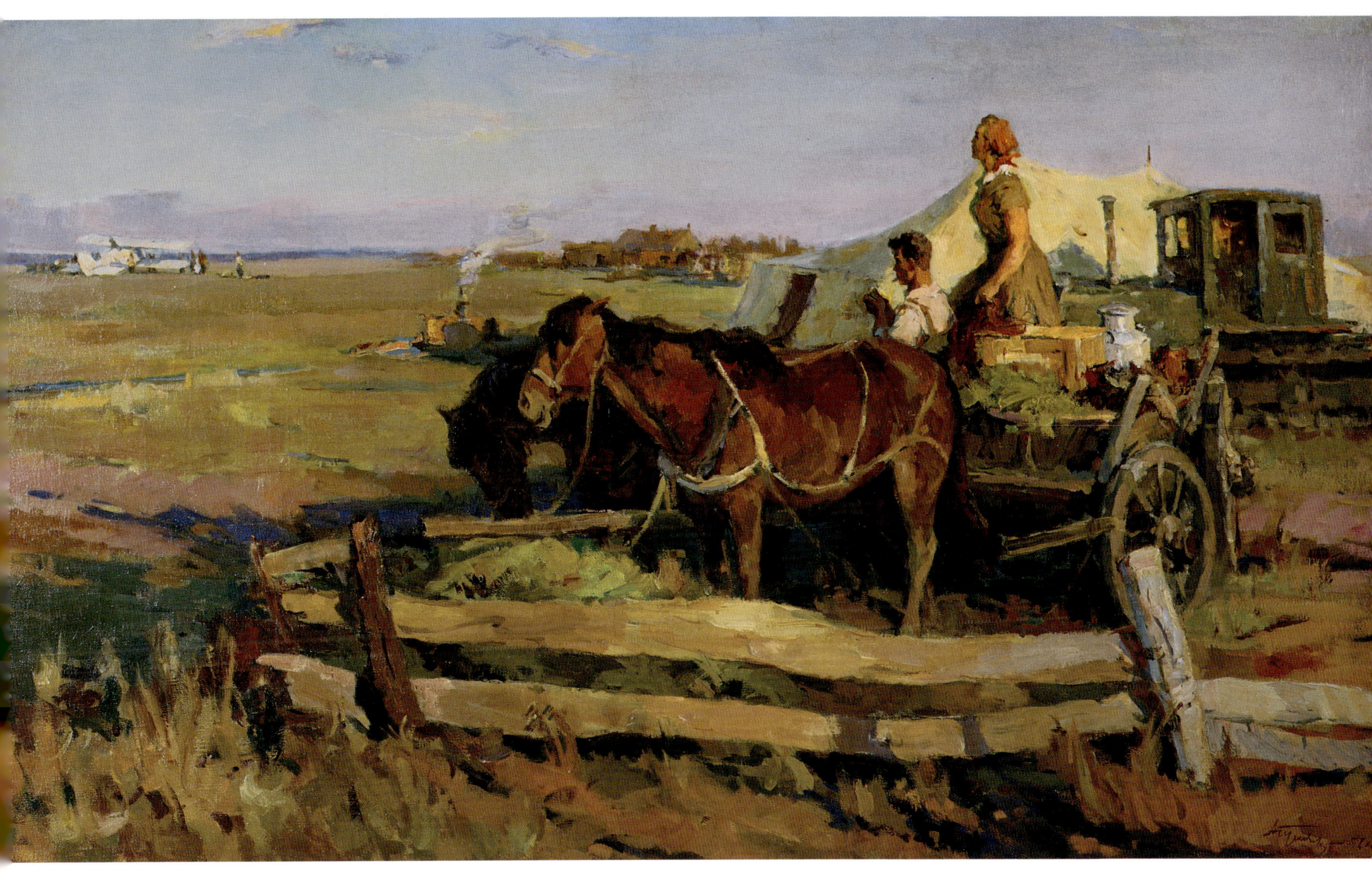

35. ***Waiting for the Mail, Virgin Lands*** 1957
Alexander Georgievich Gulyayev
31-1/4 x 53-1/2 inches
Oil on canvas
private collection

Russian Realist art dealt mostly with contemporary life rather than the nostalgic past. It was based on the human condition rather than things or appearances. Realism was taken more seriously in Russia during this period than it was in America, where radically experimentive art drew the best talent.

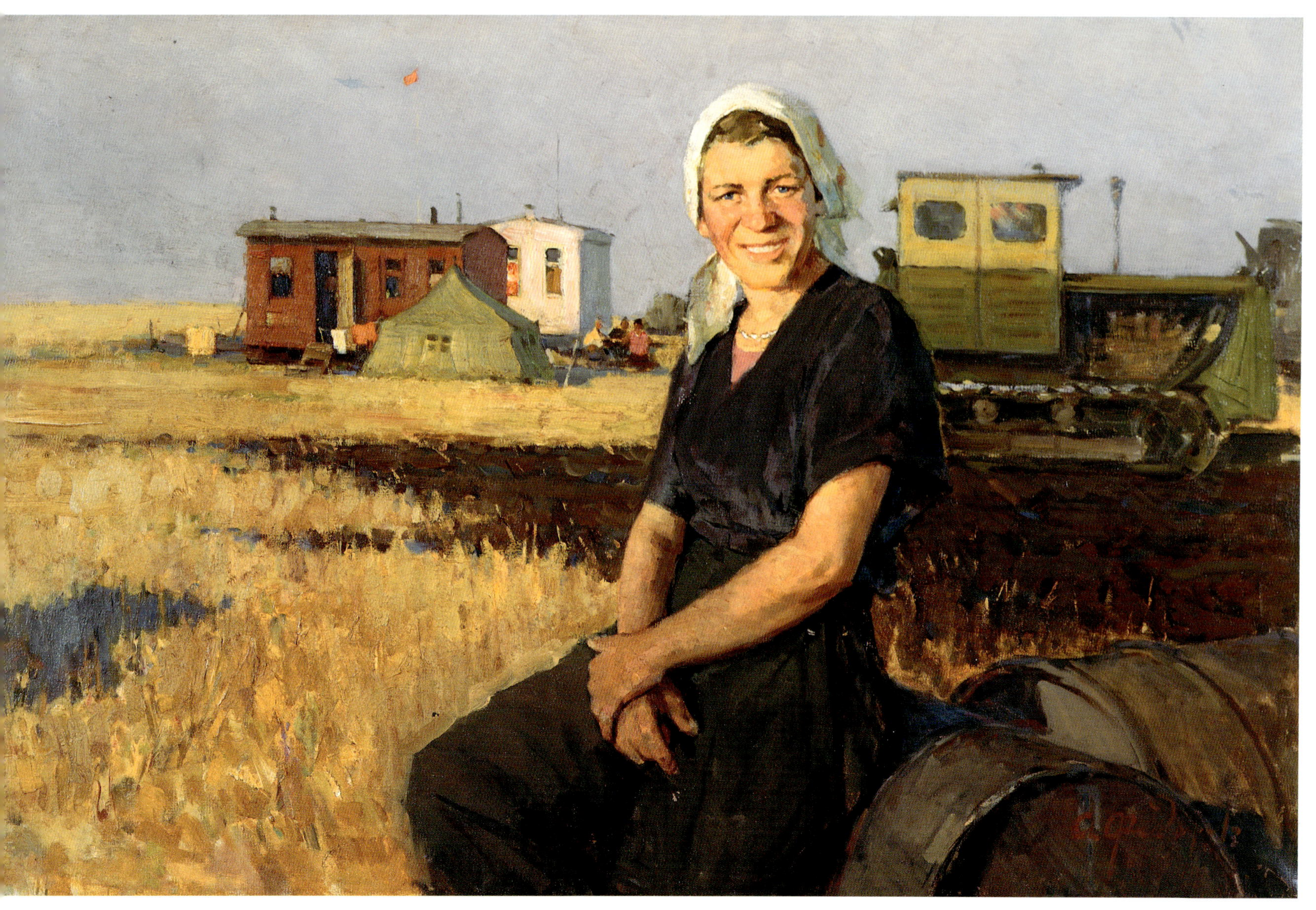

These Virgin Lands artists developed a working-class genre which featured humble laborers on the huge collective farms in every day situations. This was called *tipichnost,* or the presentation of life as it typically is, not in its extreme manifestations of angst or naive Idealism. They also incorporated the concept of *narodnost,* or the quality of popularity and accessibility derived from acting in the best interests of the people. Virgin Land Impressionism merged the two ideas effectively.

Uplifting the common man progressed to the level of a patriotic endeavor. Nearly one half of all art created during this period reflected workers and their labor. Perhaps the best comparison to Virgin Land Impressionism might be found in the art of the American West, particularly in Frederic Remington and the Taos masters, Victor Higgins, Oscar Berninghaus, Ernest Blumenschein and others. Both schools captured the sunlight, the aboriginals, the immigrants, and the pioneering efforts of breaking new ground. The epic subject was typical in both schools and both Russian and American artists did it splendidly.

36. ***Virgin Land Tractor Driver*** 1957
Alexei Viktorovich Fedorov
34 x 52-3/4 inches
Oil on canvas
private collection

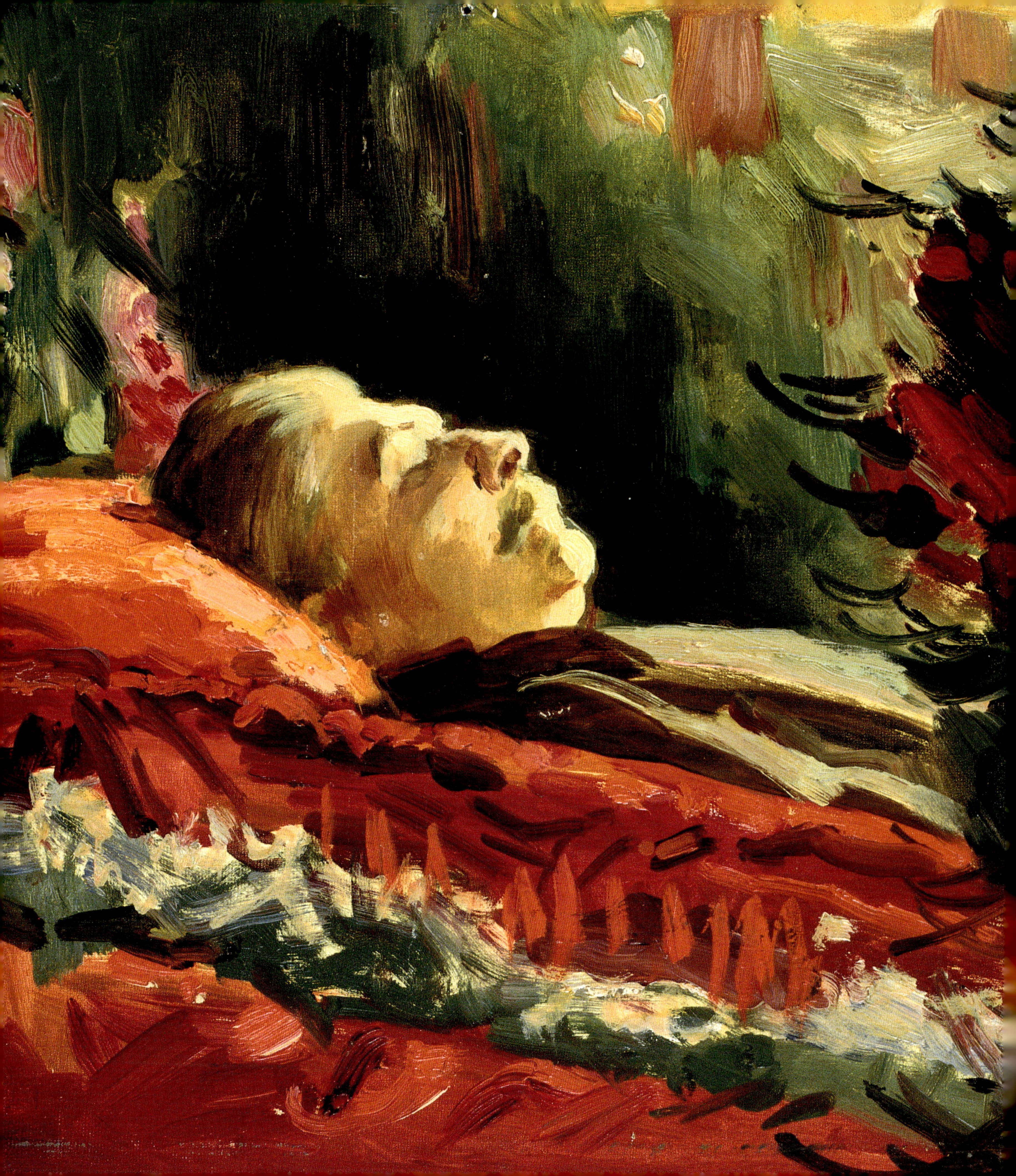

THE ART UNION: OFFICIAL ARTISTS

Soviet artists were asked to play a part in molding society, and they did so with some success. In the entire failed experience of Communism in Russia, where when one pushed the button and nothing happened, it did happen in the visual arts. Of all that Russia produced in this century, nothing, except perhaps their scientific endeavors, quite equals the indomitable creative power of their artists.

Why was it possible for the artists to succeed? Preeminently this society utilized its foremost talents. The creativity of this strong and energetic people could not be suppressed. It mattered little to what end or artistic form these talents applied themselves; with the proper motivation and opportunity they were able to work wonders. They exuded a spirit of positivism in a culture generally known for its "can't do" attitude. They were no less successful than in other periods in art history where church and state prescribed the proper means of expression. The real surprise is that such proscriptions guiding art in the mid-twentieth century would exist at all.

Instead of directions always coming from higher authorities, the Soviet artistic community tended to be critiqued from within, through colleague peer pressure. Alexander Sidorov of the USSR Academy of Arts has overstated a half-truth: "Art criticism was reduced to a concrete exposition of ideas sent down from on high; it played the role of a priest of a new belief who explained the postulates of that belief to the parishioners of the church of Socialist Realism."[51]

But the typical Official artist did not feel particularly coerced. Except for the commissions, which sometimes came from the Party officials and major salon-style exhibitions with tendentious titles like "Workers of the Soviet Utopia," aesthetic criticism usually came from the art agencies, unions and artists themselves. Anyway, painting the occasional obligatory *pompier* picture on commission or for an exhibition did not seem to infringe on what the artist really wanted to do. Only about twenty percent of their time was thus consumed in exchange for financial security. In the West, taste-makers, usually from the press, galleries and museums, have played the same role as the Cultural Ministry and the Art Union officials in keeping political correctness.

37. ***Stalin in his Coffin*** 1953
Mikael Gusen Ogly Abdullaev
10 x 14 inches, detail
Oil on canvas on board
private collection

Included in extensive state support, young Soviet artists received effective training from the reconstituted art institutes and academies. They were given subsidies, art materials, exhibitions, publications and commissions to showcase their abilities. More importantly, they truly believed in the political and social experiment to which they contributed. They felt the historical inevitability of their cause was true, at least in the early years before stagnation of the late Brezhnev era.

They were motivated by the belief that the Communist state was a perfect model for society, and they were integral cogs in the machinery of refining that society. They saw themselves as Stalin was quoted to have said, as "Engineers of the Human Soul."[52]

It matters little, in assessing the quality of their art, that they had been energized by the ideology of a corrupt, brutal and despotic regime espousing wildly outdated and ineffective theory. They were galvanized by its early successes, and the spirit of Internationalism which had begun in their own country. Life was rough, but they saw hope in having won the Greatest War and in having communized eastern Europe and China to the rightness of Marx, Engels and Lenin. They had sent Sputnik and Yuri Gagarin into space and the future looked red. They painted it with the gloss of "pink powder."[53] During these heady years, especially in the 1950s, Socialist Realist Working-Class Impressionism reached its apogee.

Historically, we find artists lending their talents and hearts to comparable purposes. Egyptian and Greek artists of genius created masterpieces to false gods. Yet collectors and museums worldwide vie with each other to acquire these *chef d'oeuvres*. To condemn Socialist Realist art for political considerations may be popular, but does not advance professional standards of art criticism. True art finds means to transcend the dogma, ideology or spirit with which it was created and speaks to all ages. Soviet Realism does the same. Matthew C. Bown has convincingly stated this case:

> But such a judgment, prompted by political or moral considerations, has no real place in the history of art; it is a relic of the Cold War; indeed, it is a mirror image of the ideologically inspired distortions of Stalin's own art historians... The nature of a regime, however reprehensible, does not dictate our response to the art produced under its aegis... Many artists in the West, and in many disciplines, have engaged in partisan fashion with the great issues of their time; art and propaganda are separate but not mutually exclusive categories. How many people looking at the Bayeux Tapestry today realize it is full of Norman lies; how many are *au fait* with all the Tudor polemic in Shakespeare's *Richard III*?[54]

Alexander Sidorov noted that Soviet art was the "maidservant of State and Party bureaucracy."[55] It is a fact that a number of mediocre artists received the highest Communist accolades because of their subservience to the dangerous ideology of *partiinost*. This meant putting the Communist Party in a central or leading role in all aspects of Soviet life. Among these were Pavel Sokolov-Skalya, Dmitri Nalbandyan and other sycophants, who achieved a level of recognition their art did not warrant. Some critics have used this to justify a view that Soviet Socialist Realism, in any form, was not a viable school of art.

CHAPTER SIX

Unfortunately, many artists saw in the idea of *partiinost* a tenet worthy of their trust. Even Western intellectuals, during this period, also felt that the Party was a more worthy advocate for social change than their own democratic governments. The noted art historian, Anthony Blount, the Queen's Keeper of Pictures, even spied for the Soviets with this belief in mind. Many Western artists, such as Pablo Picasso, Ben Shahn, Rockwell Kent, and the Italian, Renato Gusttuso, among others, placed their faith in the fiats of Communism.

As artists moved toward an unabashed acceptance of the Communist "Manifest Destiny," this led to the emergence of Socialist Realist painting during the 1930s to 1970s. So fully did the Soviet population readily believe in the rightness of the "Dictatorship of the Proletariat," that Realist artists thought they were working in the so-called Vanguard. Unlike certain Western counterparts, they were part of the society, not alien to it. Also, unlike some Western avant-garde artists, they did not show disdain for the working class. Rather they found that artistic expression could be dynamic without mystifying or intellectualizing as so many lower Manhattan artists seem to have done.

The social consciousness that was exhibited by Soviet official artists was at least as important as the technical method of creation or choice of the subject itself. They called this *ideinost*, which was the introduction of new attitudes and ideas, first approved by the Communist Party, as the chief means of expression. Since works of art are effective conveyors of ideas, the artist whose work is imbued with *ideinost* or collective conscience as defined by the Party, was the most effective and successful. This was a galvanizing force as in other great art movements which have been energized by ideas and ideologue.

Even apolitical landscape painters were encouraged to invest their work with more ideology and social significance. In Russian art historical parlance, this was called *konyunktura*, or the portrayal of subjects suggested by social and political developments. The Party and its spokesman, the KPDI, felt that there should be no neutrals in this great cause, but that every artist should be anxiously engaged.

It was a dual devotion to the Party and to the cult of Lenin and Stalin, to which many gave so much adulation. The Communist painter, Dmitri Nalbandyan remarked, "I work in the genre of the Leader," i.e. Joseph Stalin. Autocracy came quite naturally to the Russian people. "To us it may seem bizarre," wrote Bown,"but at the time to a people in the steel grip of the Communist dream, it was perfectly comprehensible."[56]

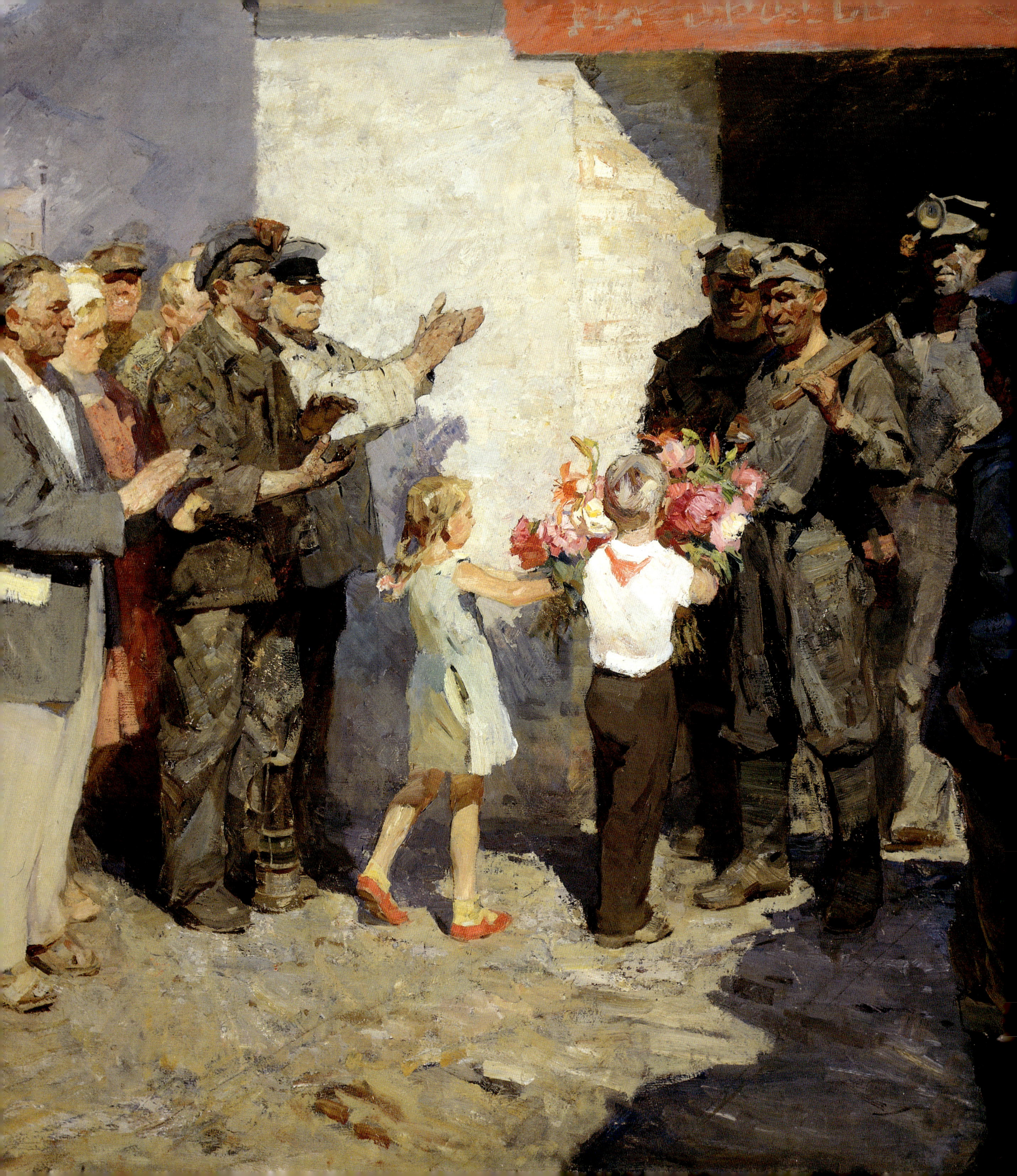

CHAPTER SEVEN

UNOFFICIAL, OFFICIAL ART

Lest one believe that Soviet Socialist Realism was mostly hard core propaganda or stylistically homogenous, it should be emphasized that most artists worked in a variety of manners. It was diverse beyond the original interpretations of any of its earliest proponents. Ironically, the basic tenets of Constructivism, the early Russian avant-garde movement, similarly extolled the glories of labor, technology and organization.

The Western myth of mechanical artists working robotically on endless paintings of Lenin or Stalin distorts the reality of the Russian art scene. For the most part, artists of the Soviet Union painted emphatically, sincerely and without much overt propaganda. For example, Muscovite Veniamin M. Sibirski's ***Greeting the Stakhanovite Champions: Winners of the Five Year Plan*** depicting a Party dignitary in the crowd as a secondary figure was not unusual for the time. They tended to paint real people lacking in pompousness, naturally conducting their lives.

In most Soviet and Russian Realism, we have an art representing the workers as they really were–unadorned by sentimentality or grandiloquence. Not that this rhetoric was never used, for in *Brigade* or team painting from the 1920s to 50s, we can find it in all its stilted didacticism. David Elliott's opinion balances the scales: "In Socialist Realism, everyone and everything was idealized. A testament to ideology rather than reality."[57] Conditions were shown in a positive light without over-idealizing. This mode was also more of a philosophical approach to art than a specific style. For the majority of artists, pink powder was employed with surprising restraint in a society which made heroes of those workers who met their quotas and used the ubiquitous *pater familiae* figures of Lenin and Stalin.

Union artists were the official artists of the day, but unlike most historical camps, they turned the definition of official art on its head. A number of important elements, which are usually ascribed to official art, were notably missing in Socialist Realist painting. Throughout the course of art history, official art commissioned by governments, religious bodies, wealthy benefactors and corporations, was characterized by smooth polished surfaces, emphasis on drawing and highly delineated forms, indirect painting techniques,[58] abundance of detail (verisimilitude), overly idealized, especially when dealing with the lower classes; officious, pompous and ceremonious subjects, grandiloquent gestures and stilted poses; and deference for the power brokers or upper classes.

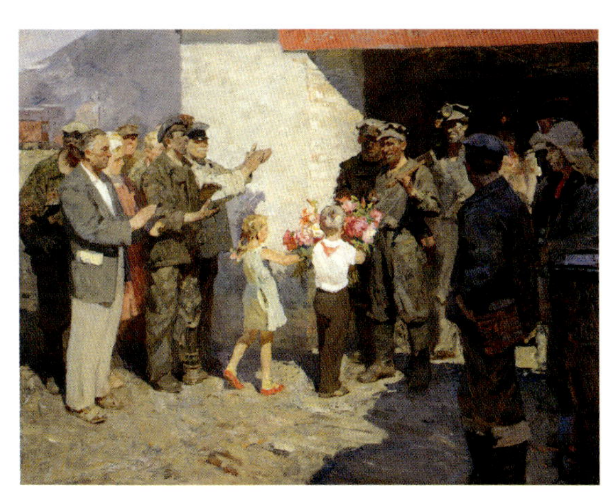

38. Detail
39. ***Greeting the Stakhanovite Champions: Winners of the Five Year Plan*** 1963
Veniamin Mikhailovich Sibirski
53 x 69 inches
Oil on canvas
private collection

In most respects, official Soviet artists tended not to paint in the manner previously described. Even though painting materials tended to be in short supply, the entire Soviet Impressionist school seemed resolute in producing thickly painted canvases, often encrusted by gobs of pigment. The typical Soviet painter expressed him/herself in broadly Impressionist/en plein-air terms – vigorous *impasto*: painterly surfaces and textured pigmentation; emphasis on *bravura*; full-bodied brushwork and implied form, direct painting; wet-into-wet, alla prima, *fa presto*, lack of pedantic detail, suggestions of particulars instead; positive but natural presentation of their subjects, lack of grandiose rhetoric, depicted in more typical fashion, except in *kartina* and *Brigade* art; and, party leaders were usually portrayed as common people.[59]

Through painterly application and direct brushwork, Soviet artists found a technical means of expressing working class issues. In Vasily M. Arapov's ***Babushka*** (PLATE 44), the class correct vision of an elderly worker for the Soviet state is painted with great power and sensitivity. Without resorting to minutia, finesse or the sophistication exemplified by cabinet painters of the nineteenth century, Arapov has instead employed a two-fisted approach to brushwork and paint application. Generally speaking, they show an Impressionists non-concern for acute definition. Also, painting was not reduced to a formula like the Neo-Impressionism of Georges Seurat and Paul Signac, until the Rough or Severe style emerged.

Soviet artists employed an economy of visual language to sustain their pictures. Igor A. Razdrogin's ***Orange Roofs in Winter*** (PLATE 40) exemplifies this incisiveness. It depicts a mother pulling a sleigh in which her child on the sleigh is shown with just a single dab of color. All is sacrificed to the general power of the figures, surface and composition. The epoch had its own stylistic answer to expressing what Proletarian art should be. Working class subjects required a working class technique–an Impressionist approach was their solution.

Without resorting to the painters mall stick and one hair brush, the Russian Impressionist-Realists attacked their canvases with surprising boldness. This is unexpected when we realize that these were official artists painting numerous official pictures. This passionate display of brushwork challenges the myth that Soviet artists were robots painting in a mechanical fashion.

On a broad scale, major artists truly painted for the people, not just to awe them. In Soviet official art, many age-old dictates were confounded. This break with tradition allowed the artists the opportunity to portray life as it really was, though not worse than it really was. This mission, despite all the tedious lectures on classical and academic verities the artists endured, was the lasting legacy of Soviet official art.

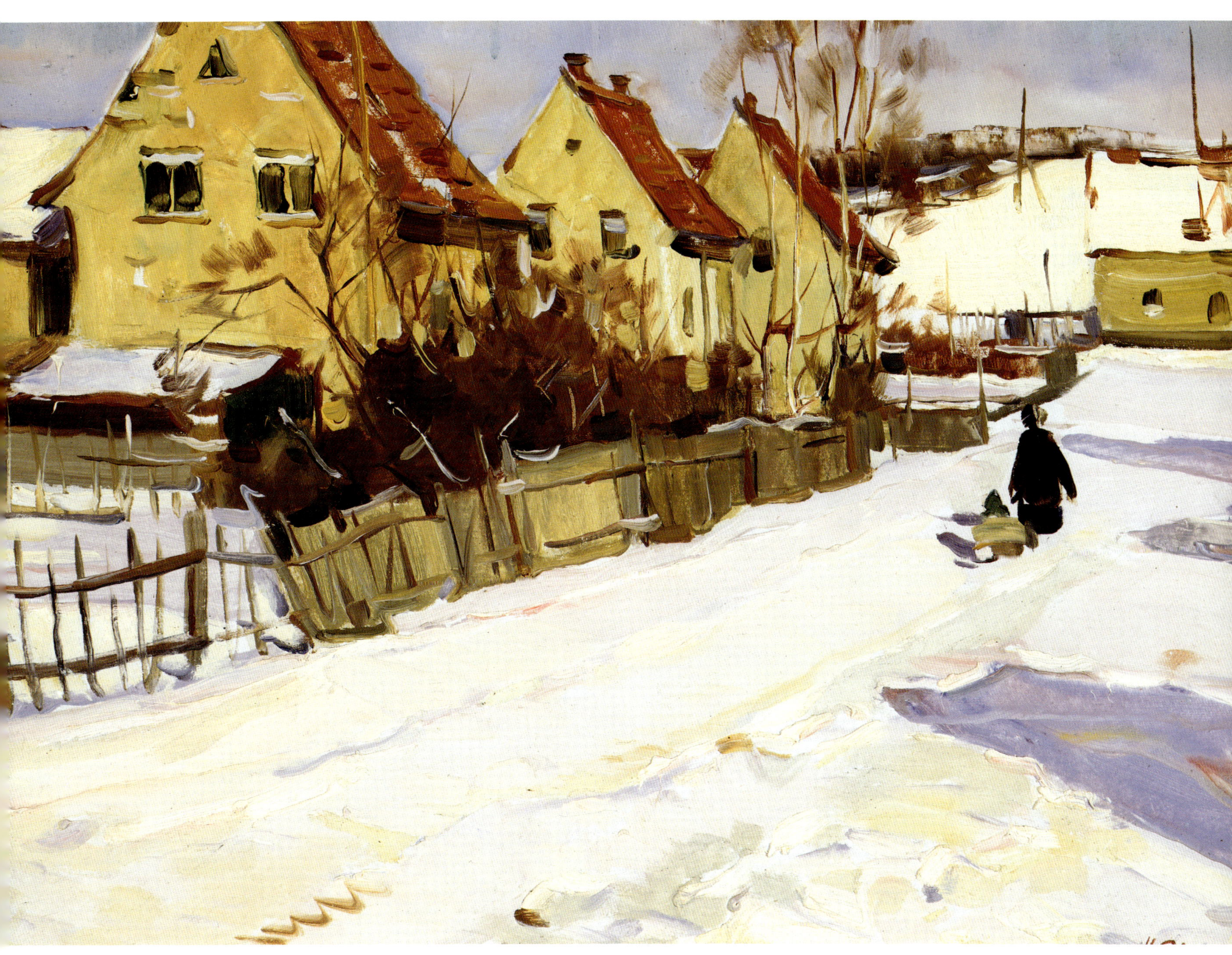

40. ***Orange Roofs in Winter*** 1960
Igor Alexandrovich Razdrogin
13-3/4 x 19-3/8 inches
Oil on canvas
private collection

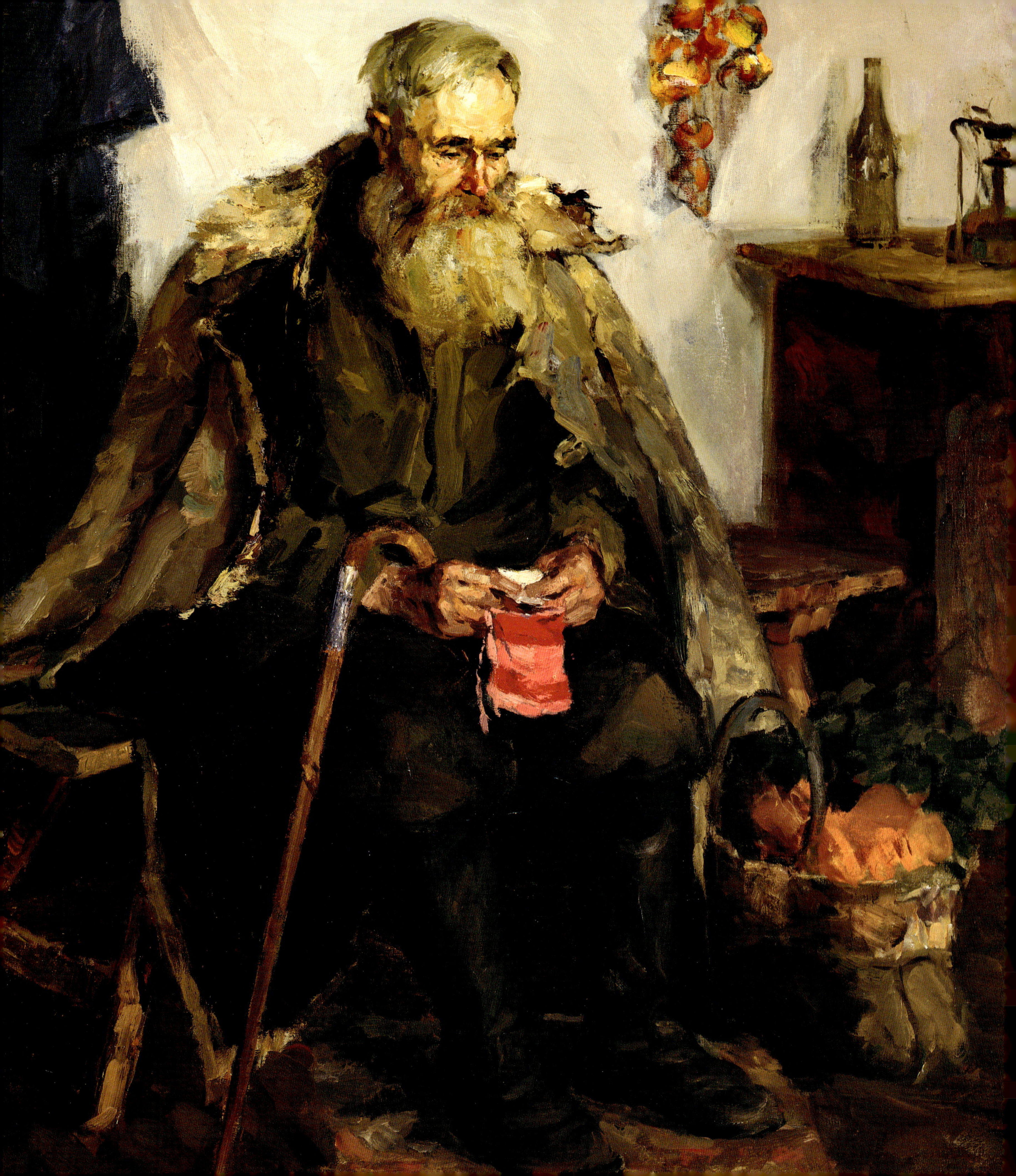

CONCLUSION

Once perceptions of reality set in, exposed first in the denunciations of Stalin in 1956, the invasion of Hungary the same year, and later, the economic drain from the Vietnam War which sapped the strength of the country, despair and doubt began to weaken the artists' creative spirits. By the end of the 1970s, the best artists of the period were graying and the climate for producing bright-eyed Socialist Realism dimmed. No longer did they truly believe in the lie of Communism. They now found the Socialist system intolerable and suffocating. Yet, ideas about the common man and the importance of labor, which transcended mere ideological Communism, still energized a number of artists working during the late 1970s and 1980s.

When Socialist Realism collapsed, art in the Soviet Union was unable to reinvent itself with every new manifestation of style that came along. Art during the Soviet period had committed itself to one form and now a vacuum drew in a slavish adoration for Western art. It fell back on its own unofficial tradition, which had for so long been based on finding ways to oppose official art rather than in being itself.

After the non-conformists had no common enemy, it became unhinged. From painful and tortured figurative paintings, to pastiches of Modernism of every variety, to heavy-handed "Stoz" political satire, a confused transitional period exists in the Russian art scene today. Even French decorative, "sweet" art and academically doodled tourist art have been revived for the foreign trade.

Never again will Russian art be as powerfully concentrated in a cohesive manner, full of purpose, for the public good as when manifested at the high point of Working-Class Impressionism. Now it is every artist for himself. But there once was a period, a Camelot of sorts, where the artists collaborated with the State, working in willing unison, to make a difference in the "soul of man."[60] It would be difficult to envision a scenario in which the scale and intensity of this cooperative effort could ever be duplicated. Thankfully, gone with it is the one party state – the tyranny of Communism.

Once a credible, non-conformist alternative to the official school became established by 1970, many of the art critics of the period jumped from the bandwagon of Socialist Realism. Little consideration and research have gone into the study of this, the declining decades of the Socialist Realist movement, even though a number of superlative artists continued to make important contributions. The 1970s and 1980s might be considered the warm after-glow of High Socialist Realism, rather than the cold cinder many critics suppose.

41. ***Everything is in the Past*** 1953
Nikolai Konstantinovich Kazakevich
54-3/4 x 38-3/4 inches, detail
Oil on canvas
Fleischer Museum Collection

Critics and art historians such as John Bowlt, Matthew C. Bown, David Elliot, Alexander Sidorov, Brandon Taylor and Sarah Wilson have already written remarkable essays on the Soviet period. More needs to be said. Their critiques, and my own, will remain preliminary at best until the end of this decade, given the general resistance of art critics.

Suzie Gablick and others have proclaimed the death of Modernism to have occurred about 1980. The same is true of Socialist Realism. It died of stagnation and enervation about the same time. The postmortem of Post-Modernist and Post-Socialist Realism literature, now acknowledges a greater melding of Western and Russian artistic aspirations. Working-Class Impressionism fitted so perfectly with the aspirations of its age that it endured for nearly fifty years. While not an earth-shaking movement in art historical terms, it was suited for its time.

Since December of 1991, when the Soviet Union died, a circle has been drawn around this political period. It is now a part of the historical past. With the official demise of the sponsoring artistic apparatus of Socialist Realism, this era takes its place in art history, even though it had been dying for more than a decade. Some hard questions need to be asked regarding Soviet Realism. After the giddiness about the demise of the Cold War, it is now time for an honest reevaluation of this significant artistic manifestation.

Many feel that fine examples of Russian and Soviet Realism will artistically inspire a younger generation of American Realists. By presenting the most noted Russian artists of their day, through their best work, it may be possible to make a change for the better in present day American Realism. The power of expression in an art for the people cannot help but influence our own artists as well as entice collectors who are presently becoming captivated enough to procure these prime Russian works.

CONCLUSION

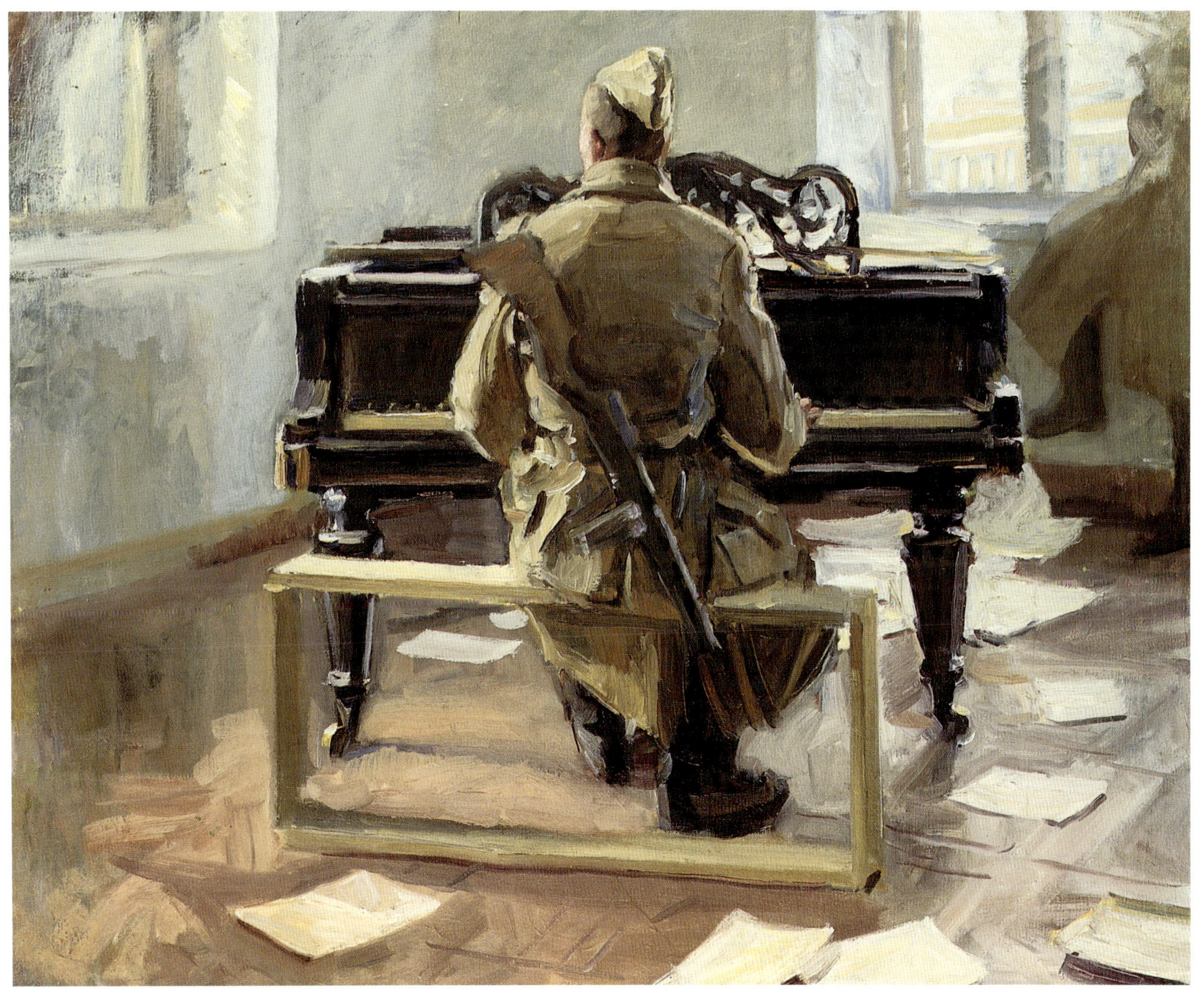

42. ***Victory Day in Berlin*** 1960
Georgi Stepanovich Melikhov
31 x 39 inches
Oil on canvas
private collection

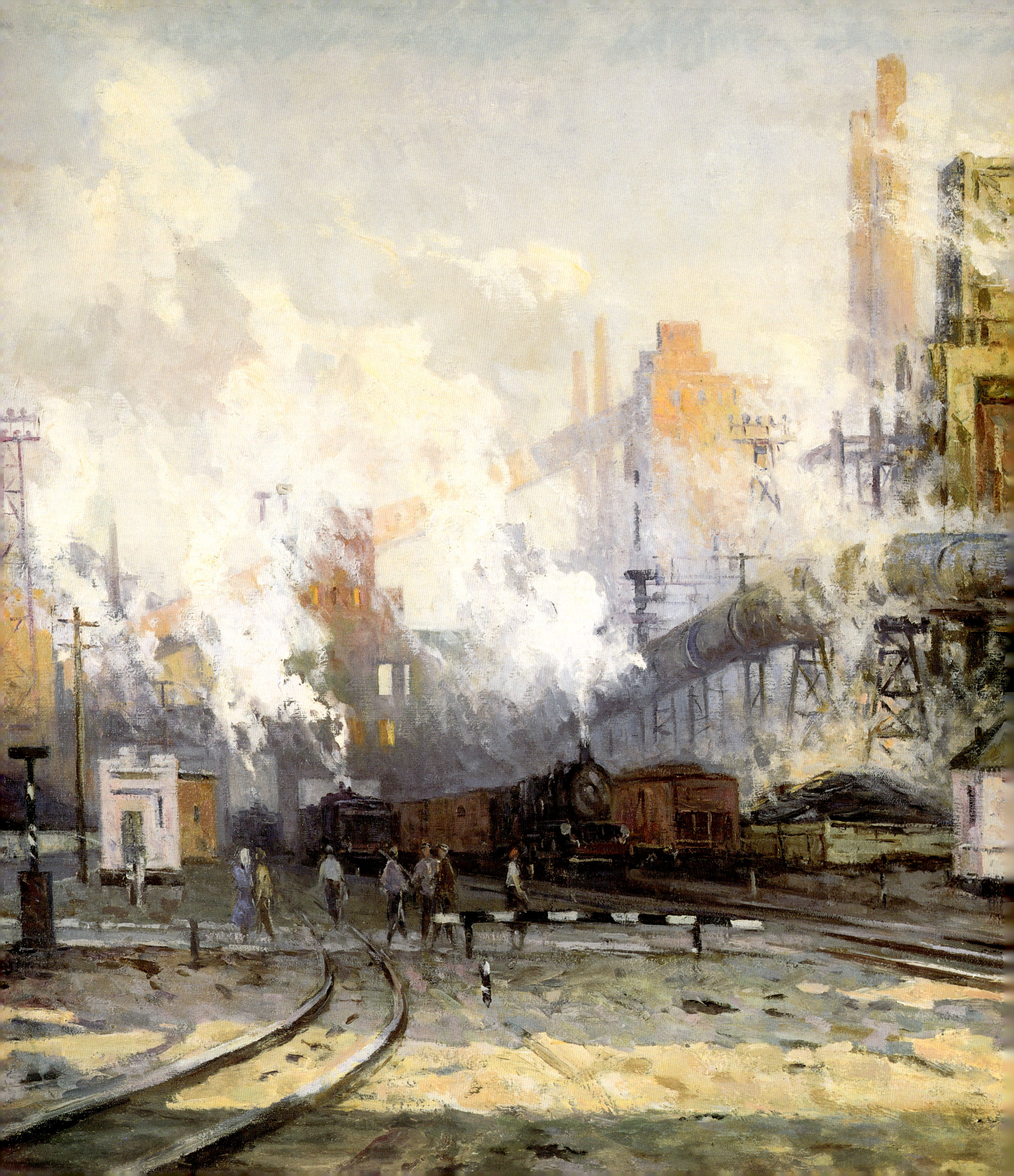

CHRONOLOGY OF SOVIET ART

PRELUDE

1848: Karl Marx and Friedrich Engels publish Communist Manifesto. Famous paraphrase from this work, "Workers of the World, Unite! You have nothing to lose but your chains."

1870: Founding of the populist art movement *Peredvizhniki* (Society for Traveling Art Exhibitions) or Itinerants/Wanderers. A number of artists concerned themselves with *narodnost*, social reform and the welfare of the common people.

Bakunin, early Russian Communist, had a vision of "the whole of European culture...transformed into an enormous rubbish heap." This line of thinking became the basis of much avant-garde (Futurist) thought.

1898: *RSDLP* (Russian Social Democratic and Labor Party) founded. *Bolsheviks* were initially a faction and became the majority group after the Second Congress in 1903. They called themselves the RSDLP (Bolsheviks) at its Seventh Congress in April of 1917. In March 1918, they changed it to Russian Communist Party (Bolshevik), and in 1925 to the All-Union Communist Party (of Bolshevik), and finally in 1952, to the Communist Party of the Soviet Union.

November 1898: *Mir iskusstva* (World of Art) was first published and continued until the spring of 1905. A loose assembly of artists self-consciously proclaiming the art for art's sake doctrine or the art for the sake of decoration. They were interested in Art Nouveau, state design, as well as music and literature. Leading members of this group included Borisov-Musatov, Alexander Benois, Léon Basket, Nikolai Roerich, Serov, Korovin and Serge Diaghilev.

1903: Founding of the Union of Russian Artists in Moscow under the direction of Leonid Pasternak of the Surikov School. This union continued until 1925. It gave a legacy of conservative Impressionism to the nascent Socialist Realist movement. Members included Sergei Vinogradov, Igor Grabar, S.V. Malyutin and Konstantin Yuon.

43. ***Azov Steel*** 1957
Konstantin Alekseevich Shurupov
35 x 44-3/4 inches, detail
Oil on canvas mounted
private collection

1910s

1914: Outbreak of World War One.

1915: Lenin wrote the article "Party Organization and Party Literature." He noted that Realism formulated to the fundamental demands of the Party and political struggle would be the highest stage in the development of Realism. The slogan "art belongs to the people" pronounced by Lenin.

15 March 1917: Czar Nicholas was forced to abdicate.

1917-22: Lenin's terror chief, F. Dzerzhinski, heads secret police, *Cheka*. The "Dictatorship of the Proletariat" begins.

16 July 1917: Romanov family shot in Ekatarinberg.

7 November 1917 (25 October, old calendar): Bolsheviks, under V.I. Lenin's direction, leads the October Revolution coup and takes over Russia in the name of International Communism. Bolshevik government established.

December 1917: Revolution inspires optimism in artistic circles.

1917-18: Closing of the Imperial Academy of Arts in St. Petersburg, destruction of plaster casts at Art Institute and firing of existing staffs.

1917-32: *Proletkult* (Proletarian culturo-educational organization), or "left" art, attempted to make a purely Proletarian culture on the ashes of Classical tradition. Their propaganda, "burn Raphael and trample the flowers of art in the name of our tomorrow," turned the Party against them.

1918: Treaty of Brest-Litvodsk ends World War One for Russian people.

1918: *Izo NarKomPros*: The art department of the People's Commissariat for Education (*NarKomPros* organized in 1917) existed until 1946. The executive committee of *Izo NarKomPros* was called the *Kollegiya*. Anatoli V. Lunacharski (1875-1933), Commissar for Education, set up painter David Shterenberg (1881-1948) as director.

1918: Infamous decree of the Soviet People's Commissars for the demolition of monuments to the Czars and their associates. The planning of monuments to the Russian Socialist Revolution signed by Lenin in 1919.

1920s

1920: *Inkhuk* (Institute of Artistic Culture) is established, headed by Kandinsky, then Rodchenko and Stepanova. The *Svomas* (Free State Art Studios) renamed *VkhUTEMAS*.

1920s: Left-wing artists in the People's Commissariat for Education squabble to obtain a monopoly in the determination of cultural policy. Among these was *Unovls* (Affirmers of New Art), an avant-garde group led by K. Malevich.

1921: Civil War is over. The Academy of Fine Arts restored in Petrograd.

1921-28: *NEP* (New Economic Policy) devised by Lenin allowing a limited amount of capitalism.

1922: *USSR* (Union of Soviet Socialist Republics) formed with 13 republics, but not the Baltic States.

May 1922: *AKhRR* (Association of Arts of Revolutionary Russia) first called Association of Artists Studying Revolutionary Life, was quickly renamed Society of Artists of Revolutionary Russia. Renamed in 1928 to AKhR (Association of Artists of the Revolution). Published journal *Iskusstvo v massy* (Art for the Masses) from 1929, and as with all groups, it was dissolved in 1932. Declared goal was to depict Red Army, workers, peasants, revolutionary activities and heroes of labor. AKhRR was the major source for inspiration for the future Socialist Realist art movement. Members included Georgi Ryazhski, Evgeni Katsman, M. Grekov, S. Ryangina, Igor Grabar, Aleksandr Gerasimov, F. Bogorodski and Boris Ioganson.

21 January 1924: Lenin dies, leaving the Soviet Union in turbulent state.

1925: Stalin becomes head of Party and advances the slogan "Socialism in One Country."

1925: *OST* (Society of Easel Painters) formed under chairmanship of David Shterenberg. Inherited the mantle of the old avant-garde, combining ideological commitment with an interest in the formal possibilities inherent in Modernism.[61] Subject of industry was central to OST as was the idea of the new Soviet person through revolutionary contemporaneity and industrial metaphors. Members included Alexander Deineka, Alexander Labas, Alexander Tyshler and Yuri Pimenov.

1925: *AKhRR: kartina* (ambitious and large thematic picture) opens the seventh AKhRR exhibition in 1925. Lunacharski declared, "The Proletariat needs the *kartina* – the *kartina* understood as a social gesture," and urged artists to strive toward, "the great social *kartina*, which will be the start of a new era in art."[62] This became the forerunner to Socialist Realism of the 1930s through '60s. Brodski and Pavel Sokolov-Skalya helped develop this panoramic genre, which later became *Brigade Art.*

1925-32: Founding of *RAPP* (Russian Association of Proletarian Writers).

August 1928-32: Stalin and 15th Party Conference launches *Piatiletka* or Five-Year Plan, followed by a period of dictatorial system of resource-allocation appears. The goal was collectivisation of farms and construction of an infrastructure for heavy industry. By 1933, over ten million peasants die of famine and persecution. Unaware, artists respond to the Five-Year Plan by painting its achievements.

1929: *VseKoKhudozhnik* (All-Russian Union of Co-operative Comradeship of Workers in the Visual Arts) was founded with the purpose of unifying visual artists.

1930s

1929-33: Liquidation of over four million landowning farmers, *Kulaks*, as a class.

1930: Deaths of Ilya Efimovich Repin (b. 1844), Nikolai Alekseevich Kasatkin (b. 1859) and Abram Efimovich Arkhipov (b. 1862) among the last of the *Peredvizhniki* (populist) painters and link with the Social Realist.

1930: At the 16th Party Congress, Stalin calls for an art "national in form and socialist in content."

March 1931-32: *RAPKh* (Russian Association of Proletarian Artists) formed by Party members of *AKhR.* It closely identified itself with the achievements of the Five-Year Plan, following the Party directive for increased political action. It began a witch-hunt of less politically motivated or tainted artists.

23 April 1932: Party Central Committee disbands all artistic groups with expectation that an encompassing state organization would be set up (not until 1957).

May 1932: The term "Socialist Realism" first appears in print in article in the Literary Gazette. It stated, "The masses demand of an artist honesty, truthfulness and a revolutionary, Socialist Realism in the representation of the Proletarian Revolution." Stalin settles on this term at a secret party at Maksim Gorki's flat on 26 October 1932.[63]

1932-present: *LOSSKh* (Leningrad Section of the Union of Soviet Artists), the first of the major artists unions to be established.

1932-present: *MOSSKh* (Moscow Section of the Union of Soviet Artists) renamed in 1938 to *MSSKh*, then renamed *MOSKh* in 1957 with the reorganization of the country-wide unions. The painting section represented half of its membership. Of these, over two to one were Stylistic traditionalists.

1932: "Artists of the Russian Federation over Fifteen Years" exhibition opens in Russian Museum in Leningrad, then moved to Moscow in June 1933. The show included work by Malevich, Pavel Filonov and other avant-garde artists, but was censored before going to Moscow as a warning to other Formalists. In a sense, it ended an era of overt Modernism in Soviet art.

1932/33-present: *InZhSA* (Leningrad, Institute of Painting, Sculpture and Architecture), now known as the I.E. Repin Institute of Art.

CHRONOLOGY

1933: Stalin, Voroshilov, Aleksandr Gerasimov, Evgeni Katsman and Isaak Brodski met to discuss painting and the new Socialist Realist art. Based upon the Itinerants and Russian Academics, it would be popular, easily understood and narrative.

1933: Beginning of the persecution and exclusion of Formalist from artistic affairs. Katsman's letters to Brodski establish the viciousness of the Realist: "Only a Realist can be a Soviet artist. Whoever is not a Realist is complete shit."[64]

1933: The United States recognizes the USSR.

1933: Two new art journals were sponsored by *MOSSKh, Iskusstvo* (Art) and *Tvorchestvo* (Creativity). Osip Beskin was editor of both magazines and was an arbiter of correctness in the visual arts. He denounced Modernism in the same year with his book, Formalism in Painting.

1934-54: NKVD (People's Commissariat for Internal Affairs) secret police replaces *Cheka* (1917-22), GPU & OGPU (1923-34) and is replaced by KGB (1954-present). Stalin shifts basis of his personal power from Communist Party to the secret police.

Summer of 1934: First All Union Congress of Soviet Writers met in Moscow and proclaim Socialist Realism as the approved means of expression for Soviet artists. Phrases surface, such as the depiction of "reality in its revolutionary development." The artist is "an engineer of human souls." Gorki proclaimed that labor should be the true hero of literature (art).

1934: Isaak Brodski made director of the All-Russian Academy of Arts in Leningrad. He reinstitutes the Academic teaching methods which were rejected in the 1920s.

1936: Abortions banned and the number of works of art with subjects depicting motherhood and maternity increase. Also, after the carnage of forced collectivisation slowed, more pictures depicting happy peasants on the *kolkhoz* (collective farms) became more widespread.

1936: Adoption of new Constitution - civil rights provisions ignored.

1936-38: The Great Purges of the top ranks of the Red Army.

Spring 1936-53: *KPDI* (Committee of Art Affairs), answerable directly to the Central Committee of the Party, took responsibility for the visual arts from *NarKomPros*. It was under the leadership of P.M. Kerzhentev, until June 1939, to oversee artistic productions. In 1953, its duties were taken over by a newly formed Ministry of Culture.

1937: Publication of Marx and Engels on Art. Engels called for a "tendentious" art devoted to the workers' cause.

November 1937: Exhibition at Tretyakov Gallery of Georgian art of Joseph Stalin's youth.

1938: Book published entitled, V.I. Lenin on Literature (Culture) and Art.

1938: First Great Exhibition of Socialist Realist art, "20 Years of the Workers' and Peasants' Red Army and Navy of 1938." Artist could pick a theme from a list of over 100 titles.

1939: *FOSKh* (Federation of the Association of Soviet Workers in the Spatial Arts) managed to unite art groups and publish a journal *Brigada Khudozhnikov* (Artists' Brigade).

June 1939: *Orgkomitet* (Organization Committee of the Artists Union) set up art unions throughout the Soviet Union. Met between 1939 and 1957, first to organize, then centralize artist unions. Headed for most of its life by Aleksandr Gerasimov, Stalin's court painter.

19 August 1939: Soviet-German Non-Aggression Pact.

1939: The Great Exhibition of 1939 emphasized, "The Industry of Socialism." Another exhibition honored Stalin's birthday, "Comrade Stalin and the People of the Country of the Soviets in Visual Arts."

1940s

30 September 1939 - March 1940: The Russo-Finnish War. Soviet war machine stalls, Voroshilov removed as Commander-in-Chief of the Red Army.

June 1940: Russia occupies Baltic States.

1940: Over ten million prisoners in slave labor camps.

1940: Gorki on Art published. Maksim Gorki called for optimism in fiction and art.

August 1940: Trotsky is murdered in Mexico.

1940: Moscow State Art Institute *(MGKhl)* formed. 1948 to present, it has been called the Surikov Institute of Art.

1941: Lucrative Stalin Prizes for Art (first and second class) were awarded. These served as examples of correct principles in Social Realism.

22 June 1941: Nazi Germany invades the USSR in spite of their secret peace pact.

1942: The death of Mikhail Vasilievich Nesterov (1862-1942), the last of the *Peredvizhniki* artists and neo-Russianist.

9 May 1945: USSR defeats Nazi Germany.

24 May 1945: Stalin's "toast to the great Russian people," in the Kremlin marks the beginning of overt Russian chauvinism and pre-eminence over the other republics. This was a reversal of the notion that culture was to be "socialist in content and national in form."

1945-50s: Eastern Europe countries become satellite vassal-states under Moscow's control.

1945: Andrei Aleksandrovich Zhdanov named Secretary to the Party's Central Committee and Chief of Propaganda Administration. A year later, Mikhail Suzlov became the head of the Department of Agitation and Propaganda. Together, they were the leading guiders of orthodoxy for Soviet art. Aleksandr Gerasimov was also a force in this same direction.

1945-present: *MVKhPU* (Moscow Higher Artistic and Technical College), or Stroganov College, founded.

1 August 1946-48: Zhdanov initiates art purges, giving name to *Zhdanovshchina Era* (1946-53), though he himself died in 1948. The reassertion of Lenin's concept of *Partiinost* campaign against dissidence from official norms and for optimistic, hard-line orthodoxy to Socialism and unification of artistic groups ended with Khrushchev's anti-Stalin speech a decade later. Although this period was one of constraint by officials, the art produced tended to be of the best quality in terms of Socialist Realist ideals.

1946: The All-Union Art Exhibition was visited by 800,000 people. Gerasimov noted how appreciated in Soviet art were "works saturated with ideas and formally complete, answering to the needs of the people, educating the Soviet person in the spirit of cheerfulness..."[65]

1947: Exhibition entitled, "Thirty Years of Soviet Representational Art" commemorated the October Revolution. The campaign against Impressionism could be seen in paintings with smoother surfaces and a more limited palette.

1947: Letter read aloud in the first session of the Committee for Art Affairs (KPDI) stated, "The Academy of Arts must wage a relentless struggle against all the various forms of toadying to bourgeois art." Two new concepts were now disdained: rootless *cosmopolitanism* and bourgeois *impressionism* in favor of the importance of Russian tradition and the academic heritage which had heretofore been considered inherently bourgeois.

5 August 1947: In the premises of the old Imperial Academy of Arts the new Academy of Arts of the USSR was established, with Aleksandr Gerasimov as president, to exercise control over the major art institutes and schools. It took orders directly from the

Committee for Art Affairs (KPDI). Later it controlled the Union of Artists and had influence on artistic research, museums and publishing. "The foundation of the Academy marked the final stage in the imposition of an authoritarian hierarchical structure on the Soviet art world."

1947: Collection of the Moscow State Museum of Modern Art dispersed.

1947-49: Beginning of *Brigade Art* or collaborative group paintings. Paintings were usually very large in scale, with cast of hundreds, and of a triumphant or ceremonious nature.

1948: Aleksandr Gerasimov and Voroshilov paid a visit to the Museum of New Western Art in Moscow and closed it. The 1930s campaign against Formalism was being waged against Impressionism's catch-all term for Modernism, Decorativism and Primitivism.

February 1949: At the third session of the Academy of Arts, critic Pyotr Sysoev made a speech, "The Fight for Socialist Realism in Soviet Representational Art." M. Saryan and others were criticized for not adhering to the Russian model of Realism.

1949: A large exhibition in Moscow celebrated the birthday of Stalin and included many episodes from the General Secretary's life.

1949: Soviet Union explodes its first nuclear weapon.

1950s

1950s: Cultural Section of the Communist Party oversaw the Ministry of Culture which oversaw art museums, State Purchasing Commission and other agencies such as the Academy of Arts of the USSR.

1950: Stalin published work entitled, Marxism and Questions of Linguistics which aided the Academic revival in art as well as language.

1950-51: Soviet control of the International Peace Movement(s) led to the giving of international Stalin Prizes for Communist sympathizers. From about 1950 onward, union artists were inspired by authorities to produce peace propaganda art. Vladimir Nekrasov's oil, "We are for Peace," was typical of this Cold War art.

1952: At the 19th Party Congress, a thaw in State control of art content and form begins.

5 March 1953: Joseph Stalin dies in the Kremlin.

1953: Infighting begins to find a successor to Stalin. Georgi Malenkov became Premier, succeeded in 1955 by Marshall Bulganin. Collective leadership until Nikita Khruschev becomes first Secretary of the Party in 1953. In 1958, he becomes Premier.

1953: Ministry of Culture founded, replacing the KPDI.
January 1954: Exhibition by Moscow artists, organized by Alexander Kamenski, echoed shift in Party policy away from ceremonious splendor of the cult of personality to Stalin.

May 1954: Ilya Ehrenburg published short novel *Ottepel* (The Thaw), becoming symbolic of the thaw in the arts in Post-Stalinist period.

June 1954: Communist Party calls for volunteers to open the Virgin Lands to cultivation. Ministry of Culture calls artists to create a visual record of this epic program.

1955: Soviet architecture takes a new path away from neo-classicism, baroque and hand-crafting in favor of functional, prefabricated forms and modernistic forms.

14 February 1956: Khrushchev denounces the crimes and misrule of Stalin in secret session of the 20th Communisty Party Congress. Period of de-Stalinization begins.

1956: Soviet Union intervenes militarily in Hungary. Revolt is bloodily put down.

31 October 1956: Delegation from the Moscow Union of Artists spoke to Moscow Committee of the Communist Party. They spoke strongly against Aleksandr Gerasimov's Stalinist policies and art.

Spring/Summer 1957: Khrushchev publishes on art For Close Ties between Literature and Art and the Life of the People and The High Mission of Literature and Art. His conservative views were not so much restrictive demands as much as exhortations to maintain Leninist principles.

1957: First man-made satellites, Sputniks I & II put into orbit. Space Age begins.

1957: *SKH SSSR* or *Soyuz Khudozhnikov SSSR* (Union of Artists of the USSR) was established, which eventually numbered over 13,000 artists. It was responsible for the implementation of Party orthodoxy. Many members were Communist members as well.

1957: International Youth Festival permitted the display of Western Abstract painting for the first time since the 1920s.

Late 1950s: The development of the Severe Style of Social Realism. Art begins to be more experimentive and less Classical.

1960s

1960: The first RSFSR Artist's Congress denounces "underground art." Expressionism and Surrealism rejected, while younger artists pressure for a broader interpretation of Socialist Realism.

1960: *SKh RSFSR* (Russian Union of Artists) subordinate to the USSR Union of Artists.

1961: Hard line campaign against Modernist and Abstract art movements begin.

1961: Yuri Gagarin becomes first man to orbit Earth.

1962: Cuban Missle Crisis.

1 December 1962: At Moscow's Manezh Gallery, Khruschev denounces avant-gardism at "Thirteenth Anniversary of the Moscow Section of the Artists' Union," especially the Abstract work of the late R.R. Falk, contemporary Ilya Belyutin and students. Press campaign against cultural deviationists begins.

14 October 1964: Khruschev ousted by the *Politburo* for being erratic, ineffectual and authoritarian.

1964: Leonid Brezhnev becomes first General Secretary of the Party. Begins his own cult of personality. His domestic policy emphasized repressive measures against dissidents.

1966: Leningrad Art Union begins full funding of 500 artists at 150-200 rubles monthly. Artist required to present at least two paintings at end of year. The building of over 300 artists' studios commences, with nothing built after 1985.

1967: Japanese art dealer, Mrs. Nakamura of Gallery Gekkoso, begins to sell Russian & Soviet art in Japan.

1967: First public exhibition in many years of unofficial artists. Development of national art schools in the Soviet Republics encouraged.

August 1968: Invasion of Czechoslovakia, put down of "Prague Spring."

1970s

14 September 1974: Non-official artists, A. Zverev, O.Y. Rabin and others held an exhibition, "First Autumn Exhibition of Paintings in the Fresh Air," in a field in Moscow. Their show was bull-dozed by the authorities and four participating artists were arrested, with some sent to mental hospitals.

1976: Moscow wide network of exhibitions by non-conformist artists held in private apartments across Moscow.

1977: Gallery established in Malaya Gruzinskaya Street in Moscow, publically exhibiting unofficial artists.

1977: The Metropolitan Museum of Art and the Fine Arts Museum of San Francisco state exhibition, "Russian and Soviet Painting." A number of official Socialist Realist artists are included, thus telling the story of Soviet art in America for the first time.

1979: Brezhnev starts Afghanistan War.

During this decade, non-official art triumphs, while Socialist Realist art becomes vilified.

Western art dealers in Europe discover the merits of Socialist Realistic painting and begin to promote it in the West.

CHRONOLOGY

1980s 14 November 1982: Brezhnev dies and is succeeded by K.V. Chernenko and Yuri Andropov. Both are elderly and die in office.

1985: Mikhail Gorbachev becomes General Secretary of the Communist Party. Process of democratization begins. *Perestroika* and *Glasnost* introduced.

7 July 1988: Sotheby holds auction of contemporary Soviet art, the first of its kind in Russia. Creates furor, prices soar for non-conformist art.

1989: Exhibition, "100 Years of Russian Art" from private collections, held in London in association with the Barbican Art Gallery and Museum of Modern Art in Oxford. Socialist Realist art is virtually ignored for Non-Official painting.

1990s 1990: The Smithsonian Institution Traveling Exhibition Service in Washington, DC organizes, "Moscow: Treasures and Traditions" show. It includes a modest component of Soviet art.

October 1990: The Springville Museum of Art in Utah exhibits 45 paintings by Vladimir Nekrasov. This exhibition is then followed by five more Socialist Realist exhibitions at the museum over the next three years.

November 1990: Overland Gallery in Scottsdale, Arizona is first gallery in America to offer Soviet official art to collectors.

1991: Matthew C. Bown publishes Art Under Stalin, which stands as the most significant book on the subject to date.

25 December 1991: The Union of Soviet Socialist Republics dissolves. This would be the official demise of "Soviet Socialist Realism," although it had been dying for years.

January 1992: The Museum of Modern Art, Oxford, exhibits the largest exhibition of Soviet official painting in the West. Entitled "Soviet Socialist Realist Painting 1930s-1960s," it includes 60 paintings which thereafter travel to museums on the continent. David Elliott, Matthew Bown and Alexander Sidorov publish a color catalogue.

Spring 1993: Overland Gallery opens in Wayzata, Minnesota to offer Russian and Soviet art.

15 January - 30 April, 1994: Fleischer Museum in Scottsdale, Arizona unveils exhibit entitled, "HIDDEN TREASURES: Russian & Soviet Impressionism, 1930-1970s. First private art museum in the United States to curate and exhibit such a show. Produced a 216 page, 113 color plate book to accompany the exhibition.

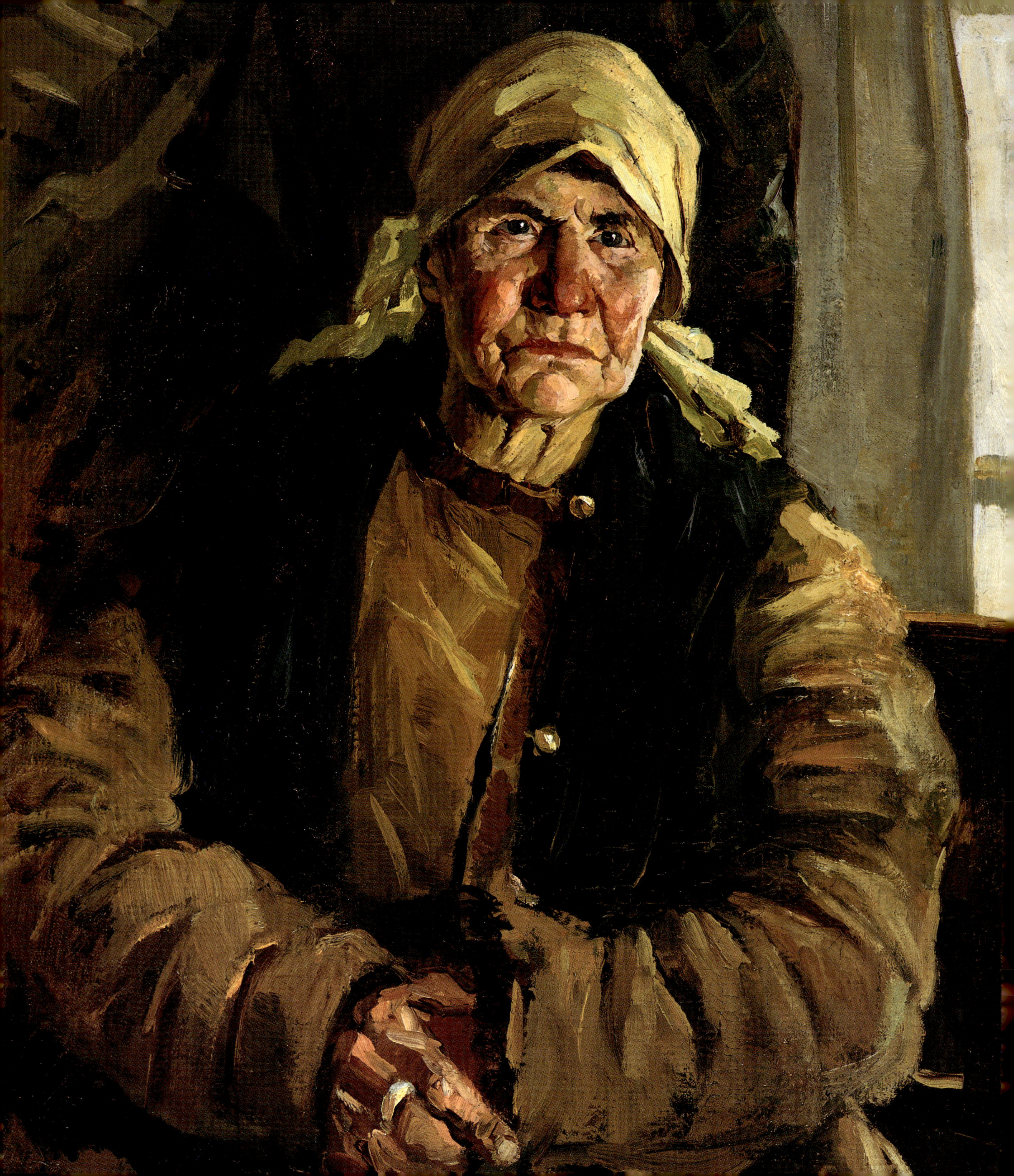

BIOGRAPHIES

Limited documentation regarding these artists
was available at the time of this publication's printing.

MIKAEL GUSEN OGLY ABDULLAEV

(19 December 1921 -) Baku, Azerbaijan

Mikael Gusen Ogly Abdullaev was a student of the Moscow State Art Institute where he studied under S.V. Gerasimov and V.A. Favorsky. Elected a Corresponding Member of the Academy of Arts in 1958, he was awarded the Order of Lenin in 1959.

Paintings by Abdullaev are remarkable for their characteristically lush colors, generalized form and emotional intensity. Being a master of drawing and possessing a capacity for arranging the color expressively, he achieves compact integrity in his compositions.

His portraits are something of an achievement, as he endeavors to penetrate the spiritual world of his models. He depicts his contemporaries, relatives, well-known people and the common man.

Since 1965, Abdullaev has been teaching art in the Azerbaijan Institute of Fine Arts in Baku. He has been a participant of numerous exhibitions, both in and out of Russia. His paintings have been shown in Prague, Peking, Paris, Berlin and Brussels.

NICKOLAI A. ABRAMOV

(24 September 1940 -) Leningrad

From 1945-50, Abramov studied at the Leningrad Art School and at the Repin Institute in Leningrad from 1950-57. His diploma work "The Evening" was finished under Ioganson's guidance.

Abramov worked in the studio of Aleksandr Gerasimov and participated in All-Union, republican and regional exhibitions from 1957-86. His works can be found in the Russian State Museum in St. Petersburg. They exhibit a powerfully Impressionist handling of paint, mixed with strong emotional content.

44. ***Babushka*** 1956
Vasily Mikhailovich Arapov
36-3/8 x 23 inches, detail
Oil on canvas
private collection

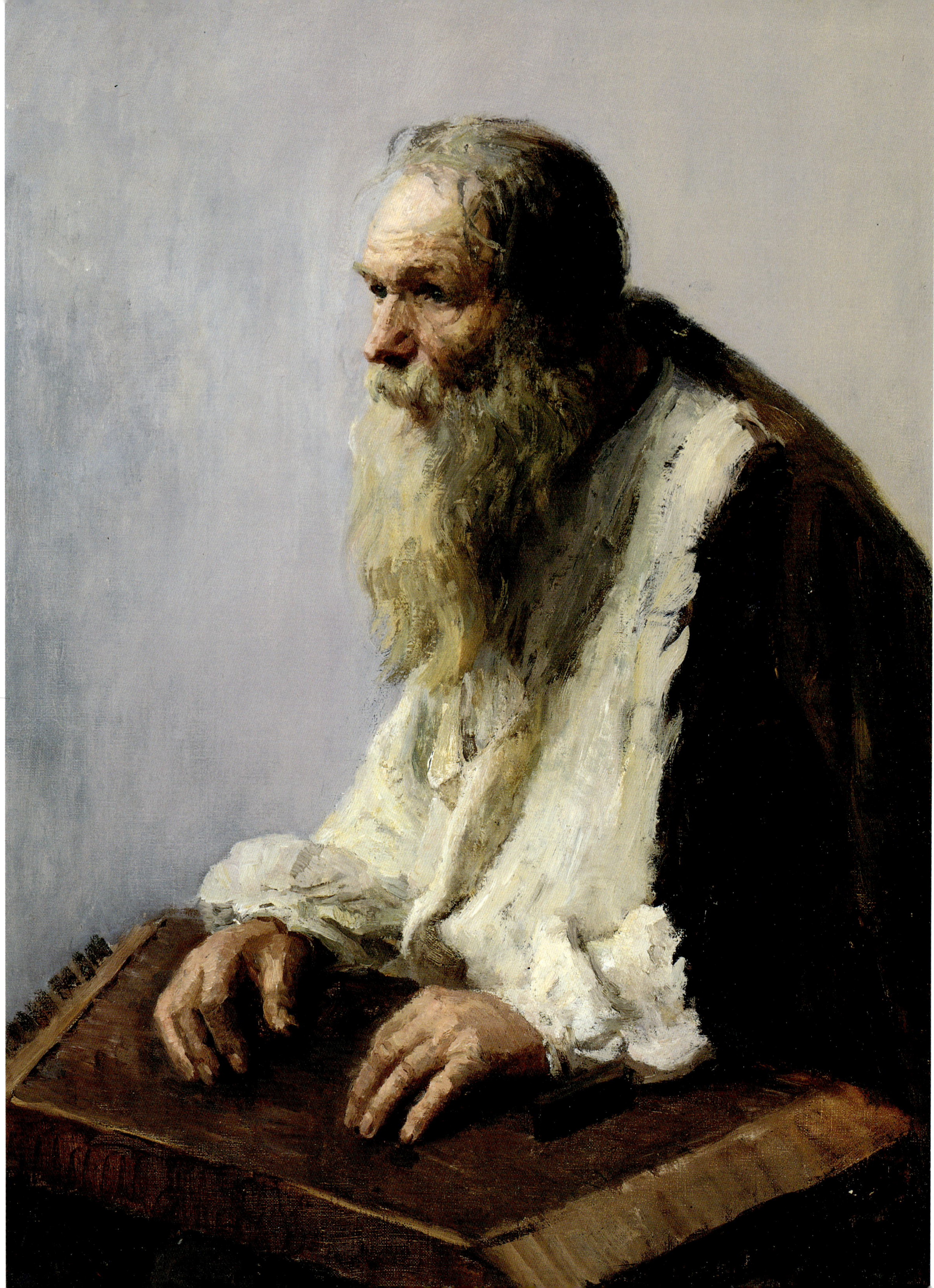

MIKHAIL KORNEEVICH ANIKEEV

(14 March 1925 -) Moscow

Following Anikeev's participation in the Great Patriotic War, his studies began in 1946 at the Art College in Kishinev, graduating with honors. Moving to Moscow in 1950, he entered the Surikov Institute under the instruction of Malkov, Korolyev and Pokarzhevski.

A fourth-year student in 1954, Anikeev traveled to Kazakhstan and created a number of pictures devoted to the cultivation of the Virgin Lands. Several of these pictures are now in museums in Tselinograd, Alma-Ata and Kokchetav.

In 1956, Anikeev graduated from the Institute. His diploma work, devoted to themes of the Revolution, demonstrated the great abilities of the young painter.

A broad variety of themes find reflection in his art, one being the image of Lenin. Labor is also the focus of his attention, with pictures full of respect toward toilers. In war themes, he tries to express peoples' responsibility for peace in the world.

Anikeev was awarded the title of Merited Painter of Russian Federation in 1965. More than 200 of his works are in museums of the former Soviet Union. A constant participant in many regional, All-Union and international exhibitions, he has had several one-man shows in Russia and the Republics. His work is contained within the Fleischer Museum Collection.

VASILY MIKHAILOVICH ARAPOV

(1 April 1934 -) St. Petersburg

Arapov graduated with honors from the Ryazan Art School in 1954 under his instructor, I. Akinchev. Between 1954-60 he studied at the Repin Institute in Leningrad. He worked in an art workshop headed by Academician Boris Ioganson and Professor A.A. Mylnikov from 1960-64. During those years, he took part in numerous local exhibits in Leningrad and republican exhibitions, as well as being admitted to the Leningrad Chapter of the Russian Artists Union.

Arapov's works are found in the Ryazan Museum of Fine Arts, the Scientific Research Museum of the Leningrad USSR Academy of Arts and private collections in the United States, England, Switzerland and Finland.

"Realism is everything to me. I like art that is truthful, spiritual and passionate. Among the Russian artists, my kindred spirits are V.A. Serov, M.A. Vrubel, A.E. Arkhipov and A.S. Stepanova. Among Western artists, I admire the works of El Greco. I am completely indifferent to abstract art."

45. ***Old Man Playing a Goulyar*** 1949
Sergei Fedorovich Babkov
31-3/8 x 23-5/8 inches
Oil on canvas
private collection

SERGEI FEDOROVICH BABKOV

(28 December 1920 - 1993) St. Petersburg

Babkov graduated from the Russian National Academy of Arts High School, under Lepilov, Newelstein, Kazakov, Zaitsev, Liberov and Naumov.

For his part in the Great Patriotic War, he received Patriotic War Orders and medals. Upon demobilization in 1946, Babkov entered the Repin Institute and graduated cum laude in 1952. Thereafter, he taught high school arts for one year, and then joined the staff of the Leningrad Branch of M.B. Grekov Military Artists Studio.

A member of the Russian Artists Union, Babkov participated in exhibits in Leningrad and other cities of his native land, in republican and national exhibitions and internationally.

"When I look through the sketches I made during the Great Patriotic War, my memory brings back ideas for new paintings. This theme is inexhaustible."

Babkov's works are found in museums in Leningrad, Moscow, Zhitomir, Volgograd, Tver, Biysk, Sevastopol, Vladimir and Stalingrad, as well as in private collections worldwide. His figurative and landscape resonate Impressionist color and surface work has stirred much emotion.

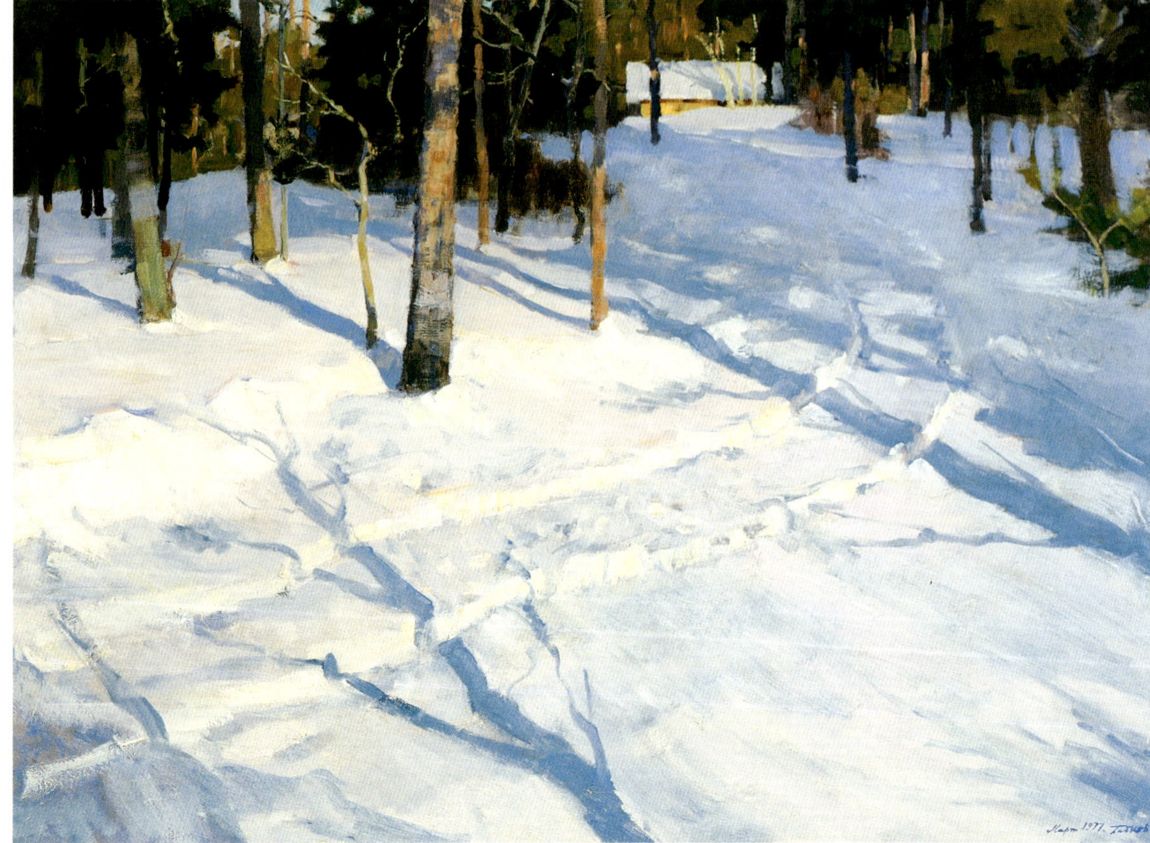

46. ***Winter Road in March*** 1977
Sergei Fedorovich Babkov
36-1/2 x 51 inches
Oil on canvas
private collection

NIKOLAI IVANOVICH BARCHENKOV

(3 December 1918 -) Zagorsk, Russia

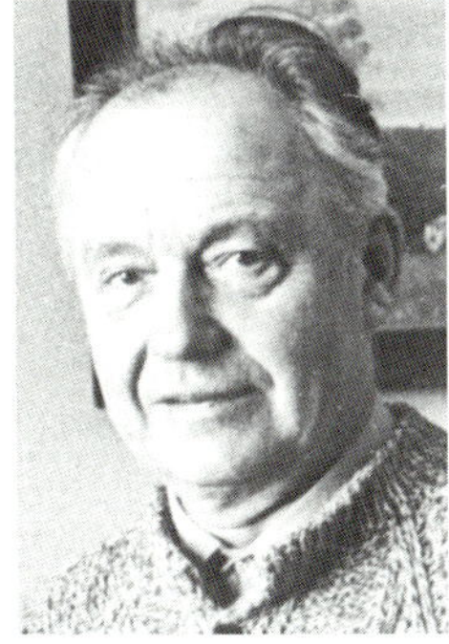

Entering the Moscow Regional Art School in 1935, Barchenkov studied under Grabar, Krymov, Gorelov and Arkady Plastov.

At graduation in 1939, Barchenkov returned home and devoted his energies to the Zagorsk Association of Artists, which is considered one of the best in the Moscow region.

Responding to World War II events, his works were shown at the All-Union art exhibitions of 1947 and 1949.

Barchenkov's main subject has been his home town. His works are humane and poetic. The architecture in his landscapes is always supplemented by human figures. In his portraits, the artist shows man in his typical environment. He devotes great attention to facial expressions and gestures. Warmth, humanism and a kind attitude toward the world are typical of his art. He looks for the beauty in life and conveys this throughout his canvases.

Barchenkov has taken an active part in Moscow regional, zonal, republican and All-Union art exhibitions since 1947. His first one-man show took place in Zagorsk in 1953 with 109 works exhibited. Since then, several exhibitions have taken place internationally.

47. ***Spring: Reading on the Porch*** 1960
Nikolai Ivanovich Barchenkov
31-3/4 x 23-5/8 inches
Oil on canvas
private collection

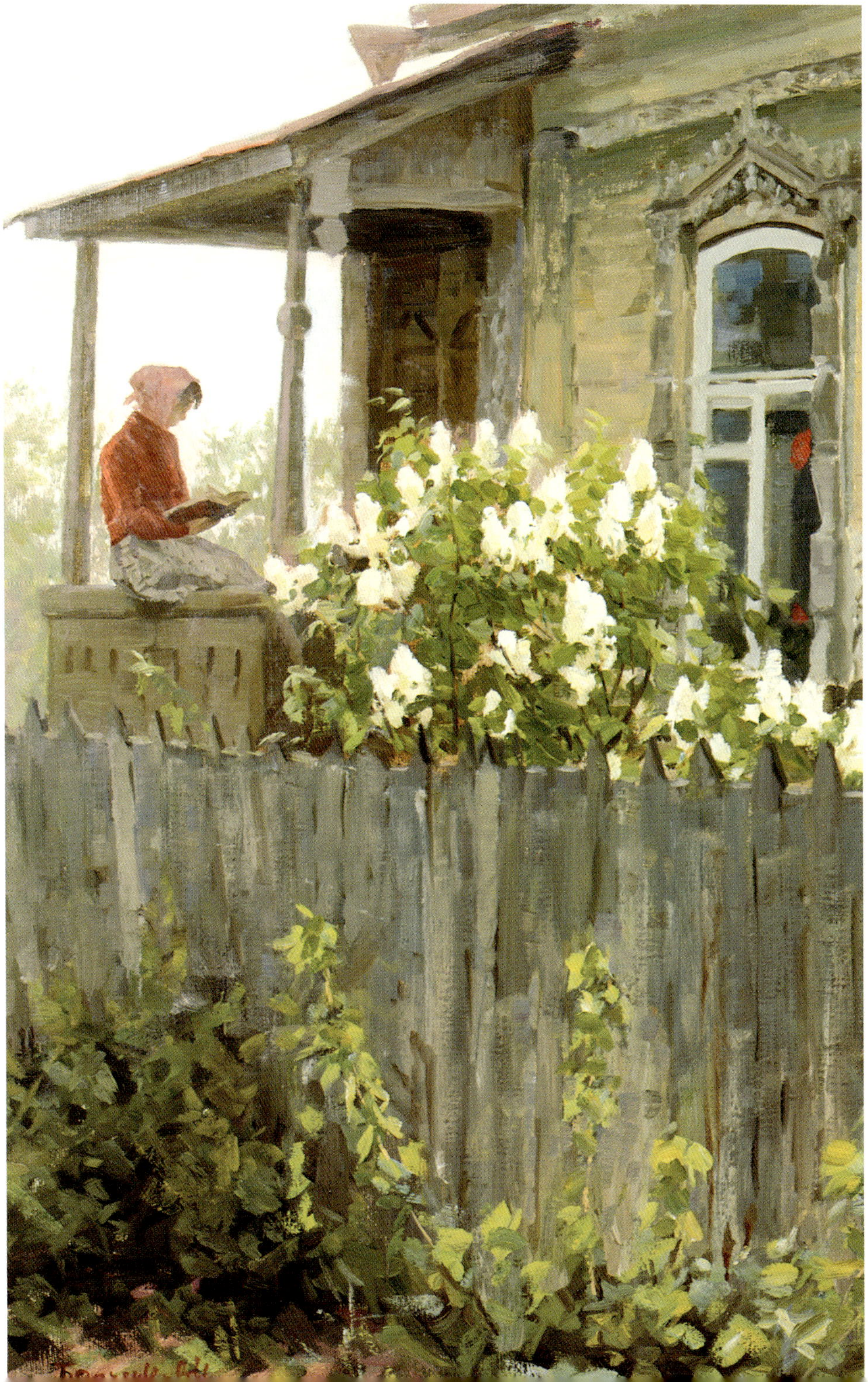

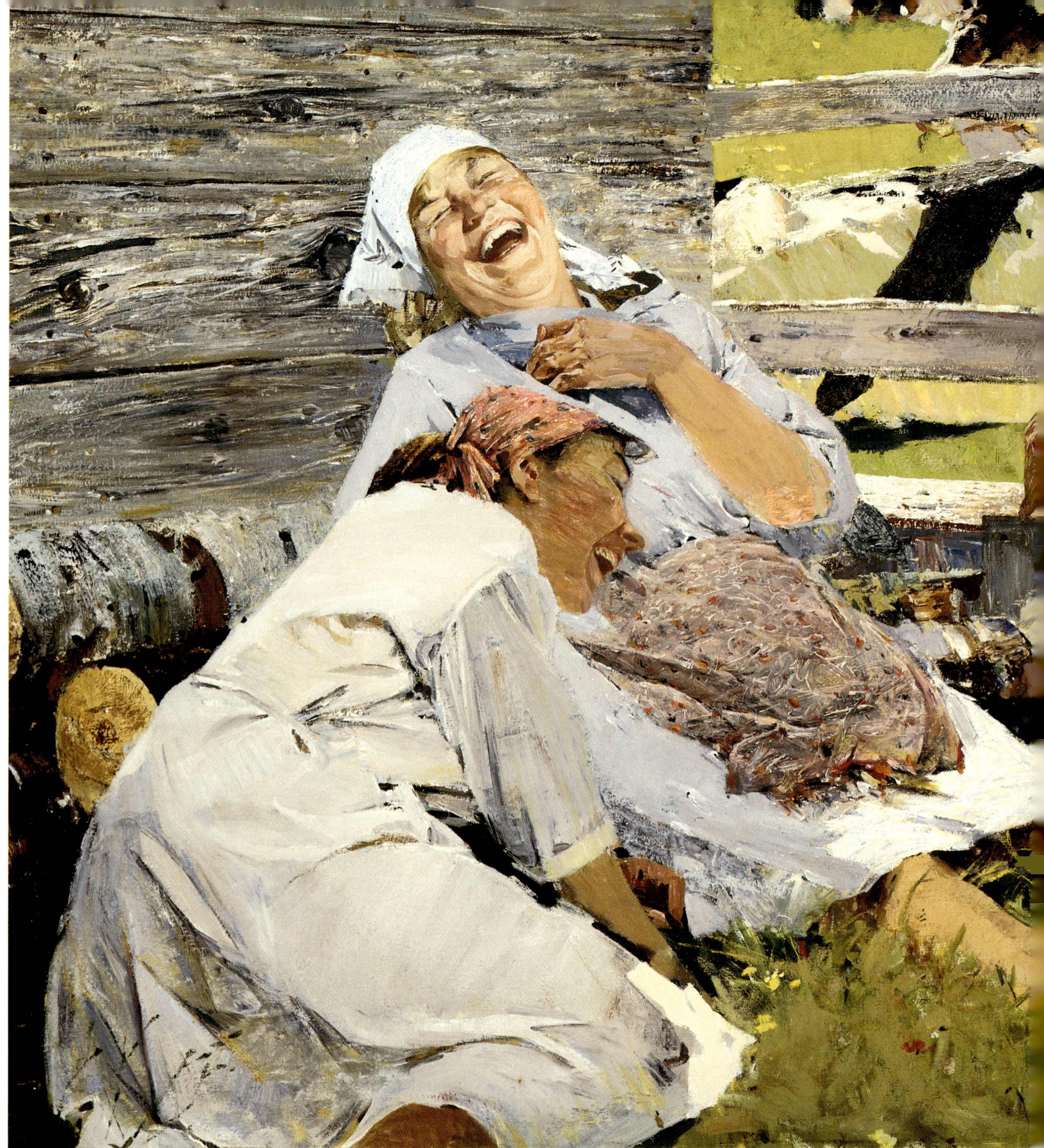

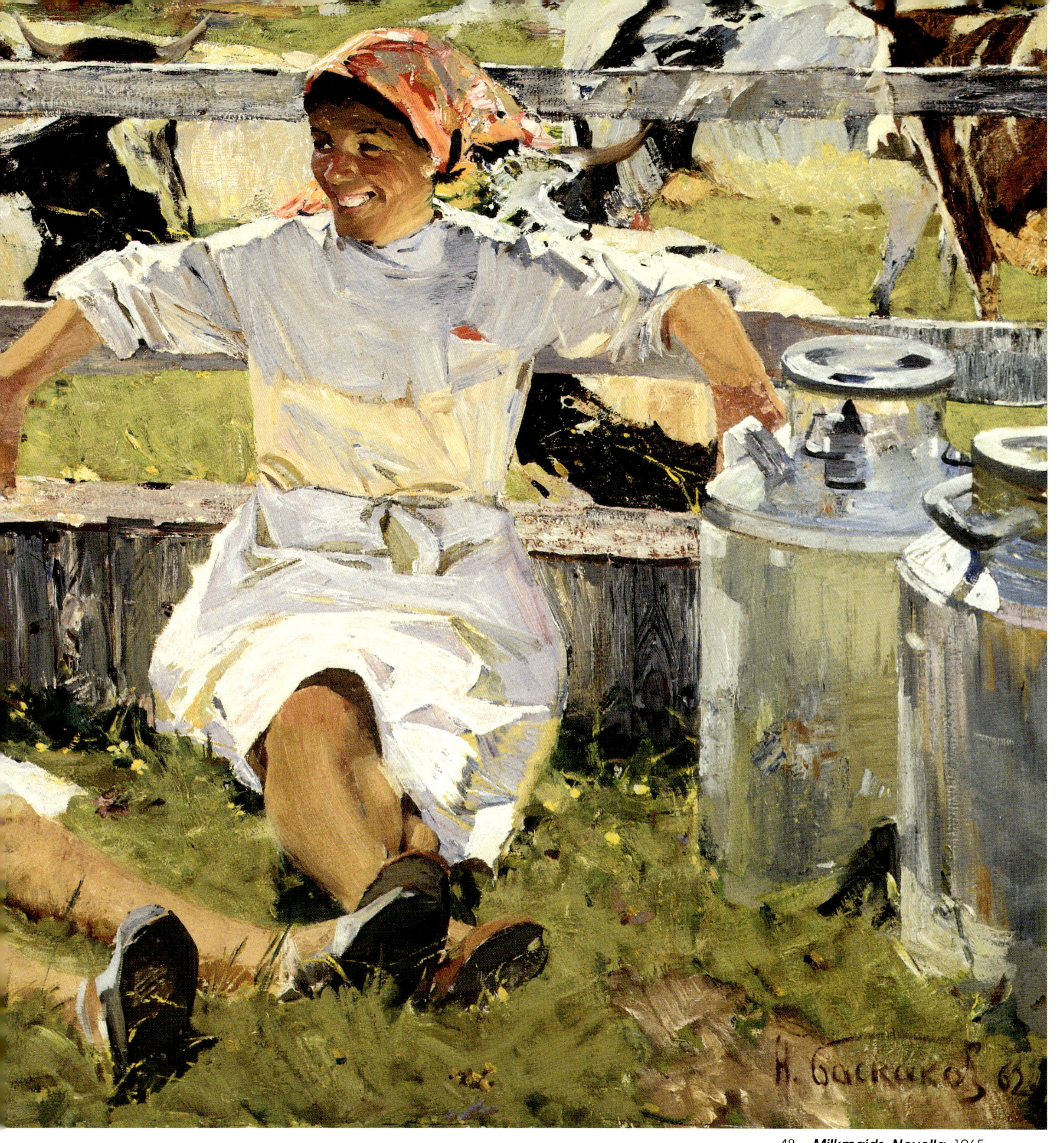

48. ***Milkmaids, Novella*** 1965
Nikolai Nikolayevich Baskakov
47 x 90-1/4 inches
Oil on canvas
private collection

NIKOLAI NIKOLAYEVICH BASKAKOV

(8 May 1918 - 1993) St. Petersburg

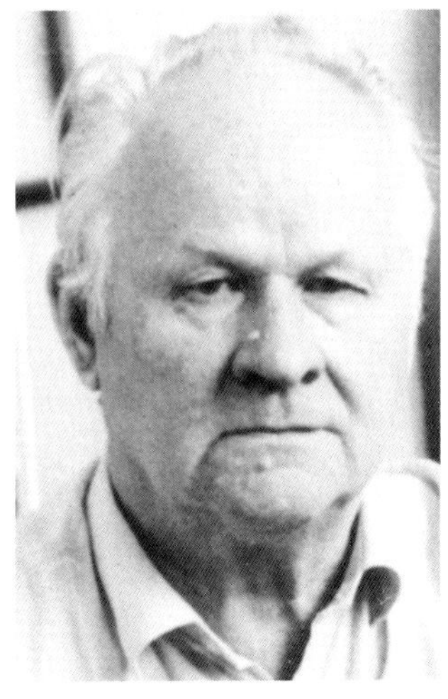

Baskakov attended the Astrakhan Art College from 1933-39. His next seven years were served in the Soviet Army before he attended the Repin Institute, Leningrad from 1945-51. His diploma work was under the guidance of Boris Ioganson. In the 1950s, a number of his genre paintings focused on the theme of work.

"The spirit of Classicism was in the very system of our education. We learned from each other and from the works of old masters, as was the case during the Renaissance and later. Rarely did our maestro correct our mistakes and make comments."

Baskakov became a member of the Leningrad Chapter of the Russian Artists Union in 1951 and participted in local exhibits in Leningrad, republican and national exhibitions and Soviet art exhibits. He thrice won the Kirov Factory Prize and was also named an honorary member of the Kirov Factory team.

"I prefer the paintings of French and Russian Impressionism. I have high regard for the antique painting, which brought forth all that is spiritual and lofty in European and Russian art."

Baskakov's works of art are found in museums in Moscow, St. Petersburg, Alma-Ata, Astrakhan, Kazan, Yaroslavl and in private collections worldwide.

ALEXEI PAVELOVICH BELYKH

(3 June 1923 -) Kostroma

An A.P. Belykh exhibition opened at the Kostroma Museum in June 1973, the 50th birthday of the painter. Given central place was a self-portrait created in 1940, though at that time, Belykh had neither artistic education or experience. At the Livny Vocational School, Belykh made his first steps as a painter under the guidance of Soviet artist, S. Volkov.

Years of study were interrupted by the Great Patriotic War as Belykh defended the Soviet Motherland. Following the war, Belykh was sent to the Moscow War Academy. In 1947, he began his work as a designer at the Moscow factory, The Red Textile-workers, while he continued to paint at an amateur painter's studio.

In 1952, Belykh took part in the All Union exhibition of Amateur Artists. Highly praised by critics, the painter was invited to enter the Surikov Institute of Art. Among his teachers were such masters as Pokargevsky, Reshetnikov and Tsyplakov.

As a student, Belykh visited the Baltic Republics, Siberia and Lake Baikal. The grandeur and scale of the Bratskaya hydro-electric power station so inspired him, that his graduation work was "First Builders of Bratskaya Electric Power Station."

Following graduation, Belykh returned to Kostroma where he worked as a teacher, and later as a professor, at the College of Art. Belykh is one of the most active participants in regional exhibitions.

In 1964, he created a number of canvases regarding people in the lumber industry. Laborers are the main theme of Belykh's work. The spirit of his characters, rarely seen motions and conditions of nature are captured on his canvases . In the picturesque harmony of nature, this painter feels the beauty of life. Portraits of his mother, milkmaids, and old collective farmers reproduce the images of the strong Soviet people. Several of his pieces are included in the Fleischer Museum Collection.

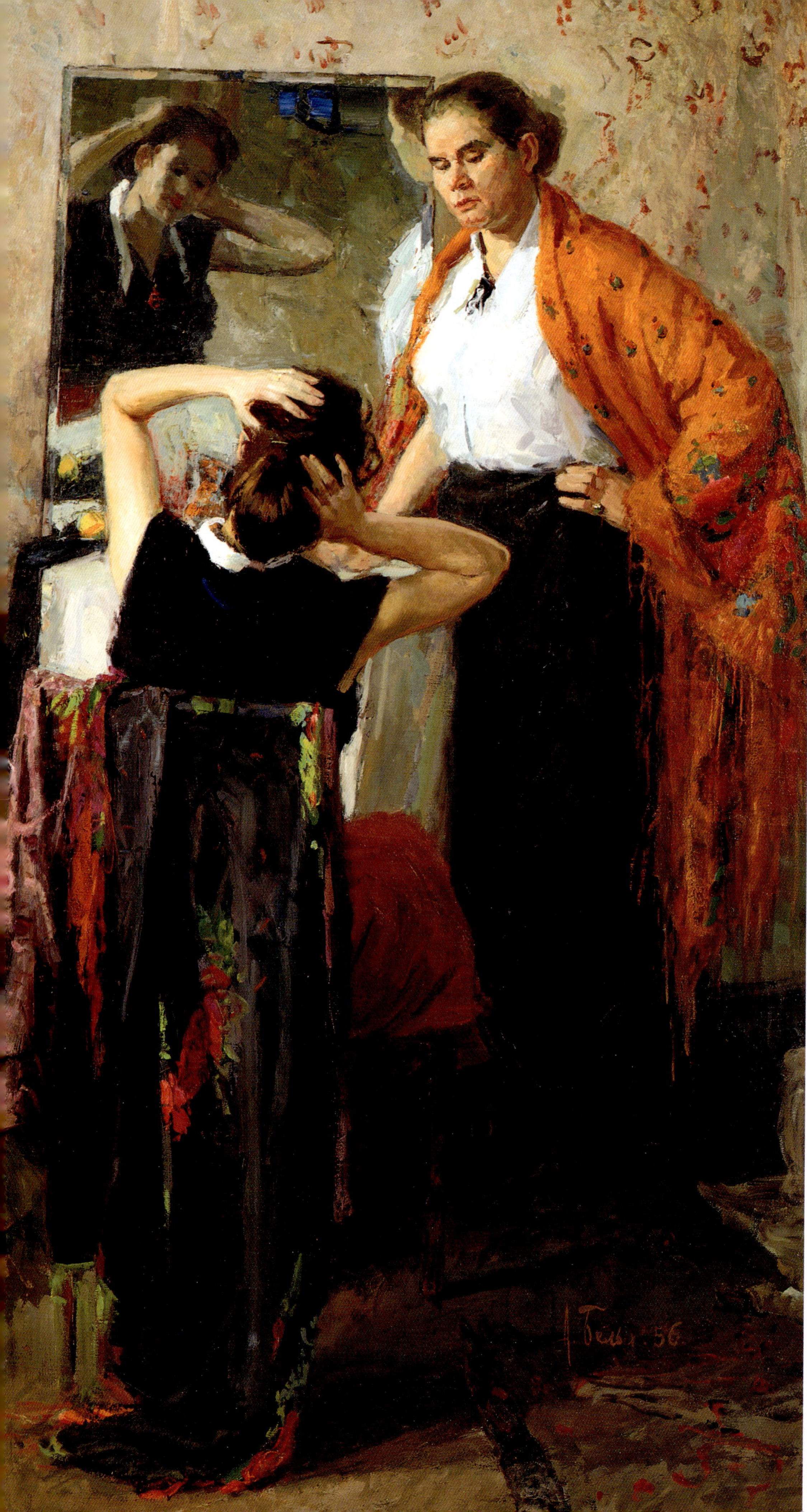

49. ***By the Mirror*** 1956
Alexei Pavelovich Belykh
55 x 31-1/2 inches
Oil on canvas
private collection

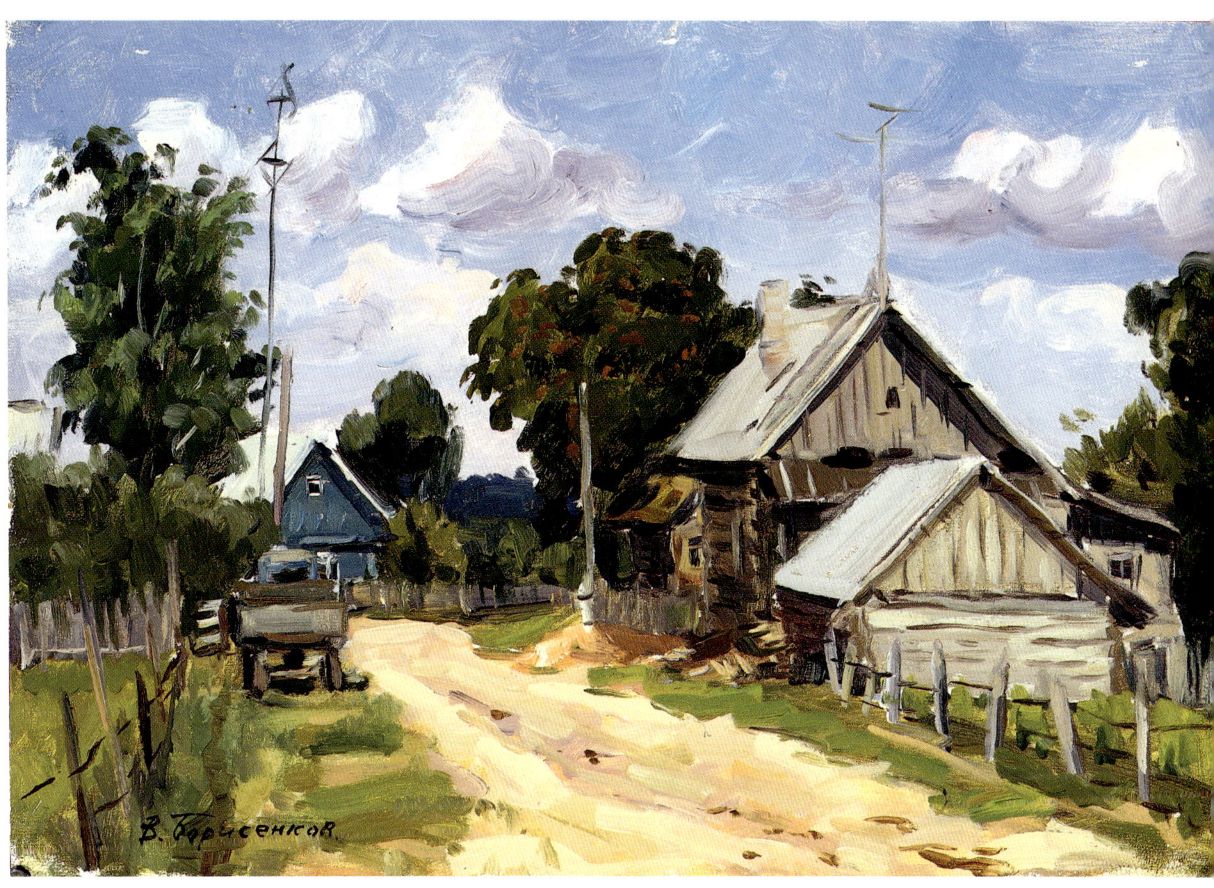

50. ***In the Village*** 1979
Vassily P. Borisenkov
13-3/8 x 19-13/16 inches
Oil on board
private collection

VASSILY P. BORISENKOV

(1 October 1924 -) St. Petersburg

Borisenkov's father was a merchant who became a farmer when the Communists "made everyone the same." His father died in the Great Patriotic War.

From 1949-54, Vasily attended the St. Petersburg Academy of Fine Arts and credits his hometown as a great inspiration to him. Borisenkov, a lover of nature, claims that the outdoors represents "peace on earth." This is one reason why he became so skilled in painting landscapes.

He often travels to Siverskaya, a community in a forested area where artists gather. There you can "touch nature and recognize yourself in nature." Borisenkov emphasizes that Russia's greaest treasure is nature. His plein-air works give testimony to this ideal. Borisenkov subjects also include the Black Sea, the Baltic republics and the Caucasus Mountains. Borisenkov likes to depict industrial scenes, in addition to landscapes.

Borisenkov is influenced by the Realist artist Sergei Ivanov, a painter of Russian and old world themes at the turn of the century.

ALEXANDER FILIPPOVICH BURAK

(10 July 1921 -) Sverdlovsk

Burak is an Honored Art Worker of the Russian Federation. His works can be found in the Tretyakov Gallery, Moscow and the Russian Museum, Leningrad. He has participated in many national and international exhibitions. Burak now lives in Sverdlovsk. His depictions of children reveal a sensitivity to an adult's world impressed upon youth.

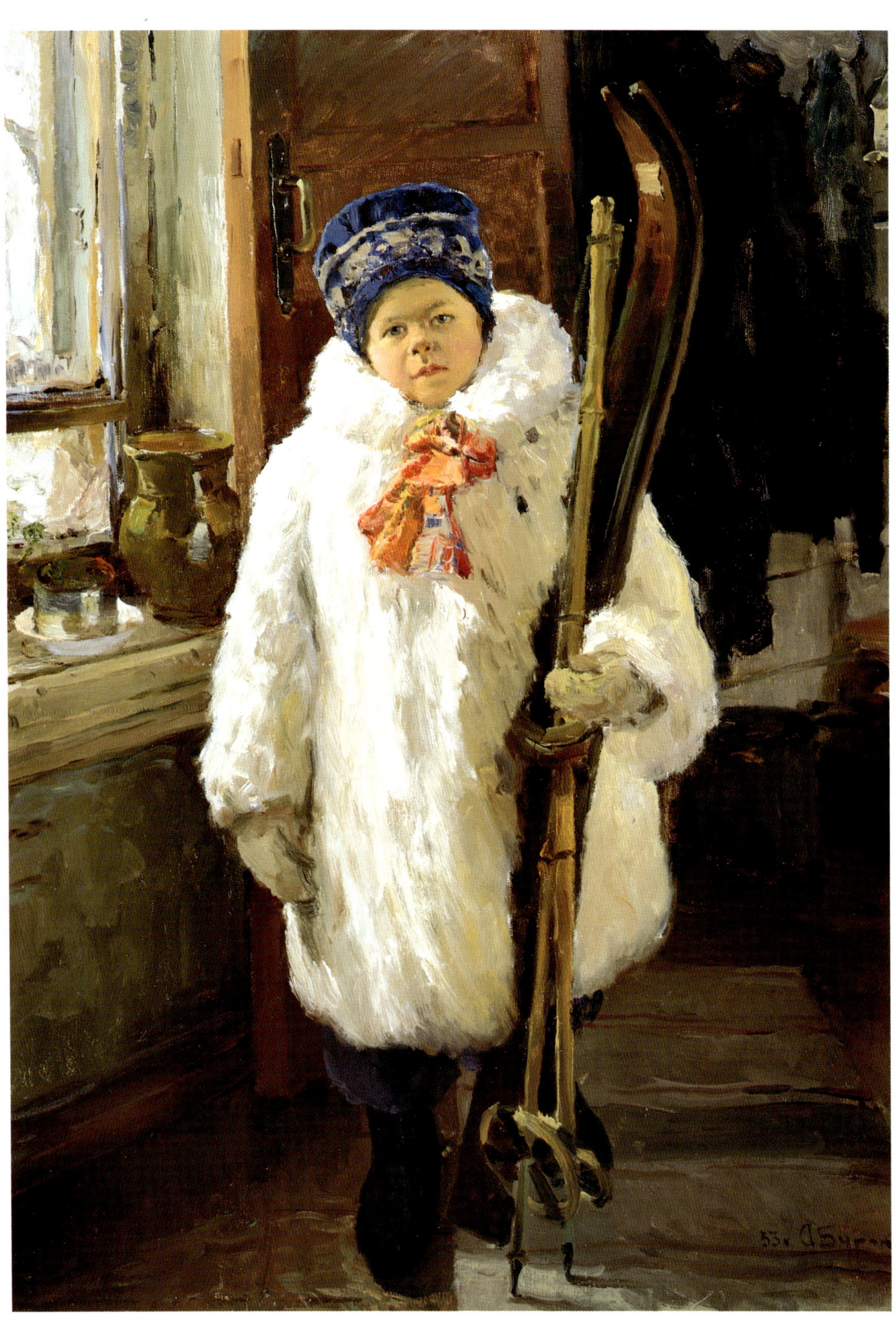

51. ***The Young Skier*** 1952
Alexander Filippovich Burak
31-3/8 x 23-1/8 inches
Oil on canvas
private collection

MAI VOLPHOVICH DANTSIG

(27 April 1930 -) Minsk

Professor Dantsig is the Merited Arts Worker of Byelorussia and member of the USSR Union of Artists. His talent for drawing was noticed and developed by his father and his first teacher, S.P. Katkov. Dantsig was a student at the Minsk Art College from 1947-1952. At the Moscow State Art Institute (Surikov Institute) from 1952-1958, fellow students were Andronov, Salakhov and Popkov who determined new tendencies in a newly-born "Rough-style" Soviet art. He strove to render the romantically harsh reality of life. It was not incidental that the term "Stern or Severe style" originated and developed during this period.

Little by little, the romantic coloring of the first undemanding landscapes changed for more expressiveness and energetic use of color. One can observe the expansive use of painting language and its simultaneous great expressiveness, generalized and enlarged forms, unusual foreshortenings, and a freer attitude toward the arrangement of space in his paintings of that period.

Dantsig created a series of paintings depicting Minsk, in which his interest to Deineka's art and industrial landscapes by Nissky is quite obvious. However, Dantsig declares his own active comprehension of modern life.

The theme of free labor becomes an important one. Paintings are full of passion and monumentality as the painter accepts everything he sees around him with great enthusiasm and joy. It is not a false fervent depiction, the painter is sincere.

Later, the painter understood that life is more complicated. He applied a new theme that demanded more responsibility and new creative methods. The war theme became part of his creative biography. Several paintings were devoted to the partisan movement. The images reflect real persons and symbols, they display the dialectics of the specific and the general, the reality and non-conventionality. The painter worked over this theme, the reconstruction of Minsk, in a number of his post-war period paintings. They were optimistic and philosophic, full of associations and complex feelings.

Mai Dantsig is a highly recognized Soviet painter. He has been awarded numerous titles and prizes and has taken part in many All-Union and foreign exhibitions. He has had the fortune to work and travel extensively. Since 1958, Dantsig has been teaching at the Byelorussian State Theatre-Art Institute.

KONSTANTIN GAVRILOVICH DOROKHOV

(6 March 1906 - 1960) Moscow

From 1923-1930, Dorokhov attended the Moscow High Art Technical Institute, under professors Brunie, Pavlinov, Kuprijanov and A. Shevchenko.

The main subject of his paintings were the laborers, for the whole country had become a huge construction site. Paintings by Dorokhov are full of spirit of the creativity and the affirmation of a new way of life, reflecting different aspects of life in the country. In the 1930s, he painted mostly portraits of his contemporaries. Dorokhov desired to stress the unity of the destiny of the individual with that of the country as a whole. An attractive image of youth with its hopes and aspirations is created in his portraits. In the 1940s and 1950s, he tackled thematic paintings, and in the late 1940s, he received public criticism from the Academy of Arts for his failure to paint in the approved Classical style.

Landscape painting of this period was also marked by some specific features. Traveling all over the country, Dorokhov creates a series of landscapes depicting various places from north to south. They depict different sides of Soviet landscapes – from miners' villages to large industrial cities.

Dorokhov was an active participant of the Great Patriotic War. Painting at the frontline, be it a rough sketch of a battle scene or a portrait of a comrade created while in a trench, he expressed the heroic resolve of the people who were fighting for their native soil.

After the war, Dorokhov once again devoted his time to recreating the dramatic pages of the Soviets struggle against Fascism and depicted the poetry of everyday life. The paintings apply to genre scenes connected with home motifs. Often the compositions combine figures of people and still lifes. His interest in the material essence of nature and things brought the painter a new manner of painting: the tonal painting of his early works gave place to energetic brushstrokes, intense colors and decorative associations with mosaic.

Dorokhov was an active participant of numerous exhibitions, both in and outside the USSR and he had several one-man shows. His works are in private collections and in more than 25 museums in the former USSR.

VASILI PROKOFEVICH EFANOV

(1900-1978) Moscow

The creative work by Efanov is one of the brightest pages in the history of Soviet representational arts. A fine portrait painter, a brilliant graphic artist and landscape painter, Efanov left a considerable art legacy. His biography closely connects with the events in the history of his country that played a decisive role in forming his outlook and personality.

Born to peasants, Efanov spent his childhood and youth on the banks of the Volga River. Upon graduation from a secondary school, Efanov entered the Samara Art Institute where he received his first professional skills. His ambition to become a painter brought him to Moscow in 1920, however his attempt to enter the *VKhuTeMas* failed. He attended the Free Academy of Arts, headed by the oldest master of Russian Realistic school, Arkhipov. During 1921-1926, Efanov was a student of a private art studio headed by Professor Kardovski, a pupil himself of I.E. Repin and P.P. Chistyakov. These two masters helped the future painter avoid modern trends and determined his Realistic way of art.

In 1928, Efanov painted his first large picture which was not perfect, but with historical-revolutionary subject, it demonstrated the painter's concern for the realities of contemporary life. Together with painters Saviski, Ioganson, Plastov, Gorelov and Moravov, Efanov took part in the creation of a panorama and series of paintings, "The Storm of Perekop" in 1934.

From 1936-1937, Efanov painted a significant work, "Unforgettable Meeting," depicting the Kremlin meeting of *CPSU* leaders and women, for which he was awarded the State Prize. The painting is now in the Tretyakov Museum.

Efanov, as an artist, is closely associated with the Party line in Soviet art. The main subject of his genre paintings were public figures and achievements of the Soviet State. His canvases show the social awakening of the Russian masses, and convey the heroic spirit of everyday life, reflecting the country's peaceful development and belief in a radiant future.

The Great Patriotic War prompted him to paint patriotic feats. "Portrait of Mother" depicts a common Russian woman who carries on her frail shoulders the war burden. Following the War, he traveled to India and Mongolia displaying the national peculiarities of these countries. Following the death of Stalin, he became more Impressionistic.

He combined his creative work with teaching activities, working as a professor of the department of painting in the Surikov Institute (1948-57) and teaching at the Moscow State Pedagogical Institute from 1957 until his death.

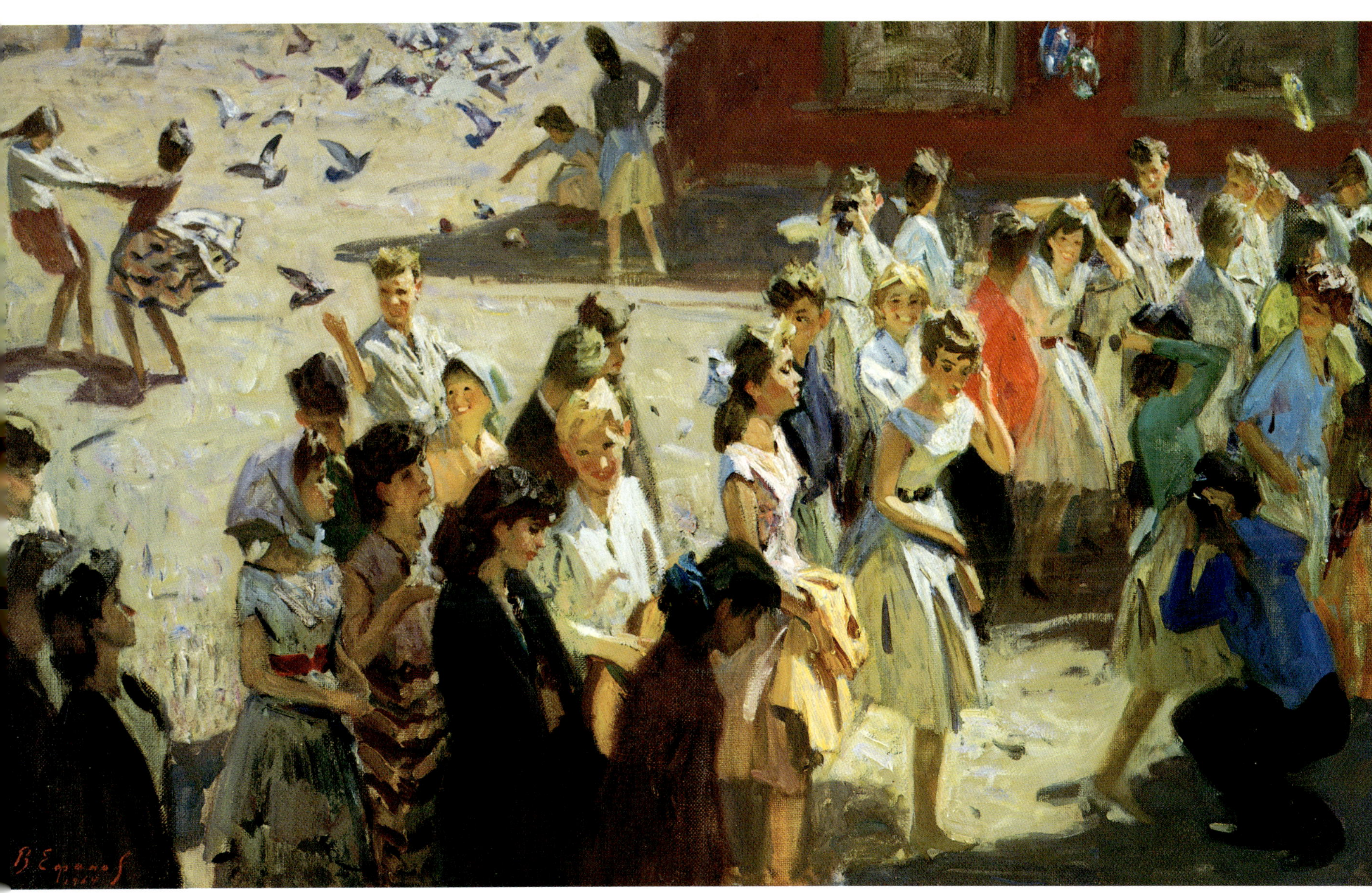

52. ***Graduation Day Red Square*** 1964
Vasili Prokofevich Efanov
30 x 48 inches
Oil on canvas
private collection

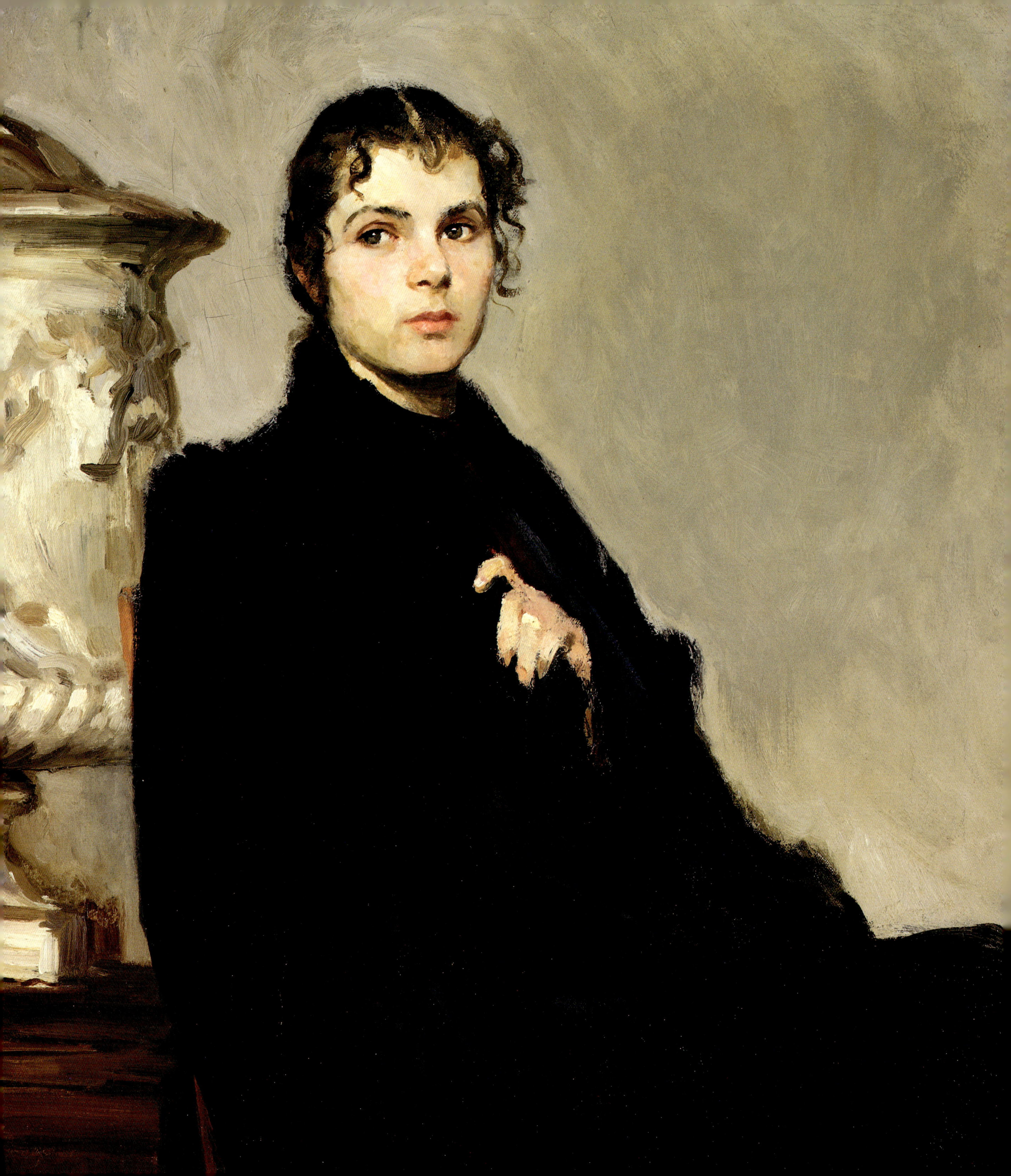

ALEXEI VIKTOROVICH FEDOROV

(31 January 1927 -) St. Petersburg

Fedorov studied at the Children's Art School of the Tauric Trade School of Arts in Leningrad from ages 6 to 14.

At the time of the Great Patriotic War, Fedorov lived in evacuation in Yaroslavl Region and Kostroma Region, where he worked in a factory.

In 1944, Fedorov attended Tavricheskoe Art School, and in 1948 he entered the Repin Institute in Leningrad, studying under Platunov, Stepashkin, Pavlovsky and Belousov. After his third year at the Institute, he majored in the Oreshnikov workshop.

At the age of 24, Fedorov began participating in republican, zonal and local exhibits in Leningrad. He held personal exhibitions in Moscow in 1970 and 1978 as well as in Leningrad in 1967. In 1953, he joined the Leningrad Chapter of the Russian Artists Union.

Fedorov's works are found in private collections throughout Italy, France, Japan, the United States and in the Leningrad History Museum.

53. ***Portrait of a Young Woman – Natasha*** 1954
Alexei Viktorovich Fedorov
35-1/8 x 27-1/8 inches
Oil on canvas
private collection

54. ***Jurors*** 1953
Alexei Viktorovich Fedorov
43-1/2 x 45-1/4 inches
Oil on canvas
private collection

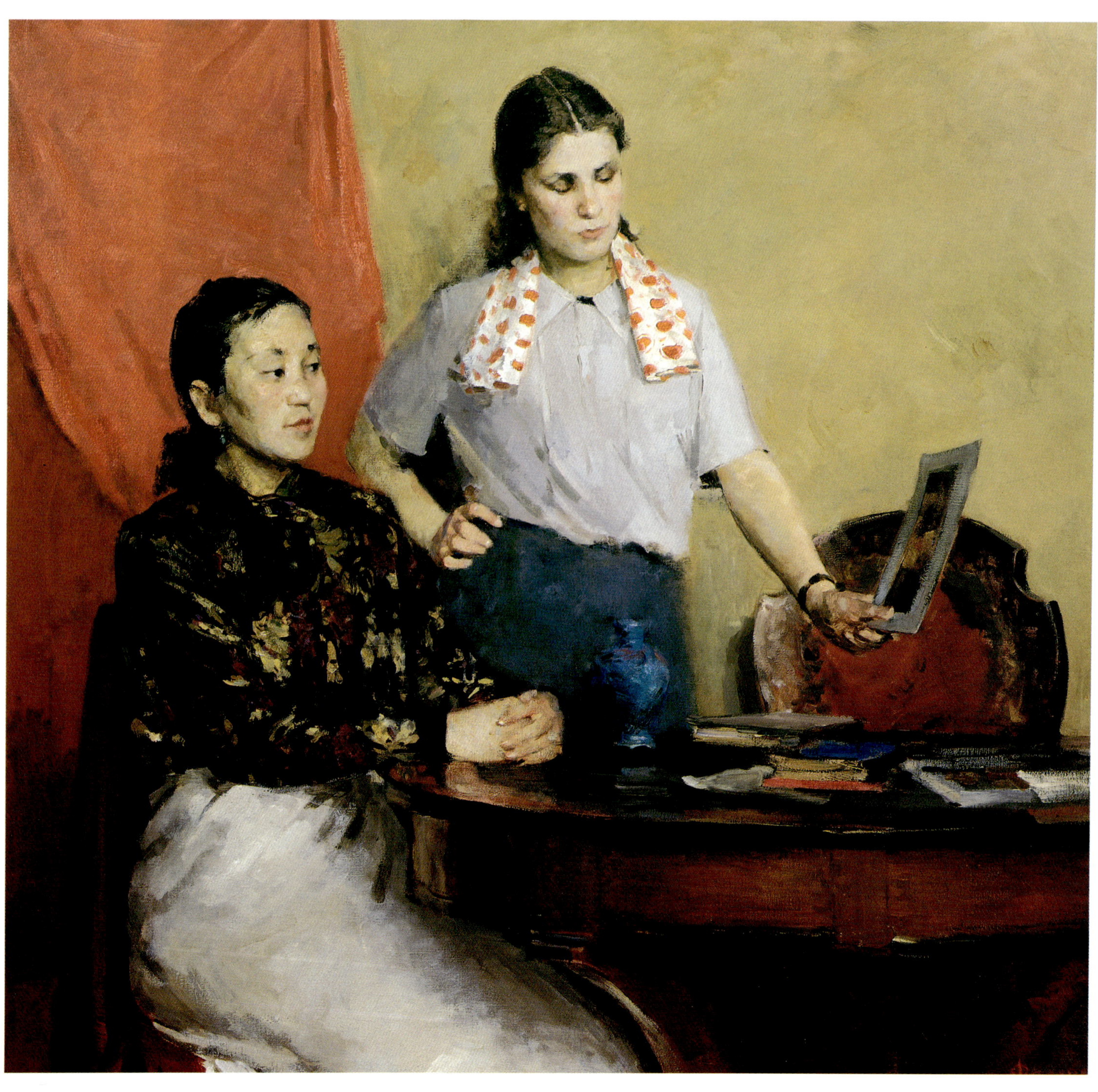

MIKHAIL D. GABUNIYA

(1 August 1928 -) Tbilisi, Georgia

After graduating from the Tbilisi Art College where he studied under the Merited Arts Worker, K.F. Kikhadze, Gabuniya entered the Repin Institute in 1949. He studied at an artistic workshop headed by Academician V.M. Oreshnikov, who influenced Gabuniya's creative outlook and work to a great extent in the painter's first subject paintings and portraits. His diploma work, "Midday," full of joyful spirits, sunny air and expressiveness, brought the painter fame and the Stalin Prize.

After graduating from the Institute, Gabuniya worked at the Tbilisi State Academy of Fine Arts, and later at the Tbilisi Art College.

He created a series of multi-figured compositions and portraits, the central theme of which the image is contemporary. These canvases are remarkable for their simplicity and clarity of intention and compositional structure. The painting vocabulary is light and airy, full of freshness and color concentration.

Through his art, be it a portrait, genre painting, or landscape, he makes the viewer believe in the painter's optimistic comprehension of life. His paintings are full of love toward man and to everything surrounding him, everything that uplifts and elevates him and makes him noble and sensitive.

55. ***Midday*** 1955
Mikhail D. Gabuniya
52 x 95-3/8 inches
Oil on canvas
private collection

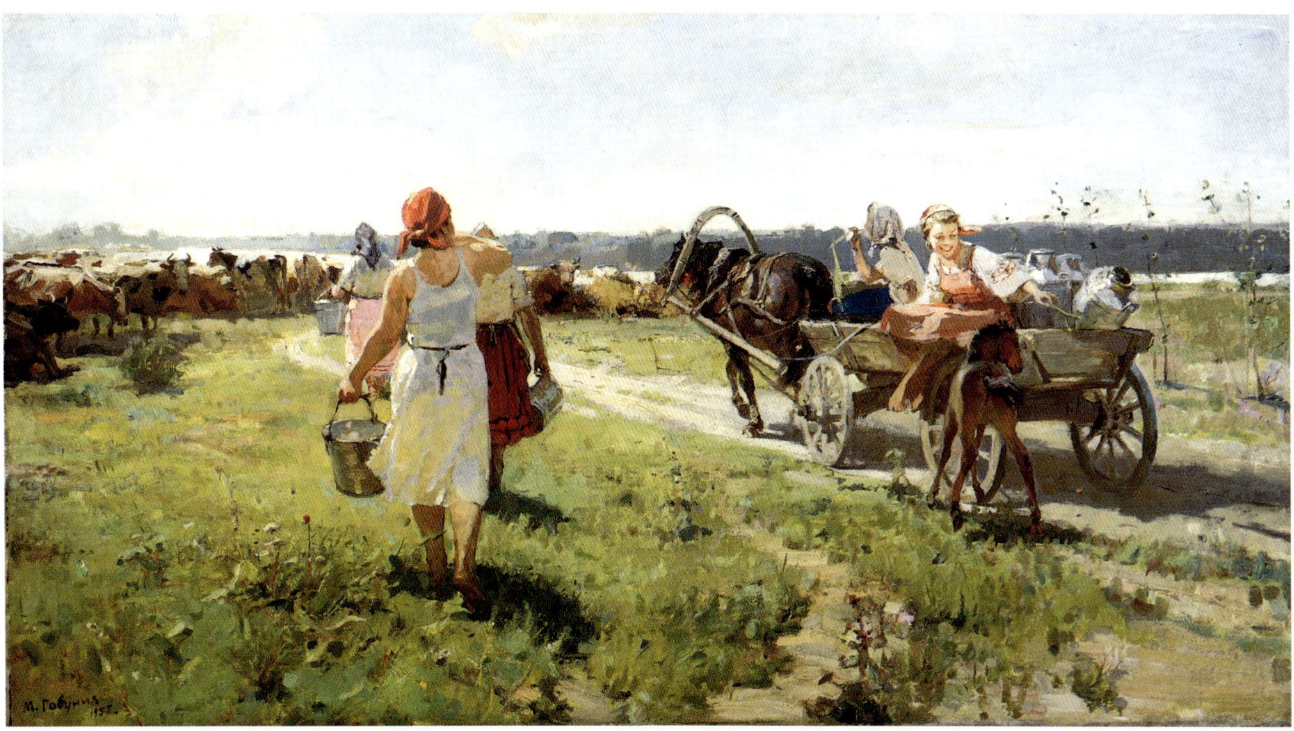

GREGORI SERGEEVICH GALKIN

(6 March 1924 -) Kharkov, Ukraine

During the Great Patriotic War in 1943, Galkin went to the front where he was severely wounded. He graduated from a secondary school in 1944 and entered the Art Institute in Kharkov where he graduated in 1951. His teachers were Shavykin and Besedin. The Renaissance Epoch, Impressionists and famous Russian painters Vasily Surikov, Valentin Serov and Piotr Konchalovsky most influenced him.

Galkin tries to depict in his canvases, the life of his childhood. The son of a peasant, Galkin was interested in the question of land, the theme of defending the Motherland, science and culture. The focus of the painter's attention is Russian and Ukrainian history and its creators.

The painter depicts historical stages of his country, its development, its tragic and triumphant pages.

Galkin believes that the Soviet system of art gave him the opportunity to obtain a good education and master his professional skills. He admits that the financial dependence on the Ministry of Culture demanded certain themes and put some restrictions on creative freedom of painters.

The works by Galkin were on display at All-Union, republican and international exhibits in America, Italy, China, Mongolia, Poland, Germany and Bulgaria. Many works are in museums and social organizations of Canada, Nepal, Italy and Poland.

ALEKSANDR MIKHAILOVICH GERASIMOV

(1881-1963) Moscow

Gerasimov graduated from the Moscow College in 1915, following studies with Archipov, Kasatkin and Korovin. He was a member of *AKhRR*, the leading group of Realist artists from 1925-1932. Gerasimov was chairman of the Moscow Artists' Union from 1937-39, and of the organizing committee (Orgkomitet) of the Union of Artists of the USSR from 1937-1954. As the first President of the USSR Academy of Arts, he presided from 1947-57 until compelled to resign by Khrushchev.

Gerasimov was awarded Stalin Prizes in 1941, 1943, 1945 and 1948. Gerasimov is the artist most closely associated with the Party line in Soviet art of the Stalin period.

In his painting ***A Russian Communal Bath***, he attempted to maintain a personal response to life that is in striking contrast to his many contributions to the Stalin cult.

In 1958 he received a Gold Medal at the World Exhibition in Brussels. His works may be seen in many Russian Museums. He exhibited in Tokyo, Cologne, Pittsburgh, Paris, Damascus, Moscow and at the World Exhibition in New York in 1947.

SERGEI VASILYEVICH GERASIMOV

(1885-1964) Moscow

Known as a painter of landscapes and thematic pictures, Sergei Gerasimov was also a book illustrator. He graduated from the Moscow Collegein 1912. In the 1920s he was a member of the artists' groups: *Makovets* 1922-25; the Society of Moscow Painters (*OMKh)* 1926-29; and the Association of Artists of the Revolution (*AKhr)* 1931-32. He taught at the Moscow *VKhu TeMas/VKhuTeIn* from 1920-29, at the Moscow Polygraphic Institute from 1930-36, at the Surikov Institute from 1936-50, as director from 1946-48, and at the Stroganov College (*MVKhPU*) 1950-64. He was chairman of the Moscow Artists' Union in 1939-52. In the post-war years Gerasimov, as chairman of the Moscow Artists' Union and director of the Surikov Institute, he came under fierce attack from the Academy of Arts because of his relatively liberal views on art. In 1948 he was compelled to resign as director of the Surikov Institute. Although he painted a number of well-known thematic pictures, he was above all a landscape painter and as such had considerable influence on young artists. In the Khrushchev thaw, he was made First Secretary of the newly-formed USSR Union of Artists, a post he held until his death.

PAVEL PHILIPPOVICH GLOBA

(7 January 1918 -) Moscow

Born in the Ukraine, Globa studied at the Omsk Artistic-Pedagogical Tekhnikum in Siberia from 1933-1937 and at the USSR Academy of Arts in Leningrad, from which he graduated in 1940.

From 1939-45, he was a member of the Grekov Studio of Military artists.

Globa lives in Moscow and paints portrait and landscapes. He has exhibited widely in the USSR.

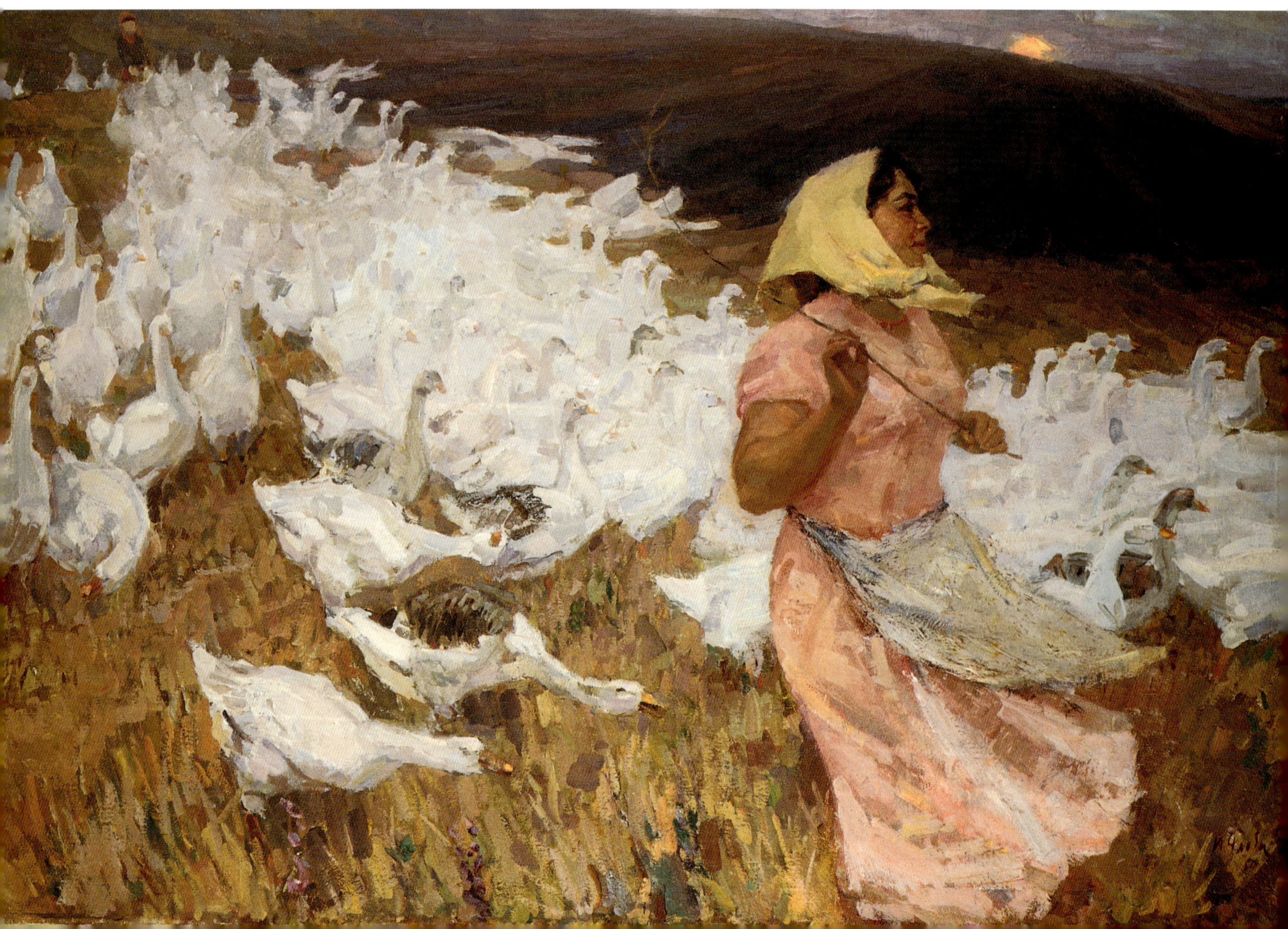

ALEXANDER GEORGIEVICH GULYAYEV

(11 September 1917 -) St. Petersburg

Alexander Georgievich Gulyayev was born in Rubtsovsk, Altai Territory. In 1932, Gulyayev graduated from middle school and entered the Tashkent Trade School of Arts. After studying under the direction of Volkov, Markova and Kurzin, Gulyayev progressed to the Russian All Academy of Arts in Leningrad in 1937. Here he studied under the instruction of Cheptsov, Stepanshkin and Ovsianikov.

Gulyayev voluntarily joined the Red Army in 1941 during the Great Patriotic War. He received the Patriotic War Order and eleven medals, including the Labor Veteran Medal, for his service during the war. After being wounded, he was demobilized in December of 1942 and resumed his study.

Gulyayev graduated from the Repin Institute in the Osmerkin workshop in 1946, and soon became a member of the Leningrad Chapter of the Russian Artists Union. He participated in numerous national, republican, zonal and local exhibits in Leningrad.

56. ***Galya of the Birds*** 1950
Pavel Philippovich Globa
54 x 79 inches
Oil on canvas
private collection

NIKOLAI KONSTANTINOVICH KAZAKEVICH

(5 May 1934 -) Minsk

Kazakevich spent his childhood among woods, meadows and fields of Byelorussia. The beauty of nature forever left a mark on his mood and creative activity.

During the Great Patriotic War, he lost his parents and found his home in an orphanage not far from Minsk.

In 1955, he graduated from the Minsk Art School and became a student at the Byelorussian State Theatre-Artistic Institute. His professors were Shevchenko, Suchoverkhov and Malishevskiy. He studied art under V.K. Tsvirko and soon became a remarkably talented draftsman.

In his creative work, he was greatly influenced by landscape painters Bialinitskiy-Burylja, Plastov, Ivanov, Mikhail Vrubel and Issac Levitan, the masters Rembrandt, Michelangelo Buonarroti, Van Gogh and the French Impressionists.

Kazakevich became a member of the USSR Union of Artists in 1963.

In his compositions, he used the human figure like a subject that is a part of a landscape. The colorist is sensitive to the nuances of tone in nature. At the same time, his vigorous brushwork gives the painting life and movement. He is concerned not only with the elements of visual experience, for him the poetry of Byelorussian landscape is always at the heart of his work.

In his portraits, he brings all colors harmoniously together trying to express his own attitude toward the characters.

Kazakevich considers himself to be a successful painter. He took part in a number of exhibitions, not only in the former USSR, but in Czechoslovakia, Hungary, Poland, France, Germany, Finland, Austria and Yugoslavia.

In 1986, he was awarded the Order of Friendship Among People, and in 1987, he became the Merited Arts Worker of Byelorussia.

His work is included in the Fleischer Museum Collection.

NIKOLAI ALEKSEEVICH KHAN

(10 December 1924-1981) Kiev

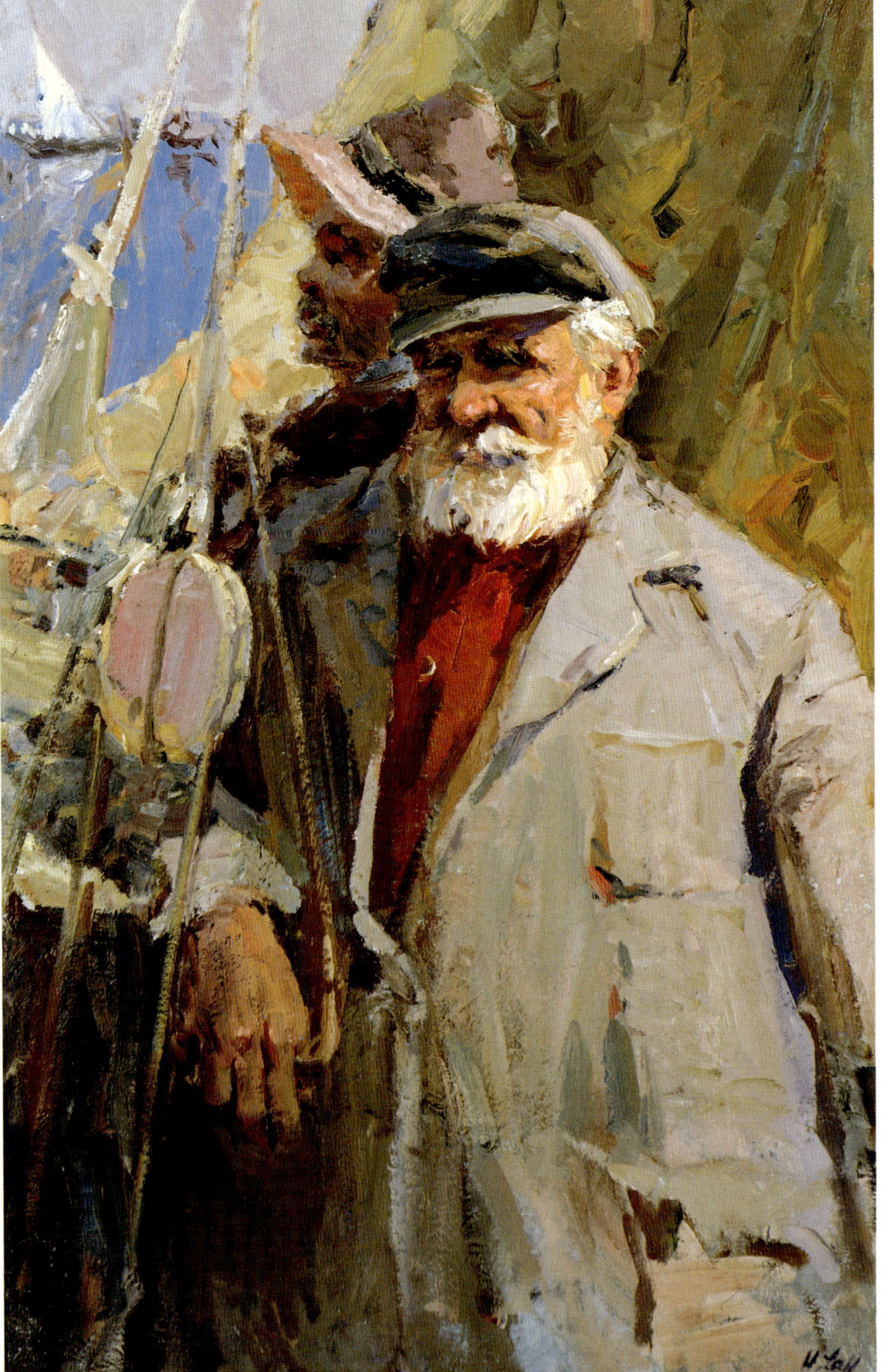

In 1945, Khan graduated from the Alma-Ata-College and in 1952 from the Kiev Art Institute, the studio of Shovkunenko.

A painter who lived and worked in Kiev, Khan was known above all for his pictures of the sea and sailors' lives. He also painted scenes of the Ukrainian countryside. In 1966, he made a mural in the Zoo Museum of Science of the Ukraine.

Khan was a member of the Union of Artists of the USSR and a Honored Artist of Ukrainskaya. Khan participated in All-Union, Ukranian, Regional exhibitions. In recognition of his achievements, he was awarded a Ukrainian State Prize posthumously.

57. ***An Old Russian Fisherman*** 1956
Nikolai Alekseevich Khan
42 x 27-3/8 inches
Oil on canvas
private collection

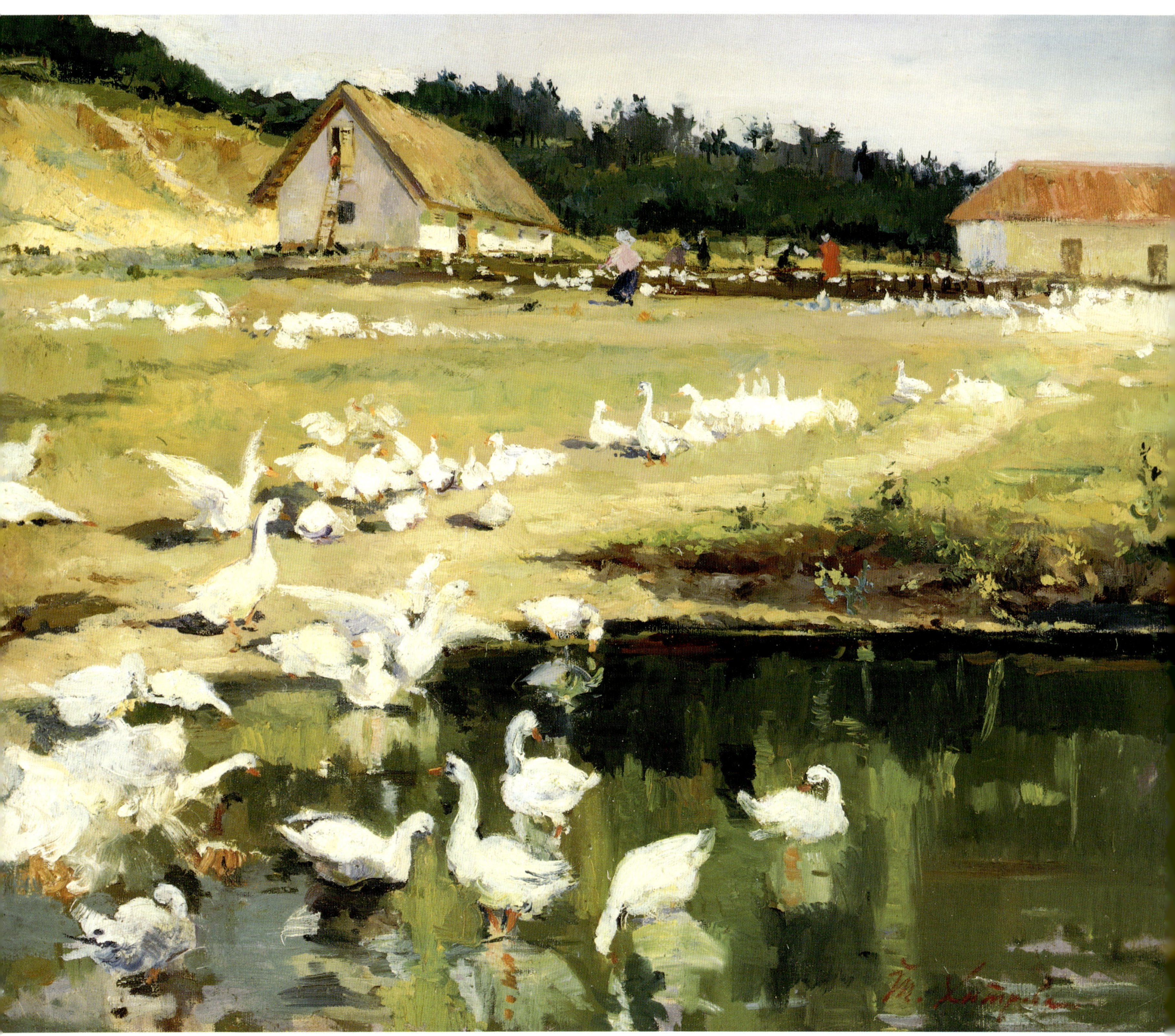

TAMARA ALEXANDROVNA KHITROVA

(1913-1991) Kiev

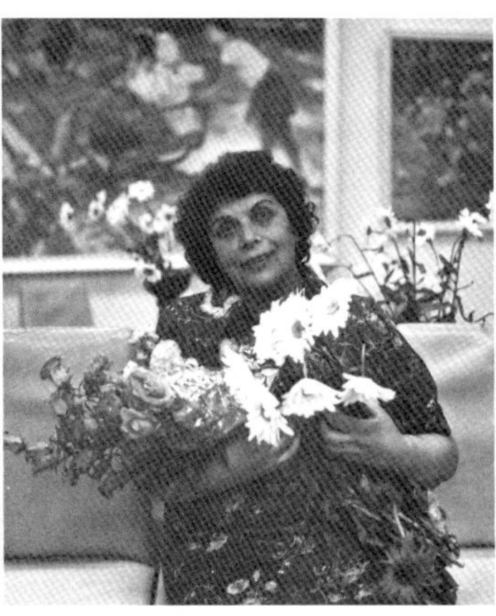

From 1931 to 1934, Khitrova was a student of the Odessa Artistic Institute. She was taught by Volokidin, who influenced her artistic direction. Khitrova was directed to the Kiev State Artistic Institute for continuation of her studies in 1934. At the studio of well-known Ukrainian artist, A. Shovkunenko, she developed the laws of color and composition. She worked out her own creative style, utilizing the Realistic viewpoint.

Following graduation from the Institute in 1940, Khitrova received first prize for her graduation work at the Second All-Union Exhibition and was given membership of the Artist's Union of USSR.

Khitrova attended the Lievov Artistic School until 1941. At the beginning of the German invasion, the painter was evacuated to Siberia. She worked in Novosibirsk and Tomsk, where her following paintings appeared at various shows. During this time she participated in the creation of political posters, helping the cause. Khitrova moved into Kharkov, where she worked at studios of the Artists' Union.

In 1945, with the artist's team, she was sent to the Ukrainian front line to inspire the soldiers to heroism and to ensure victory. Painting portraits of soldiers, officers and partisans, she subsequently exhibited a series of war heroes in Kiev. "For Valiant Labor in Great Patriotic War 1941-45," Khitrova was conferred a medal and an honorary diploma by Presidium of Supreme Council of Ukraine.

Khitrova skillfully connected the decorative soundness of palette with realistic form of her works. The compositions are vitally simple and clear for everyone. She also reveals a talent in still lifes, landscapes and subject pictures. Children are found as subjects in her works as well.

In 1983 she was made an Honored Artist of the Ukraine. Contemporaries called her "the painter by god." Khitrova died in 1991. She was buried in Baikhov Cemetery in Kiev. Her works are contained within the Fleischer Museum Collection.

58. ***Geese Farm*** 1946
Tamara Alexandrovna Khitrova
28-1/2 x 34-1/8 inches
Oil on canvas
Fleischer Museum Collection

59. ***Apple Blossoms on the Dnieper River*** 1950
Yuri Vasiljevich Kiyanchenko
46 x 78-3/4 inches
Oil on canvas
private collection

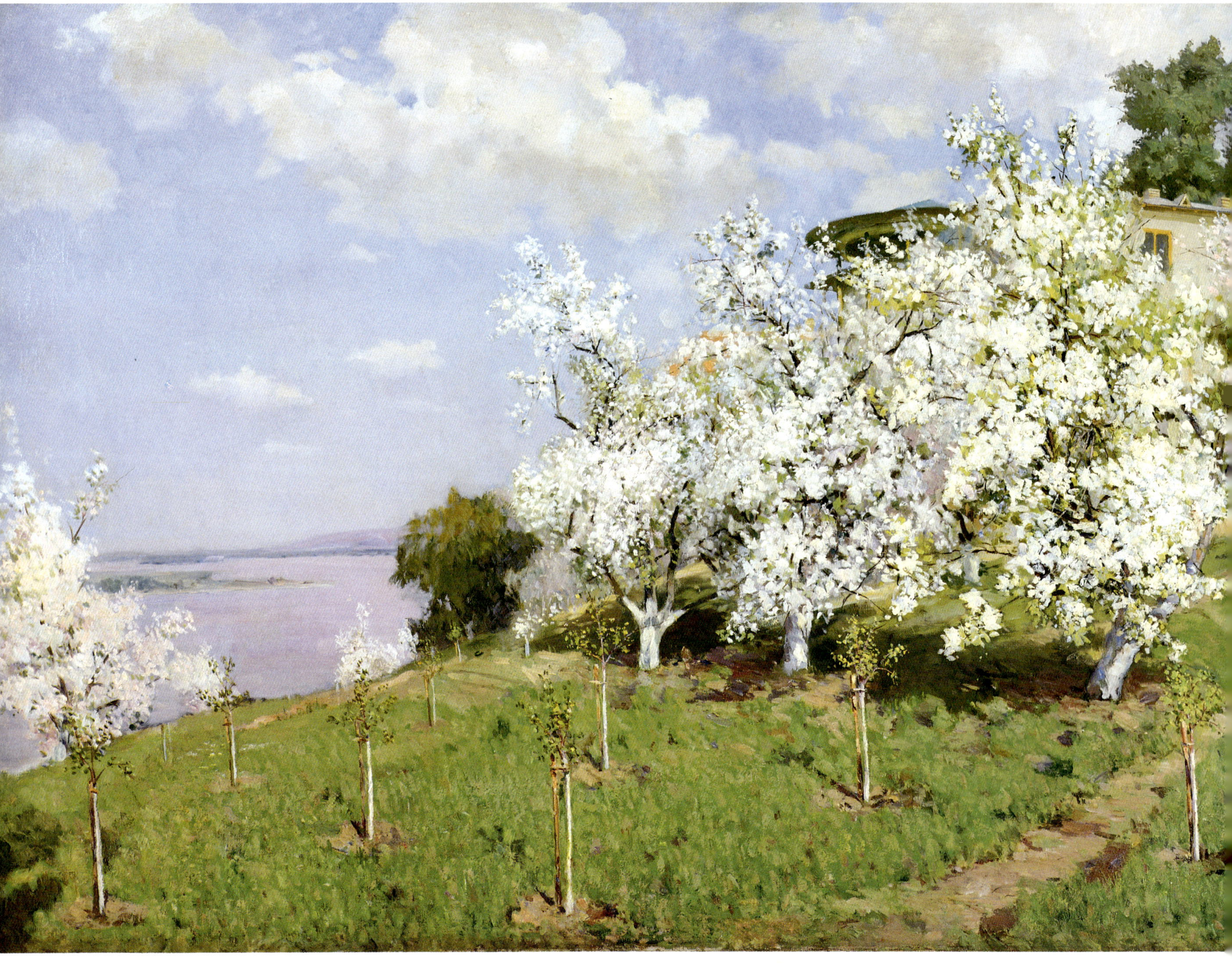

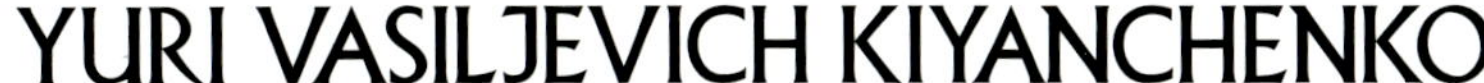

YURI VASILJEVICH KIYANCHENKO

(25 May 1911 -1989) Kiev, Ukraine

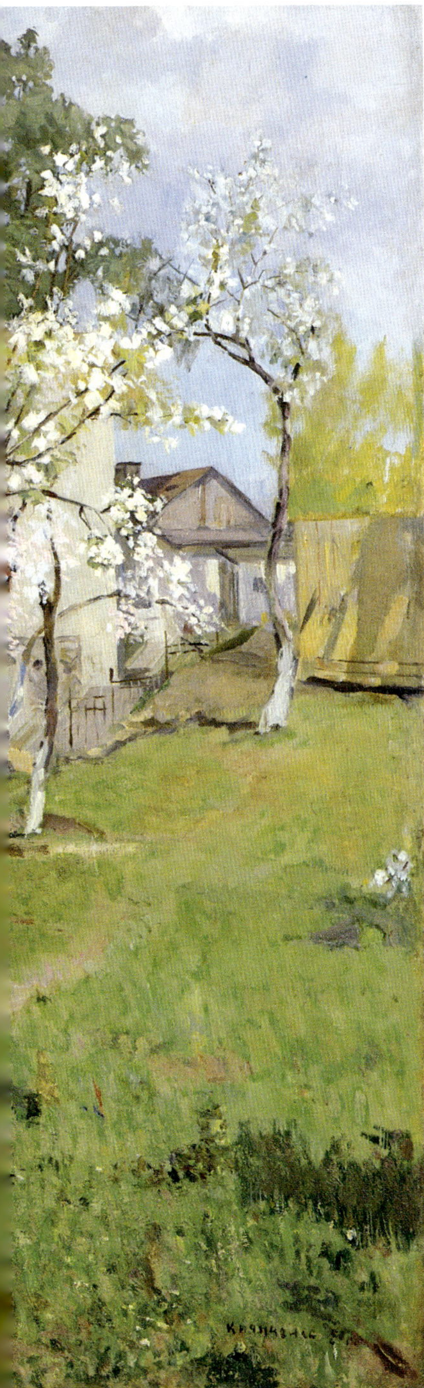

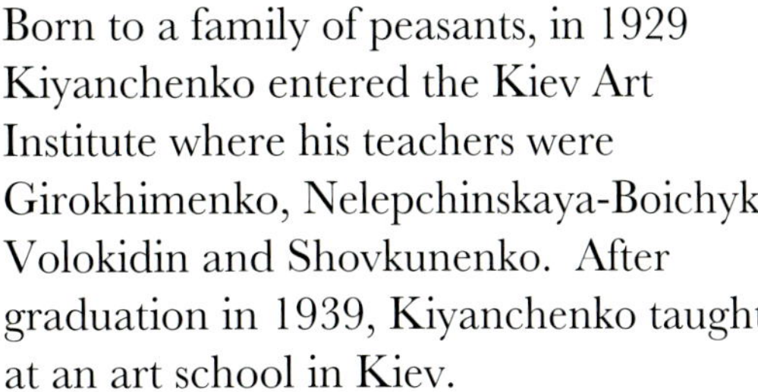

Born to a family of peasants, in 1929 Kiyanchenko entered the Kiev Art Institute where his teachers were Girokhimenko, Nelepchinskaya-Boichyk, Volokidin and Shovkunenko. After graduation in 1939, Kiyanchenko taught at an art school in Kiev.

Joining the army in 1941, he fought at the frontline, was taken prisoner, but managed to survive. Since 1945, Yuri Kiyanchenko lived and worked in Kiev.

His creative work was greatly influenced by Russian Realistic painters Repin, Surikov and Serov. He worked with enthusiasm at the Hermitage, copying the paintings of El Greco.

Throughout his career his main interests were subject paintings connected with the history of Ukraine, which demonstrated his high professional skill and brought him fame.

A subject painting, "Summer Day," (1947) was on display at one of the Republican exhibitions and caused a large interest and a negative reaction of the representatives of the official art, due to the depiction of a nude woman. The painting, denounced by Nikita Khruschev, is now in the Odessa Art Museum.

Total ideological view of art certainly affected Kiyanchenko's creative activity, but his paintings devoted to the image of Lenin were painted with a sincere belief in "A kind Tsar," which has always been typical of Russian painters.

Portrait painting is another sphere of his professional interest. A sizeable part of his portraits are devoted to historical images and Cossacks' military leaders of the time of Bogdan Khmelnitsky. The painter never ignored landscape painting, in which different places of Ukraine are depicted with great love and sympathy.

Paintings by Kiyanchenko are in museums of the former USSR and in private collections throughout the world.

FYODOR DMITRIEVICH KOLESOV

(21 September 1919 -) Nizhany-Nogorod (formerly Gorki)

In 1936, Kolesov entered the Gorki Art School and in 1939 he was called for service in the army. After demobilization, he completed his studies at Gorki Art School in 1949, and he became an active participant in the artistic life of the town by exhibiting his works. Since 1957, he has been a member of the Union of Artists of the USSR.

He preferred to paint the portraits of pre-revolutionary Russian writers and artists, as well as the portraits of his contemporaries. These paintings are vibrant because of a specific plastical manner of painting and firmdrawing. Kolesov participated in exhibitions in the Gorki region, the Volga zone and the whole of Russia.

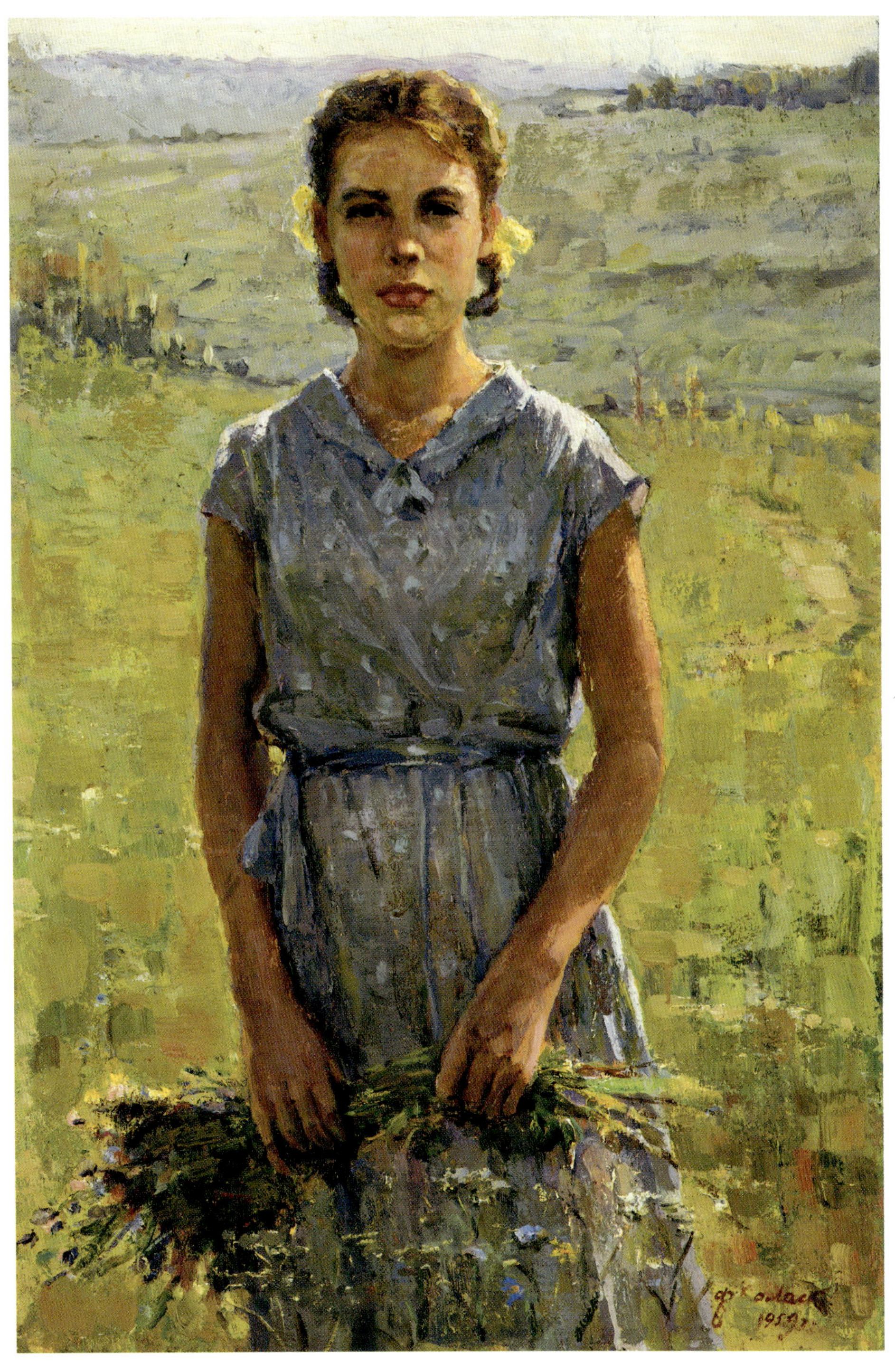

60. ***A Girl with Flowers*** 1959
Fyodor Dmitrievich Kolesov
30-3/x24 x 20-1/2 inches
Oil on canvas
private collection

ALEXANDER IVANOVICH KOMAROV

(18 August 1918 - 19 July 1987) Tver, Russia

Komarov lived and worked in Leningrad, graduating from the Repin Institute. He participated in major exhibitions of the Soviet Union during the 1950-1980s. His works are in the State Russian Museum in St. Petersburg and in other museums in Russia.

61. ***Coming from the Lake*** 1950
Alexander Ivanovich Komarov
34 x 44-5/8 inches
Oil on canvas mounted
private collection

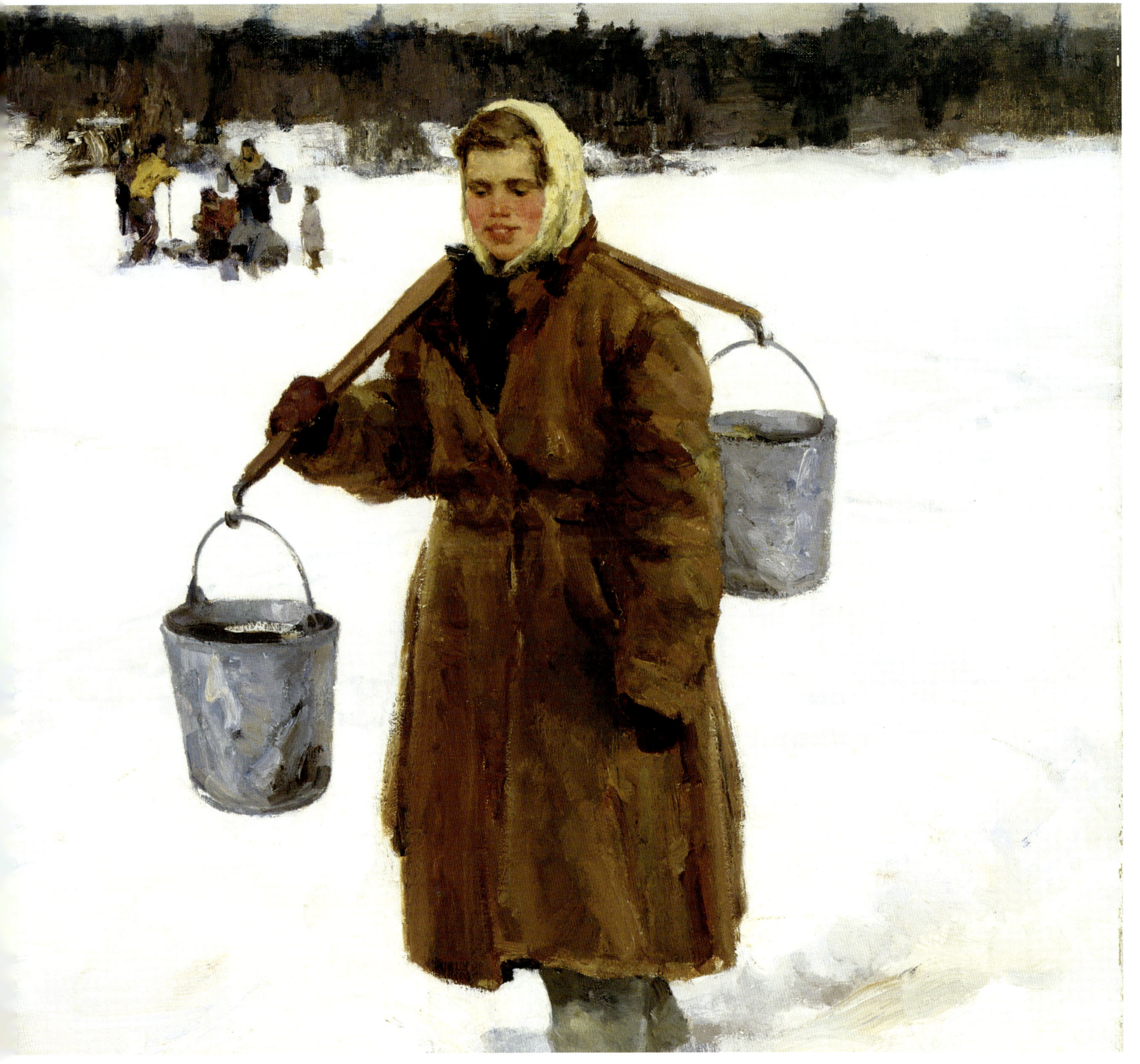

MIKAIL A. KOSTIN

(1918 - unknown) Rostov-on-Don

Mikhail Kostin graduated from the Moscow State Art Institute during the Great Patriotic War. At the end of the 1940s, he taught at the Vladivostok Art College and was chairman of the local union of artists. In the 1950s he returned to Moscow, where he lived and worked until his death.

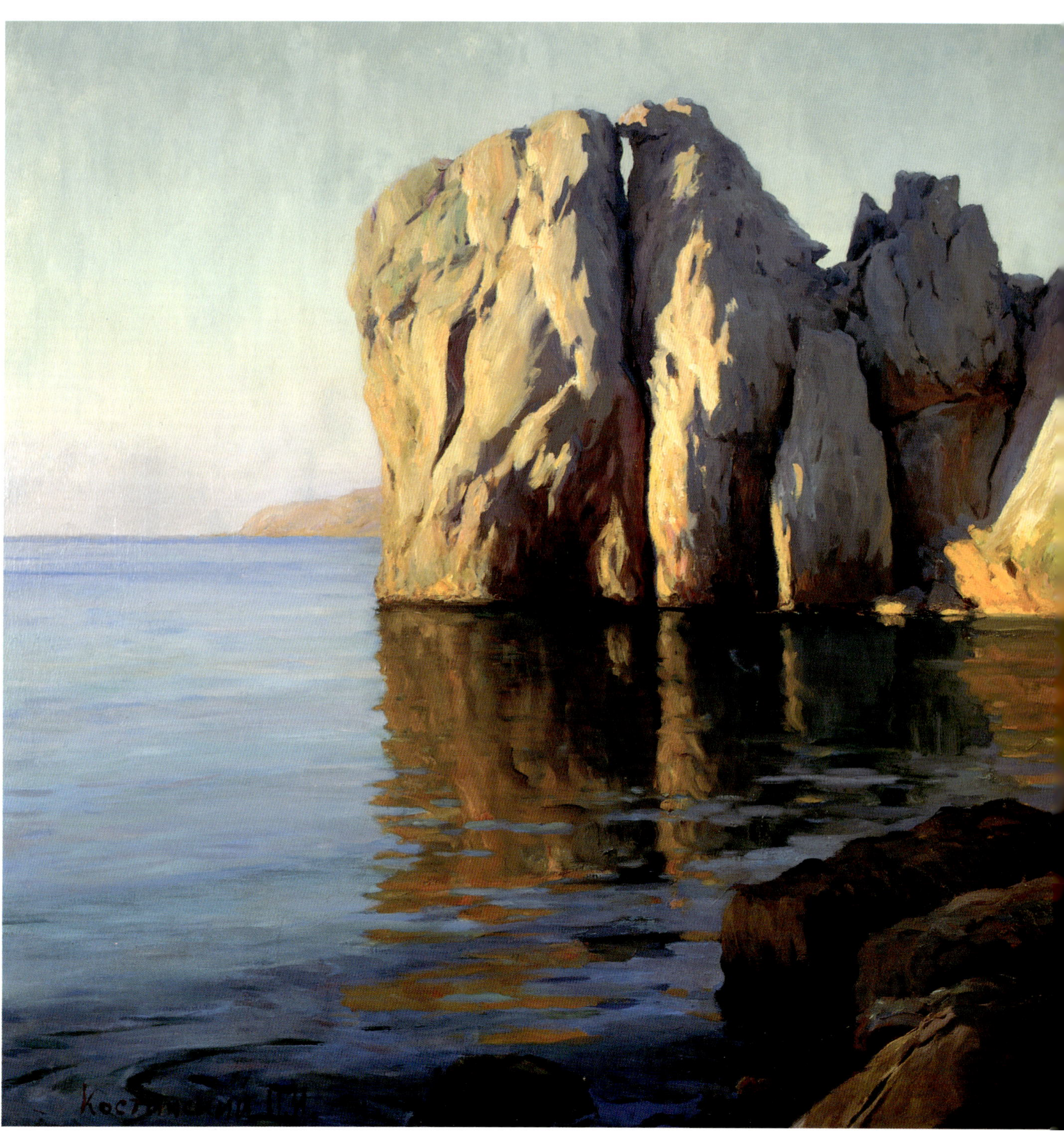

PETR IVANOVICH KOSTINSKY

(21 November 1916 -) Moscow

Born in the town of Maikop into the family of a railroader, Kostinsky lost his father very early. His mother, a village teacher, encouraged his interest in drawing at a school studio where she taught.

Kostinsky studied at the Rostov-on-Don Art College, from which he graduated in 1939. His first teachers were Chernykh, Neiphel and Oreshkin. After graduating from the college, Kostinsky entered the Academy of Arts in Moscow, but was called to military service and studied at a School of Junior Aviaspecialists. Following the War, Kostinsky was appointed Chief Artist of the State Central Museum of the USSR Armed Forces.

In 1950, he was admitted to the Moscow Artists Union and has been an active participant of Moscow, republic and All-Union art exhibitions. His works have been displayed at foreign art exhibitions in Japan, Sweden, Canada and West Germany.

Kostinsky's sphere of interest is marine landscapes which reflect different moods of the sea. In his pictures, dedicated to the Baltic Sea, Kostinsky describes sea toilers and their everyday life.

Kostinsky's landscapes depicting Moscow suburbs stand out for their expressiveness and violent colors. One of the painter favorite subjects is trees, as he considers them symbols of nature's grandeur.

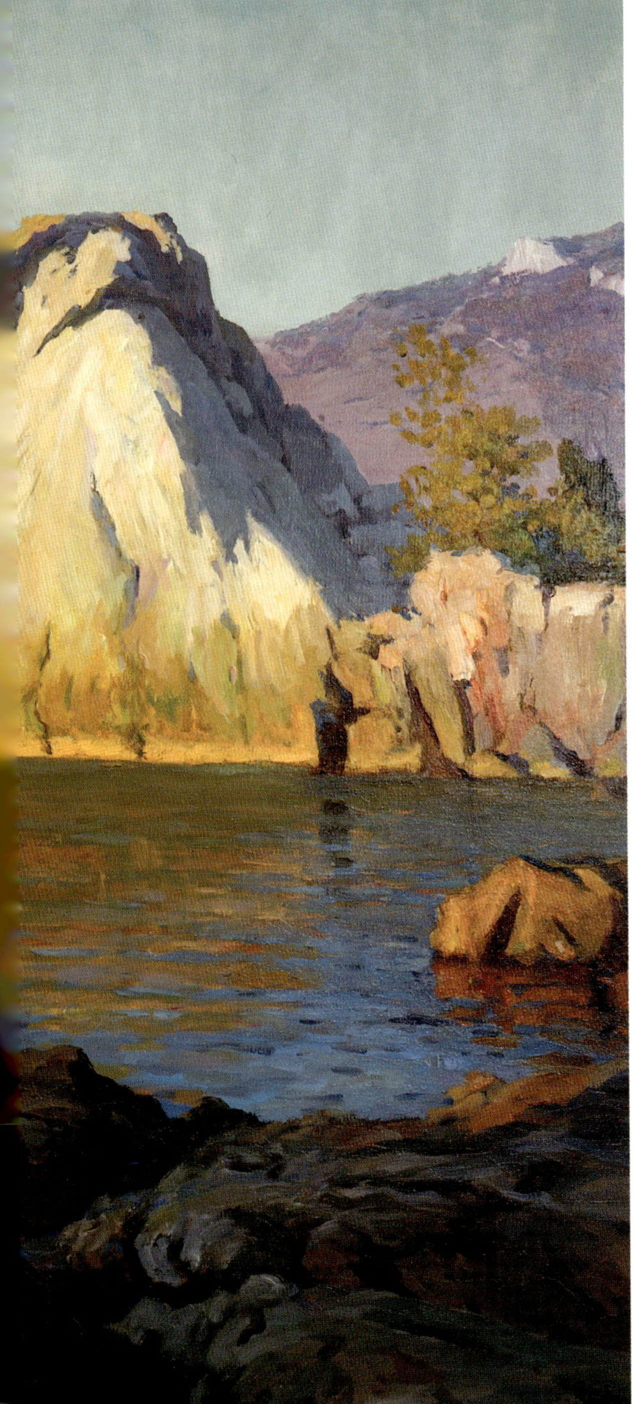

62. ***Morning at Gurzuf*** 1958
Petr Ivanovich Kostinsky
45 x 66-1/8 inches
Oil on canvas
private collection

ZINAIDA MIKHAILOVNA KOVALEVSKAYA

(13 December 1902 - 1972) Samarkand

It was only natural that Kovalevskaya's ambition to develop her creative inclinations and her bent for drawing brought her to the Kazan Art Tekhnikum, where she studied from 1922-24. She attended classes run by Nicolai Fechin and Pavel Benkov. She began a close relationship with Benkov, and when he had decided to settle in the ancient town of Samarkand in central Asia, Kovalevskaya followed him. She worked in the ethnographic department of the Uzbek State Scientific Research Institute and then as a teacher at the Samarkand Art College which was set up by Benkov, from 1932-44.

In 1943, Kovalevskaya defended her diploma work as an external student at the Leningrad Art Institute.

From 1930, Kovalevskaya has participated in art exhibitions. In 1953 she had her first solo show. Kovalevskaya received the title of People's Artist of Uzbekistan in 1964 .

Kovalevskaya worked on subject pictures and potraits, as well as still lifes and landscapes. Kovalevskaya painted scenes of Uzbek life, the happiness of free labor, the joy of motherhood, unpretentiousness of a child's soul. One of the main characteristic features of her artworks is their national coloring. The painter knew the national characters and national psychology of Uzbek people very well. Kovalevskaya's artworks are in the museums of Uzbekistan and Tatariya and in private collections.

ENGELS VASILYEVICH KOZLOV

(24 March 1924 -) St. Petersburg

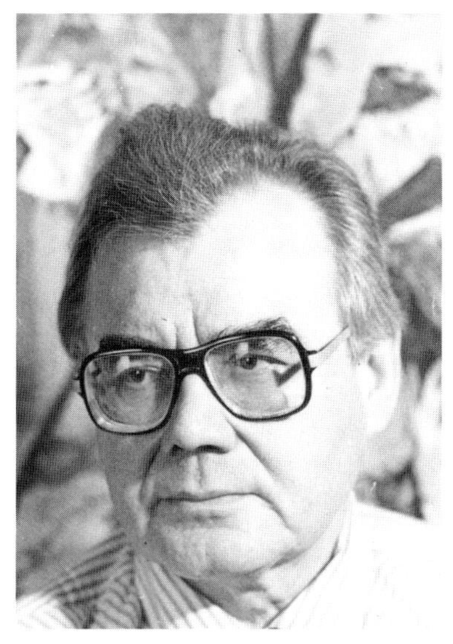

At age 11, Kozlov attended the Children's Art School in Syktyvkar and graduated from high school the year the Great Patriotic War ended. He then studied at the Department of History at the Komi State Pedagogical Institute and at the Yaroslavl Art School before moving to Leningrad in 1949.

One year later, Kozlov entered the Repin Institute and studied under Mikhailov, Valtsev and Stepashkin. Kozlov also studied in the Neprintsev workshop. Kozlov comments on Neprintsev, "His desire to infuse us with the sense of contemporaneity, so we could leave their images for our decendants was the principal content of our education, supported by a solid professional training. Our professor demanded that we peer into the model, form, motion and pictorial relations; that we understand everything and reflect it on the canvas in the clearly explicit complete form."

From 1953 on, Kozlov had an active role in the national, zonal, and republican exhibitions and in local exhibits in Leningrad and Syktyvkar, as well as in Turku, Finland and Philadelphia, USA. Kozlov graduated cum laude from the Institute in 1956. His wife is artist G.A. Smirnova.

He became a member of the Leningrad Chapter of Russian Artists Union in 1957, and for the next 34 years, Engels was a member of the Communist Party. He received the Honors of the Order of Friendship of Nations, the Medal for Labor Valiance, USSR Academy of Arts and USSR Council of Ministers diplomas, and a Kirov Factory Prize in Leningrad.

From 1961-63, Kozlov worked in the V.M. Oreshnikov art workshop. Throughout his career, he received many honors: Honorable Art Worker of Komi in 1971; Honorable Artist of Russia in 1978; National Artist of Komi in 1982; and National Artist of Russia in 1987. Engels has held personal exhibits in Syktyvkar, Leningrad and Moscow.

He has authored various articles on art in *Khudozhnik* magazine. He was the subject of numerous publications and articles in the personal exhibit catalogs. The album-monograph, *E.V. Kozlov*, was published in 1991 in Leningrad.

"The master's hand uses paints to communicate his mental tension, his spiritual disposition, enthusiasm in his heart and his love. Perhaps we should also believe in our humble pride, that the eyes of the future world will see our time reflected on our canvases."

Kozlov's works of art can be found in Leningrad, Syktyvkar, Orenburg, Briansk, Petrozavod and Smolensk.

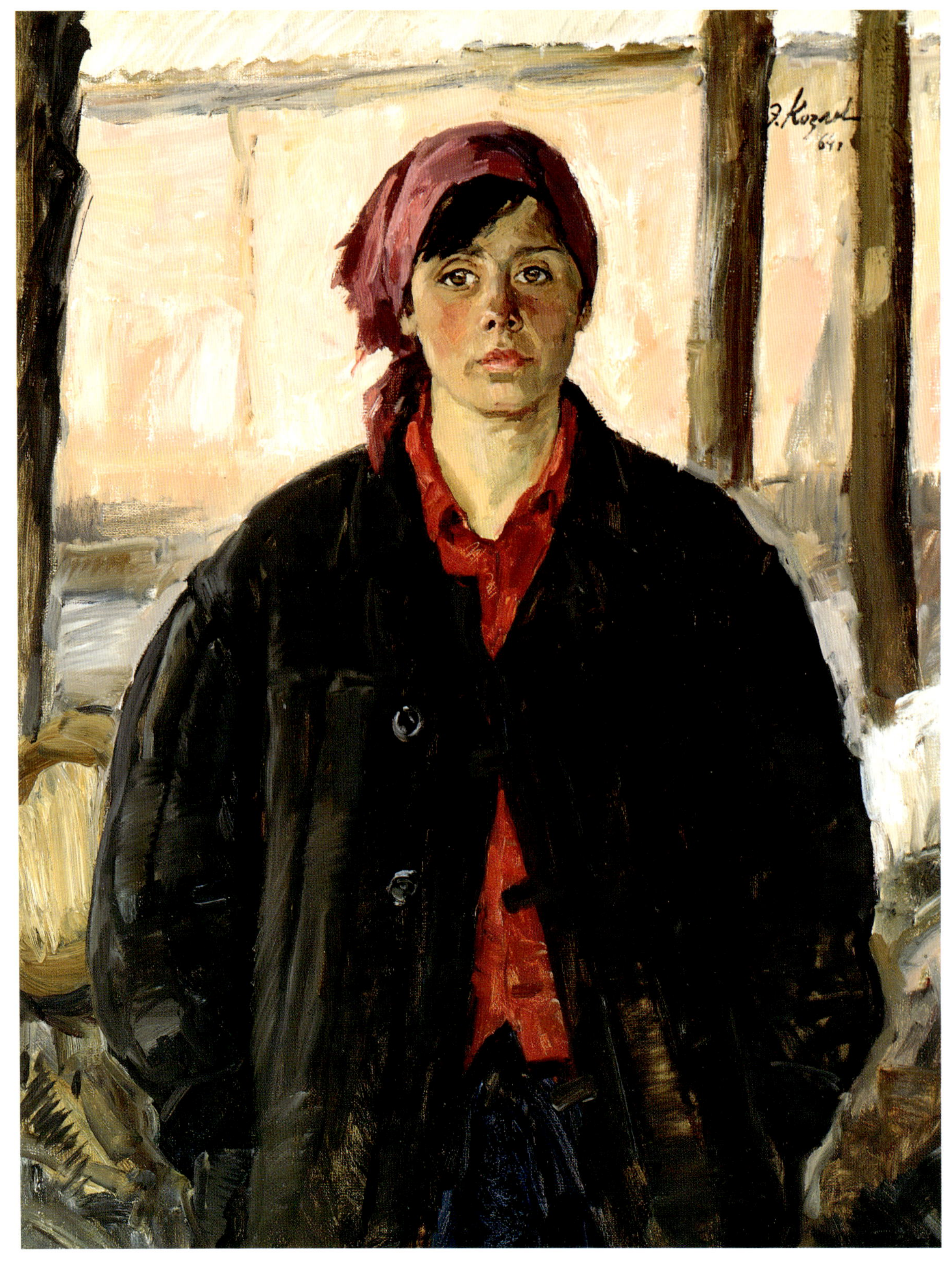

63. ***Portrait of the Coal Miner, Freda*** 1964
Engels Vasilyevich Kozlov
39 x 31 inches
Oil on canvas
private collection

64. ***The River Usa*** 1965
Engels Vasilyevich Kozlov
43-1/2 x 78 inches
Oil on canvas
private collection

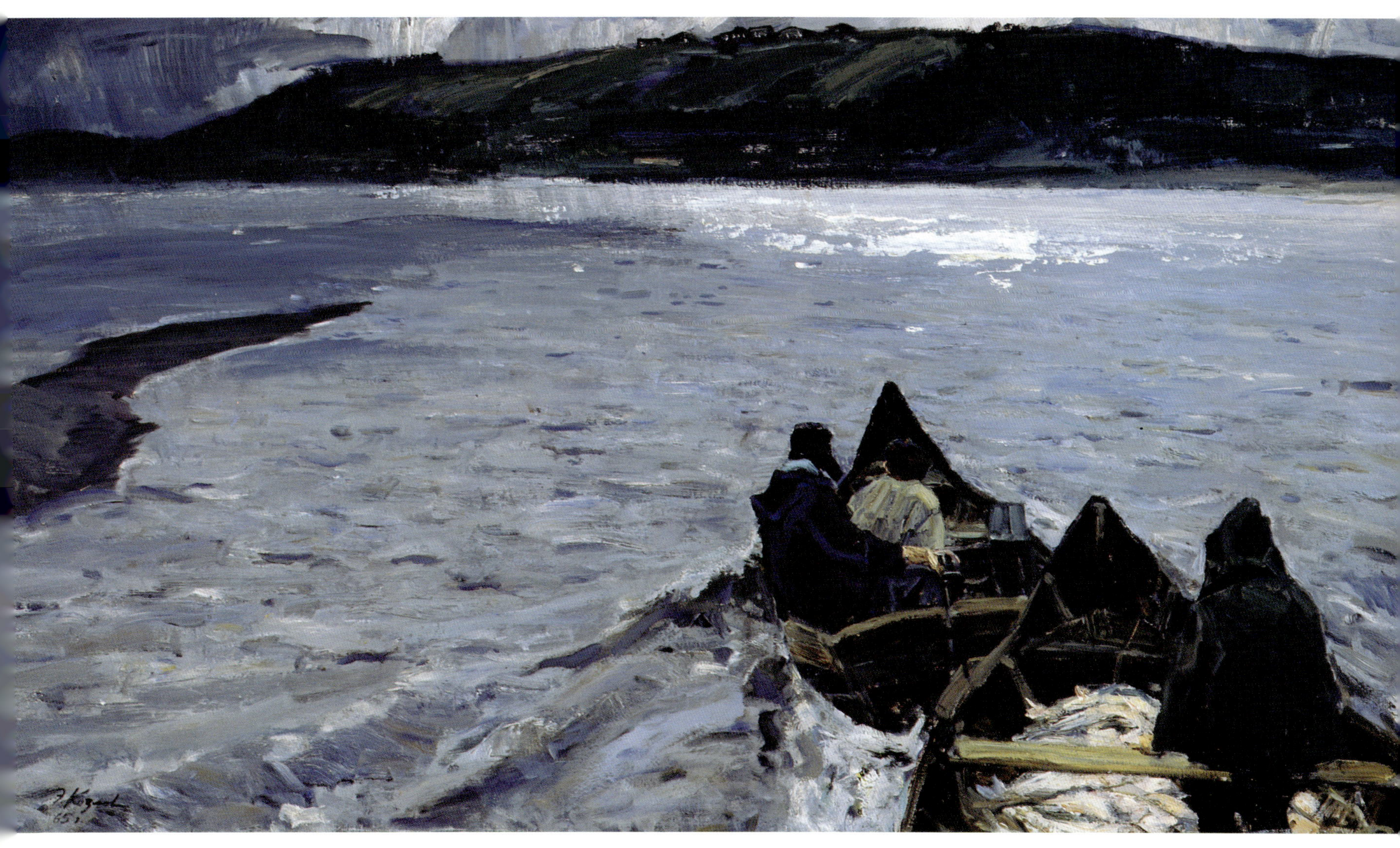

LEONID KUZOVKIN

(9 April 1921 -) Lipezk

Kuzovkin graduated from the "1905" College of Art in Moscow in 1947 where his teachers included Petrovich, Belyanin and Baksheev.

In 1950, he became a member of the Union of Artists. He held one-man shows in Sergiev Posad, Zagersk in 1971, 1981 and 1993. His primary work focuses on portraiture. Many of his paintings are in museum collections and the Russian Ministry of Culture.

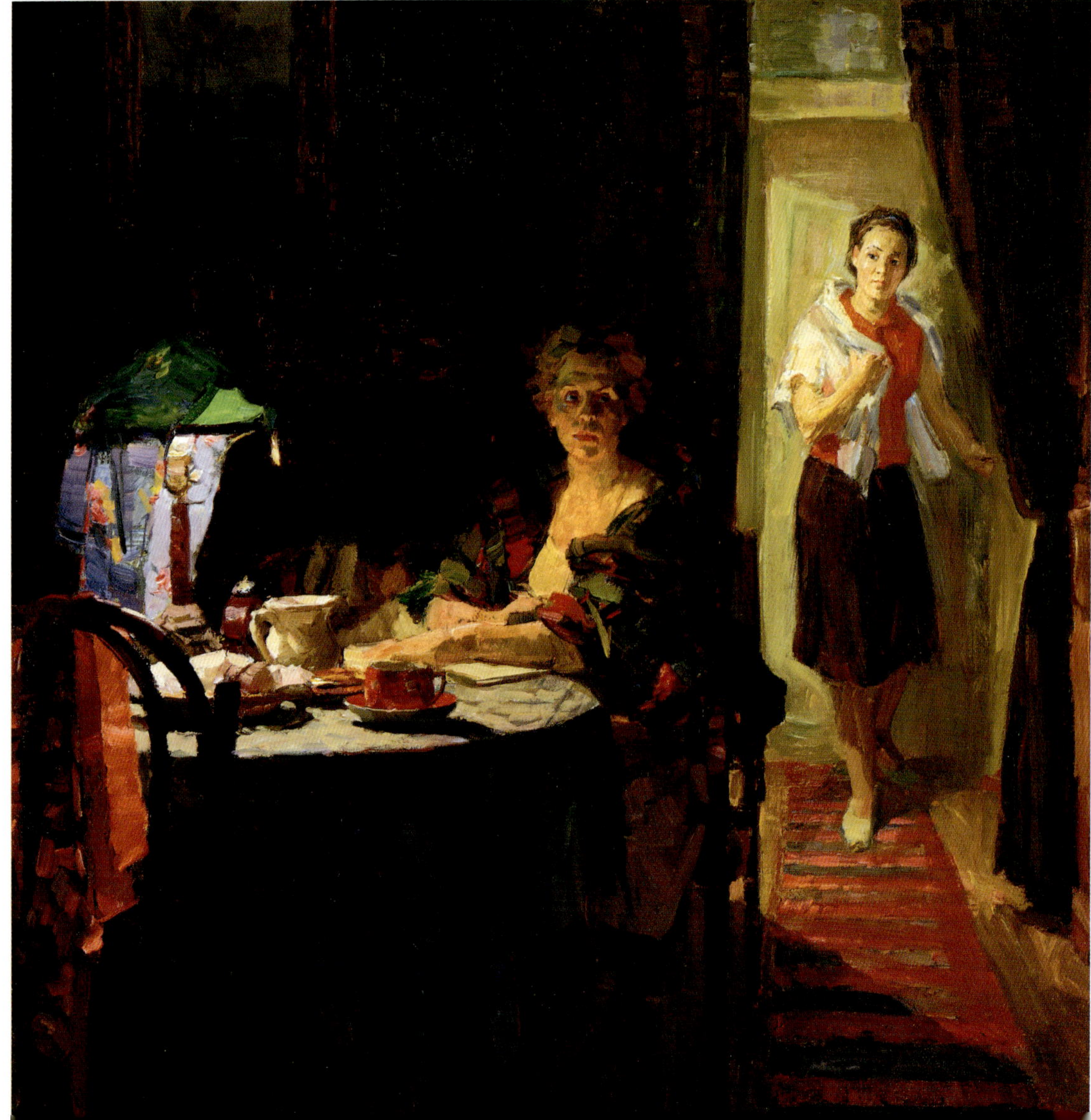

65. ***The First Date*** 1957-62
Leonid Kuzovkin
39 x 41-1/8 inches
Oil on canvas
private collection

ALEXANDER IVANOVICH LAKTIONOV

(17 May 1910 - 1972) Moscow

Alexander Laktionov, the People's Artist of Russia, and member of the Academy of Arts, was born in Rostov-on-Don. In 1926, he entered Rostov Art Secondary School, graduating with high honors in 1929. He entered the Leningrad Academy of Art and started an artistic workshop headed by Isaak Brodski in 1932. From 1938-44, Laktionov was a post-graduate at the Academy. Laktionov was Brodski's favorite pupil and an arch-exponent of the Classical style which came into its own after the war.

Before the war, Laktionov worked mainly as a portrait painter, acting often as a graphic painter. In his drawings, the exactness of characteristics, and freshness of life impressions are evident. His wife and relatives were often his models.

During the war, Laktionov lived and worked in Tamarkend where the Academy of Arts was evacuated and where the painter made several landscapes and portraits. He was awarded a Stalin Prize in 1948 for ***A Letter from the Front***.

Following the war, he lived in Zagorsk, whose atmosphere contributed to executing numerous landscapes which are full of tenderness to Russian nature and old architecture.

Laktionov's main interest during the '60s and '70's were portraits of his contemporaries. He painted several portraits of Leonid Brezhnev.

Laktionov participanted in art exhibitions at home and in Romania, Poland, Germany, Belgium, France and England.

BORIS MIKHAILOVICH LAVRENKO

(6 May 1920 -) St. Petersburg

Boris Lavrenko was born in Rostov-on-Don. At the age of 16, Lavrenko entered the Rostov Trade School of Arts and took part in local art exhibits through 1948.

Lavrenko became Master Sergeant of the 199th Bradenburg Infantry Regiment during the Great Patriotic War from 1941-45. He received the Patriotic War Order and numerous medals including the Victory over Germany medal.

In 1946, Lavrenko graduated from Rostov and entered the Painting Department at the Repin Institute in Leningrad. Under the guidance of Pavlovsky, Frenz, Serebriany and Ioganson, he graduated with a degree in painting six years later.

From 1952 on, Lavrenko took part in all major art exhibits in Leningrad, as well as republican and national exhibitions in Moscow. He became a member of the Leningrad Chapter of the Russian Artists Union in 1953, and in 1954, he began teaching at the Repin Institute. The Institute named him a docent in 1962, and in 1976 he became a professor. He published several articles on the methodology of teaching the collections of scientific articles in *Iskusstvo* magazine.

"My credo is the unity of truth and beauty, the truth of beauty and the beauty of truth." Lavrenko was the subject of a monograph by A.I. Roshchin, published in Leningrad in 1989; articles in the exhibit catalogs - *Iskusstvo* and *Khudozknik;* the *Sovetskaya Kultura* newspaper and others.

In 1972, Lavrenko held personal exhibits in Leningrad, Moscow and Rostov-on-Don. That same year, he joined the Communist Party, of which he was a member until it disbanded in 1991.

In 1976, he was named Honorable Artist of Russia; in 1980, he received the M.B. Grekov Silver Medal for his pictures depicting the Great Patriotic War.

His thesis, *The Contribution of B.V. Ioganson and His School to the Formation and Development of Soviet Thematic Painting*, was published in 1983, the year Lavrenko earned his Ph.D. in Study of Art.

"I met Americans back in 1945 in occupied Berlin. The Americans and we, the Russians, are very similar in nature and in our attitude toward life and people. I feel great affection for them."

Lavrenko's works of art are found in the Russian Museum in Leningrad, in museums and private collections in Ashkhabad, Briansk, Vladimir, Orel, Rostov-on-Don, Moscow, Leningrad, England, France, Japan, West Germany, Colombia, Turkey and the United States. Lavrenko works in St. Petersburg.

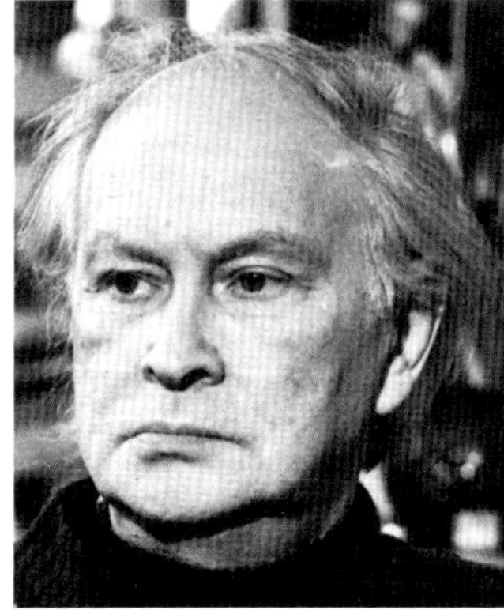

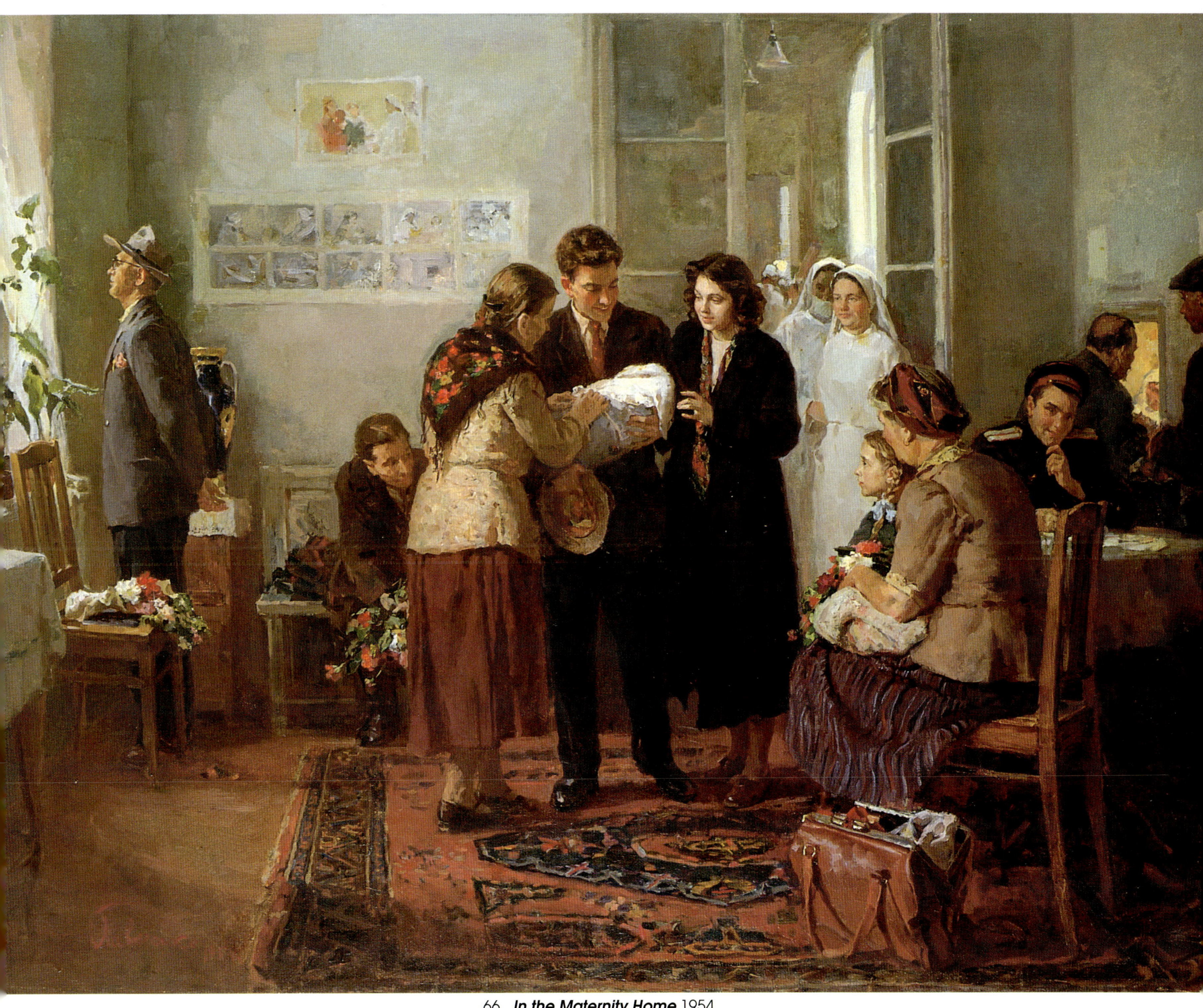

66. ***In the Maternity Home*** 1954
Boris Mikhailovich Lavrenko
48 x 61 inches
Oil on canvas
private collection

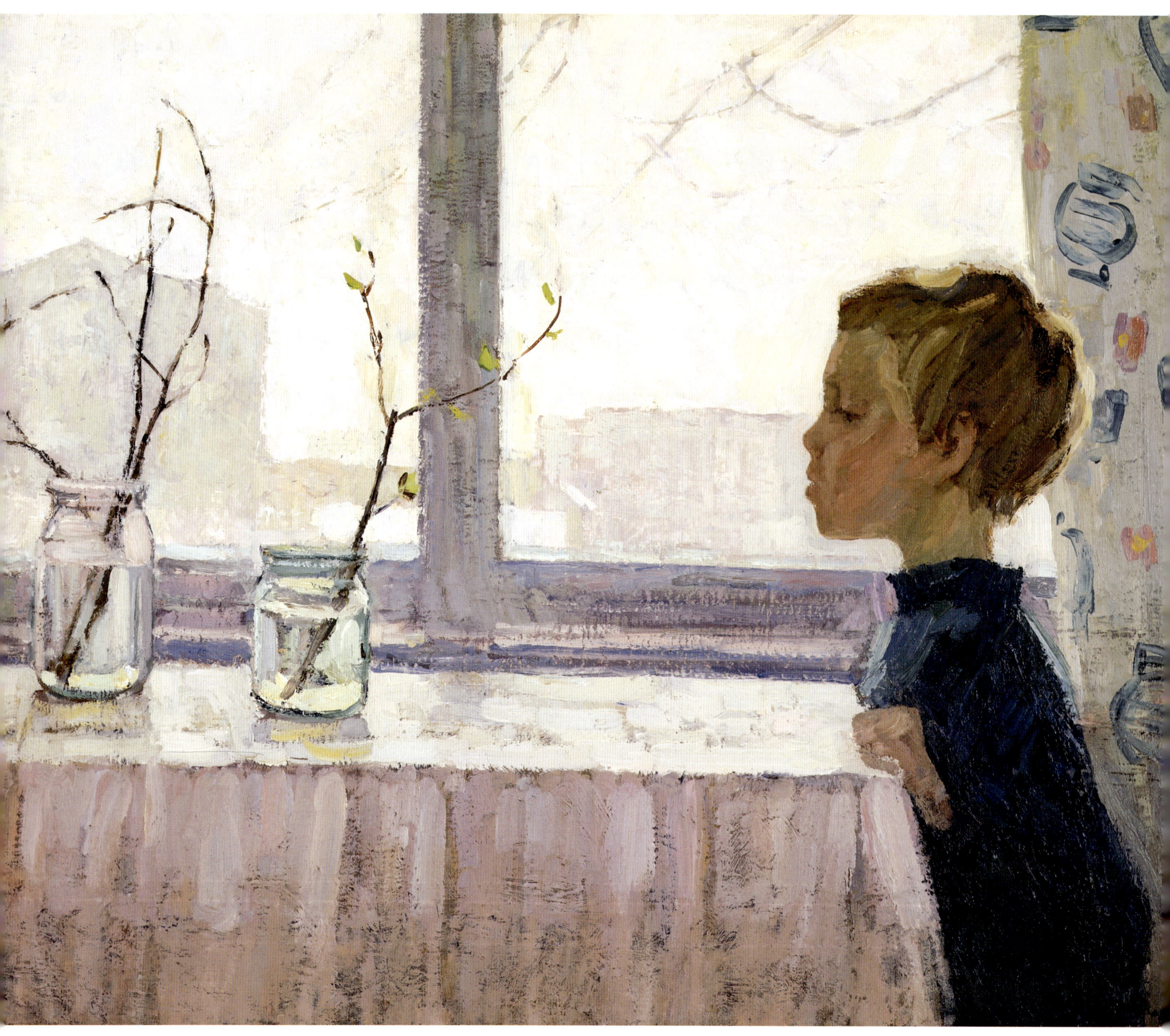

YELENA LEONIDOVNA LEONOVA

(12 July 1929 -) Moscow

In 1978 Leonova's first solo exhibition took place. She was born to the family of the well-known Soviet writer Leonid Leonov, where she was acquainted with the works of Russian art and literature as a child.

Drawing became a serious occupation for her only in 1943 when returning from the evacuation, she went to Moscow secondary school specializing in art. In 1947, Leonova entered the V.I. Surikov Art College where her teachers were Kotov and Reshetnikov. Her graduation picture *Children in the Theater* was in the exhibition of graduation works of the students of art colleges of the whole USSR in 1954.

In 1958 she became a member of the Union of Artists of the USSR and has regularly participated in numerous exhibitions. Her first works were genre pictures following the traditions of the Soviet painters. Far from perfect, they revealed what would later develop in the artist's works, a sincere, human and lyrical understanding of the world.

Recently she has preferred to paint still lifes which are simple and beautiful. She likes to paint windows, following the traditions of Russian artists of the fin de sie`cle, such as Dobuzhinsky, Kustodiev and Zhukovsky. To paint a window is to show someone's life on the background of a landscape. It is a way of revealing the artist's philosophy of life. While the village windows in the pictures of Leonova show her admiration of the beautiful scenery and country life, the city windows are often associated with sad thoughts of human life. The idea of loneliness of a human being in a big city is expressed. All the details have symbolic meaning.

All the works of the artist are full of poetical understanding of the world. The composition is always perfectly developed. The color range is noble and not very bright. The details are accurately chosen. Everything that is depicted is significant. The idea of the picture is always clear, although the techniques and the subjects vary greatly. The colors of her pictures reflect certain emotional conditions. Her landscapes are full of light, air and the sun, but the shapes are always distinct and never covered with the spots of light.

She has her own creative attitudes, her own way of looking at the world and this way is both sincere and analytical. Her pictures tell us much about Russia, the people, their lives, thoughts and feelings. Although the genres she uses are sometimes underestimated by art critics, one should remember that there are no unimportrant genres in painting.

67. ***The Beginning of Spring*** 1961
Yelena Leonidovna Leonova
31-1/4 x 38-1/4 inches
Oil on canvas
Fleischer Museum Collection

ANATOLI PAVIOVICH LEVITIN

(16 November 1921 -) Moscow

Anatoli Levitin, the People's Artist of Russia, developed his aptitude for drawing in the Central House of Artistic Education of Children in Moscow. Later on, he was sent to Leningrad to study at a Secondary Art School at the Academy of Arts, from which a future painter graduated in 1941 with high honors.

In the autumn of 1941, Levitin was a cadet of the Leningrad Artillery-Technical College. From 1942-45, Levitin was at the front.

On demobilizing, Levitin came back to Leningrad and entered the Department of Painting of the Repin Institute. He studied art under professors Zaitsev, Fogel, Ovsyannikov and Ostova. He majored at the artistic workshop headed by Professor Ioganson. Painters that influenced his creative work were Russian Realists Ilya Repin, Valentin Serov, Issac Levitan, Mikhail Vrubel, as well as French painters, Van Gogh, Claude Manet, Sisley and Italian painters.

The main genres that the painter worked in was subject pictures and portraits. The main characters of his pictures were people, common and outstanding, young and old, his contemporaries and the heroes of the past. The painter depicted everyday situations connected with labor. Some pictures belong to the genre of historical subject pictures, the main themes of which are the Revolution of 1917 and the Great Patriotic War.

Pure landscapes are rare in his work. The painter considers landscape an element of any subject picture which contributes to understanding the theme and characters of people. He often gets impressed by the ordinary objects or faces. The ability to be amazed by things, to feel the full force of their impact is one of the most characteristic, determining and charming traits of Levitin's art. His art is dominated by positive characters, the leading one being that of a master. A master is not necessarily an artist. It is anyone who has achieved perfection in his work. The ideas projected in his pictures take their beginning in his personal life: the events, impressions, information and feelings. He rejects speculativeness in art, as well as invention and constructionist subjects based on abstract rationalistic schemes.

Levitin is a participant of numerous exhibitions. His works are in the collections of Russian Museum, Leningrad, and the Tretyakov Gallery, Moscow. Levitin's paintings are also in private collections in France, Japan and the United States.

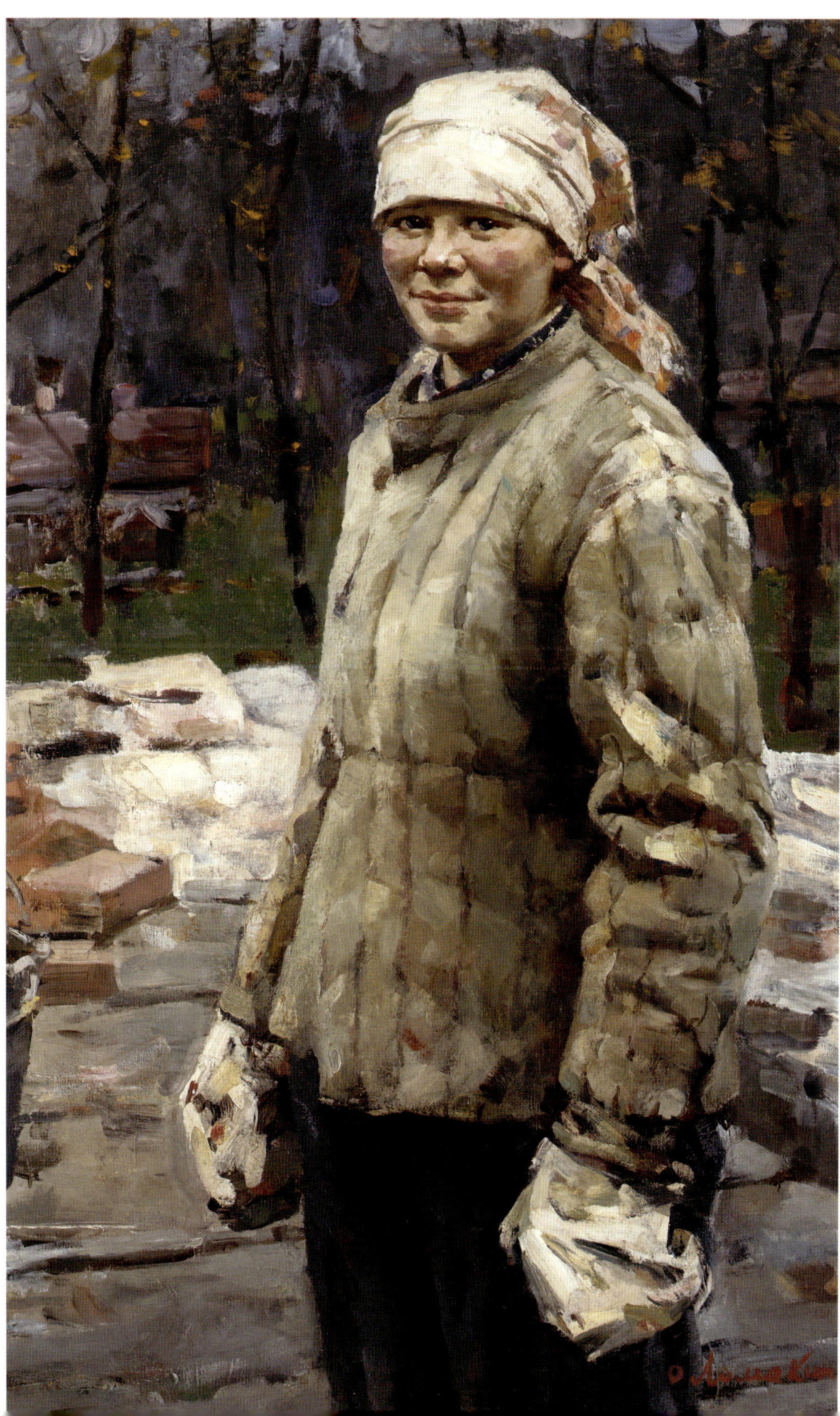

68. ***Road Worker: Nina*** 1954
Oleg Leonidovich Lomakin
143 x 92 inches
Oil on canvas
private collection

OLEG LEONIDOVICH LOMAKIN

(26 August 1924 -) St. Petersburg

Lomakin was born in Krasny Kholm, in Tver Region. At the age of 16, he studied at the High School of Arts in Leningrad and continued his stay until the school was evacuated to Smarkand in February 1942. He enlisted in the Great Patriotic War in 1942, was seriously injured the following year, and received the First Class Patriotic War Order and the Medal For Bravery. In 1944, he returned to the High School of Arts, which had relocated back to Leningrad.

Oleg graduated from the I.E. Repin Institute of Painting, Sculpture and Architecture in the B.V. Ioganson workshop in 1952. Among his teachers were Scholokhov, Bernstein, Anisovich, Mikhailov and Zaitsev. "The best memories I have are associated with Zaitsev, both as a man and as a teacher." In 1952, he also joined the Leningrad Chapter of the Russian Artists Union.

In 1978, Lomakin won a Kirov Factory Prize and in 1981 he was named Honorable Artist of Russia. He has participated in national, republican and local exhibits in Leningrad, and international exhibits in Finland, Germany, France, Spain and Japan.

Authored by N.G. Moiseyeva, Lomakin's album-monograph was published in Leingrad in 1991. Lomakin comments, "I am a realist. I like to paint interesting people. I like landscapes, too. I have painted many subjects, but I like working on portraits the most. It seems to me that the graphic art should be diversified. Everybody sees in his own, different way. And this diversity, this 'dispute', can result in interesting productions. However, I think that the sense of life, the presence of live nature, is indispensable in painting; for nothing is more beautiful than nature."

His work is included in the Fleischer Museum Collection.

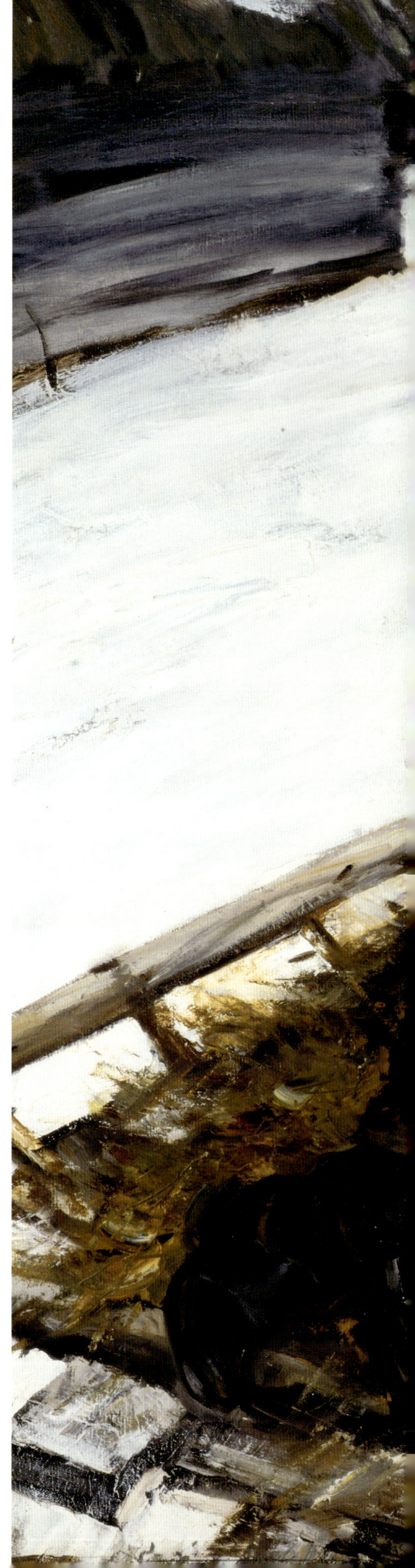

69. ***Returning from the Front*** 1969
Oleg Leonidovich Lomakin
54-3/4 x 70-1/2 inches, detail
Oil on canvas
private collection

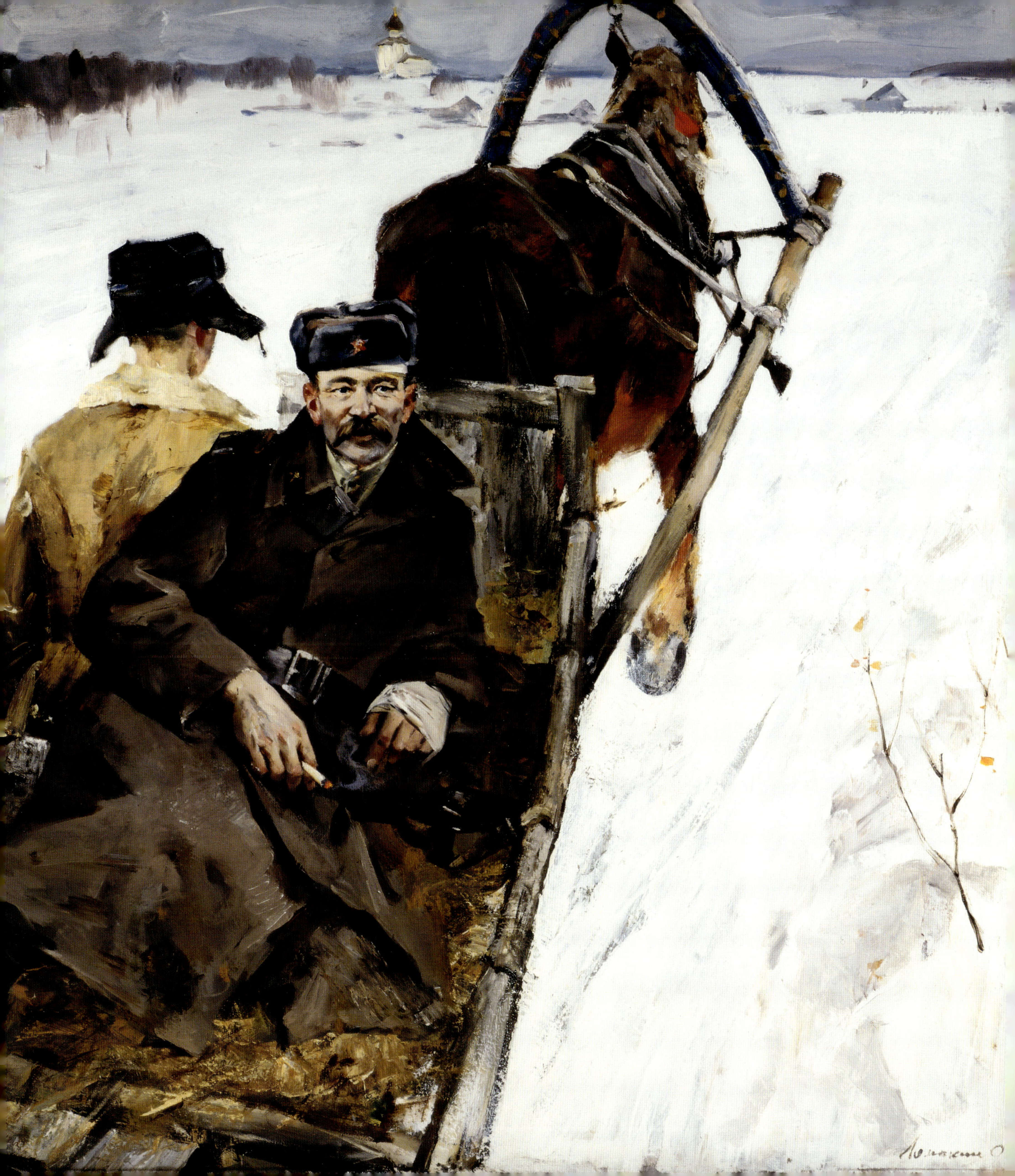

PAVEL GEORGIEVICH MARKOV

(28 August 1910 - 1978) Moscow

A genre painter, Markov graduated from the "1905" College of Art in Moscow. He was a member of the Union of Artists of USSR. Markov participated in republican, regional exhibits. He lived and worked in Pavlovski Posad, Moscow Region, until his death in 1978.

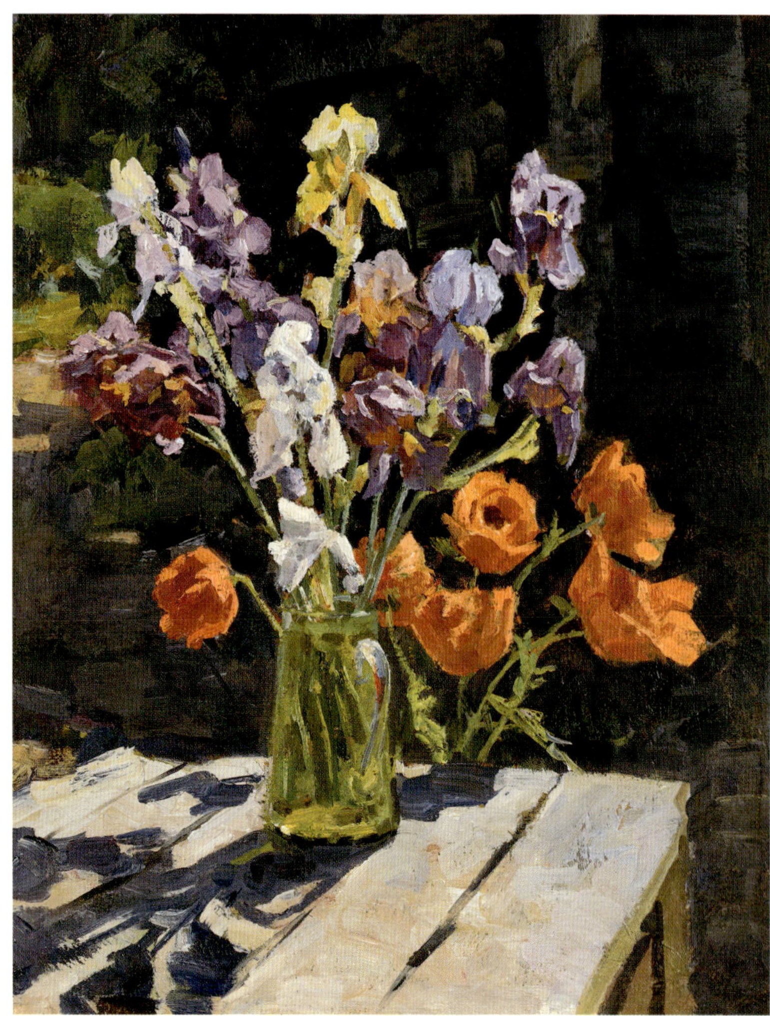

70. ***Irises and Poppies*** 1950s
Pavel Georgievich Markov
32-3/4 x 25-7/8 inches
Oil on canvas
private collection

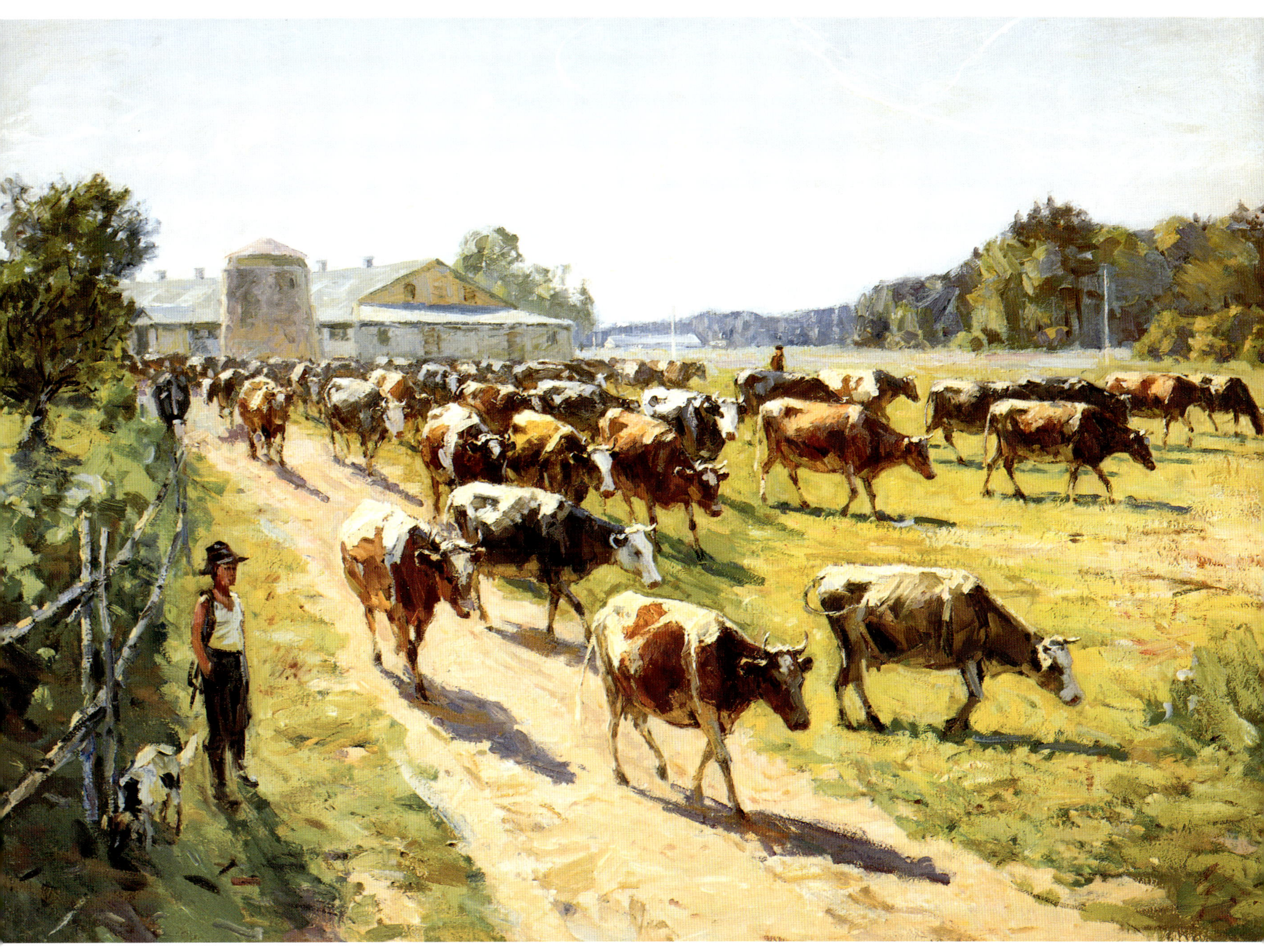

71. ***Morning on the Collective Farm*** 1950s
Pavel Georgievich Markov
36 x 52-3/8 inches
Oil on canvas
private collection

AMIR MAZITOV

(12 November 1928 - March 1992) Kazan, Tatarstan

Mazitov lived and worked in Kazan, Tatarstan. He was an Honored Artist of the Russian Federation. Mazitov was Lenin's *KomSoMol* prize laureate and the region's prize laureate of Yaroslavl *KomSoMol.*

Graduating from Surikov Institute for the Arts in Moscow in 1955, he participated in All-Union, republican and regional exhibitions. A member of the Union of Artists of USSR, his works are represented in Kazan Museum of Art.

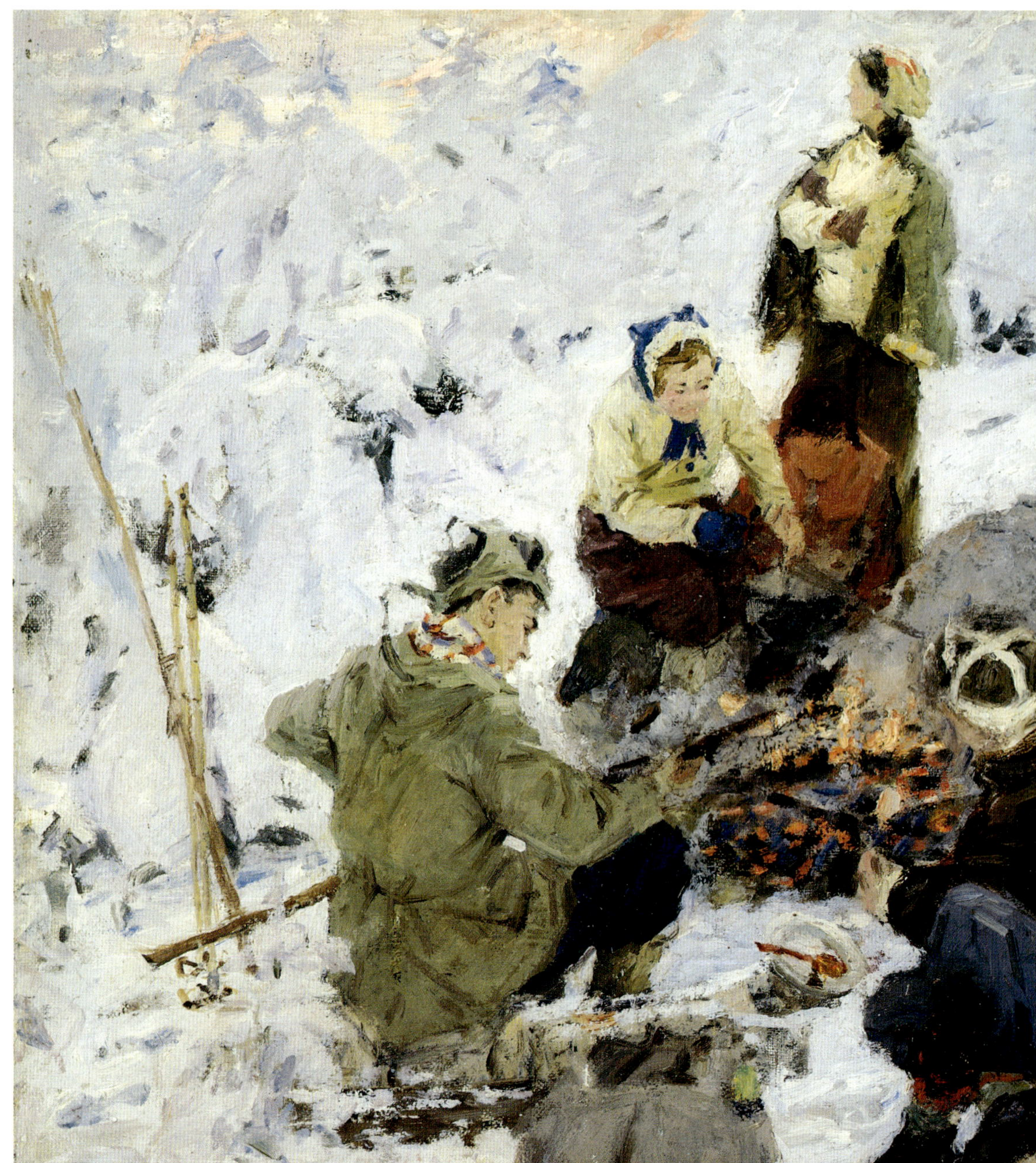

72. ***Around the Campfire*** 1950
Amir Mazitov
20 x 32 inches
Oil on canvas
private collection

GEORGI STEPANOVICH MELIKHOV

(1908-1985) Kiev

A painter of historical and contemporary Ukrainian subjects, Georgi Melikhov was born in Kharov in 1908; he died in Kiev.

He studied at Kharkov Art Institute from 1933-34 and at the Kiev Art Institute from 1935-41. Melikhov taught at the Kiev Art Institute from 1945-66.
In 1948 he was awarded a Stalin Prize for his painting *The Young Taras Shevchenko Visiting the Artist K.P. Bryullov.*

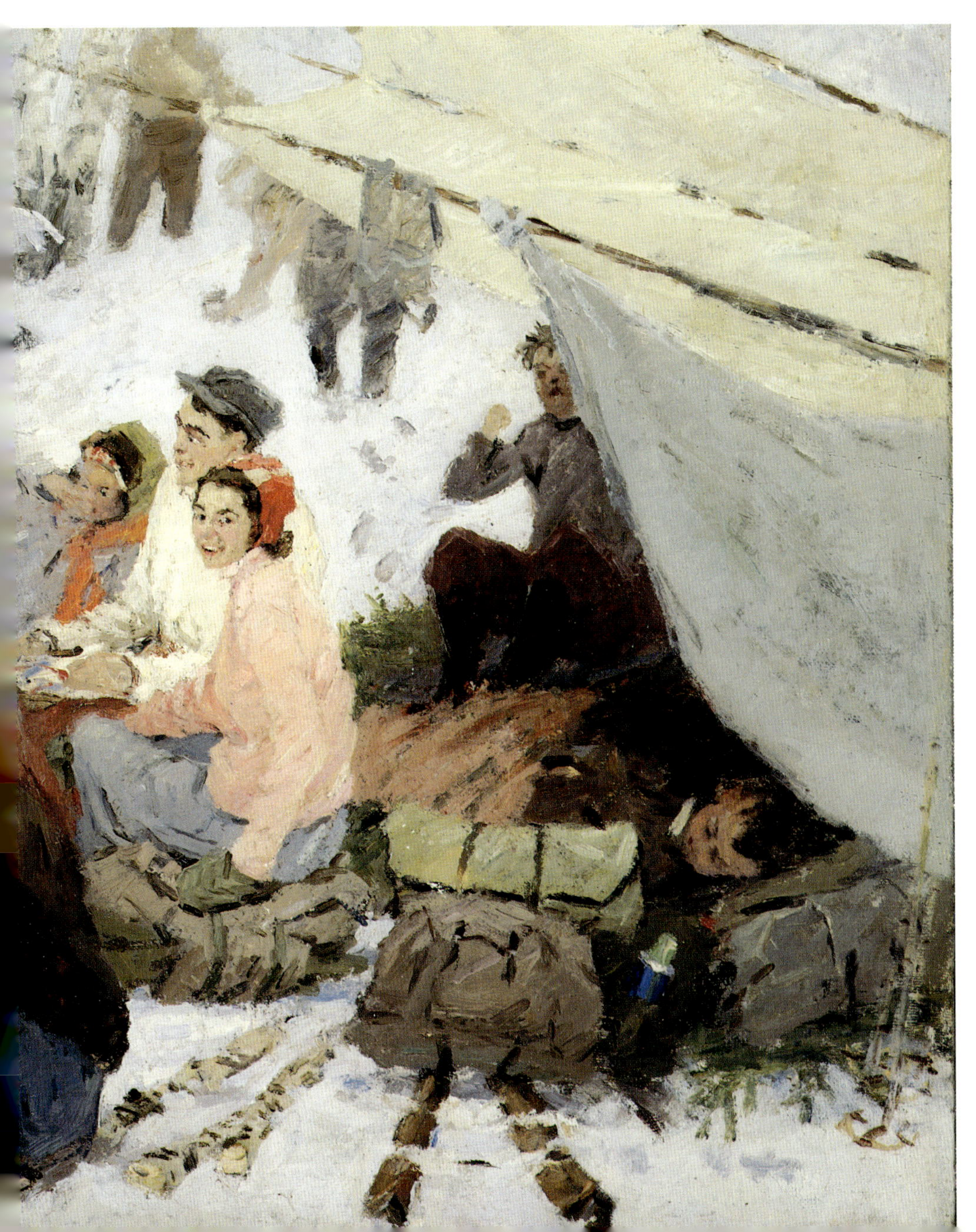

EVGENI N. MOSIN

(7 November 1923 - March 1992) Katherinberg

Mosin lived and worked in Sverdlovsk (now Katherinberg). He was a member of the Union of Artists of USSR. Mosin participated in All-Union, republican and regional exhibitions. His works are represented in museums of Moscow, Sverdlovsk and the Fleischer Museum.

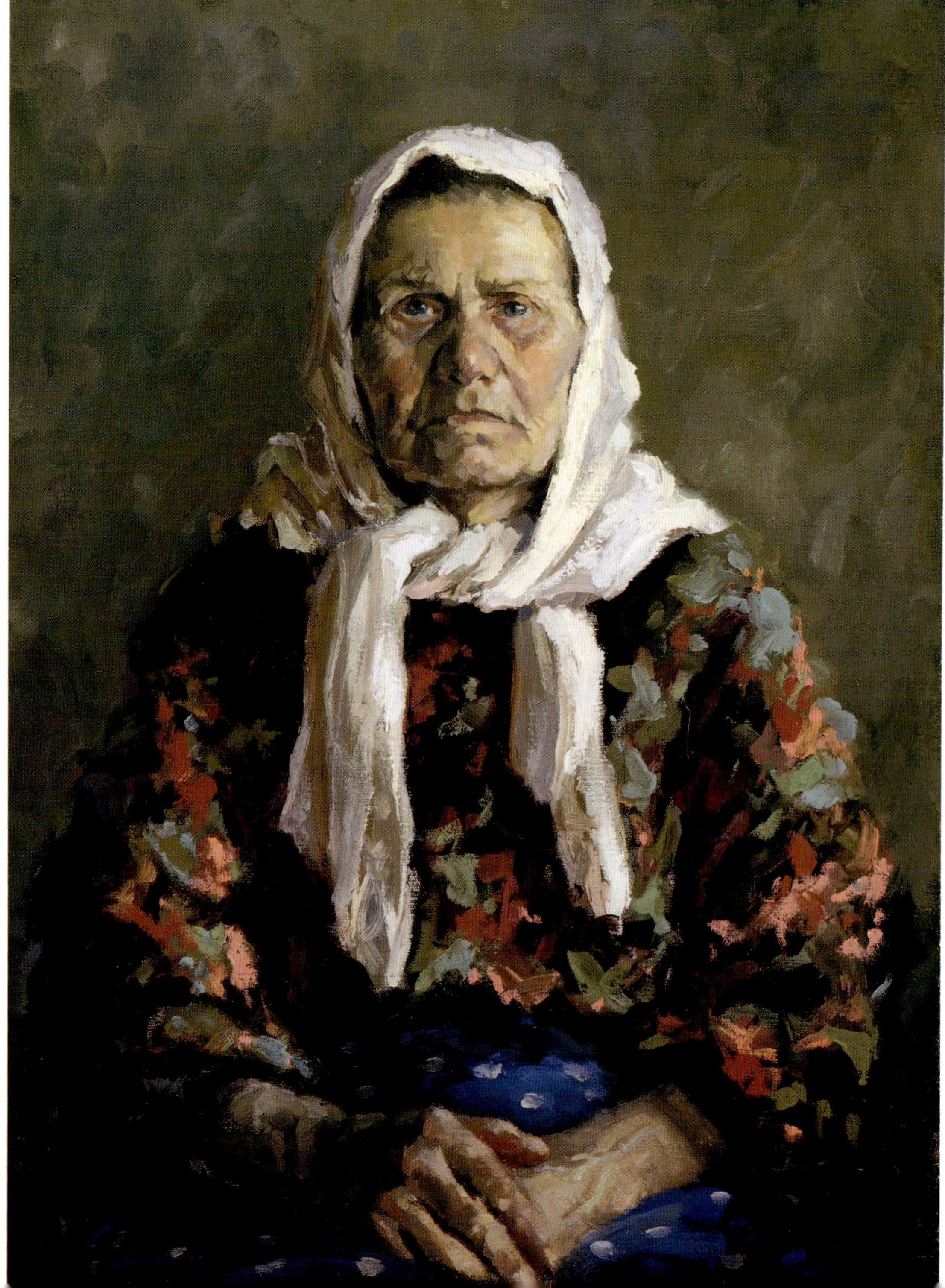

73. ***A Native of Yekaterinburg*** 1957
Evgeni N. Mosin
26-1/8 x 19-3/4 inches
Oil on canvas
Fleischer Museum Collection

VASILI KIRILLOVICH NECHITAILO

(9 January 1915 - 1980) Moscow

Nechitailo graduated from the Moscow State Art Institute, named after Surikov, where he studied at Sergei Gerasimov's Studio. In 1944, he became a member of Union of Moscow Artists. In 1948-56, he was a professor at the Moscow State Art Institute. He was awarded People's Merited Artist of Soviet Union in 1965. Twice he received the State Award of Repin and became a member of Art Academy. Nechitailo worked in Spain, Bulgaria, Italy and participated in republican and All-Union exhibitions. Museum collections include State Tretyakov Gallery, State Russian Museum, Kiev Museum of Russian Art, State Art Museum of Turkmenia Republic, Art Museum named after Vereshagin in Nikolaev, Museum of Fine Arts in Volgograd and others.

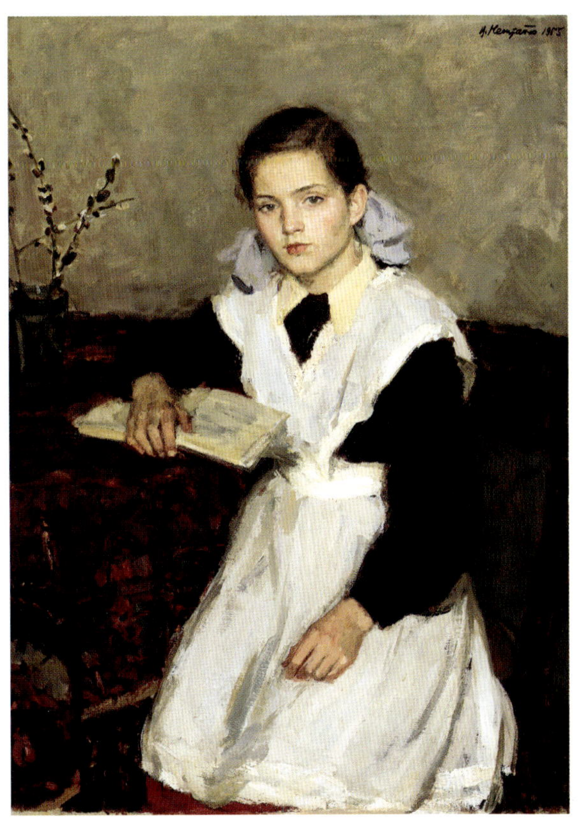

74. ***School Girl, Ksyusha*** 1955
Vasili Kirillovich Nechitailo
39-1/4 x 28-1/2 inches
Oil on canvas
private collection

VLADIMIR ILYCH NEKRASOV

(1924 -) Moscow

Vladimir Nekrasov studied at Moscow's Surikov Institute and fought on the Ukrainian front. He began exhibiting in 1953 and became a member of the Union of Artists in 1957. In 1955 he visited the Virgin Lands and painted bold oil sketches of this experience. He has produced paintings from his travels to Burma and Italy in the 1960s.

In 1979, Nekrasov was rewarded with a personal exhibition. His works have been sold to museums in Moscow, Omsk, Smolensk and Alma-Ata. Currently, Nekrasov is a professor at the Surikov Institute in Moscow.

75. ***Resting in a Trailer in the Virgin Land (study)*** 1955
Vladimir Ilych Nekrasov
19-3/8 x 27-1/4 inches
Oil on board
private collection

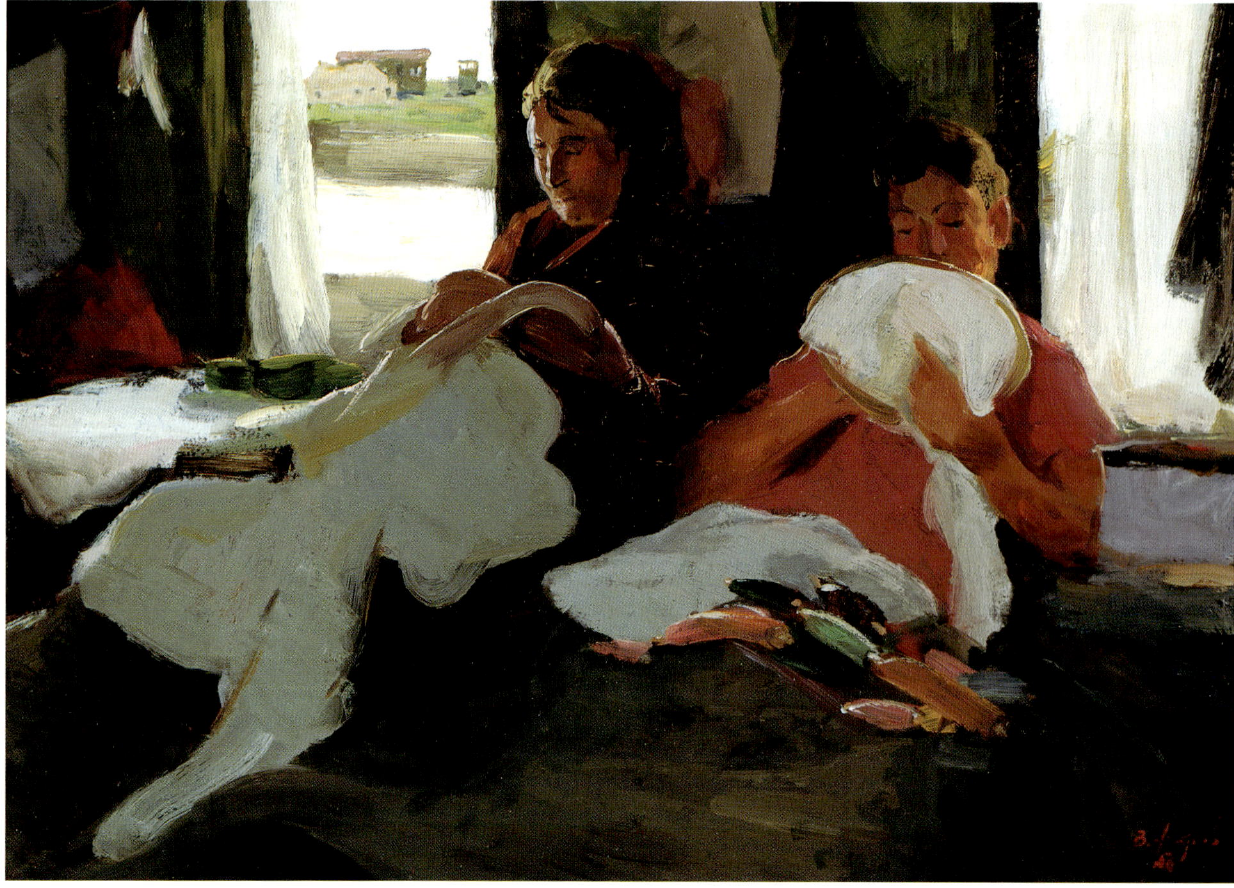

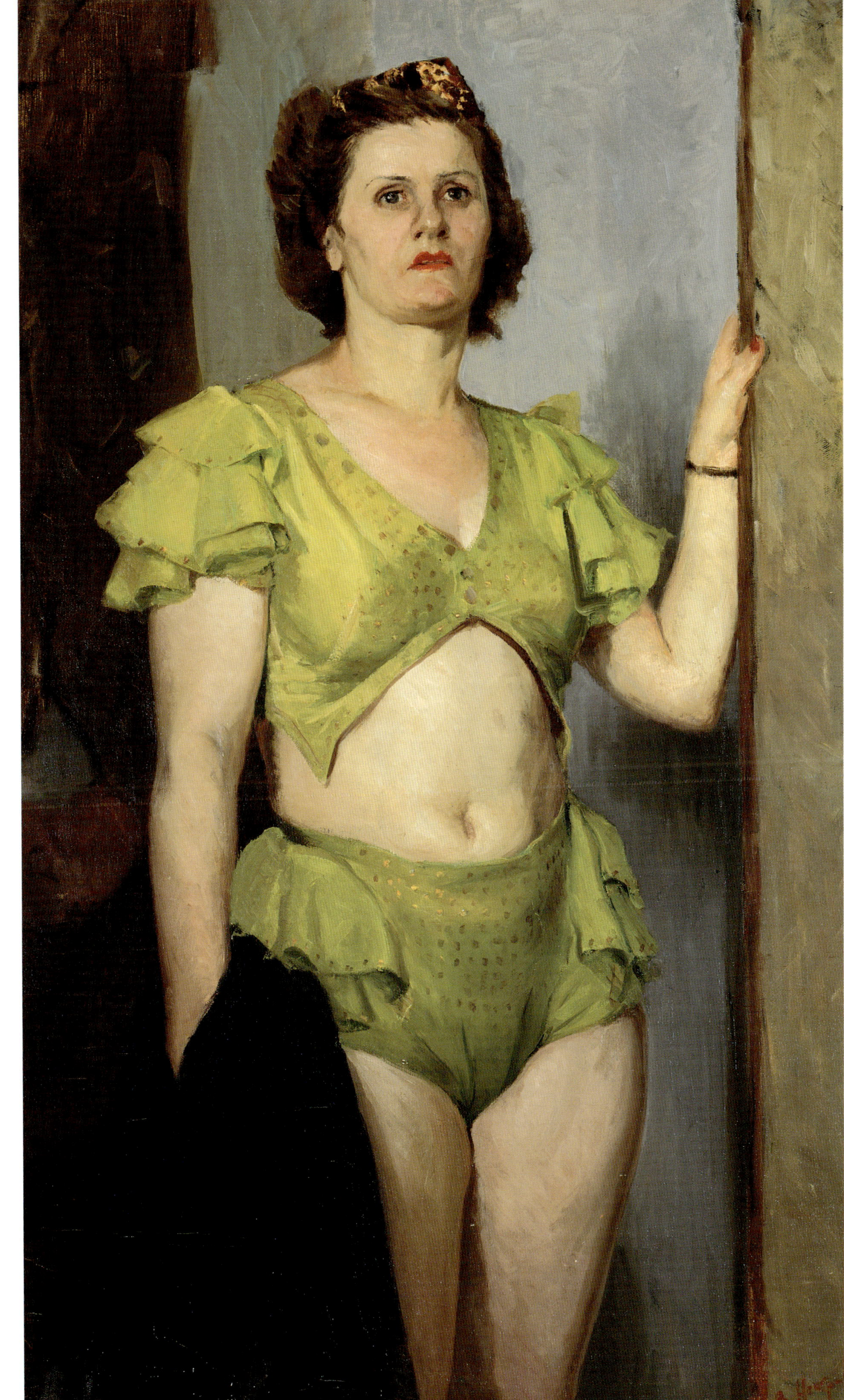

76. ***Actress of the Circus*** 1951
Vladimir Ilych Nekrasov
42 x 26 inches
Oil on canvas
private collection

ANATOLI YUREVICH NIKICH-KRILICHEVSKI

(1918 -) Moscow

The artist was born in Petrograd in 1918. He studied at the Moscow State Art Institute (Surikov) from 1935-42. Nikich-Krilichevski currently works in Moscow painting his favored still life subjects.

NIKOLAI IPPOLITOVICH OBRYNBA

(2 March 1913 -) Ukraine

Nikolai Obrynba was born in Epifan near Tula. In 1919, his family moved with him to the city Kobelyaki in the Ukraine. In 1925 he started to paint flowers and butterflies on trunks in a furniture workshop, which were sold with great success on street markets. Between 1928-31 he studied at the Art and Industrial Academy in Kiev.

In 1931 he joined the Art Society Red Ukraine. His first paintings show the daily life at the Kolhoz where he also lives. From 1931 to 1932 he worked in Poltava; in 1932 in Leningrad; from 1933-36 in Kharkov. In the summer of 1937 he made paintings and sketches of horses at Dubrovka. In 1942-43 he joined the partisans in Byelorussia where he continued to draw, depicting the soldiers as his subject matter. From 1944-50 he worked in the studio of the painter of war scenes M.B. Grekov.

Since 1960, Obrynba has traveled in France and Italy, and he is still actively painting at this present time.

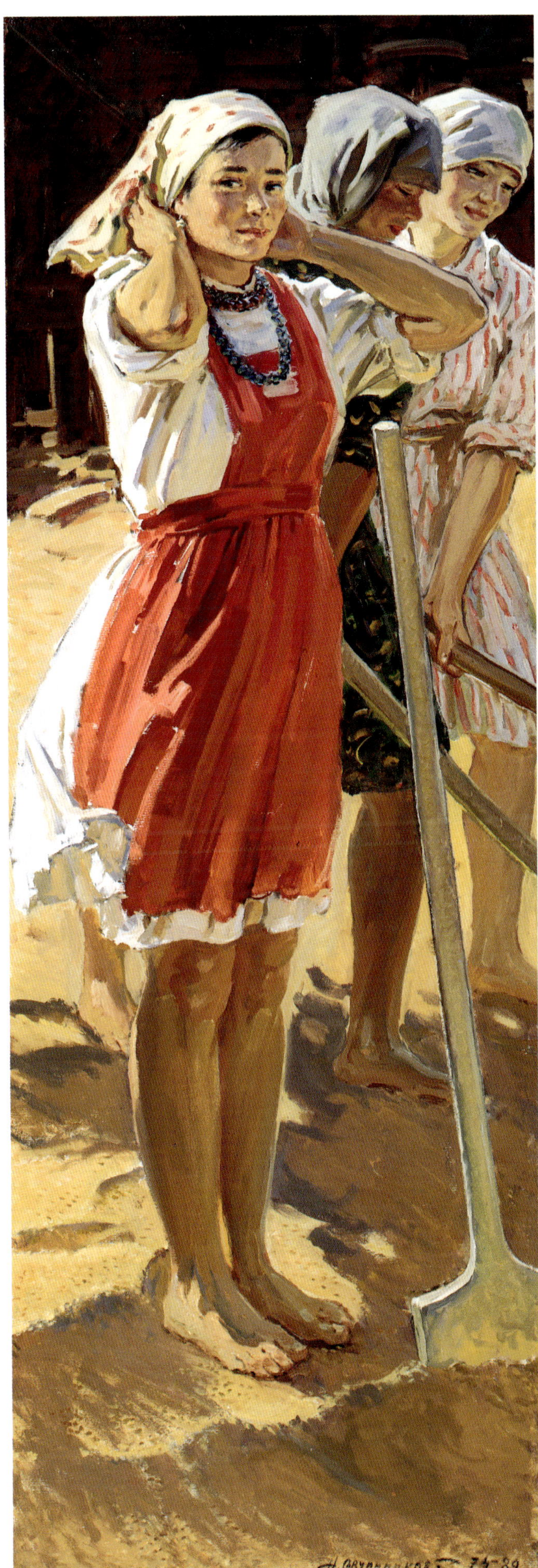

NIKOLAI VASILIEVICH OVCHINNIKOV

(1918 -) Chboksary

Ovchinnikov was born in the village of Mizhuli to the village school teacher. He became a *KomSoMol* member in 1930 and entered the Alatyr School of Art in 1934 where his instructors were F.S. Bykov, A.M. Tagayev-Surban and V.K. Timofeyev. Ovchinnikov participated in the Chuvash Autonomous Republic exhibition in 1935. From 1937 to 1939 he attended the Repin Institute, where he met I.I. Brodski and was instructed by B.A. Vogel and V.A. Gorb.

Ovchinnikov was called to service in the Red Army from 1939-41 and he participated in World War II until 1945 when he was demobilized. During his tour of duty he participated in exhibitions, became a Communist Party member and a member of the Union of Artists of the USSR.

Returning to the Repin Institute, he entered the studio of R.R. Frenz where he received the Lenin Scholarship. Completing his studies in 1951, he defended his graduation thesis to S.V. Priselkov, F.F. Fedorovsky, the picture was highly appreciated by B.V. Ioganson, I.A. Serebriany and A.L. Kaganovich. The artist taught at the Repin Institute from 1953-54 and participated in the Union of Artists of the USSR until 1959, when he moved to Chboksary.

Awarded numerous titles including Honored Artist of Russia and People's Artist of Russia, Ovchinnikov held a one-man exhibition in 1963.

77. ***On the Threshing Floor*** 1975
Nikolai Vasilievich Ovchinnikov
70-1/2 x 25-1/8 inches
Oil on canvas
private collection

VLADIMIR MITROPHANOVICH PETROV

(21 July 1920 -) Tashkent

Vladimir Petrov studied at Astrakhan Art College from 1934-39 and afterwards at the Latvian Academy of Arts in Riga. Upon graduation in 1949, he moved to Tashkent where he continues to work. He has painted innumerable thematic pictures.

78. ***Construction of Refinery: Industrial Scene*** 1955
Vladimir Mitrophanovich Petrov
43 x 54-3/4 inches
Oil on canvas
private collection

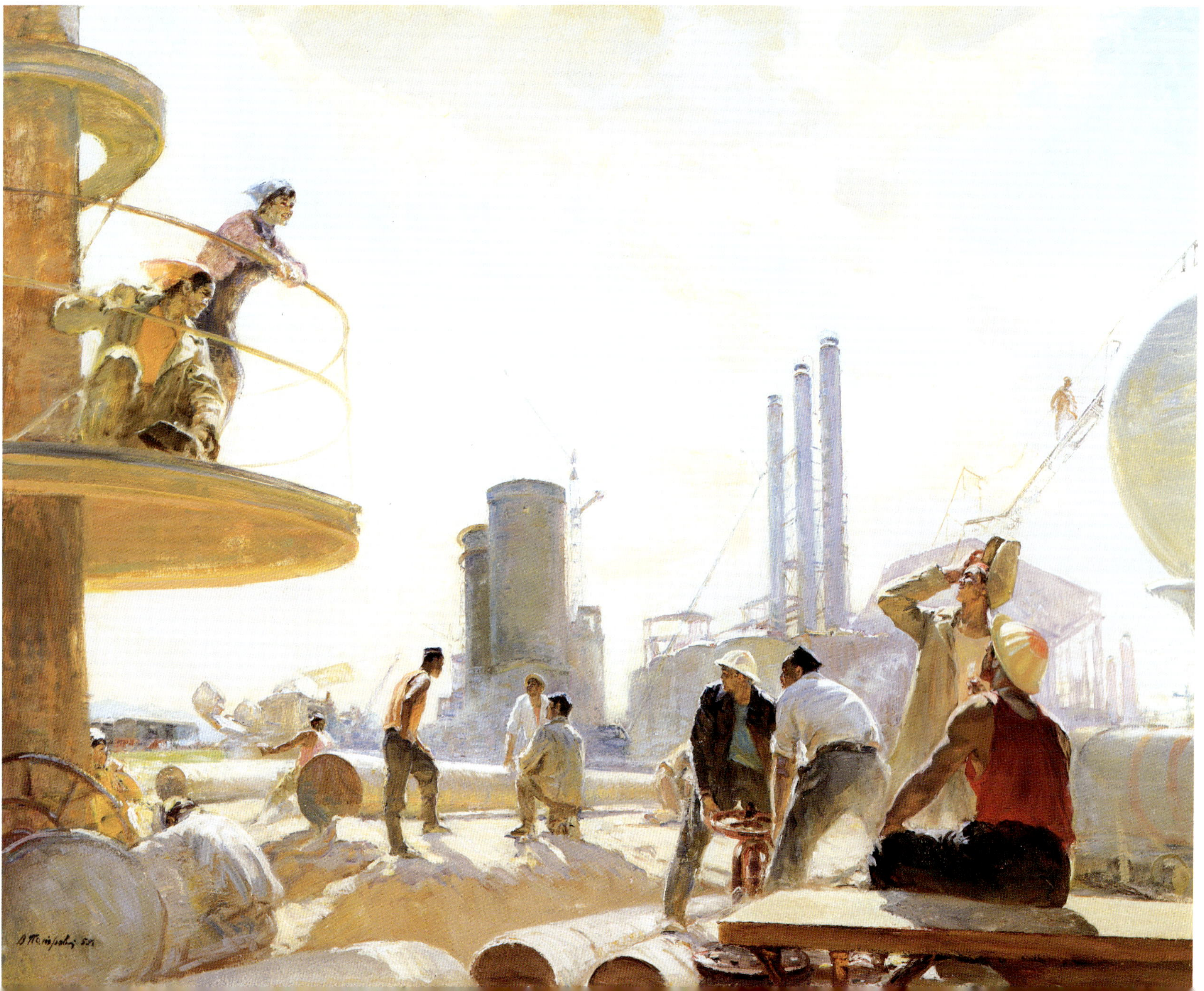

VSEVOLOD MIKHAILOVICH PETROV-MASLAKOV

(29 April 1930 -) St. Petersburg

"I began drawing, as everybody does, in early childhood. But evidently, my interest in nature and animals turned out to be dominant in my intent to become an artist." Petrov-Maslakov attended an art school for children. In Leningrad when the Great Patriotic War began, "Circumstances were such that I found myself alone in the hardest time. I couldn't even think of painting then."

In 1944, he received the Medal For Defense of Leningrad. That same year he entered the Academy of Arts High School of Arts. Upon graduation in 1950, he entered the Repin Institute. He graduated in 1956 while in the Oreshnikov workshop.

Since 1956, he has participated in local exhibits in Leningrad, zonal, republican and national exhibitions and in Soviet art exhibits in Italy, Germany, Japan, Finland, Poland, Bulgaria and the United States.

In 1957, Petrov-Maslakov became a member of the Russian Artists Union. He became a teacher at the Mukhina School of Art and Industry in Leningrad, working in geological expeditions.

"The invitation to visit Alaska was like a blessing to me. By the initiative of Robert White, a group of seven artists were painting pictures for a museum in Alaska about the discovery of Alaska and the contribution of Russians to its exploration. We were working selflessly and with inspiration. We wanted to communicate the beauty and uniqueness of the world that opened up for us. The most valuable reward for our endeavor was the delightful response that we received from the visitors of the exhibit at the University at Sitka after we finished our job. Throughout the entire duration of our stay, we were surrounded by cordiality, hospitality, sensitivity and care."

An Honorable Artist of Russia and recipient of numerous Ministry of Culture and Artist Union diplomas and medals, including the Yuri Gagarin Medal, Petrov-Maslakov's works of art are found in many museums and private collections in Moscow, Leningrad, France and America.

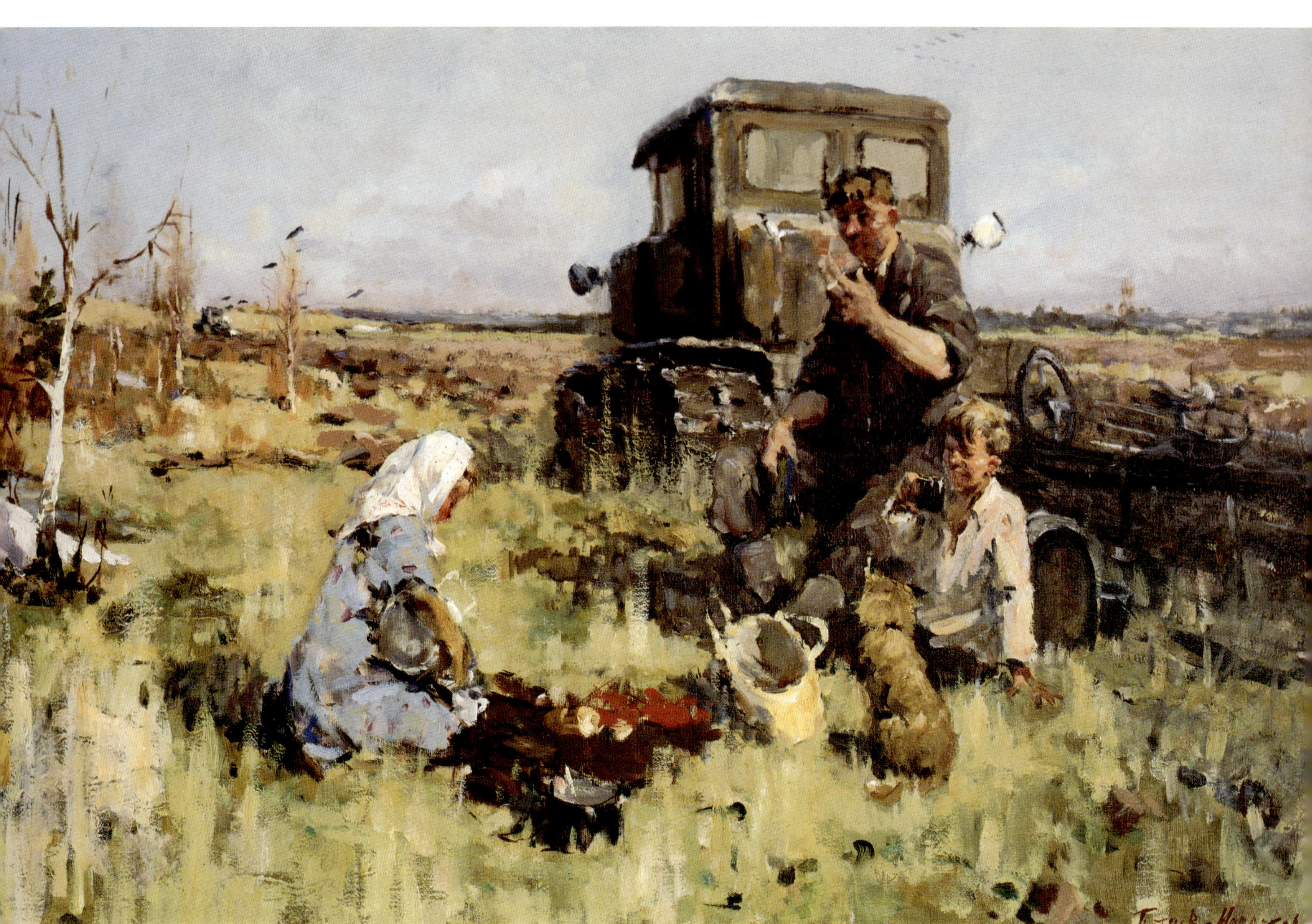

79. ***Lunch in the Field*** 1956
Vsevolod Mikhailovich Petrov-Maslakov
25-1/2 x 39 inches
Oil on canvas
private collection

GENNADY MIKHAILOVICH PETRYGIN-RODIONOV

(3 April 1928 -) Leningrad

Petrygin-Rodionov graduated from the Repin Institute in Leningrad in 1961, under the leadership of Evsei Moiseyenko.

Since 1966, he has been a member of the Union of Artists of USSR. He participated in all the significant All-Union, republican and regional exhibitions. His works are in museums of Kazakhstan and Leningrad.

80. ***Sun in the Hand*** 1975
Gennady M. Petrygin-Rodionov
55 x 55 inches
Oil on canvas
private collection

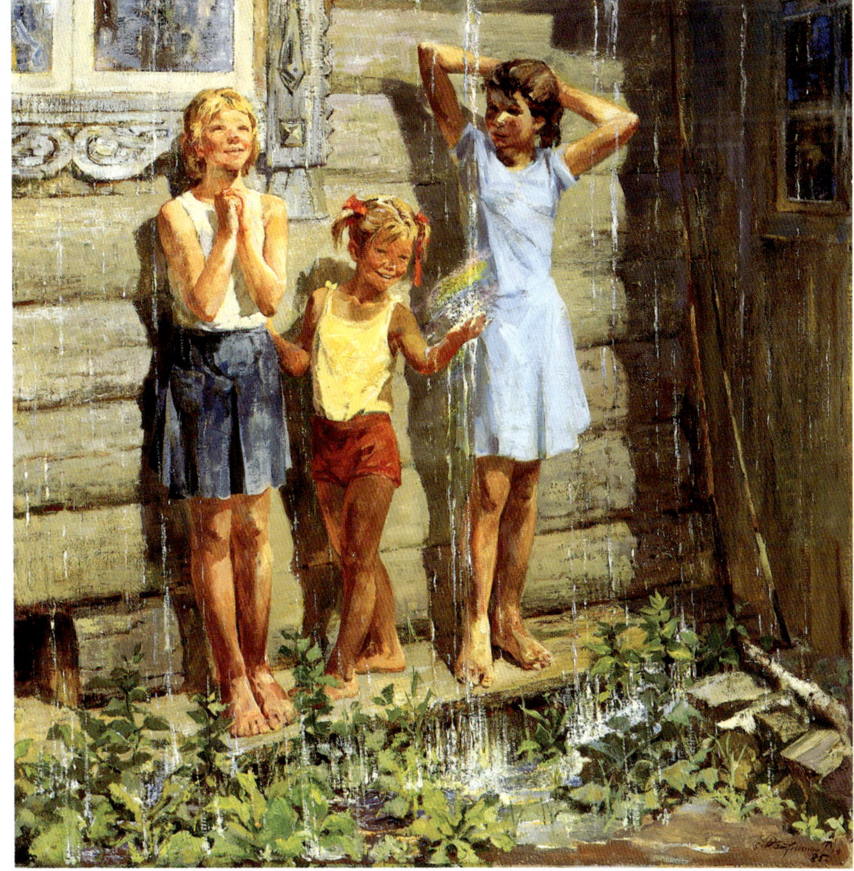

YURI STANISLAVOVICH PODLYASKI

(5 June 1923 - 1987) Khabarovsk

A painter of harvest scenes, workers and landscapes, Podlyaski graduated in 1949 from the Repin Institute of Painting, Sculpture and Architecture.

An Honored Art Worker of RSFSR, this talented artist has worked in various genres, and was represented at national and international exhibitions.

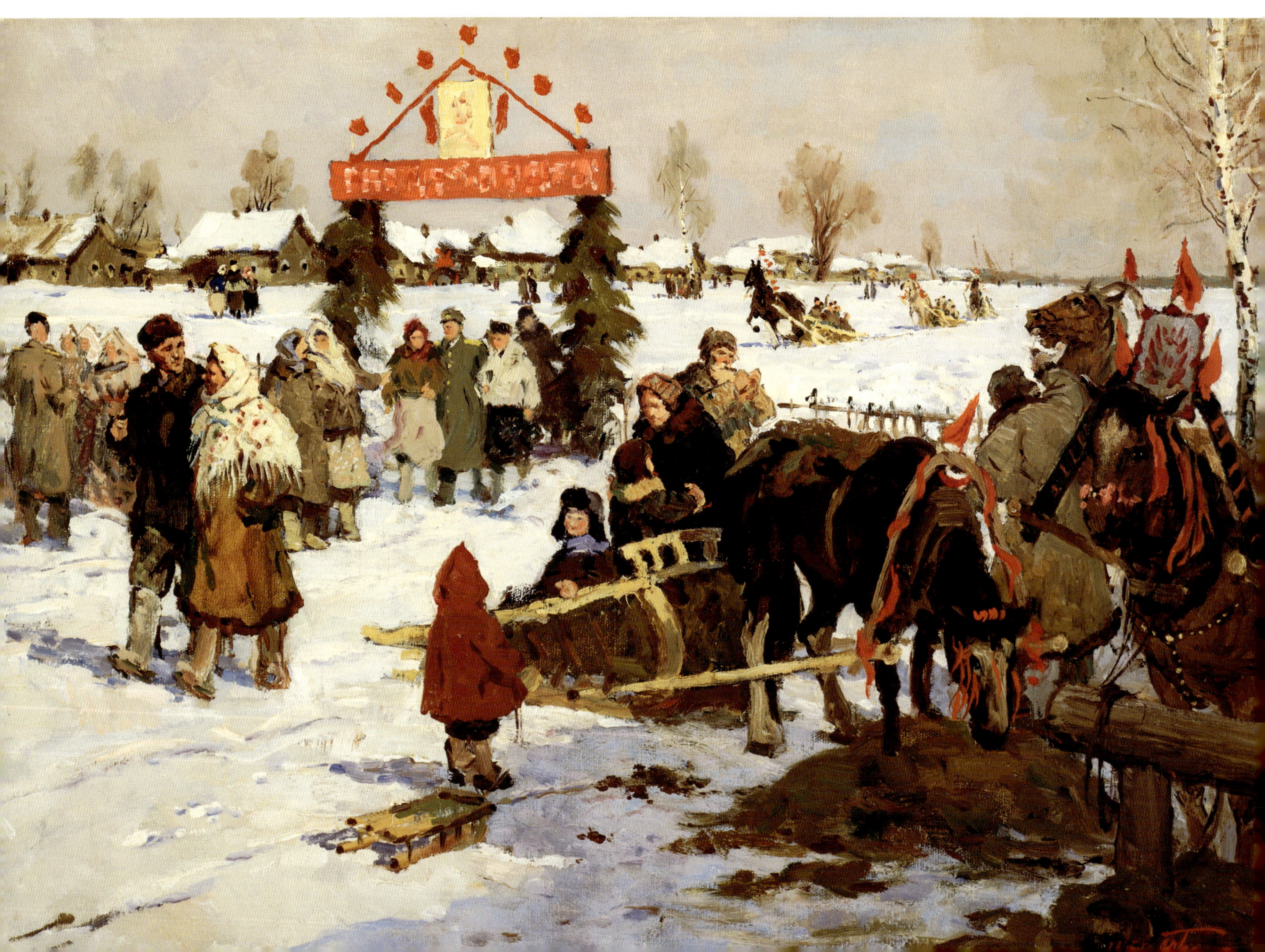

IGOR ALEXANDROVICH RAZDROGIN

(7 December 1923 -) St. Petersburg

Razdrogin received a professional education only after the Great Patriotic War when he entered the Repin Institute where he studied art at an artistic workshop headed by B. Ioganson.

On graduation in 1952, Razdrogin continued his post-graduation courses and in 1956, he defended his research work and received the title Candidate of Science (Art Critic). Since that time, Razdrogin has been teaching at the Repin Instutute where he is a Professor of the Merited Arts Worker. His influences were the Russian Realists Surikov, Serov, Repin and Korovin.

His main theme is the nature of Russia, its small towns and villages and common working people. Depicting people, the painter tries to express the individuality of each model, its character, its inner beauty and high intellect.

The years of the Great Patriotic War, in which he participated in the defense of Leningrad, have always been in the painter's memory. He tries to depict the stern war years, heroism and courage of the Soviet people defending their Motherland. The pictures are satiated with deep emotions and are colored with strong, patriotic feelings.

Razdrogin has been a participant of numerous art exhibitions, both in and out of Russia. His works are in the museums of Russia, Tretyakov Gallery, Smolensk Picture Gallery and Leningrad Museums. His paintings are in private collections in America, France and Japan.

81. ***Sun on Election Day in the Village*** 1950
Yuri Stanislavovich Podlyaski
20-3/4 x 29 inches
Oil on canvas
private collection

ERIK I. REBANE

(13 March 1922 -) St. Petersburg

A graduate of the I.E. Repin Institute, Rebane majored in the Oreshnikov workshop. In 1948, Rebane participated in his first Moscow exhibition. His first international exhibition occurred in Tokyo in 1974. His works are contained within the collections of the Fleischer Museum, as well as museums in Moscow, Leningrad, Poltava, Osaka, Khabarousk, Kiev and Tbilissi .

SEMON ARONOVICH ROTNITSKI

(28 December 1915 -) St. Petersburg

Rotnitski was born in Minsk, Byelorussia where, at the age of eight, he studied art at the Marx Palace of Culture Art Studio. He received a prize and diploma at a republican exhibit of children's art.

In 1926, his family moved to Tula, Russia. Four years later, Semon worked at the Tula Arm Factory Palace of Culture Art Studio until 1934, during which time he graduated from middle school and trade school. Semon entered the Russian National Academy of Arts Institute in Leningrad. From 1934-37, he studied at the preparatory department of the Institute, until becoming a student from 1937-41. During this time, he participated in local, republican and national art exhibitions.

When the Great Patriotic War began, Rotnitski joined the military. One year later, he became a member of the Communist Party. In 1945, Rotnitski was demobilized to resume his education. In 1948, he completed his study at the I.E. Repin Institute. That same year, he joined the Leningrad Chapter of the Russian Artists Union.

For twelve years, Rotnitski taught at the Kazan Trade School of Arts, during which he was also a director of the school. In 1953, he was elected a member of the Tatar Artists Union management, and in 1957, he was named Honorable Art Worker of Tatarstan.

In 1960, Rotnitski moved to Leningrad and became a teacher at the V.I. Mukhina Higher Trade School of Art and Industry in Leningrad in 1965 where he taught for 16 years. In 1970, he became a docent of the Painting Faculty.

Semon Rotnitski has held personal exhibitions at the Mukhina Higher Trade School of Art and Industry in Leningrad, 1981; the Summer Garden Coffee House in Leningrad in 1985; and in the Leningrad Artist Union in 1991.

"Truthful and deep penetration into the character is what I believe to be the artist's main objective. The whole life is too short for it. It takes talent and hard work. As for the results, they will be evaluated by the contemporaries and descendants," says Rotnitski. The artist believes his duty is to "be able to see the beauty of nature and man and to communicate this beauty to the spectator."

Rotnitski's works are found in major museums in Moscow, Saint Petersburg, Samara, Kazan, Tver, Perm, Pskov, Kislovodsk, Krasnoyarsk, the Fleischer Museum and in private collections in the Soviet Union and the United States.

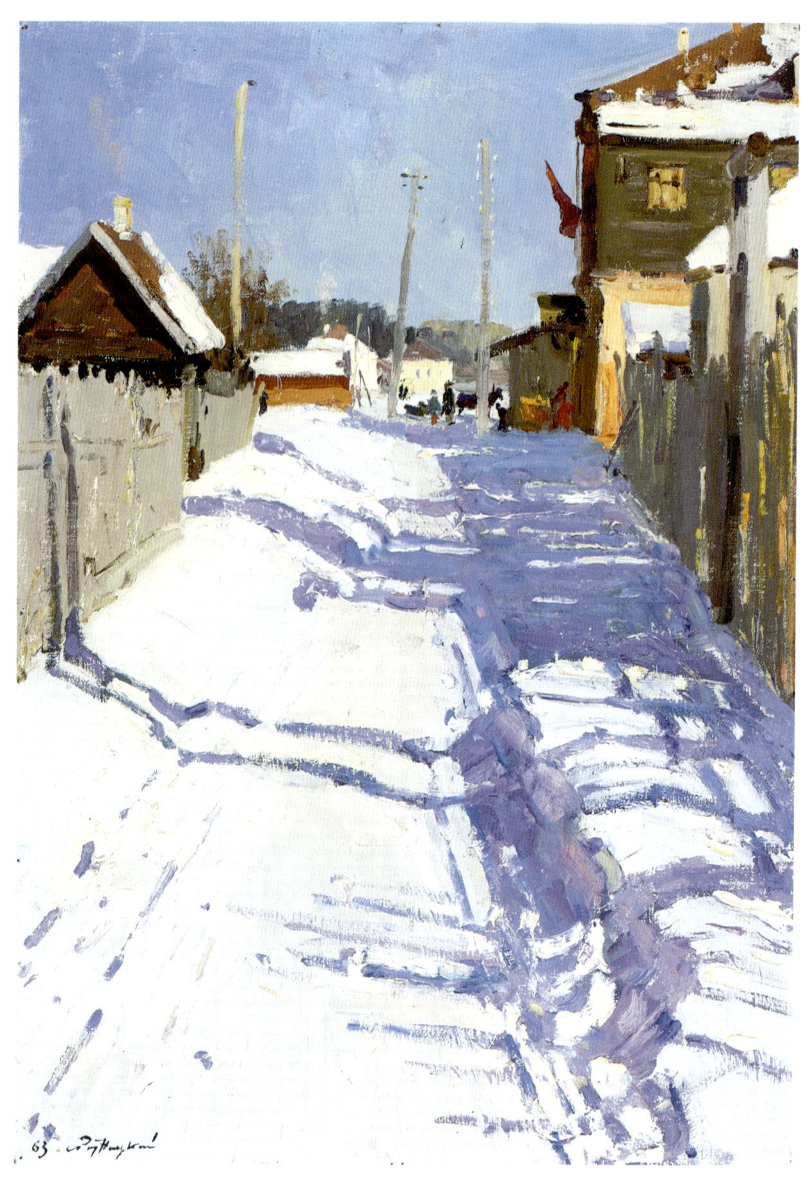

82. ***Celebration in the Kholui Settlement*** 1962
Semon Aronovich Rotnitski
27-1/2 x 19-1/2 inches
Oil on canvas
private collection

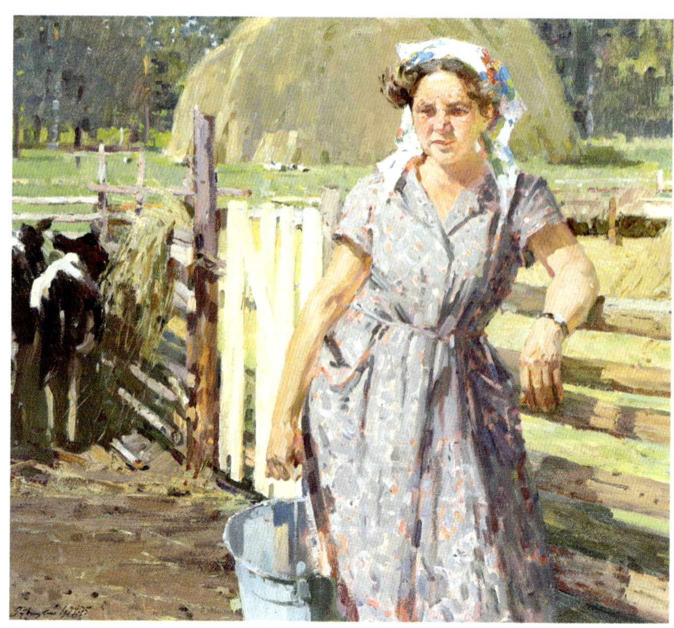

83. ***Calf Caretaker: Milkmaid*** 1972-75
Semon Aronovich Rotnitski
43 x 47-1/8 inches
Oil on canvas
private collection

ZOYA ALEXANDROVNA SAMOILENKO

(31 December 1924 -) Kiev

Before the Great Patriotic War, Samoilenko studied at the Kiev Art School and after the war in 1946, she entered the Department of Painting of the Kiev Art Institute. Her first teacher was the painter, K.N. Yeleva. Later she studied under Melikhov, Yerchikovski, Kostetski, Grigoriev and Trokhimenko.

In 1952, Samoilenko graduated from the Institute and was soon admitted to the Ukrainian Union of Artists.

In her creative work, Samoilenko was greatly influenced by Krichevski, a Soviet Ukrainian painter who was a professor at the Kiev Art Institute, but had to give up her post after the war as she was on bad terms with the demands of official art.

The main themes of her works are life in all its manifestation, labor, leisure time and young people. She works in genre paintings, depicting people in different situations, seasons, in joy and grief, trying to depict emotions and inner tension. Samoilenko traveled the country for inspirational material.

She admits that many of her paintings were made according to the orders from the Ministry of Culture. The system of orders gave her the opportunity to earn their living.

The main part of Samoilenko's pictures were sold to the Ministry of Culture or Soviet Museums. Her pictures were on display at different home and foreign exhibitions in Germany, Japan and Sweden.

84. ***The Son: Seryozha*** 1957
Zoya Alexandrovna Samoilenko
31-1/4 x 23-1/2 inches
Oil on canvas
private collection

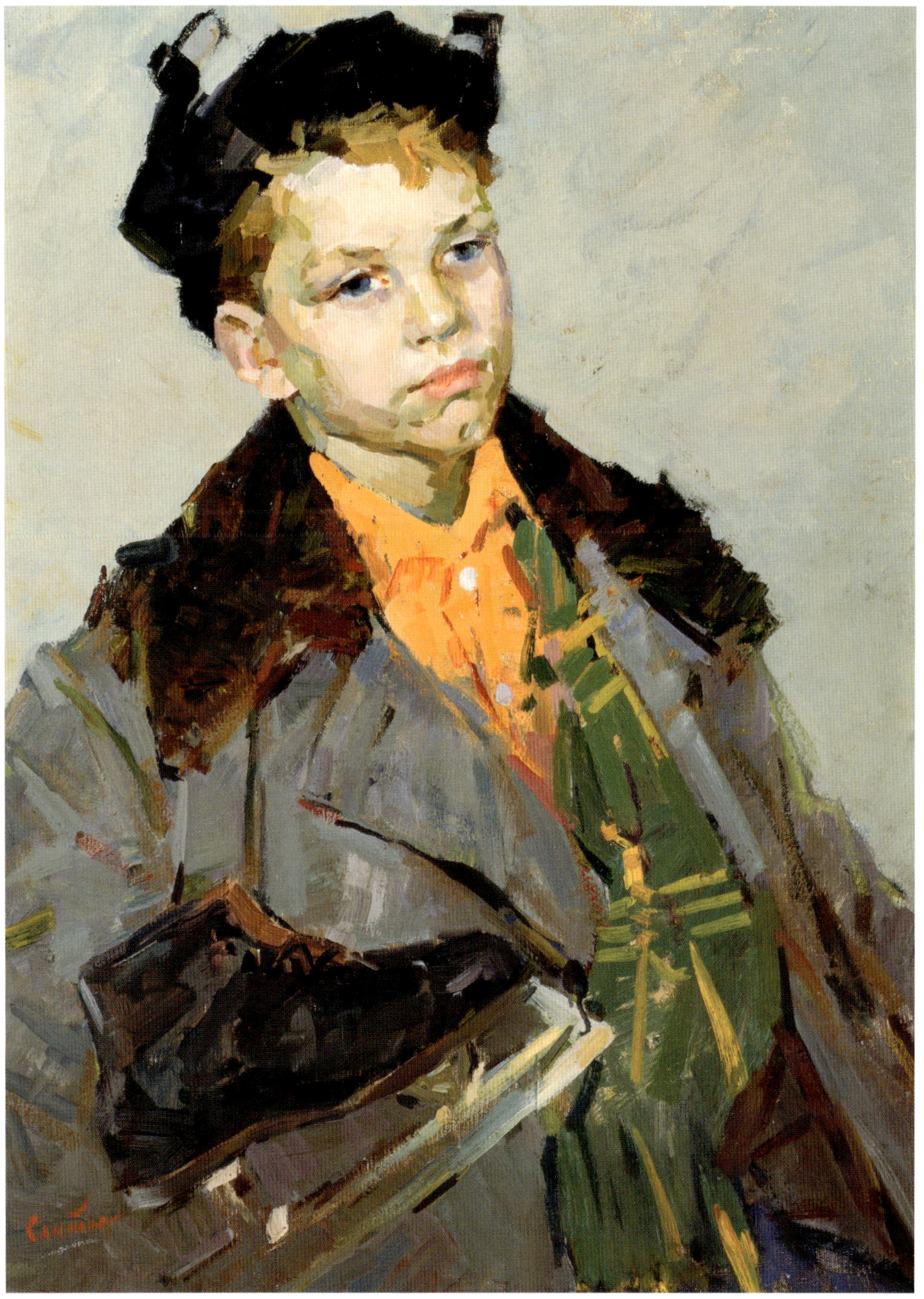

FEDOR VASILIEVICH SHAPAEV

(16 April 1927 -) Moscow

Born in Pokoj Village in the Saratov Region, Shapaev studied at the Surikov Institute for the Arts in Moscow, graduating in 1955. There he worked in the studio of Ryazhski, then under the leadership of Maximov and Gavrilov.

Shapaev became a member of the Union of Artists in 1960. His works are in museums of Arkangelsk, Voronez, Rybinsk, Ivanov, Vladikavkaz, Pereslavl-Zalesski and others. Throughout his artistic life he participated in All-Union, republican and regional exhibitions in the Soviet Union, Czechoslovakia, Bulgaria and Turkey. He has had three one-man exhibitions.

Currently living and working in Dmitrov, Moscow Region, he is an Honored Artist of the Russian Federation.

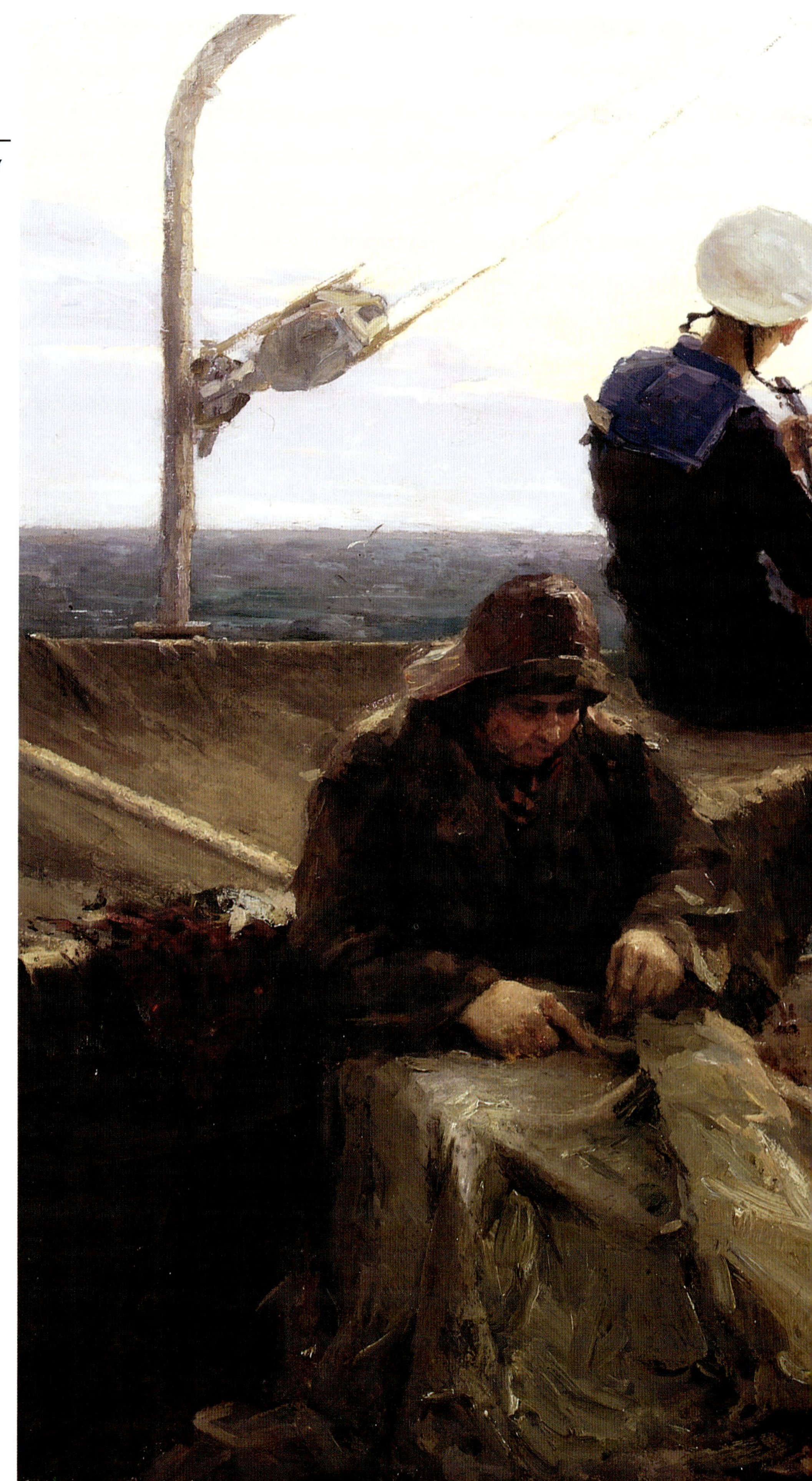

85. ***Not Far from the Motherland*** 1955
Fedor Vasilievich Shapaev
48-1/2 x 78 inches
Oil on canvas
private collection

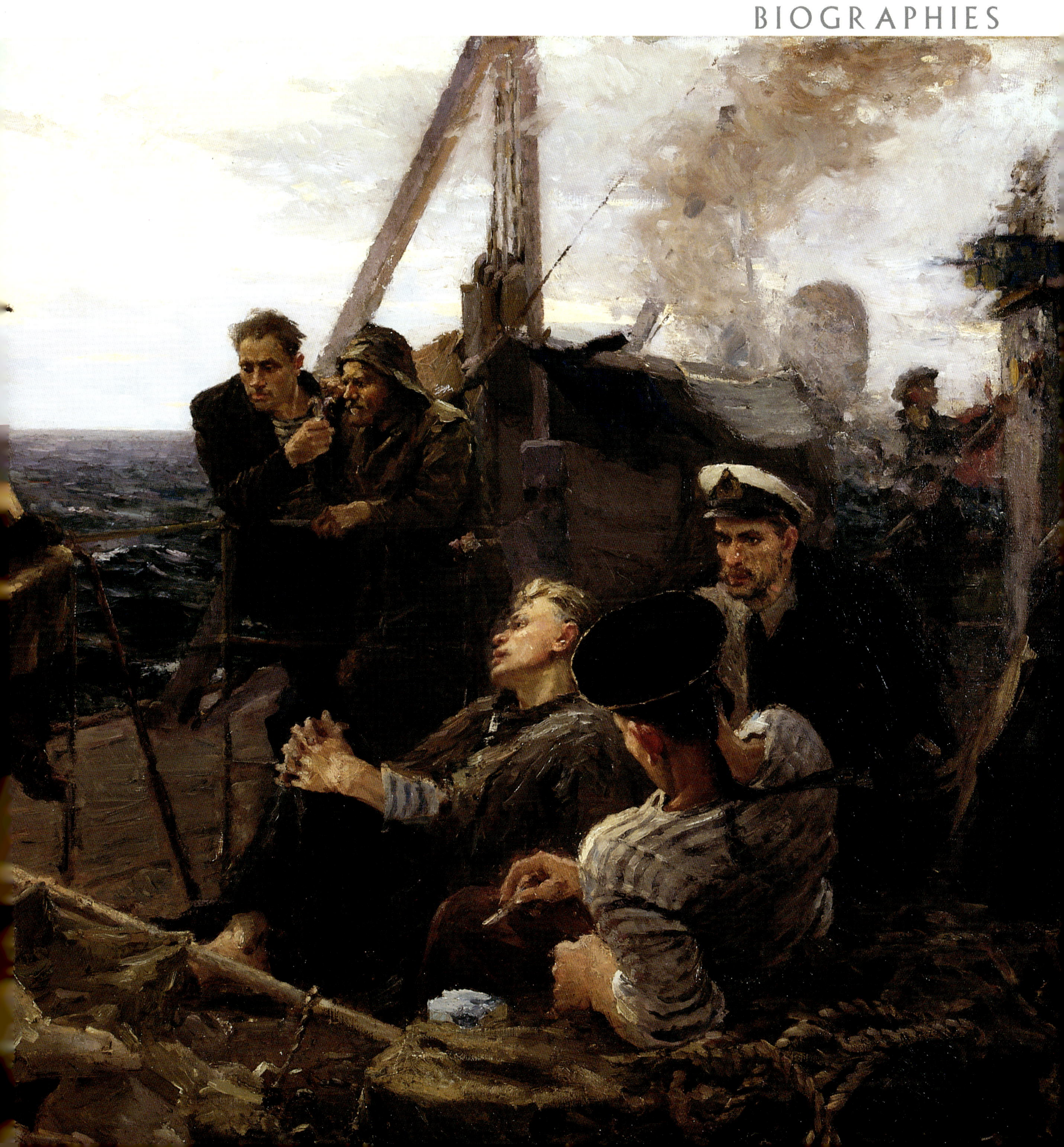

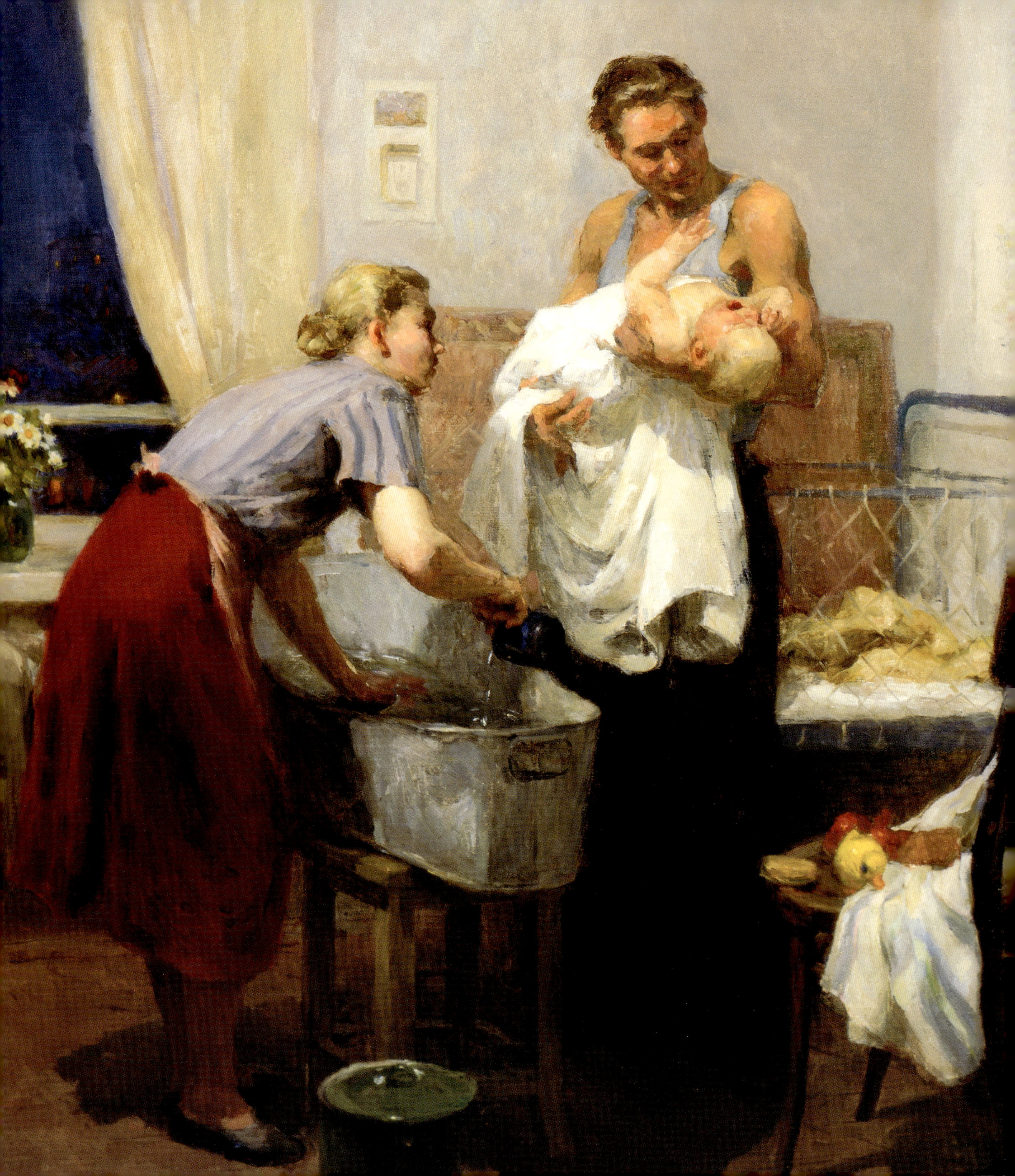

VALENTINA SHEBASHEVA

(unknown -) Moscow

Valentina Shebasheva attended the Surikov Institute in Moscow during the 1950s. Her forté is domestic genre, intimate views of family life.

86. ***At Home*** 1955
Valentina Shebasheva
47 x 35-3/4 inches
Oil on canvas
private collection

DMITRI IVANOVICH SHMELYOV

(24 October 1919 -) Nizhny Novgorod (Gorki)

Born in the town of Tambov, Shmelyov entered an art school in 1934.

Called to service in the Red Army in 1938, he was demobilized in 1939 and began work as a decorator. From 1941-46, he again served in the army and participated in military action, for which he was awarded several medals. After the war, he returned to work as a decorator. He studied art from 1950-56. While a student in 1955, he ventured into the Virgin Lands.

Since 1958, Shmelyov has been living in Gorki where he has participated in many exhibitions. He prefers portrait painting, often in a historical setting, capturing the human destiny.

His work is contained within the Fleischer Museum Collection.

87. ***The Mechanic*** 1959
Dmitri Ivanovich Shmelyov
31-1/4 x 23-1/4 inches, detail
Oil on canvas
Fleischer Museum Collection

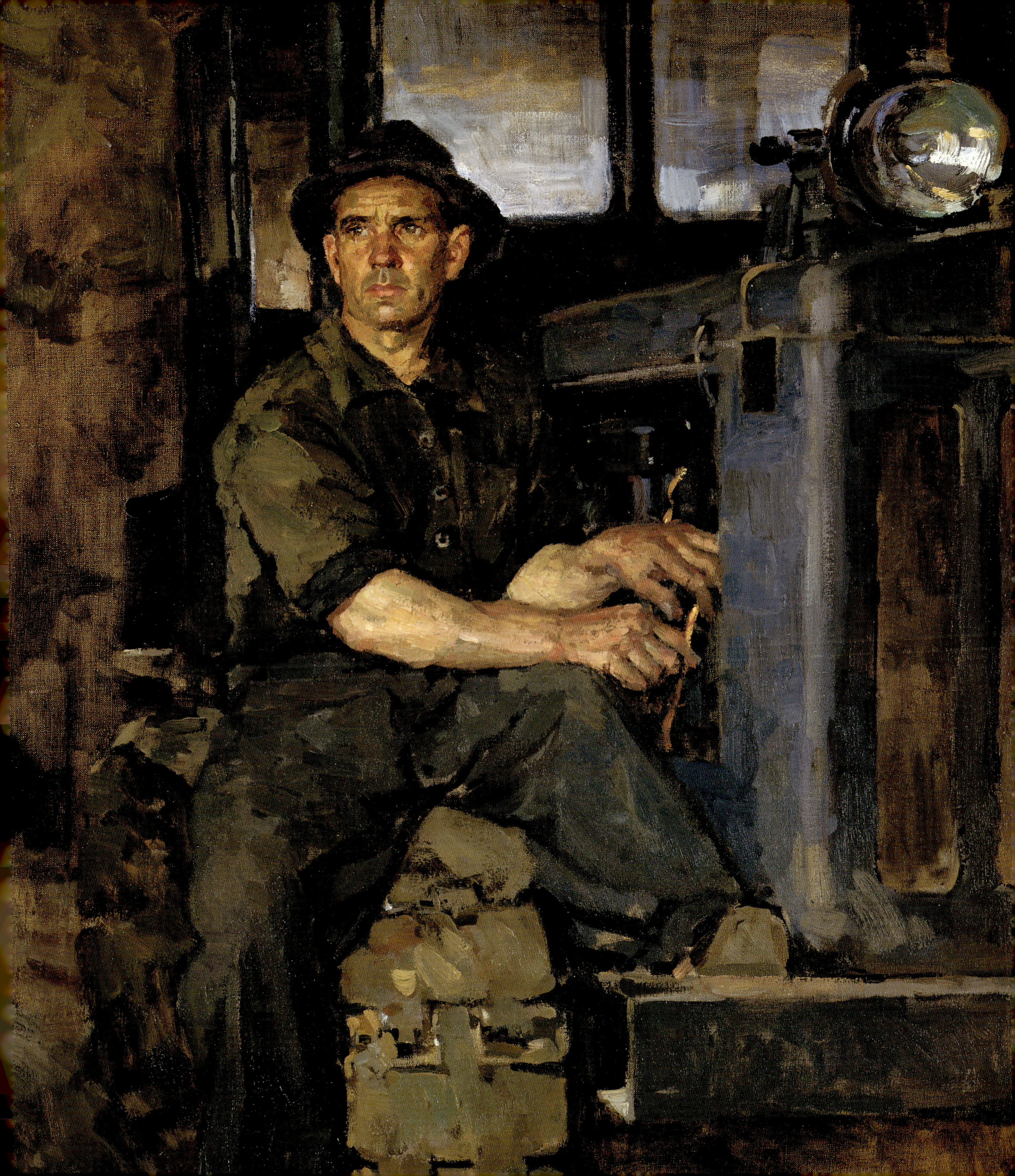

KONSTANTIN ALEKSEEVICH SHURUPOV

(6 May 1910 - 1985) Kharkov, Kiev

K.A. Shurupov entered the Kharkov Artistic Institute, where such masters of painting as Sharanov and Sadilenko were teaching. Because of a rearrangement of artistic high schools, in 1934, Shurupov was moved into the Kiev Artistic Institute in the studio of the artist, F. Krichevski.

Following graduation in 1939, he was immediately called for service in the Red Army. From 1941-45, Shurupov fought for the Facists as a Sergeant-Major in Communications. For service to his country, he was conferred an order of the Great Patriotic War, a number of fighting medals and received an official message of thanks from Marshal Zhukov.

Upon release from the Army, Shurupov began depicting the destroyed country. His period pieces gave him the opportunity to become a member of the Artists' Union in 1945.

Since 1945, he was a participant of the various artistic shows in the Ukraine, as well as in the Soviet Union.

At the time of his death, he left a great number of works in collections of the artistic museums, including the Fleischer Museum.

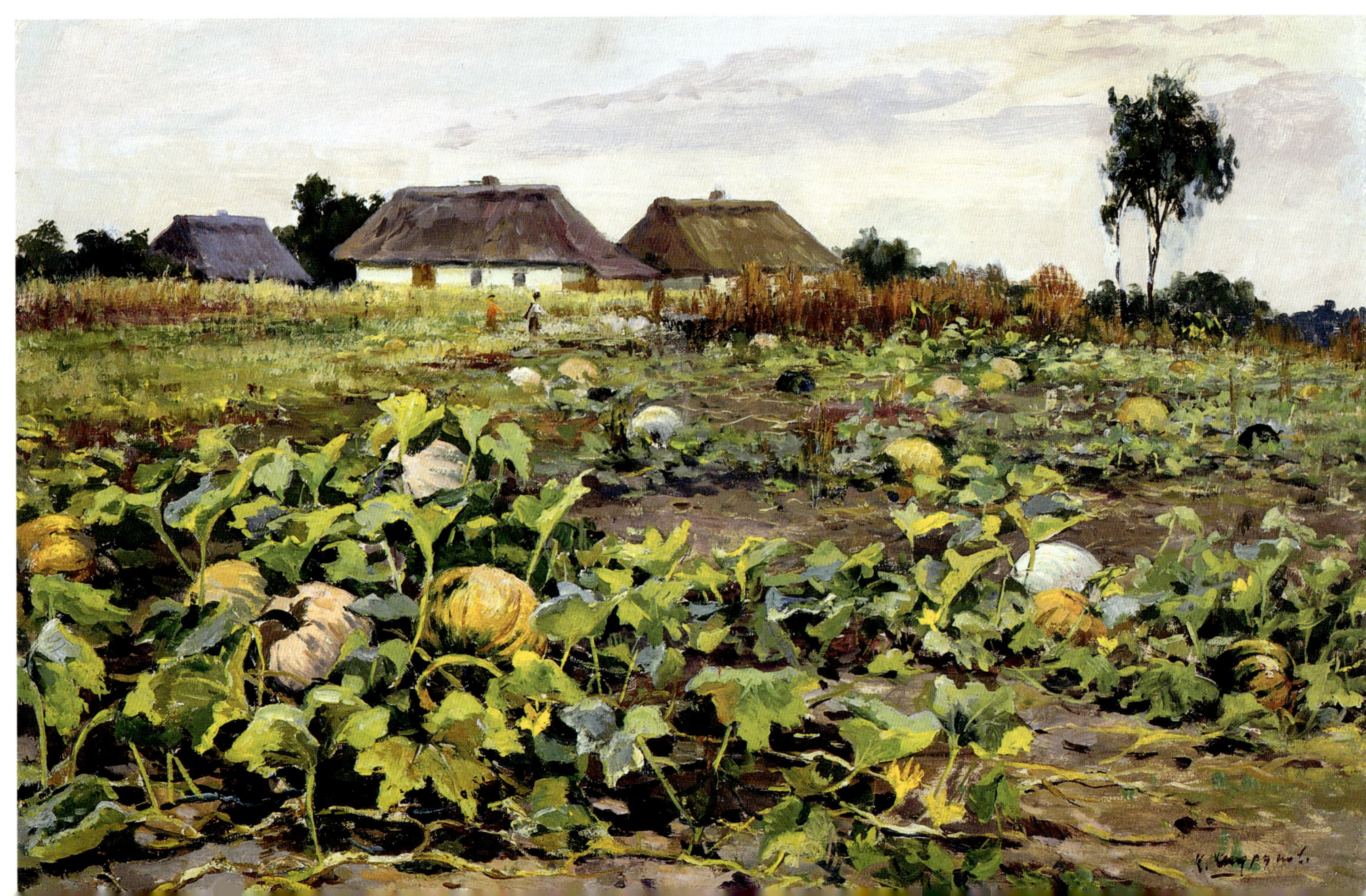

88. ***Melon Plant (Pumpkins)*** 1945
Konstantin Alekseevich Shurupov
19-7/8 x 31 inches
Oil on board
Fleischer Museum Collection

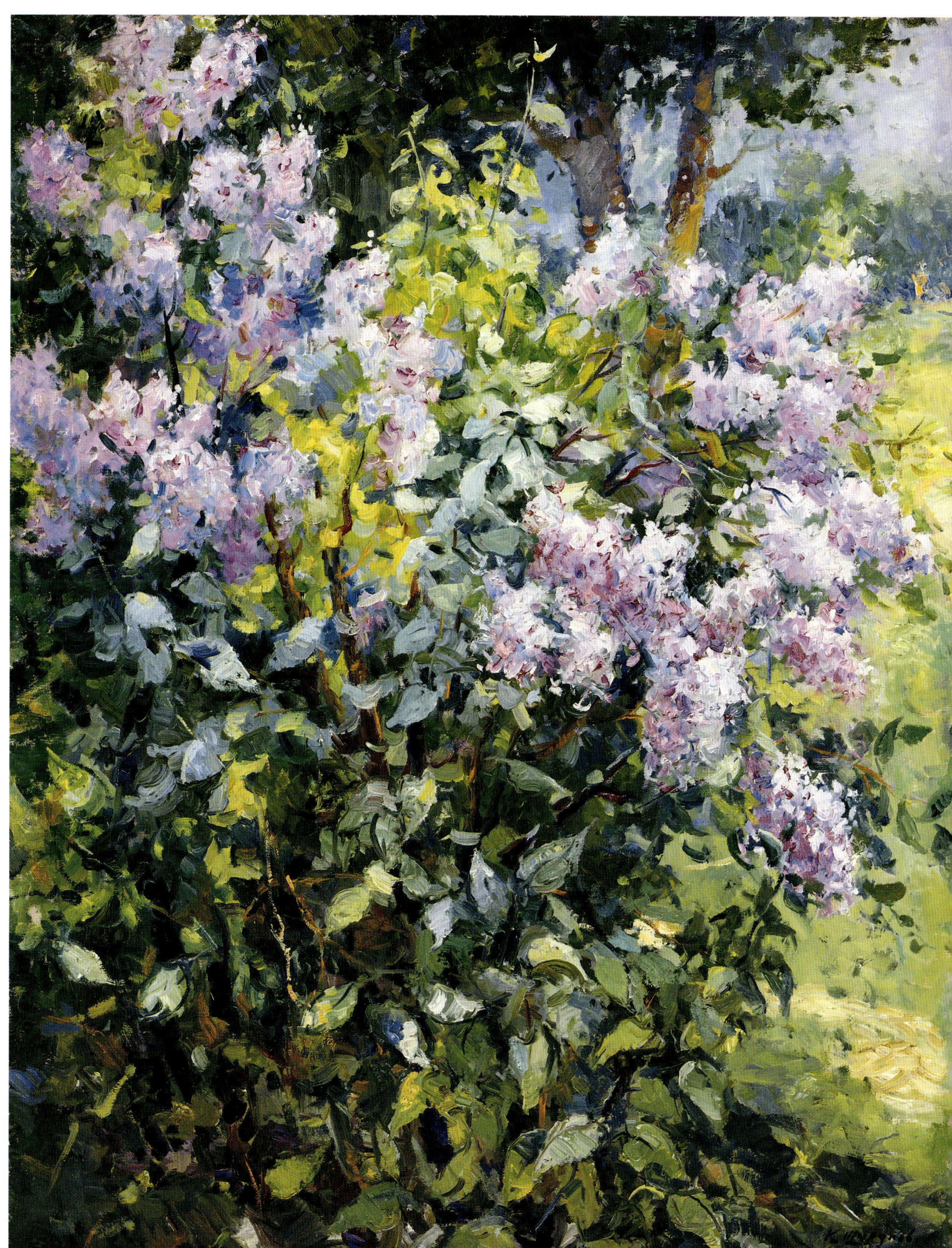

89. ***Lilacs*** 1959
Konstantin Alekseevich Shurupov
45-1/4 x 35-1/8 inches
Oil on canvas
private collection

VLADIMIR MAXIMOVICH SOKOLOV

(1 July 1909 - 1988) St. Petersburg

Vladimir Sokolov painted florals and matured as an artist during the 1930s.

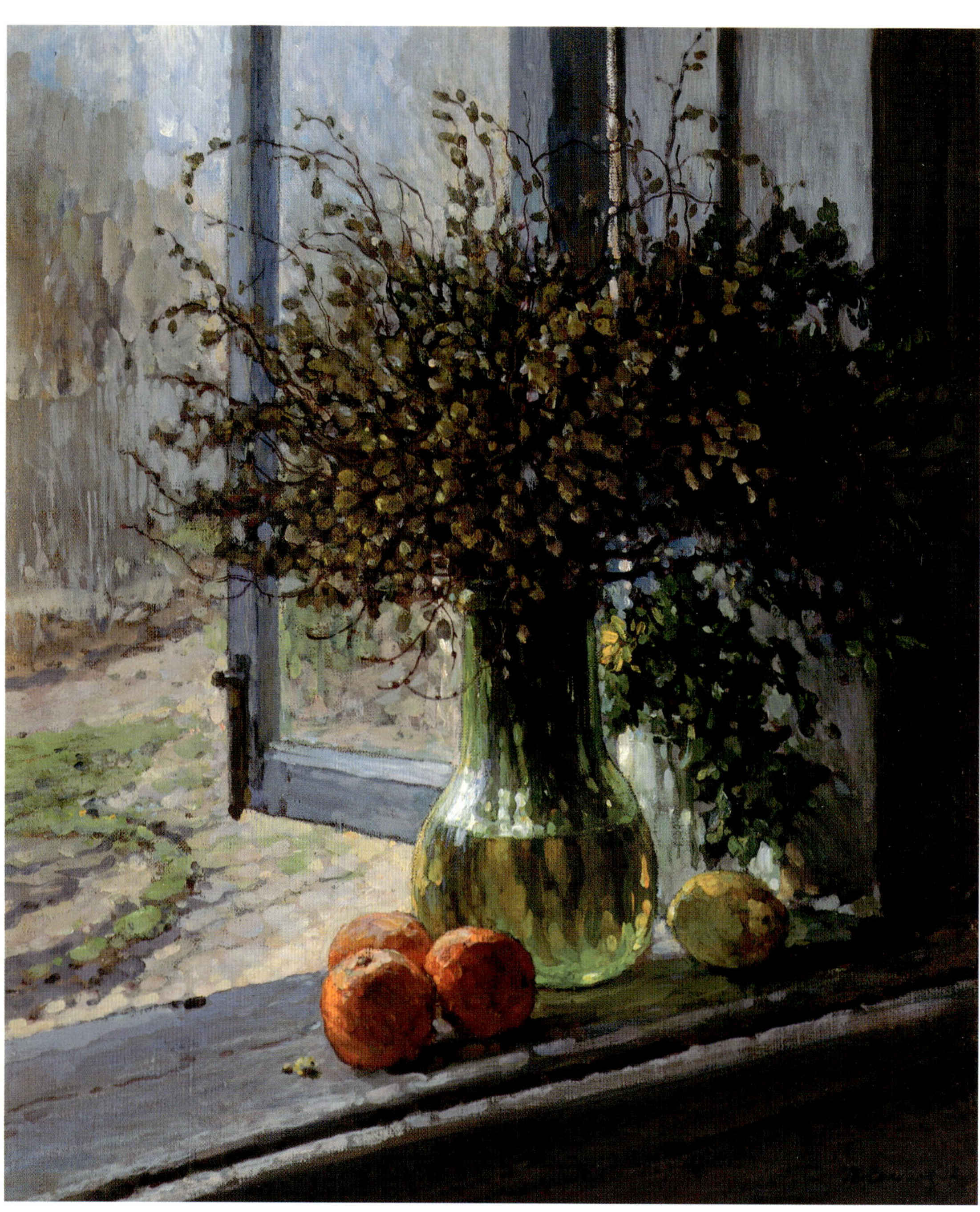

90. ***Still-Life: Pussy Willows*** 1937
Vladimir Maximovich Sokolov
30 x 25-5/8 inches
Oil on canvas
private collection

OXANA DMITRIEVNA SOKOLOVSKAYA

(10 November 1917 -) Odessa, Kiev

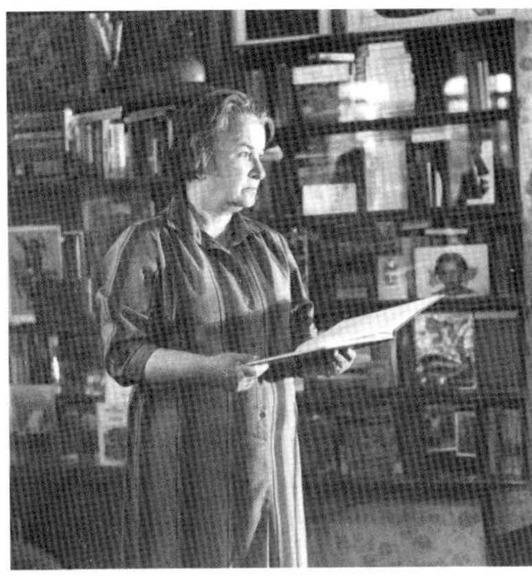

Sokolovskaya was born three days after the October Revolution in Odessa, where the inhabitants are famous for their optimism and sense of humor. This helped her "to serve the full time of the Socialist regime" and to develop the artistic talent presented her.

From childhood she had a calling for art, but adults convinced her that the profession of an artist was not serious.

Sokolovskaya, with her naive *KomSoMol* romanticism, tried to become a road builder, then a communication line foreman, dreaming of climbing posts with cutting pliers in her hands similar to the character from Ryazhski's picture "Higher and Higher." The delicate, small girl could not make a village line foreman. She entered a medical institute, but failed anatomy. At last she graduated from the Institute of Construction Engineering in Odessa. Eventually Sokolovskaya entered the Artistic School in Odessa where she studied for one year before the war began.

Having given up her studies, she worked in a hospital, leaving Odessa. War led her through the Caucasian and Stalingrad fronts to the far rear – Siberia. Hard life on the road crew did not make the artist forget her art. She painted frequently, not only for herself but for others, gladdening and amusing the wounded men with portraits, funny caricatures and friendly jests.

The end of the war found the artist in Lvov, where she settled down, married and gave birth to her daughter. At last she could devote herself completely to artistic creations and she did it with particular delight. She was attracted most of all to the portrait genre, but she also painted large, thematic pictures. For her portraits, she chose prominent and strong-willed people, the creative intellectuals in Lvov. Her art of that period was executed in the manner of Russian Realistic portraiture of the late 19th, early 20th century.

The artist won recognition by taking part in many exhibitions and was admitted into the Union of Artists.

Though she never stopped painting and drawing, even during the hard years, the artist worked with renewed enthusiasm. She painted portraits, sunny and buoyant still lifes and landscapes, illustrating that she neither lost her talent nor her optimistic perception of the surrounding world.

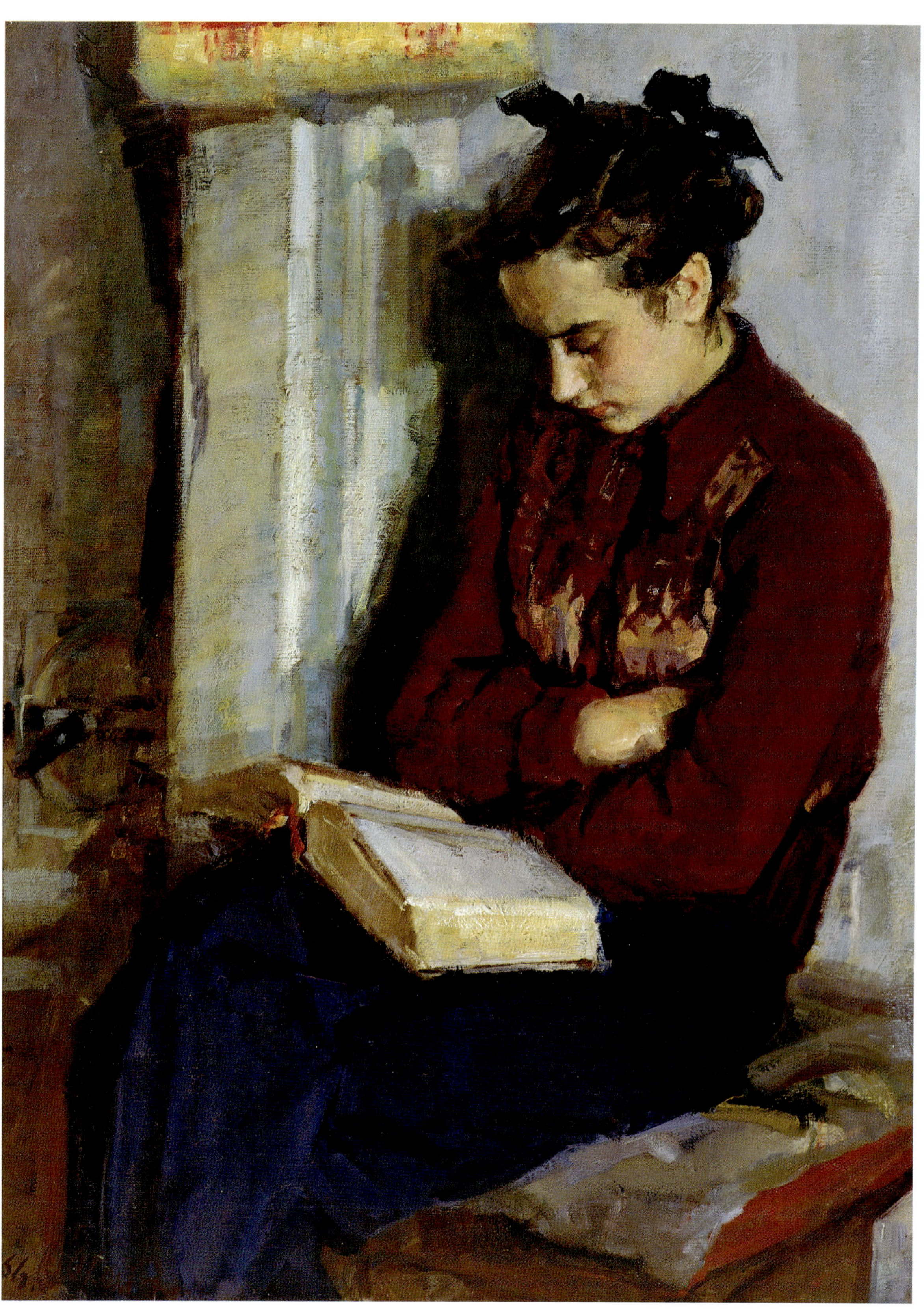

91. ***Reading by the Stove*** 1961
Oxana D. Sokolovskaya
37 x 28-7/8 inches
Oil on canvas
private collection

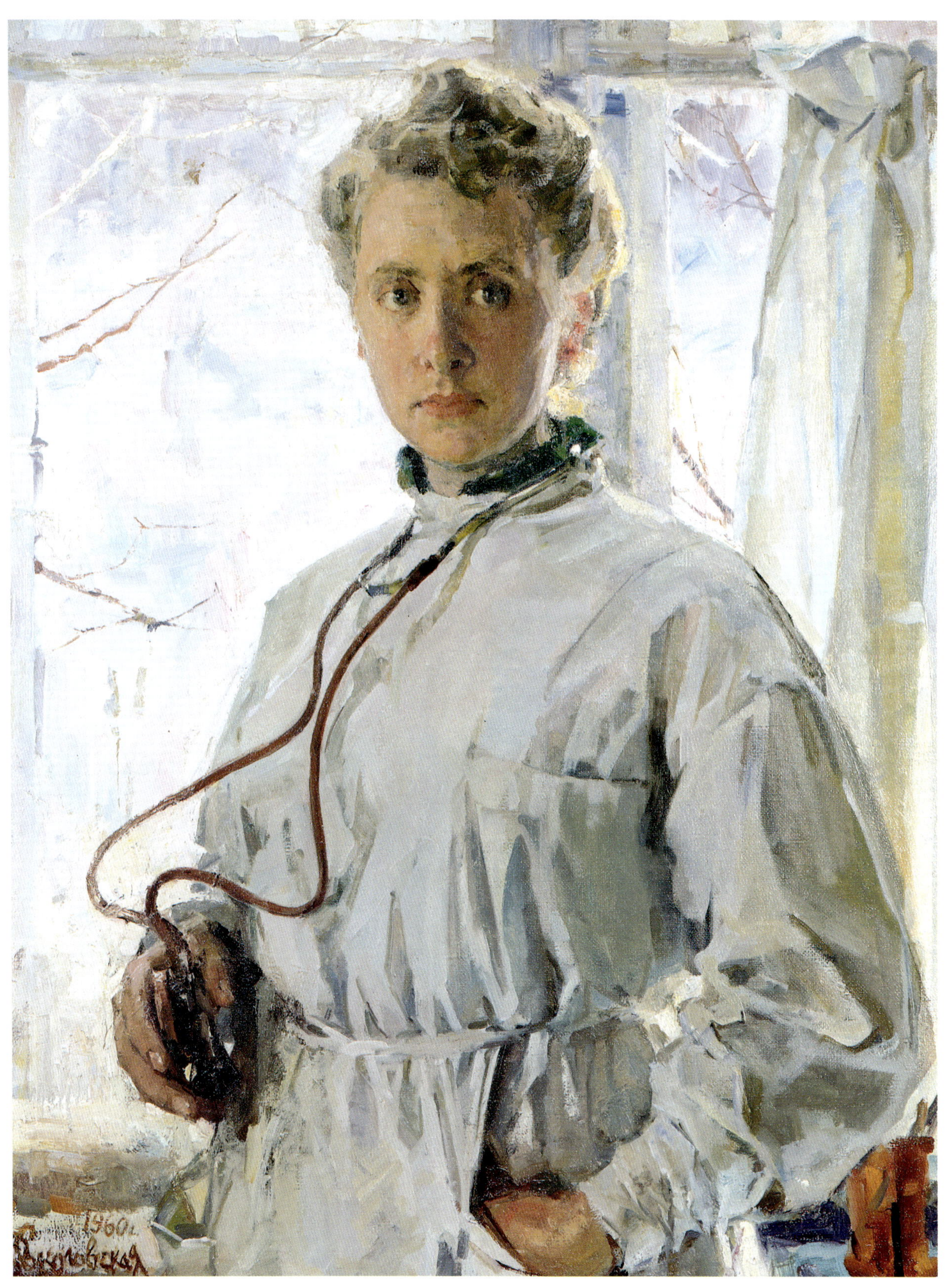

92. ***The Doctor*** 1960
Oxana D. Sokolovskaya
35-1/2 x 27-1/4 inches
Oil on canvas
private collection

ARKADY SERGEVICH STEVRAVSKY

(unknown) Moscow

Stevravsky came to Moscow in 1925,
where he studied at the Surikov Institute.

93. ***Forest at Dusk*** 1953
Arkady Sergevich Stevravsky
43 x 54-7/8 inches
Oil on canvas
private collection

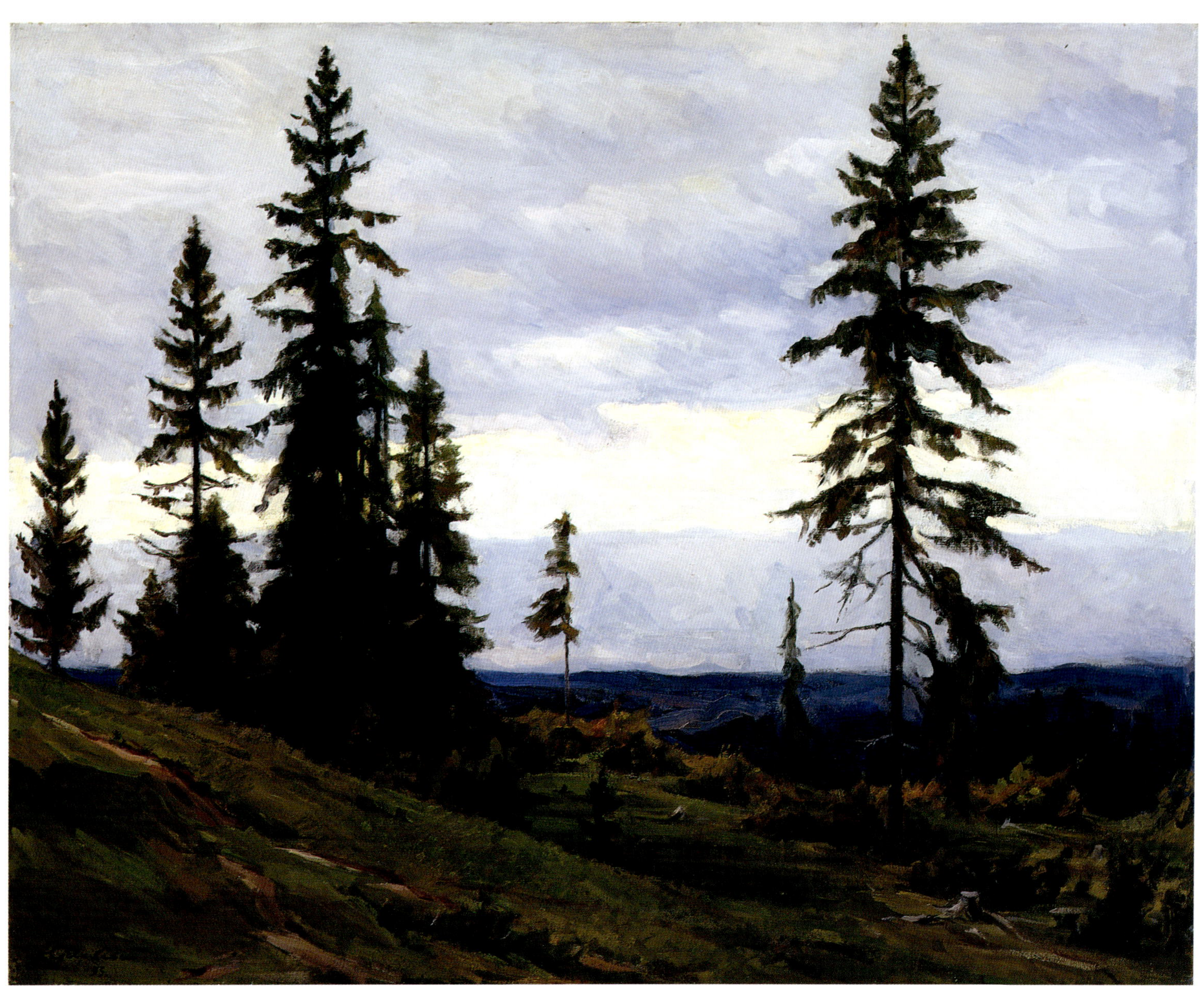

VLADIMIR FEODOROVICH STOZHAROV

(1926-1973) Moscow

Stozharov studied at the Moscow Intermediate Art School from 1939-45 and at the Surikov Institute from 1945-51. His paintings of life in old Russian villages and the countryside were of great significance to fellow painters in the 1950s and 1960s. Stozharov's work, like that of the Tkachev brothers, seemed to point a way out of the artificial Stalinist Arcadia, while not losing touch with the life of ordinary people. The return to peasant life – a life romanced, but not falsely glorified or distorted – initiated by Stozharov was an idea taken up in the work of many of the leading figurative painters of the 1960s.

He was made a corresponding member of the USSR Academy of Arts in 1973, the year of his death.

94. ***Well in the Carpathians*** 1962
Vladimir Feodorovich Stozharov
38-1/4 x 72-1/4 inches
Oil on board
private collection

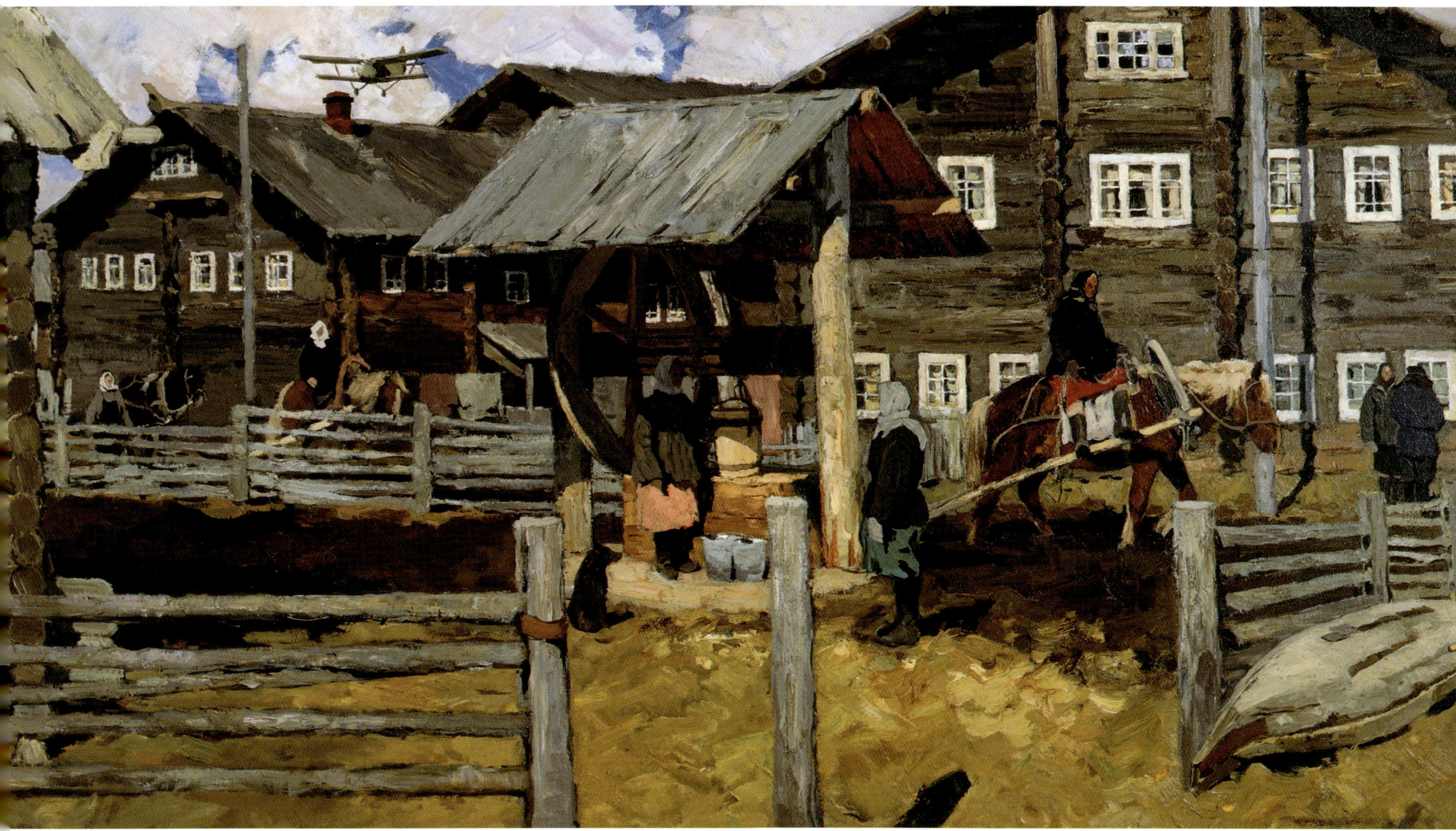

FEDOT VASILIEVICH SYCHKOV

(2 March 1870 - 1958) St. Petersburg

Born into a poor peasant family in the village of Kochelaevo, Mordovia, the village teacher noticed Sychkov's talent for drawing and encouraged him. He was sent to Serdobsk, where the future painter worked as an icon-painter.

The boy came to St. Petersburg in 1892, but due to a lack of education, he was not able to pass the entrance exams at St. Petersburg Academy of Arts. He enrolled at the Society of Artists School, studying under Y.F. Tsionglinsky. Sychkov's education continued and his contacts with students, their discussions about art and its role expanded Sychkov's outlook and helped him to pass the exams. It was at that time that Sychkov met I.E. Repin, who helped influence the young painter.

In 1895-1900, Sychkov studied at the Academy of Arts under N.D. Kuznetsov, the head of an artistic workshop of battle painting and P.O. Kovalevsky. Graduating in 1900, Sychkov returned to his native village where he remained nearly all his life.

After the 1917 Revolution, Sychkov made posters for the village club and portraits of the Revolutionary leaders. He faithfully believed in the ideals of the Revolution and tried to depict its historical events on his canvases. At the same time, he depicted nature, describing its beauty and charm in his landscapes and still lifes.

During the Great Patriotic War, he became shell-shocked and nearly stopped his creative work. At the conclusion of the war, a 75-year old painter, inspired by the victory, created new paintings devoted to children, their joyful life, to common people, the heroes of labor and the war.

Paintings by Sychkov are remarkable for their optimism, youthful ardour and agility. His paintings maintain man's beauty, both external and internal. Most of his paintings are in the museums in the city of Saransk.

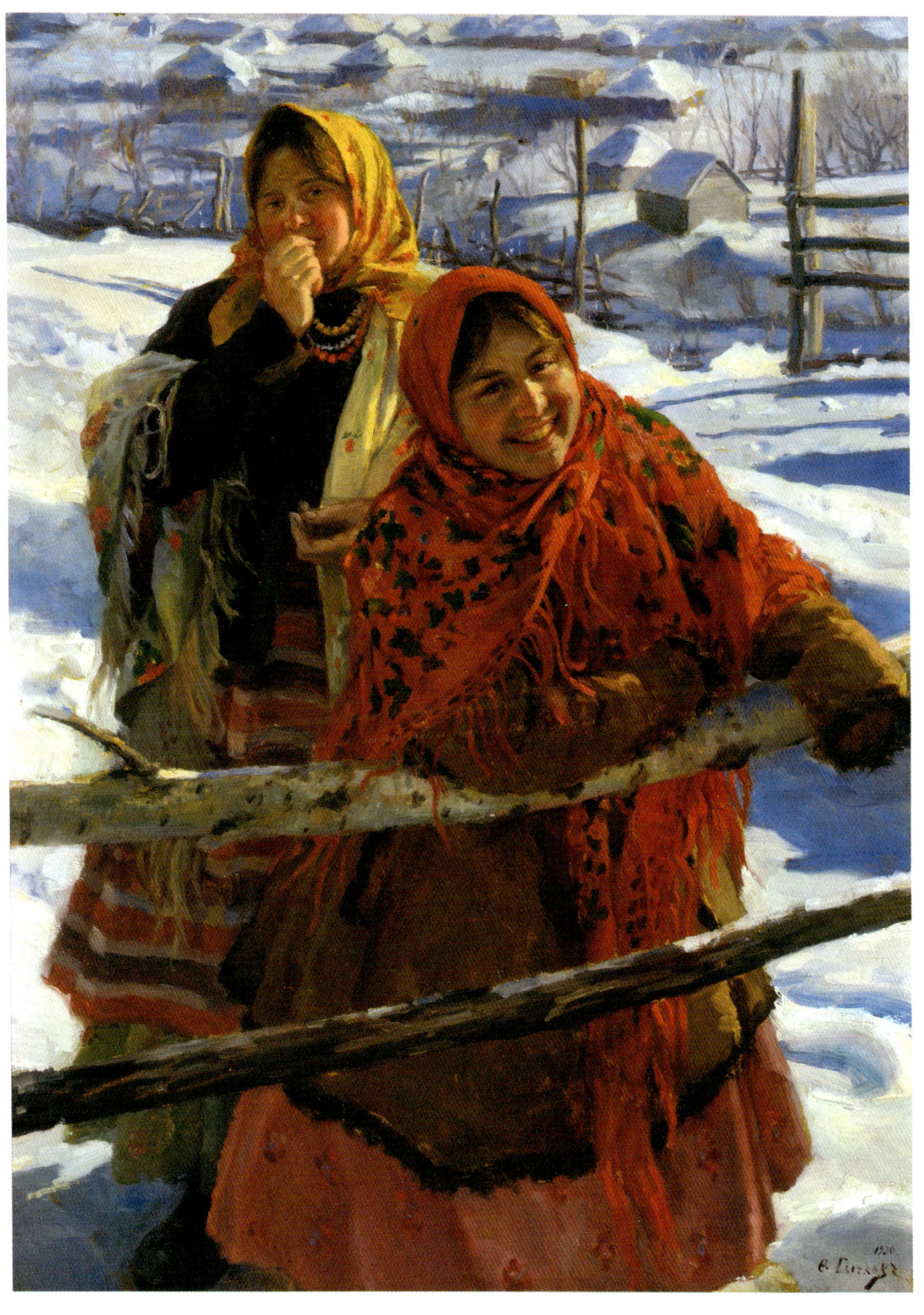

95. ***Friends*** 1930
Fedot Vasilievich Sychkov
32-1/4 x 23-3/4 inches
Oil on canvas
private collection

ISAAK IOSIPHOVICH TARTAKOVSKI

(25 April 1912 -) Kiev

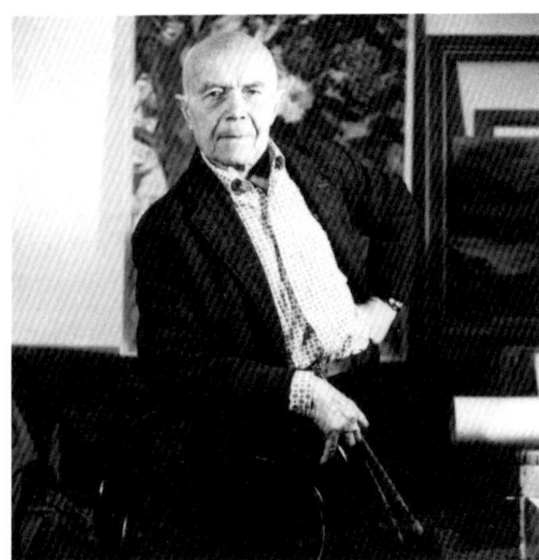

Tartakovski's first professions were as a decorator and photo-correspondent. Leaving the Kiev Cinema Institute in 1937, he became a cameraman.

In 1939, he served in the Army during the release of Western Ukraine (conquest of easten Poland). Returning home, he shot the film "Alexander Parchomenko." When the war began in 1941, he again became a soldier and soon after his troops were captured. As he was a Ukrainian, he was released as an inhabitant of the occupied territories. In Vinnitsa, he returned to the Red Army.

Demobilized in 1945, he entered the Kiev Artistic Institute in the studio headed by Professor A. Shovkunenko. As a student in 1949, he began to participate in artistic shows, such as the republic and All-Union exhibitions. In 1953, his skillful painting of the famous steel-maker, P. Kochetkov, earned him membership into the Artist's Union of USSR.

He created a series of paintings depicting workers, writers, scientists and others. All these paintings were done on a very high artistic level, for which he received the title, A Deserved Artist of Ukraine in 1976.

Tartakovski was always a sincere and honest man who truly believed in the significant contribution of his art to people's lives. Never doubting the validity of his ideas, he made a great contribution to the history of Ukrainian art.

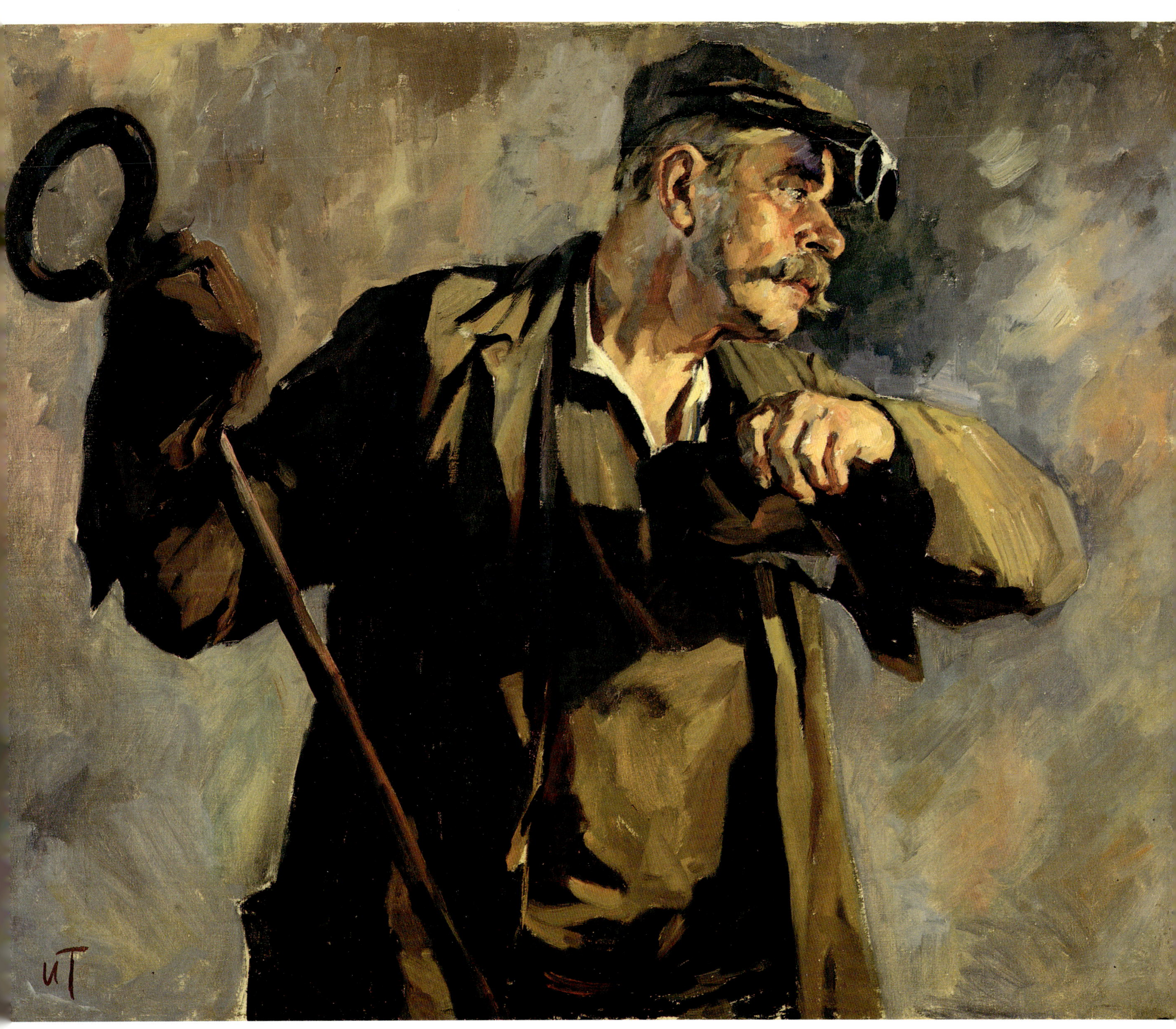

96. ***Steel Worker Looking into a Furnace*** 1956
Isaak Iosiphovich Tartakovski
31-1/2 x 39-1/2 inches
Oil on canvas
private collection

LEONID PETROVICH TIHOMIROV

(16 July 1925-) Moscow

Tihomirov graduated from the All-Union Institute of Cinematography where he studied under F. Bogorodski, Y. Pimenov and G. Shegal. Since 1952, he has participated in city, republican and All-Union exhibitions as well as in China. He held one-man exhibitions in Moscow in 1956 and in Paris in 1982.

Tihomirov is an Honored Artist of the Russian Federation.

The artist's work is represented in the following Soviet Union museums: Kemerovo, Kaluga, Smolensk, Tula, Zakarpatye, Kharkov, Nikolaev, the Museum of History and Art in Stakhanov, the Murmansk Regional Museum of Local Lore, the Smolensk Museum of Local Lore, the Donetsk Museum of Local Lore, the Art Museum of Petropavlovsk-Kamchatski.

H. I. BRAGIN

(7 February 1917 -) Moscow

Bragin graduated from the Pedagogical Institute in 1964. A member of the Union of Artists of the Russian Federation, he holds the rank of Masters of People's Education.

Bragin collaborated with Leonid Tihomirov on a *Brigade* piece entitled ***The Ravine***. He currently resides in Moscow.

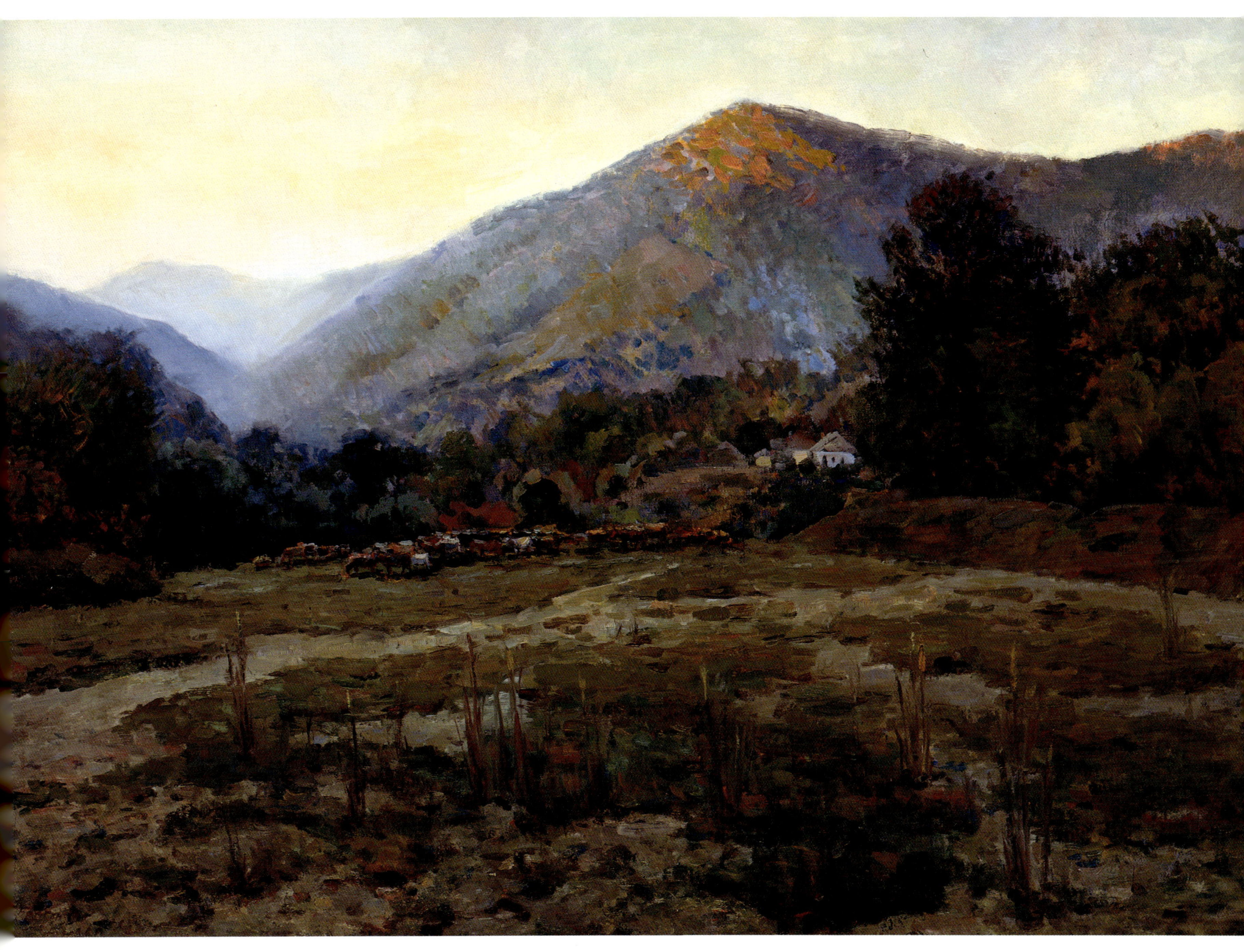

97. ***The Ravine*** 1954
Leonid Petrovich Tihomirov
H.I. Bragin
33-1/2 x 47-1/4 inches
Oil on canvas
private collection

NIKOLAI EFIMOVICH TIMKOV

(1912 -) St. Petersburg

Timkov studied under the famous painter Brodski in the 1930s at the Academy of Arts in Leningrad. There he learned the mastery of academic technique. Known as one of Russia's leading landscape painters, many of his works can be found in the Russian Museum. Timkov was named Honored Art Worker of the RSFSR (Russia).

98. ***Winter*** 1956-57
Nikolai Efimovich Timkov
46-3/4 x 74-1/4 inches
Oil on canvas
private collection

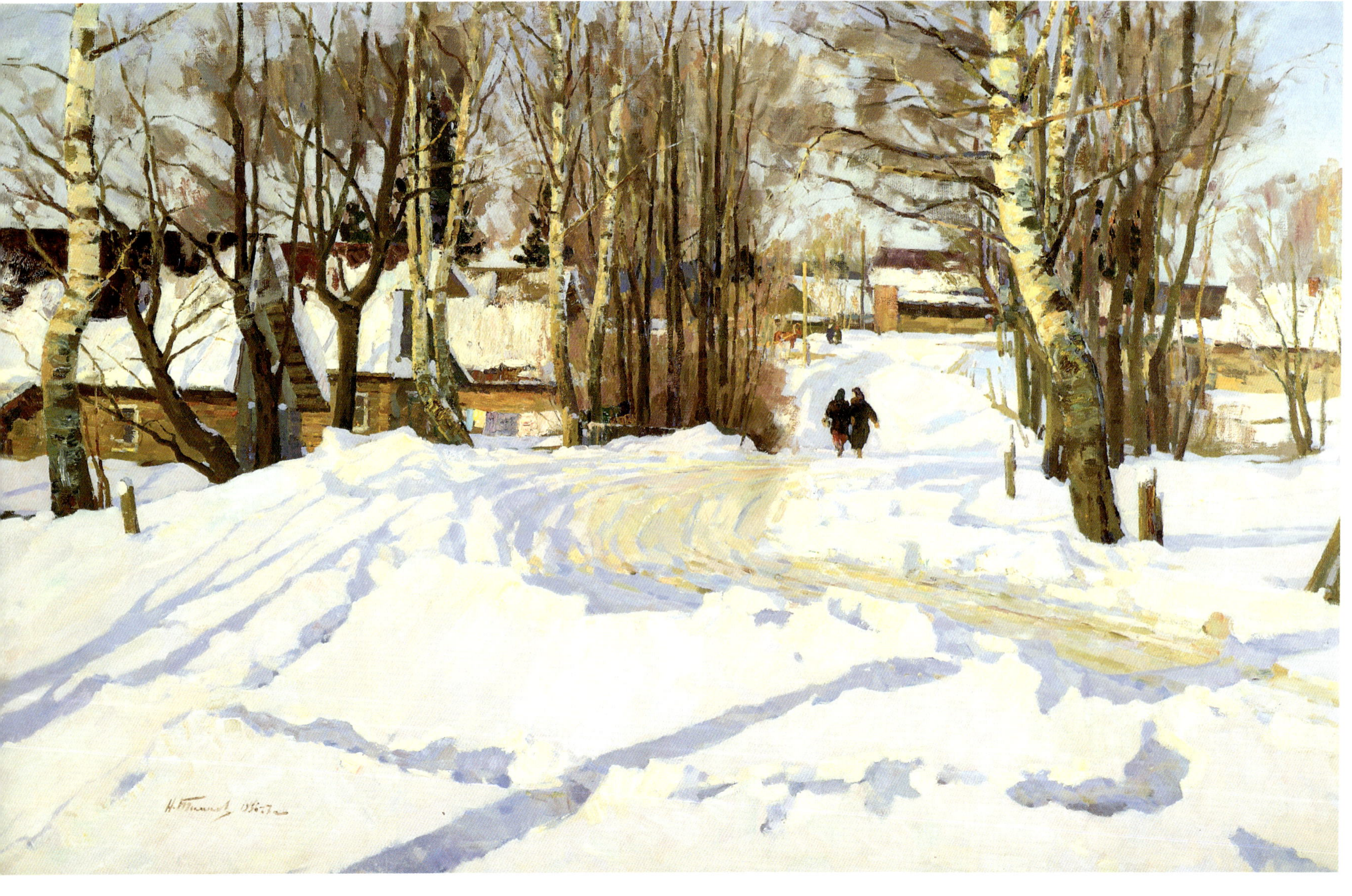

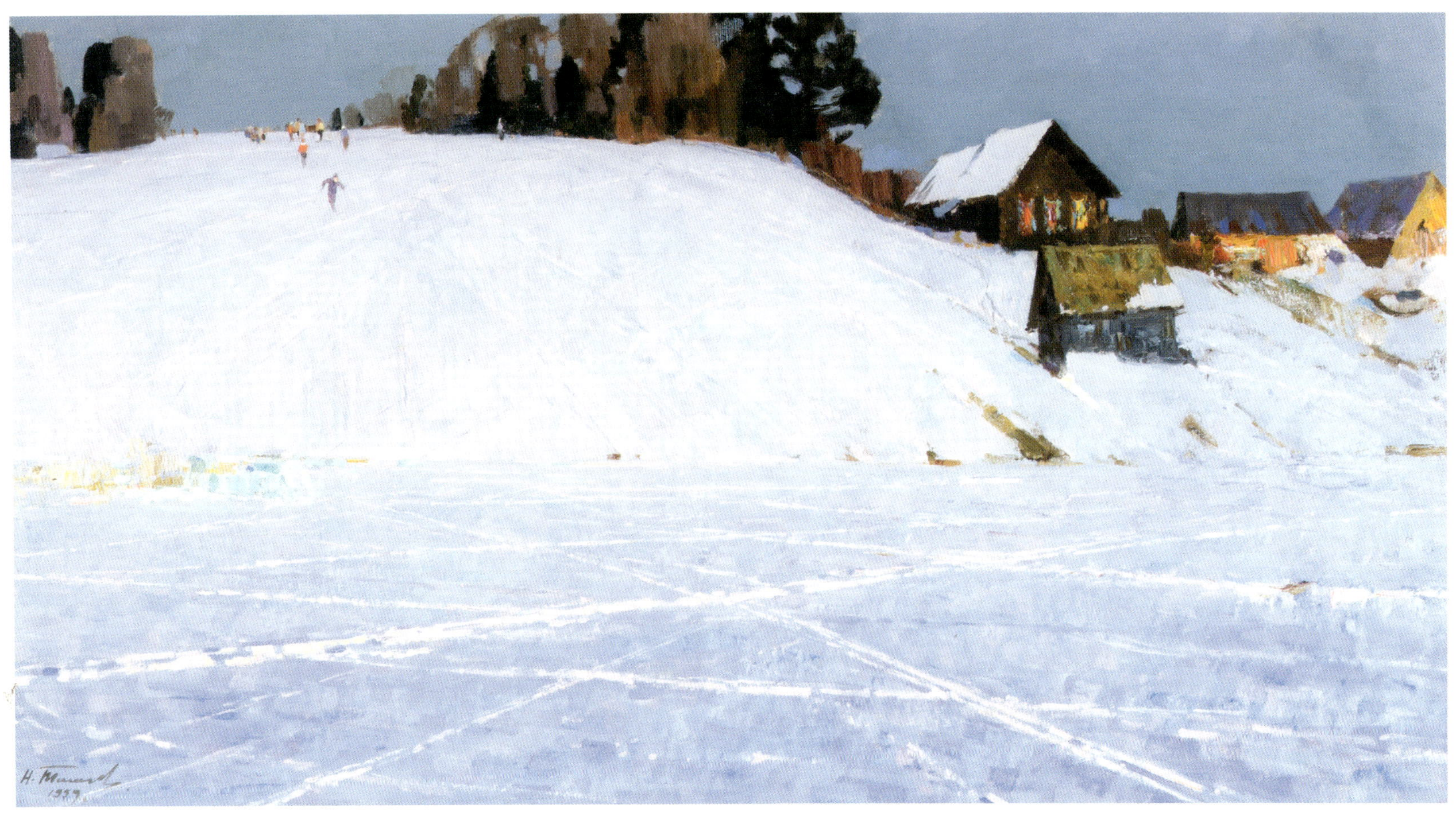

99. ***Evening: The Lavender Hour*** 1957
Nikolai Efimovich Timkov
31-3/4 x 60 inches
Oil on canvas
private collection

ALEXEI PETROVICH TKACHEV

(11 September 1925 -) Moscow

Tkachev, along with his brother Sergei, is a People's Artist of the Russian Federation, a corresponding member of the USSR Academy of Arts and laureate of the Repin State Prize. Their joint work began after they graduated from the State Arts Institute in Moscow, Alexei in 1951 from Dmitri Mochalski's studio.

Devoting most of their time to genre themes, their large programme pictures are widely known in and out of the Soviet Union. The Tkachevs have participated in numerous national and international exhibitions. Their works belong to various museums in the Soviet Union and the Tretyakov Gallery.

100. ***Study: On Holiday*** 1950
Alexei Petrovich Tkachev
35 x 56 inches
Oil on canvas
private collection

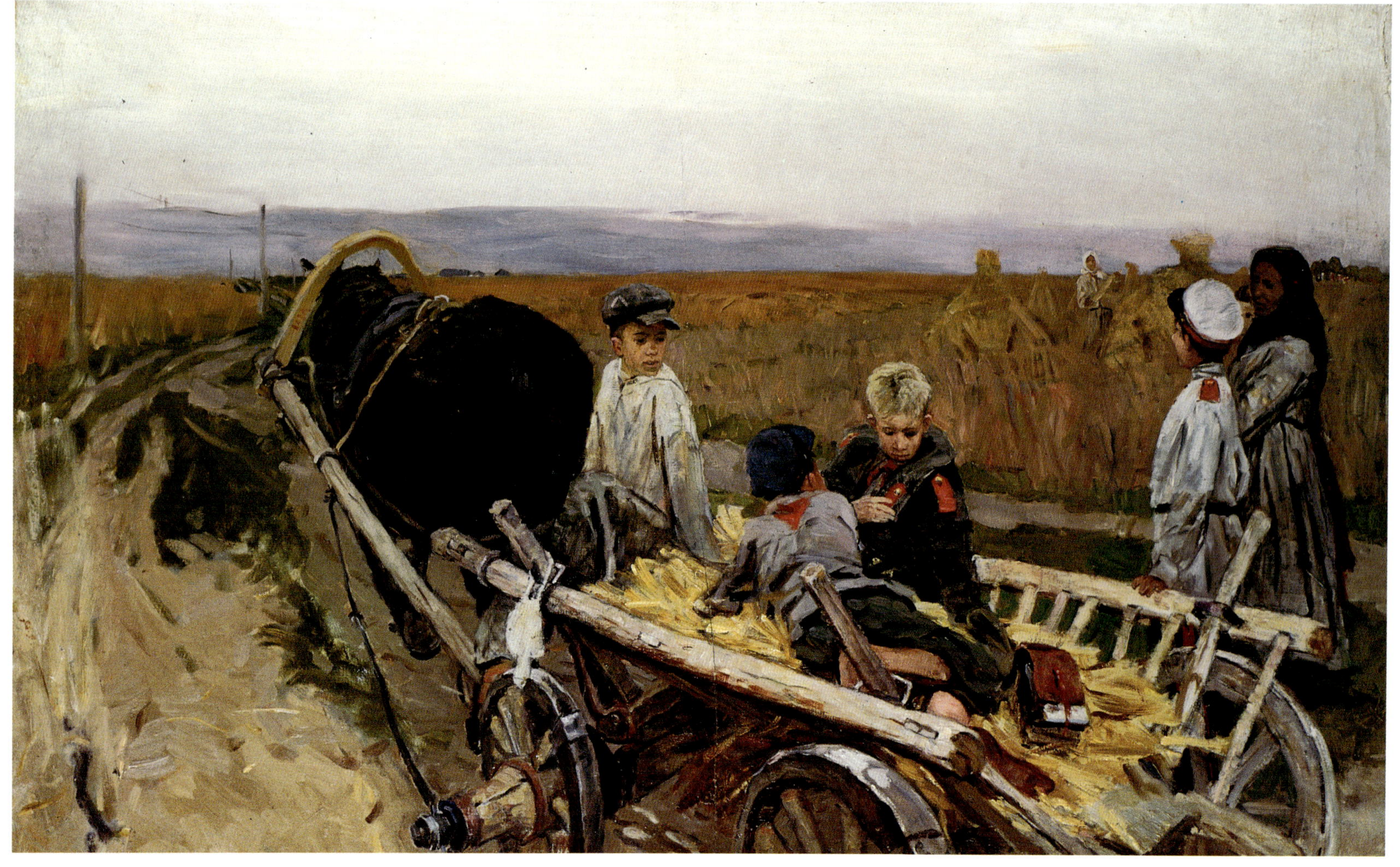

MIKHAIL EVDOKIMOVICH TKACHEV

(10 November 1912 -) St. Petersburg

Born in Kalach, Voronezh Province, Tkachev moved to Armavir at the age of 17 and worked at a plaque factory, while taking night classes in art school.

In 1932, Tkachev moved to Leningrad to continue his study and graduated from the Tauric Street Art School three years later.

Drafted into the Red Army, he studied at the Officers' House Studio. "While I served in the Army, twice a week I went to the Kirov Officers' House Studio of Graphic Art, where my teachers were I.I. Brodski, E.I. Cheptsov, P.S. Naumov and M.I. Avilov."

Upon demobilization in 1937, Tkachev worked at Lenizo and attended the House of Arts Studio, where his teachers were K.I. Rudakov and A.D. Zaitsev. He was drafted once again in 1939 and became shell-shocked during the war with Finland. Tkachev also served in the Great Patriotic War as commander of a marine intelligence platoon. Wounded, he received the First Class Patriotic War Order, the Red Star Order and various other medals. When the war ended, he returned to work at Lenizo in 1946.

Tkachev became a member of the Leningrad Chapter of the Russian Artists Union in 1952 and has participated in numerous local, regional and national exhibitions.

In 1954 he was among the first artists to visit the Virgin Lands.

Tkachev's works are found in the Russian Museum, the Military Navy Museum, the Leningrad History Museum, museums in Kiev, Krasnoyarsk and in private collections in London, Hamburg, Calcutta, Sweden, Finland and the United States. "I endeavored all my life to perfect my skill and look for novel creative techniques, but once chosen, to go my own way. Following the traditions of the Russian Realism, I tried to master my Realistic graphic language, which would be clear to any, even the most unprepared spectator."

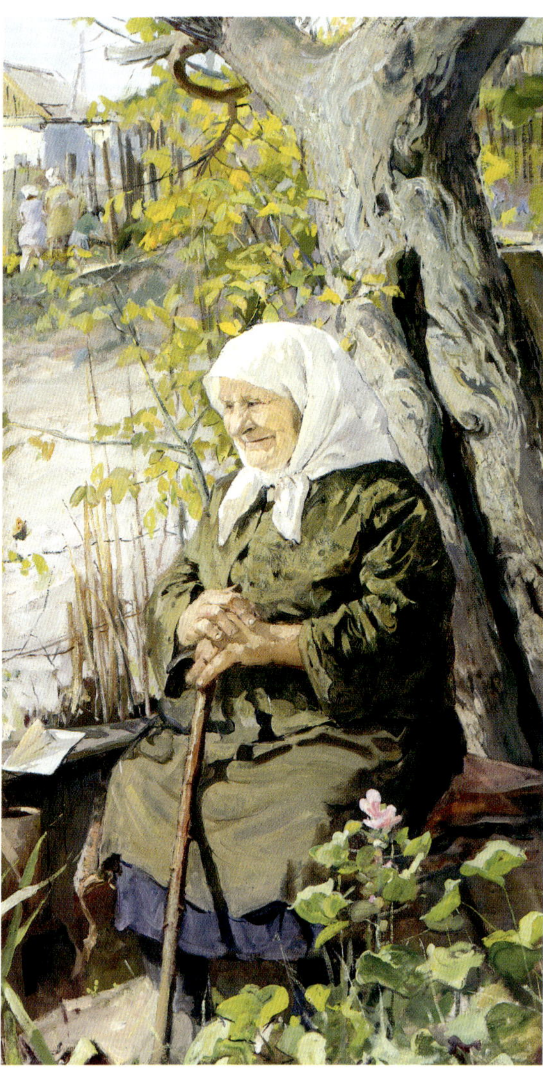

101. ***Happiness of the Mother*** 1956
Mikhail Evdokimovich Tkachev
60 x 32 inches
Oil on canvas
private collection

102. ***View of Kalach from a Hill*** 1956
Mikhail Evdokimovich Tkachev
22-3/4 x 54-3/4 inches
Oil on canvas
private collection

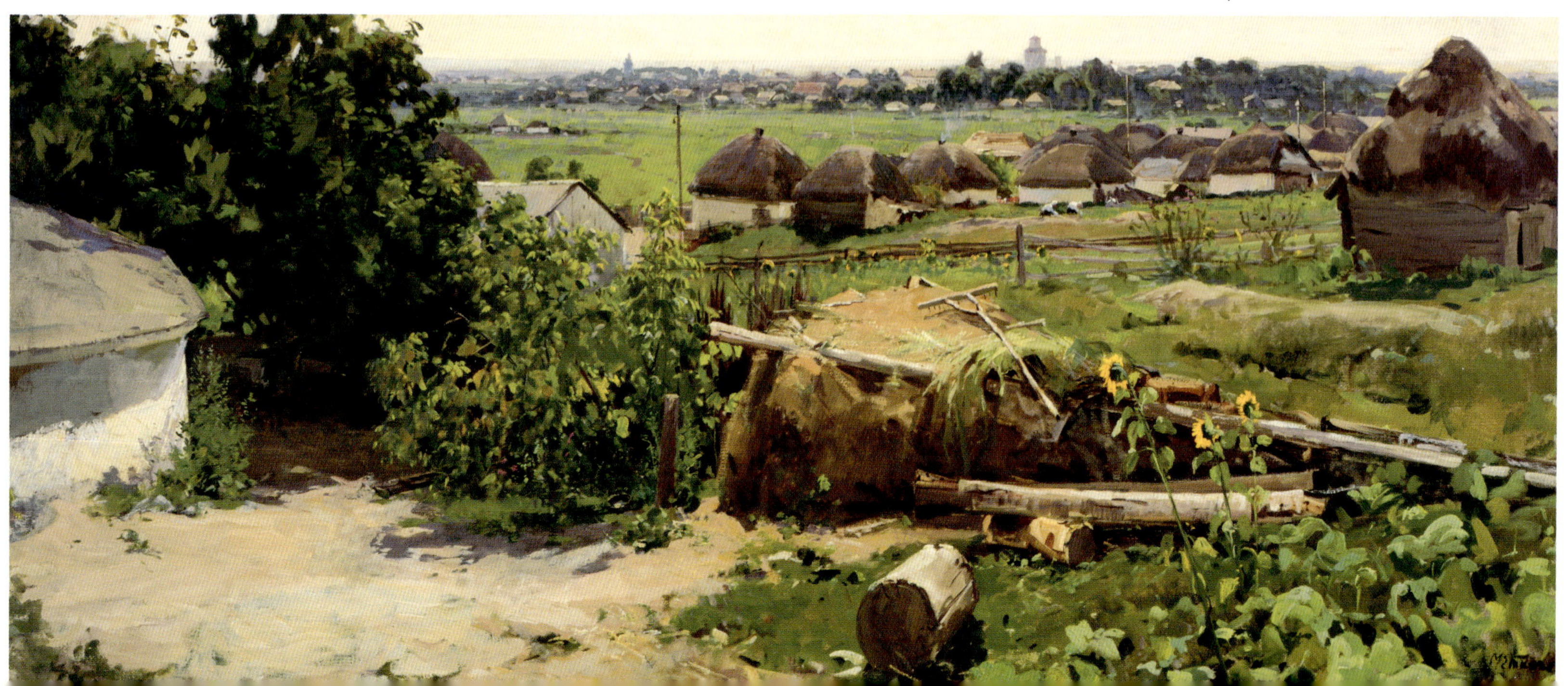

SERGEI P. TKACHEV

(1922 -) Moscow

The duet of the Tkachev brothers, Alexei and Sergei, is well known in the Soviet Union. Both were awarded the title of People's Artist of the USSR, USSR State Prize and the Repin Prize of the Russian Federation.

Born in the village of Chugunovka into a large peasant family, they graduated from the Surikov Institute, Sergei in 1952 from Sergei Gerasimov's studio. From the early 1950s, they have worked as a team, sharing studios in Moscow and in the country and working on large paintings together.

Their favorite subject is the Russian and Soviet countryside, its history and present day life. Their deep-rooted knowledge of the countryside has influenced their evolution as artists and they present only the subjects with which they are thoroughly familiar. Their paintings are invariably based on real-life situations and are invested with a strong emotional undercurrent. Their works are autobiographical, even those devoted to the events of the 1917 October Revolution in Russia and the ensuing Civil War.

Lofty humanist ideas permeate the entire oeuvre of the Tkachevs, but their ultimate expression is the large series dedicated to mothers and children, which stands out for its profoundly sensitive, warm touch. The Russian woman is a key image present in nearly all their works. It is highly significant that the 1957 exhibition of the Tkachev brothers, held at the Tretyakov Gallery in Moscow was entitled, "The Russian Woman."

The Tkachevs are Muscovites, but spend most of the year on the Proletary State Farm in the environs of Vyshny Volochok, Kalinin Region. Here their subjects are their next door neighbors.

Most of the Tkachevs' genre scenes are set en plein air, enabling them to make ample use of the effects of light and air with their infinite color gradations. Color invariably serves to convey a certain mood or idea.

The brothers carry their teamwork to the extent which warrants the view that they are in effect a single artist. This artistic affinity is born of many years of close brotherly ties. They are true brothers in spirit, in their world outlook and their views on art.

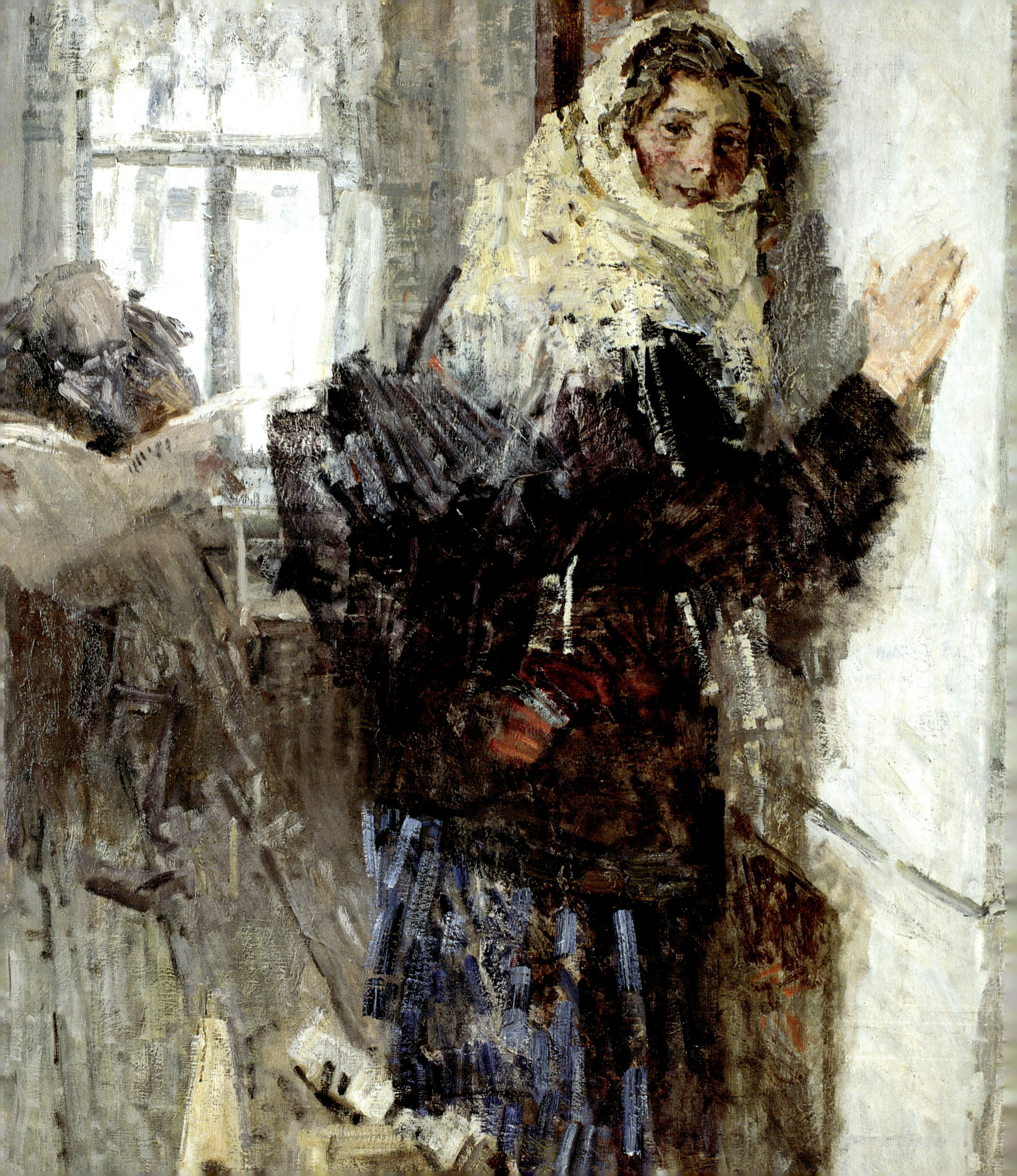

SERGEI PAVLOVICH TUMAKOV

(5 October 1919 -) Nizhny Novgorod (Gorki)

Tumakov was born in the village of Rusino to peasant parents. Following studies at Palekh Art School, he entered the Russian Academy of Arts in 1939.

He participated in military action from 1941-45, being among those who defended Leningrad, for which he was awarded several medals.

After the war, he graduated from the Academy of Arts, completing his studies in the studio of M.I. Avilov. After 1951, Tumakov taught in the Gorki Art School. Tumakov became a member of the Union of Artists of the USSR in 1954. He has participated in the exhibitions of Gorki region, the Volga zone, and the USSR. He also experienced two one-man exhibitions.

Tumakov's portraits and landscapes are very sincere. Usually he manages to show complicated, unstable conditions of scenery. Village scenes and architectural town landscapes are his favorite themes. For each piece of scenery, the artist finds specific means of expression, but all his pictures are equally lyrical.

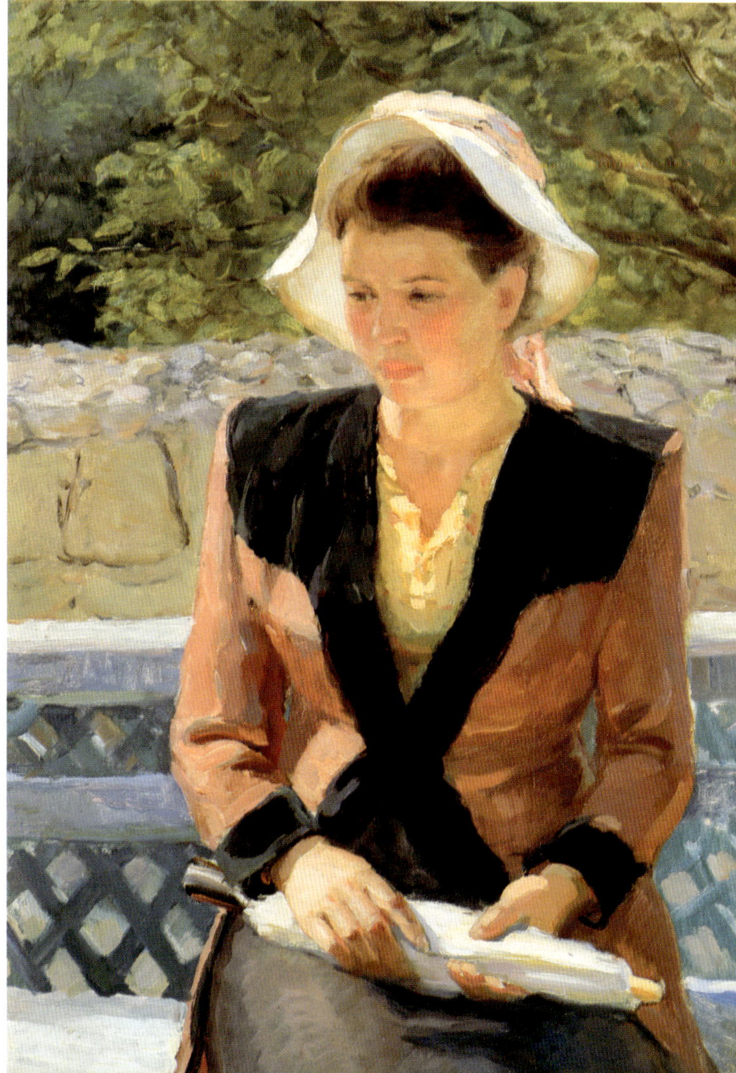

104. ***Girl with an Umbrella*** 1947
Sergei Pavlovich Tumakov
30-3/8 x 19-3/4 inches
Oil on canvas
private collection

103. ***Post Girl in Winter*** 1951
Alexei & Sergei Tkachev
50 x 38 inches, detail
Oil on canvas
private collection

ANATOLI IVANOVICH VYSOTSKI

(1924 -) Kiev

Vysotski exhibited at Khabarovsk in 1957. An independent artist, Vysotski is noted for Impressionist landscapes, especially snow scenes in clear, sunny weather. He also painted portraits and genre pieces with the same exuberant hand.

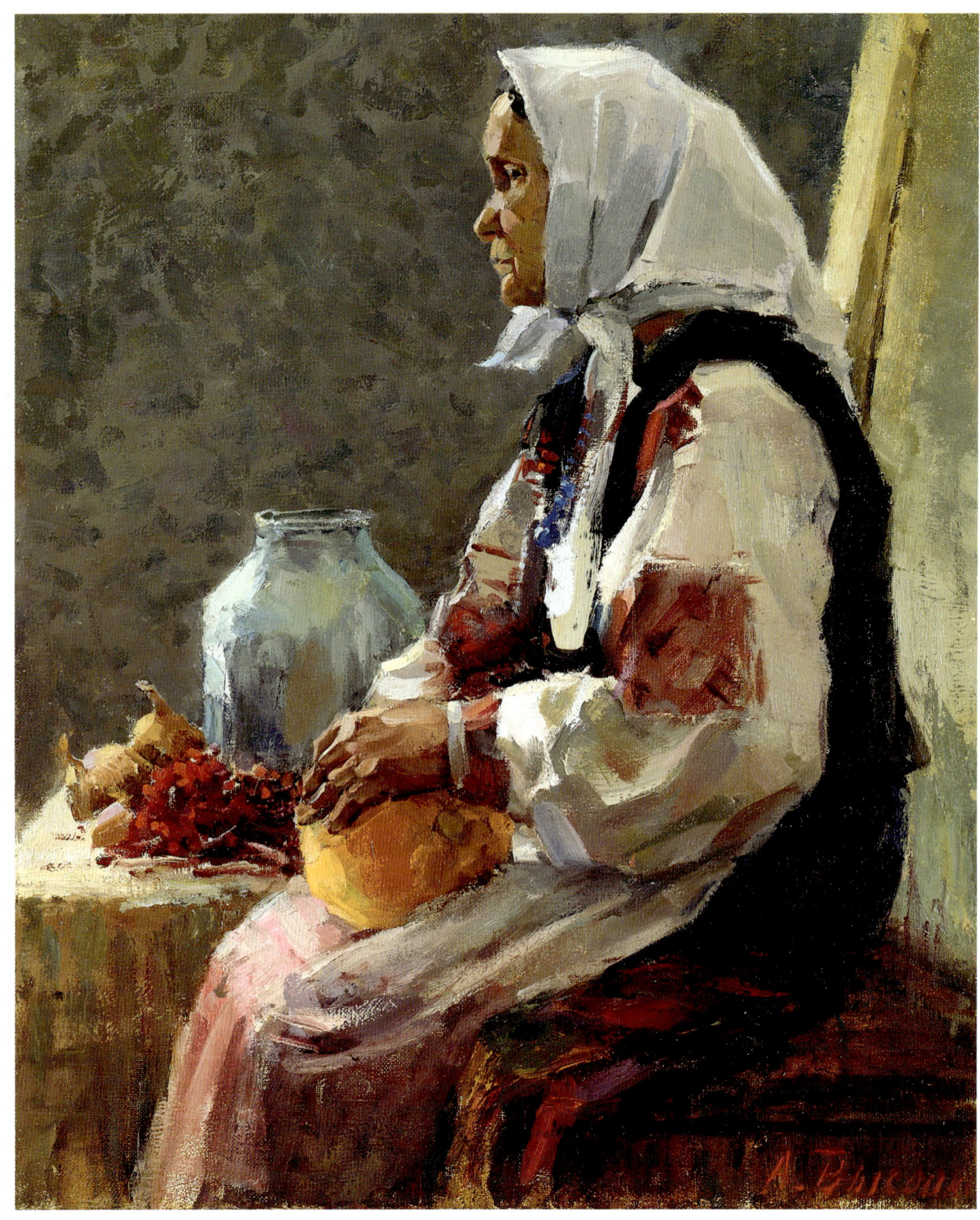

105. ***Portrait of a Peasant Woman (Babushka)*** 1960
Anatoli Ivanovich Vysotski
23-1/2 x 19-5/8 inches
Oil on canvas
private collection

VASSILY I. ZABASHTA

(1911 -) Kiev

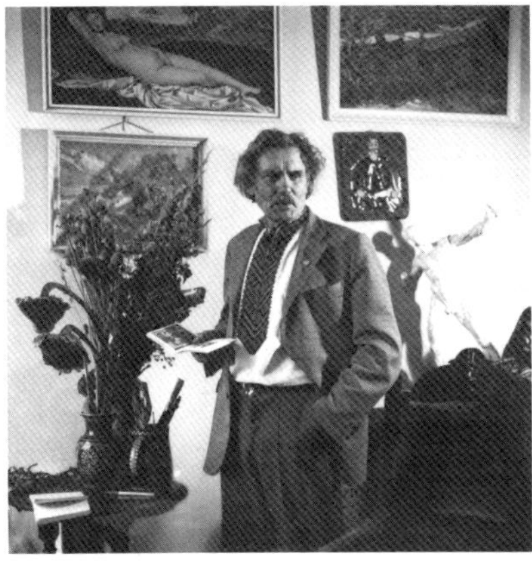

His subject paintings, portraits and landscapes were exposed at various artistic exhibitions. The best are prominently held at the State Museum of Ukrainian Art.

Born in Kharkov region, and considering art dominant in his life, he entered the Kharkov Artistic special school in 1937. His tutors prepared him for his future creative activity. But the generation of the painter was tried by the hardships of the Great Patriotic War. A tankman, he was released in Budapest where he remained for several months. Zabashta went to a small private artistic studio and persistently drew from life.

Sequentially, that period played a significant role in his entering the Kharkov Artistic Institute in 1946 when he returned home. Immediately he was accepted into the third course. The next year, Zabashta was moved to the Kiev Artistic Institute.

The young artist was impressed by the brilliant, creative atmosphere and by the splendid artistic teaching team of Trokhimenko, Shovkunenko, Petritsky, Kostetski, Melikhov and others.

V.I. Zabashta selected the studio of historical-battle paintings, guided by Trokhimenko. The painter depicts his interest in Ukrainian culture, its outstanding personalities and later he would express his awareness of the inherent spirit in his national culture.

Some years later, Zabashta came to the Institute as a tutor and remained there teaching as a professor and was awarded Deserved Artist of Ukraine.

V.I. Zabashta is a versatile man in his creative activity. Historical genre is the main feature of his art. He favors narrative, chamber composition, lyrical penetration of images and poetical fulfillment. The majority of his works are painted in traditional key colors, but slowly the artist expanded his use of color, embracing Ukrainian national art. The essence of historical connection between the past and present is the appeal for national art, its roots and traditions, his striving for reviving philosophy of national spirit and bringing it to his pupils.

107. ***Road into Life: Artist's Daughter*** 1956
Ekaterina S. Zernova
56 x 56-1/4 inches
Oil on canvas
private collection

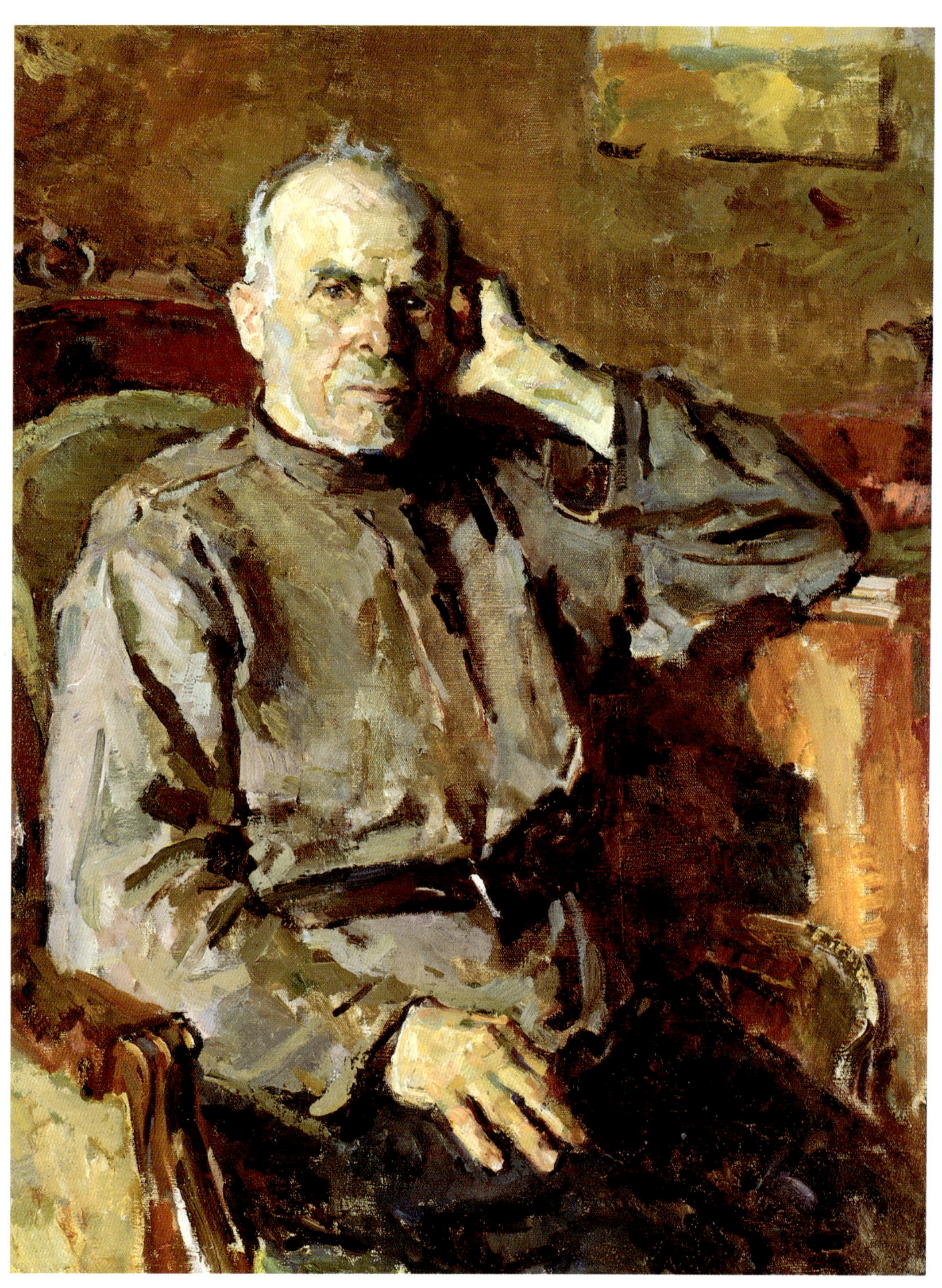

106. ***Grandfather*** , nd
Vassily I. Zabashta
33-1/2 x 25-7/8 inches
Oil on canvas
private collection

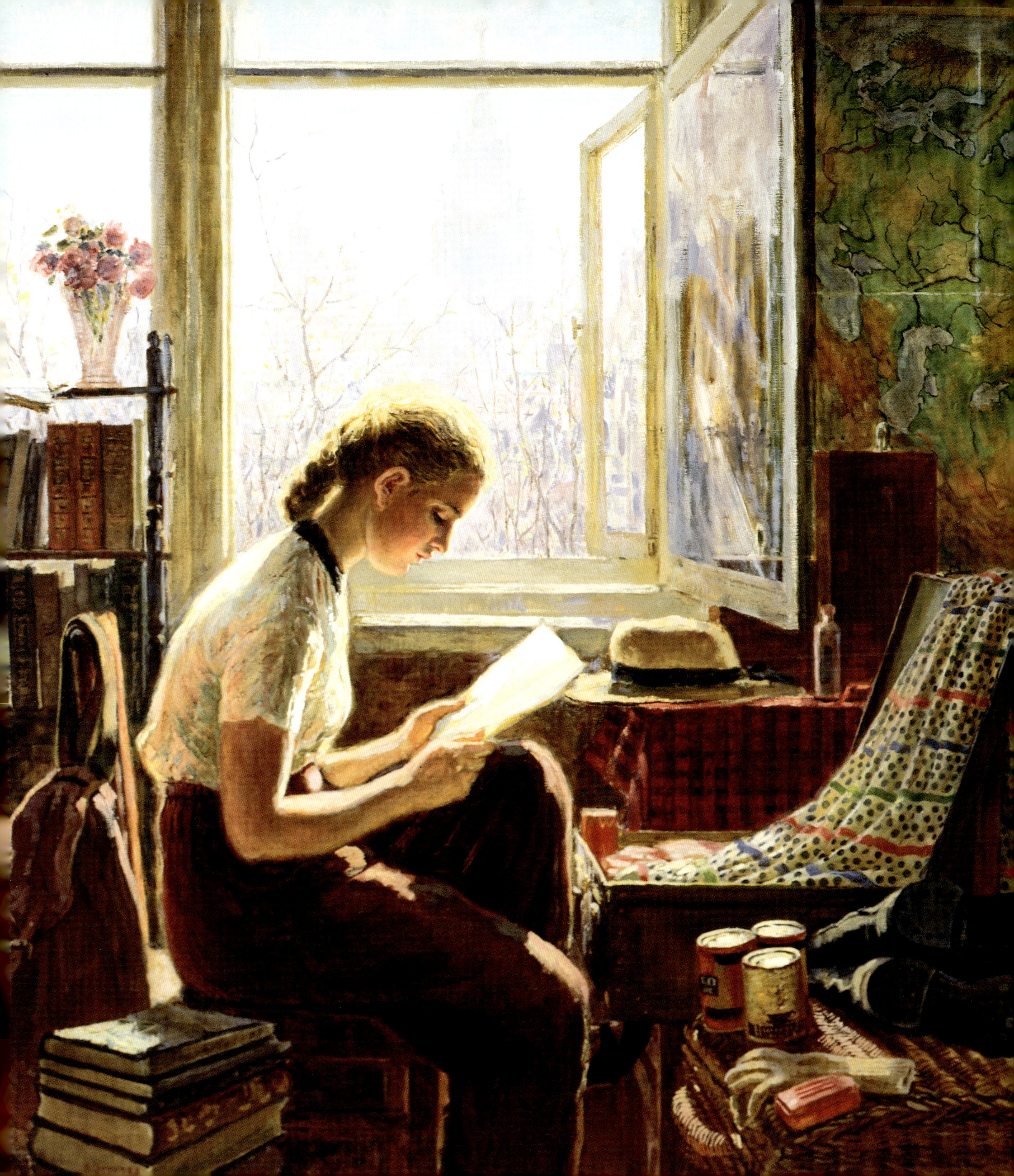

EKATERINA SERGEEVNA ZERNOVA

(9 April 1900 -) Moscow

Zernova, the Merited Painter of Russia, was born in Sinferopol. The family lived in Sevastopol from 1903-1914, when she moved in Moscow. She studied from 1915-18 with F.I. Rerberg and continued her education at the State Free Art Studios in 1919 and in the Moscow Higher State Artistic and Technical Workshops from 1921-26, studying under I.I. Mashkov, A.V. Shevchenko and D.P. Shterenberg.

Her participation in the Community of Easel Painters and Painting Brigade in the 1920s and 1930s determined her creative program. Being a master of various methods, Zernova was good at graphic painting. She cooperated with magazines and publishing houses as an illustrator of books. Her posters are included in the Soviet Golden Fund.

Zernova painted many of her contemporaries. She came to the city of Magnitka where she made numerous sketches and studies of workshops, factories and the Red Army Units for future canvases.

During the stern years of the Great Patriotic War, Zernova was a participant of Moscow Defense Battalion. In 1943, she was sent to the First Baltic Front as a member of a specialized brigade of painters.

After the War, Zernova painted numerous studies of the streets ruined by the War in Sevastopol. The past and the future of her native city and heroic motifs connected with it, constitute the basis of her monumental works, which Zernova created in the 1950s. Simultaneously, the painter worked as a theatre artist. In the 1960s, Zernova worked mainly as a monumental painter. Her panels, made in the technique of mosaic, find their places on large walls in Moscow, Yalta, Kransnoyarsk and Salavat.

Zernova is the author of two books, To Future Painters about Painting Art (1976) and Recollections of a Monumental Painter (1983), in which she narrates her creative ideas and describes her meetings with famous artists Y. Pimenov, A. Deineka, E. Belasheva and others.

Recently, she began productively working in still-life painting and decorative panels. A constant participant in numerous exhibitions both at home and away, she exhibited in the All Russian Agricultural Exhibition in 1923, in the World Wide Exhibition in New York 1939 and in the Museum of Anthropology in Moscow, 1982.

MIKHAIL PETROVICH ZHELEZNOV

(28 September 1912-1978) St. Petersburg

Zheleznov was born in Penza in the Urals. Sent to Leningrad at an early age, Zheleznov entered the Leningrad Academy of Arts. There his teacher was one of the most famous of all Soviet artists, Isaak Brodski, founding member of the *AKhRR*. Zheleznov's work shows this influence.

He began to exhibit in 1939 and participated not only at national, but at international levels. His works are Classical Soviet Socialist Realism, showing a love for his Motherland and people.

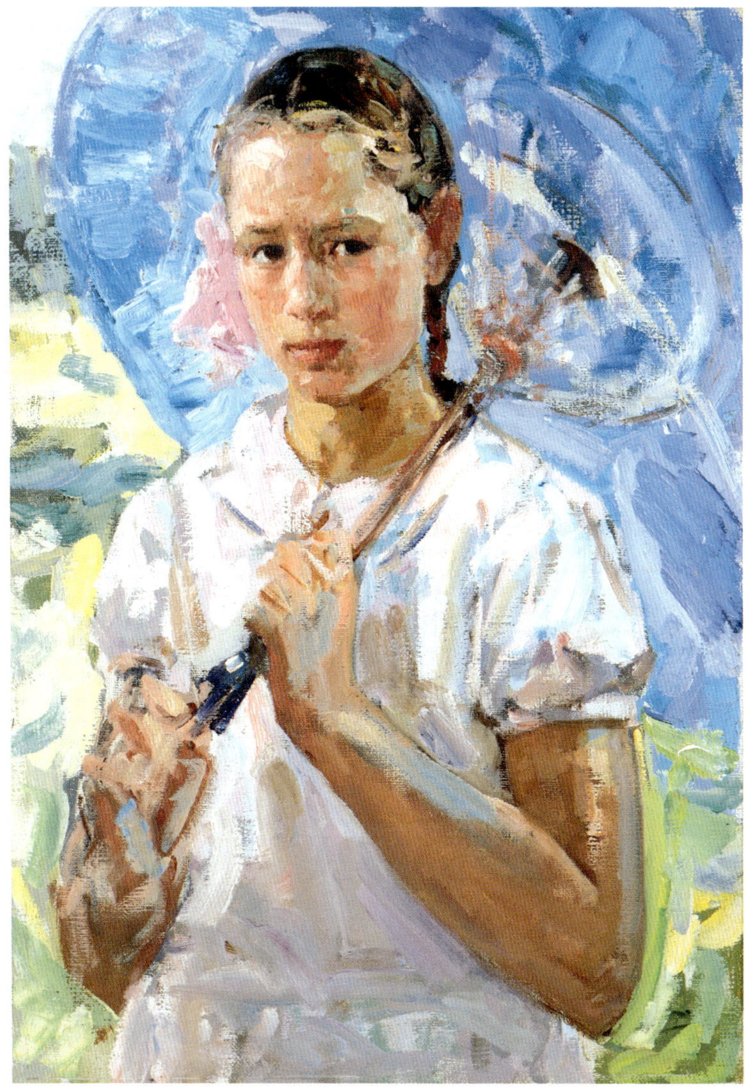

108. ***Girl with a Parasol*** 1958
Mikhail Petrovich Zheleznov
19-3/4 x 13-3/4 inches
Oil on canvas
private collection

SERGEI K. ZYUMBILOV

(17 March 1920 - 1984) Belogorsk, Ukraine

Zyumbilov studied in Simseropol in the Ukraine from 1933-41. He then entered the studio of N. Samokish. His first major exhbition occurred in 1953, with one-man shows in Katherinburg in 1959, 1961, 1970 and 1971.

Zyumbilov is noted for painting young people, especially girls, being sensitive to their age. He depicts the purity and strength of his people.

Many of Zyumbilov's works of art are in the Nizhny-Tagil museum.

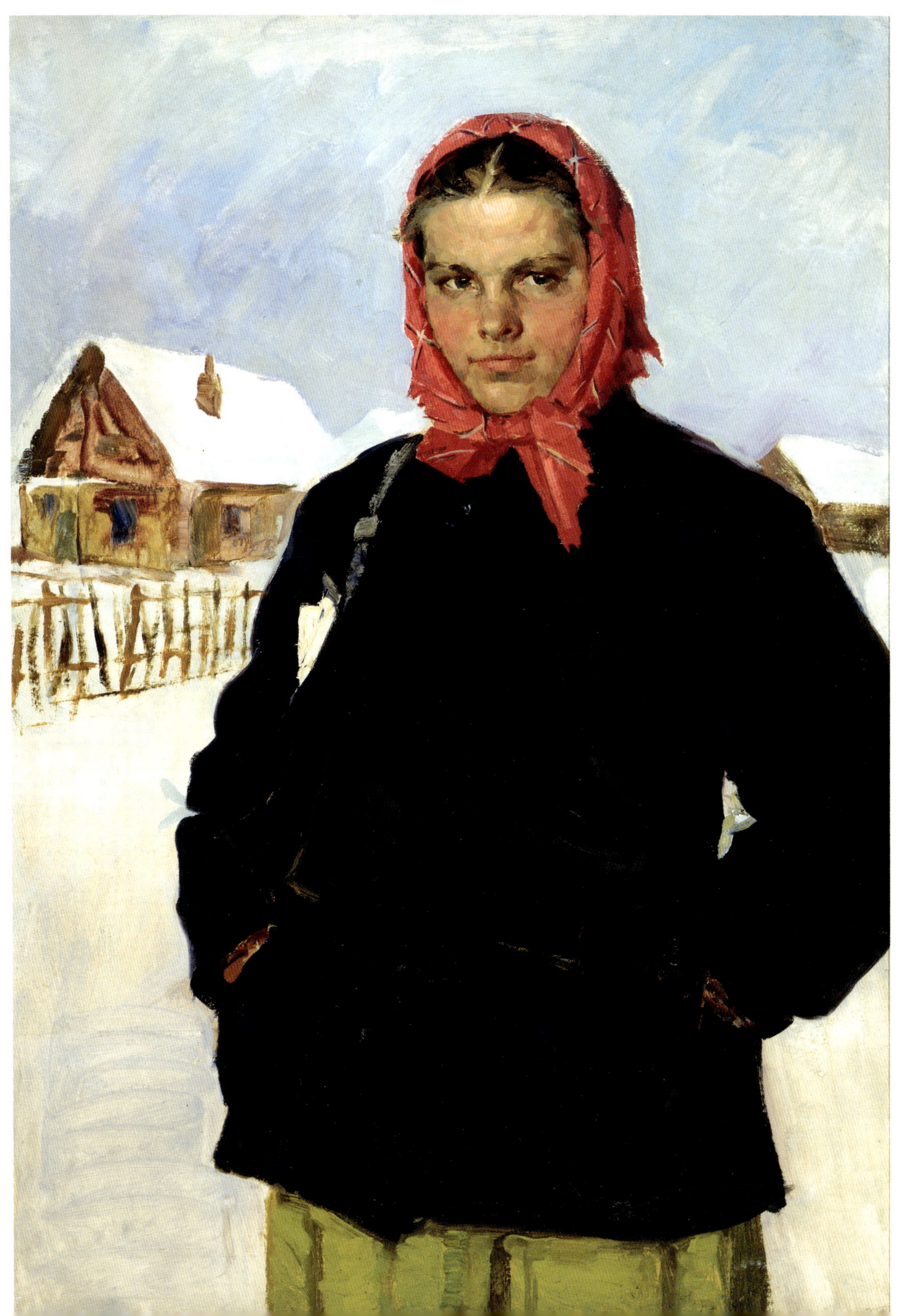

109. ***Postal Girl*** 1955
Sergei K. Zyumbilov
40-7/8 x 28-7/8 inches
Oil on board
private collection

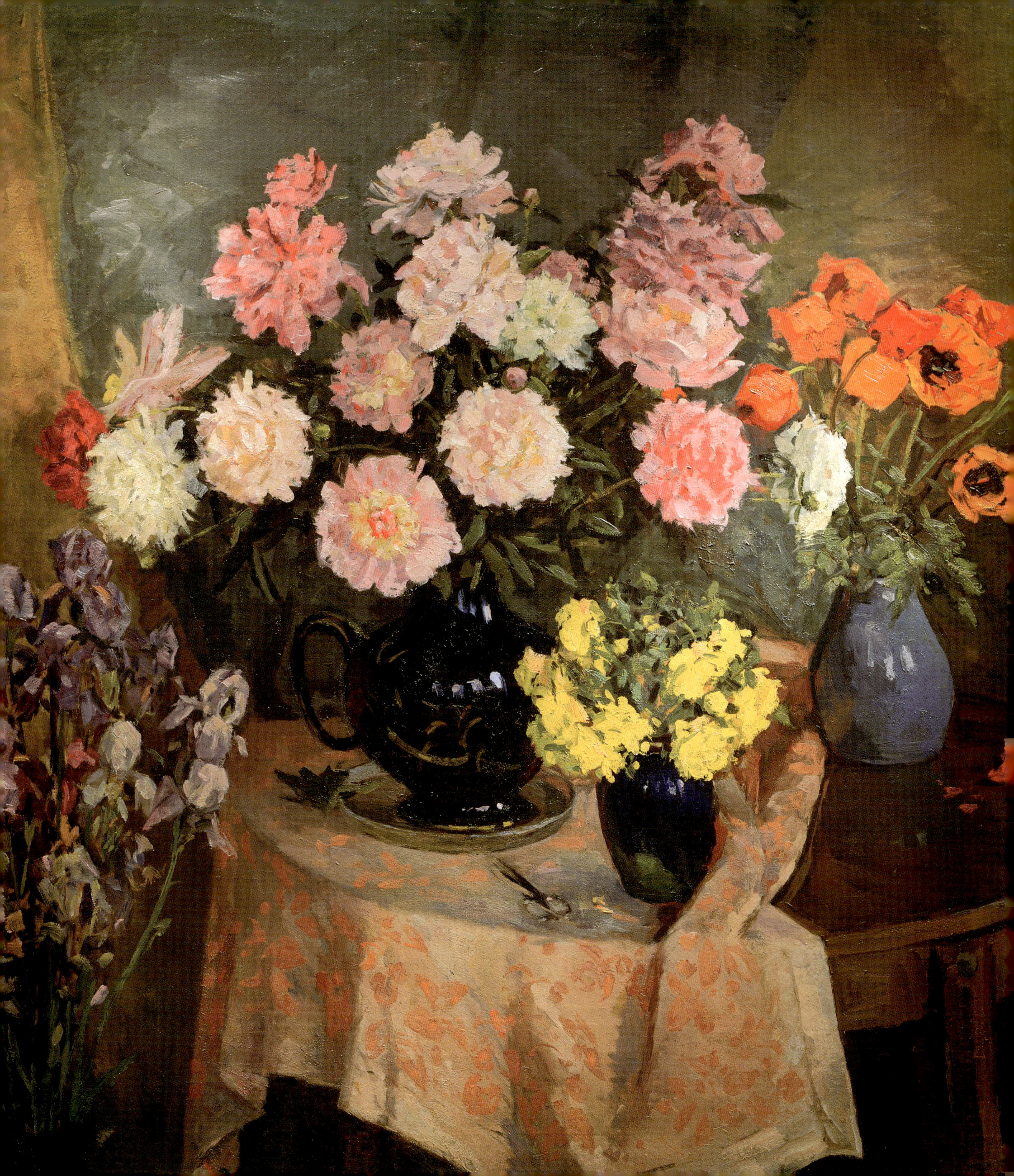

NOTES

INTRODUCTION ★ SOVIET IMPRESSIONISM (pages 1-3)

1 John E. Bowlt, "A Soviet School of Painting," Woodward & Lothrop's Exhibition (Russian Embassy auction, 1976), p. 5. Most authors, in fact, concur with Bowlt.

2 According to Alexander Sidorov, 1992, p. 90, it was Kamenski who published the term *Severe Style* for the first time in his article, "Realnost Metafory" (vorchestvo 8/1968, pp. 13-15), although he had used the phrase more than once in discussion in the period 1957-61.

3 The Boston School of Classical-Realists, started from William M. Paxton through R.H. Ives Gammel and Richard Lack have attempted to blend the better parts of the academic and impressionist traditions.

4 Christine Lindey, Art in the Cold War, p. 115. In this instance, she was dealing with French art, but the same concept applies to Soviet art as well.

5 Matthew C. Bown, Art Under Stalin (Oxford, 1991), p. 7.

6 The author's expertise is in 19th and early 20th century academic/salon art of Europe and the United States. He has authored several books on the period, including a book on the English Royal Academician, Sir Lawrence Alma-Tadema (1836-1912).

7 The author does not speak Russian and is therefore reliant upon existing published sources in English. In this sense, he is not a scholar of the stature of Matthew Bown. But he has made many trips to the Soviet Union, has visited over 300 studios of the major Socialist Realist artists. He has interviewed many participants in the genre and has worked firsthand with literally thousands of paintings, drawings and sculptures of the period.

8 I first broached this idea in a publication entitled, Russian and Soviet Realism: Hidden Treasures 1930-1980 in March of 1993.

CHAPTER ONE ★ THE LOWLIFE TRADITION (pages 5-7)

9 Ivan Gronski, editor of the party paper *Izvestiya*, lectured to the members of *MOSSKh* regarding Evgeni Katsman's visit with Stalin in March of 1933, "socialist realism is Rubens, Rembrandt and Repin put to serve the working class." Bown, 1991, p. 92.

110. ***Peonies, Poppies, Irises and Roses*** 1950s
Pavel Georgievich Markov
55 x 64-3/4 inches, detail
Oil on canvas
private collection

10 See Valkenier, 1989, p. 186. E. Melikadze, a member of the neo-Stasovite team, would agree: "What visual art of another country in the nineteenth century can be compared to the art of ...Repin, Surikov or the *Peredvizhniki* in general? ...Maybe French art? ...Yes, we do give his due to the marvelous artist (Courbet), but the ideological depth of his work, his treatment of the life of contemporary France, cannot be compared with that of Repin."

11 By the late 1940s in Russia, Manet, Degas, Monet, Pissarro, Sisley and Renoir, among others, were placed on the "enemy list," but by this time, the die was cast in favor of their influence. See Valkenier, 1989, pp. 185-86.

12 Those who are most reminiscent of Soviet Impressionism include: Alfred Mitchell, Hanson Puthuff, Edgar Payne, William Wendt and Donna Schuster.

13 Dmitri V. Sarabianov, "Russian and Soviet Painting," 1977, p. 19.

CHAPTER TWO ★ PROTO-SOCIALIST REALISM: AKHRR (pages 9-11)

14 V. Lenin at the Second All-Russian Congress for Political Enlightenment, 1921, from M. Lifshits (editor): Lenin o kulture i iskusstve, Moscow, 1938, p. 243. Quoted in John E. Bowlt, "A Soviet School of Painting," 1976, p. 5.

15 A.V. Lunacharski, O teatre i dramaturgii. Izbr. stat., 1, Moscow, 1958, p. 737. As quoted in Catherine Cooke, "Socialist Realist Architecture: Theory and Practice," Bown and Taylor, ed., p. 89.

16 Declaraction of the Association of Artists of Revolutionary Russia *(AKhRR)*, 1922. From I.Matsa, et al, editors: ovetskoe iskusstvo za 15 let, Moscow-Leningrad, 1933, p. 345. Quoted in John E. Bowlt, "A Soviet School of Painting," 1976, p. 6.

17 Bown, 1991, p. 46.

18 Brodski was only an example to some. Others he so antagonized, that he was driven out of *AKhRR* in 1928.

19 Bown and Taylor, p. 5.

20 Dr. Gabriel Weisberg calls these artists Naturalists, though they in no way expressed themselves in a botanical or illustrative manner.

21 Most art unions were formed in the 1940s, but not fully organized until 1957 (at a point of apex for the style, Socialist Realism), which thereafter went into decline.

CHAPTER THREE ★ DEVELOPMENT OF SOVIET IMPRESSIONISM (pages 13-24)

22 Bird, p. 257.

23 R.C. Williams, Artists in Revolution, London, 1978, p. 188.

24 V.I. Lenin, "Party Organization and Party Literature," in his V.I. Lenin on Literature and Art, Moscow, 1978, p. 25.

25. Joseph Stalin, 1925.

26. Boris Groy's, The Total Art of Stalinism, Princeton University Press, 1992, p. 34.

27. Andrei Zhdanov, 1934 writers conference as transcribed in the Union's constitution, see Bown, 1991, p. 90. See David Elliott, "Engineers of the Human Soul: Painting in the Stalin Period," Soviet Socialist Realist Painting 1930s-1960s, 1992, p. 5, for Zhdanov's actual words: "First, we must know life in order to be able to depict it truthfully–not scholastically, lifelessly or merely as 'object reality'; we must depict reality in its revolutionary development."

28 Igor Grabar, 1934 writers conference.

29 Bird, p. 258.

30 Russian Art of the Avant-Garde, Theory and Criticism 1902-1934, ed. John Bowlt, New York, 1976, p. 266.

31 Matthew C. Bown, typescript on Soviet art, 1993, p. 18, author's possession.

32 Andrei Zhdanov in a speech given to noted musicians, 1948.

33 Bird, p. 263.

34 We do not mean pictures of large size, but rather of monumental or significant subjects to the Communist Party.

35 Matthew Bown, note to the author, September 1993.

36 As quoted by Elizabeth Valkenier, 1989, p. 178.

37 Matthew Bown in a note to the author, October 1993, wrote: "I would put it like this: in the 1920s, the *AHhRR* artists, as you say rejected Post-Impressionistic excess, as well as Picasso, etc. By the end of the 1930s, even the broken colour and lively surface of First-Wave French Impressionism could cause offense–not so much to artists as to critics and art bureaucrats."

38 Bowlt, 1976, p. 7.

39 Zhdanov died in 1949, but things really did not loosen up much until after the death of Stalin. Actually, artists were able to produce avant-garde pictures during this period, but certain criticisms of exhibitions, especially on Sergei Grigoriev's work, had a chilling effect on Soviet painting. Bown feels that the effect of Zhdanov was profound and even innovative to a degree: optimist post-war subjects, highly finished style and new genre of everyday life appeared.

40 Bown, 1991, p. 206.

CHAPTER FOUR ★ SOVIET WORKING-CLASS IMPRESSIONISM (pages 33-41)

41 Bowlt, 1976, p. 8.

42 Bown, 1991, p. 91.

43 Bown, 1991, p. 223.

44 Alexander Gerasimov's inaugural speech to the All-Russian Academy of Art, October, 1947.

45 Interview with the artist in St. Petersburg, June 1992.

46 Bird, 1987, p. 274.

CHAPTER FIVE ★ ART OF THE VIRGIN LANDS (pages 43-53)

47 "The Works of Soviet Artists in the Spring and Summer of 1954," Sketches & Pictures from the Virgin Land, Moscow, 1955, p. 5.

48 Sketches & Pictures from the Virgin Land, Moscow, 1955, p. 11.

49 Sketches & Pictures from the Virgin Land, Moscow, 1955, p. 5.

50 A. Zhdanov, Doklad o zhurnalakh, p. 38, as quoted in Alexander Kamenski, "Art in the Twilight of Totalitarianism," Bown and Taylor, ed., p. 158.

CHAPTER SIX ★ THE ART UNION: OFFICIAL ARTISTS (pages 55-57)

51 Alexander Sidorov, forward, Art Under Stalin, p. 12.

52 Zhdanov quoting Stalin at writers conference, 1934. See Elliott, 1992, p. 5.

53 Interview with Engels Kozlov in St. Petersburg, 22 February 1993.

54 Bown, 1991, p. 227.

55 Bown, 1991, p. 226.

56 Bown, 1991, p. 176.

CHAPTER SEVEN ★ UNOFFICIAL, OFFICIAL ART (pages 59-60)

57 Elliott, 1992, p. 13.

58 The term implies the layering of different types of pigment, viz. scumble, impasto, glaze, etc., in order to arrive at the quality of representation or executive finish required for the commission.

59 It is true that official Soviet artists were often tendentious toward portraying the Party in the best light. This area of all the "official" paradigms suited Soviet art well, especially as seen in portraits and conversation pieces.

CONCLUSION (pages 63-64)

60 The author has painted the scene with "pink powder" and an abundance of nostalgia. Most Union artists reminisce about the "good old days" when they had power and privilege. The author does not believe that at the hegemony of power in their hands was at all good or preferable to the Western model. But it had certain strengths in organization, philosophy and aesthetic, which we can learn from.

CHRONOLOGY (pages 67-77)

61 Bown, 1991, p. 42.

62 Bown, 1991, pp. 46-47.

63 Bown, 1991, p. 89.

64 Katsman letter to Brodski dated 3 August 1934. Quoted in V. Manin, "Istoriya iz Istorii," *Tvorchestvo*, 7/1989, p. 12. See Bown, 1991, p. 93.

65 Bown, p. 206.

66 Bown, p. 174.

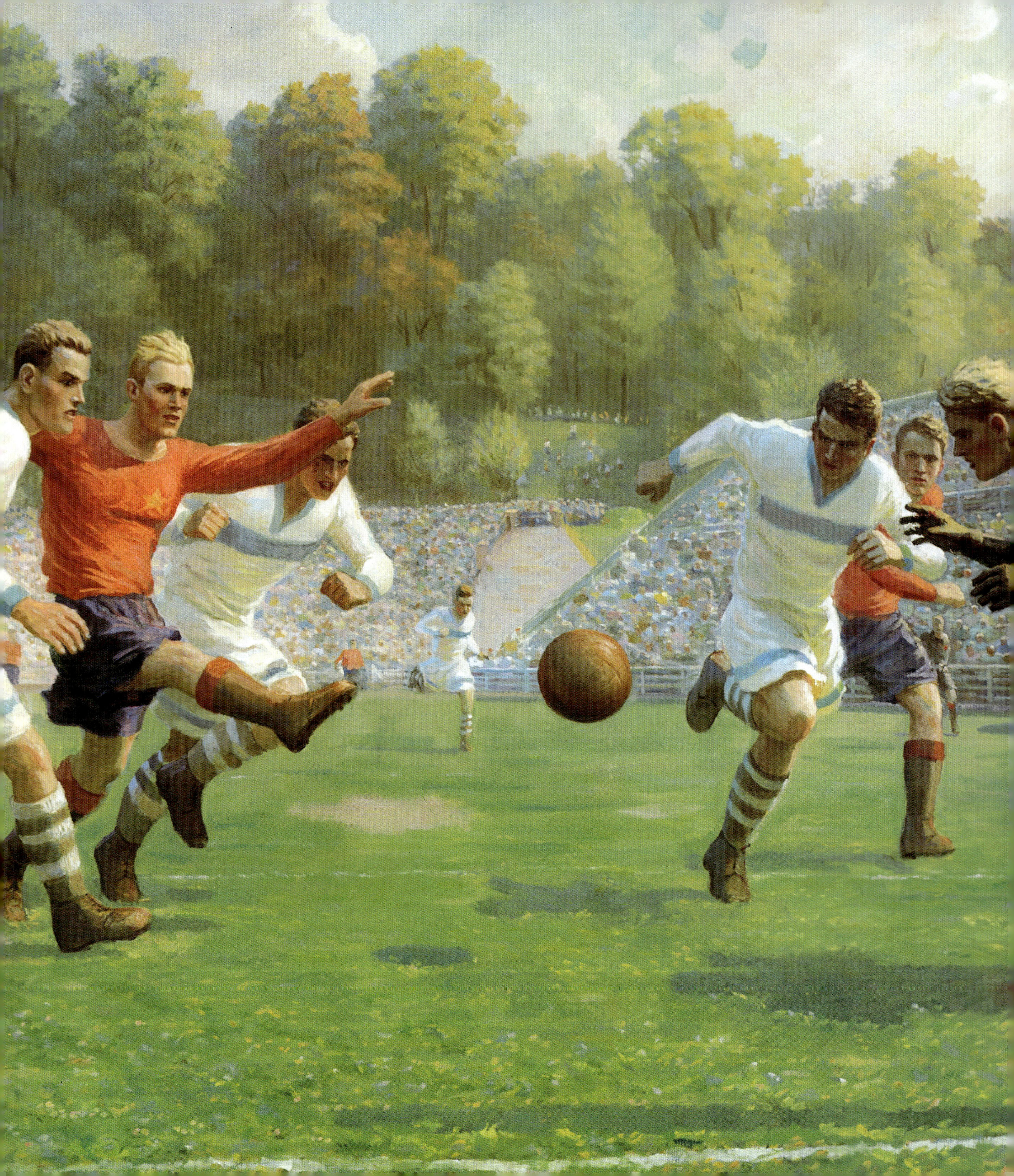

BIBLIOGRAPHY

SELECTED TITLES, ENGLISH LANGUAGE

Anonymous, "The Works of Soviet Artists in the Spring and Summer of 1954," Sketches & Pictures from the Virgin Land, The Soviet Artist, Moscow, 1955.

Anonymous, "Fifty Years of Painting USSR," National Museum of Modern Art, Tokyo. Exhibition catalogue, October 28-December 10, 1967, sixty-eight pieces from 1930s-1960s.

Beletsky, P. and Vladich, L., Ukrainian Painting, translated by Yuri Pamfilov, Leningrad, Aurora Art Publishers, 1976.

Bird, Alan, A History of Russian Painting, Oxford, Phaidon, 1987.

Bown, Matthew Cullerne, Contemporary Russian Art, Oxford, Phaidon, 1989.

Bown, Matthew Cullerne, Art Under Stalin, Oxford, Phaidon, 1991.

Bown, Matthew Cullerne, "How is the Empire? Painting in the Non-Russian Republics," Soviet Socialist Realist Painting: 1930s-1960s, Museum of Modern Art, Oxford, 1992, pp. 19-27.

Bown, Matthew Cullerne, Taylor, Brandon (editors), Art of the Soviets: Painting, Sculpture and Architecture in a One-Party State, 1917-1992, Manchester University Press, 1993.

Bowlt, John E. (editor), Russian Art of the Avant-Garde, Theory and Criticism, New York, Viking Press, 1986.

Chen, Jack, Soviet Art and Artists, London, Chiswick Press, 1944.

Elliott, David, New Worlds: Russian Art and Society 1900-37, London, Thames and Hudson, 1986).

Elliott, David, "Engineers of the Human Soul: Painting of the Stalin Period," Soviet Socialist Realist Painting: 1930s-1960s, Museum of Modern Art, Oxford, 1992, pp. 5-17.

Golomstock, Igor, Totalitarian Art, London, Collins Harvill, 1990.

Groys, Boris, The Total Art of Stalinism: Avant-Garde, Aesthetic Dictatorship and Beyond, translated by Charles Rougle, Princeton, New Jersey, Princeton University Press, 1992.

Günther, H. (editor), The Culture of the Stalin Period, London, 1990.

James, C.V., Soviet Socialist Realism: Origins and Theory, London, Macmillan, 1973.

Jelagin, J., Taming of the Arts, translated by N. Wreden, New York, Dutton, 1951.

Johnson, P. and Labedz, L., Khrushchev and the Arts, Cambridge Massachusetts, MIT, 1965.

111. ***Soccer Football Match*** 1949
Andrei Korotkov (Kiev, b. 1902)
45-1/4 x 72 inches, detail
Oil on canvas mounted
private collection

Kemenov, Vladimir, The USSR Academy of Arts, Leningrad, Aurora Art Publishers, 1982.

Lehmann-Haupt, Hellmut, Art under a Dictatorship, New York, Oxford University Press, 1954.

Lindey, Christine, Art in the Cold War, London, Herbert Press, 1990.

London, K., The Seven Soviet Arts, London, Faber and Faber, 1937.

Roberts, N. (editor), The Quest for Self-Expression: Painting in Moscow and Leningrad 1965-1990, exhibition catalogue, Columbus, 1990.

Rubissow, Helen, The Art of Russia, New York, Philosophical Library, 1946.

Sarabianov, Dmitri V. (introduction), Korotkevich, E. Yu., and Uspenskaia (catalogue), and Bowlt, John E., (translation, foreword and bibliography), Russian and Soviet Painting: An Exhibition from the Museums of the USSR presented at the Metropolitan Museum of Art, New York and the Fine Arts Museums of San Francisco, New York, Rizzoli, 1977.

Swanson, Vern G., Russian & Soviet Realism: Hidden Treasures 1930-1980, exhibition catalogue, Minneapolis, Overland Fine Arts, 1993, 26 pages.

Taylor, Brandon, Art and Literature under the Bolsheviks: Cultural Policy and Practice in the Soviet Union, Volume I, 1991, Volume II, 1992.

Valkenier, Elizabeth, Russian Realist Art, Columbia University Press, 1989.

112. ***Young Pioneer at the Door*** 1955
Fedor Vasilievich Shapaev
58-1/2 x 27 inches,
Oil on canvas
private collection

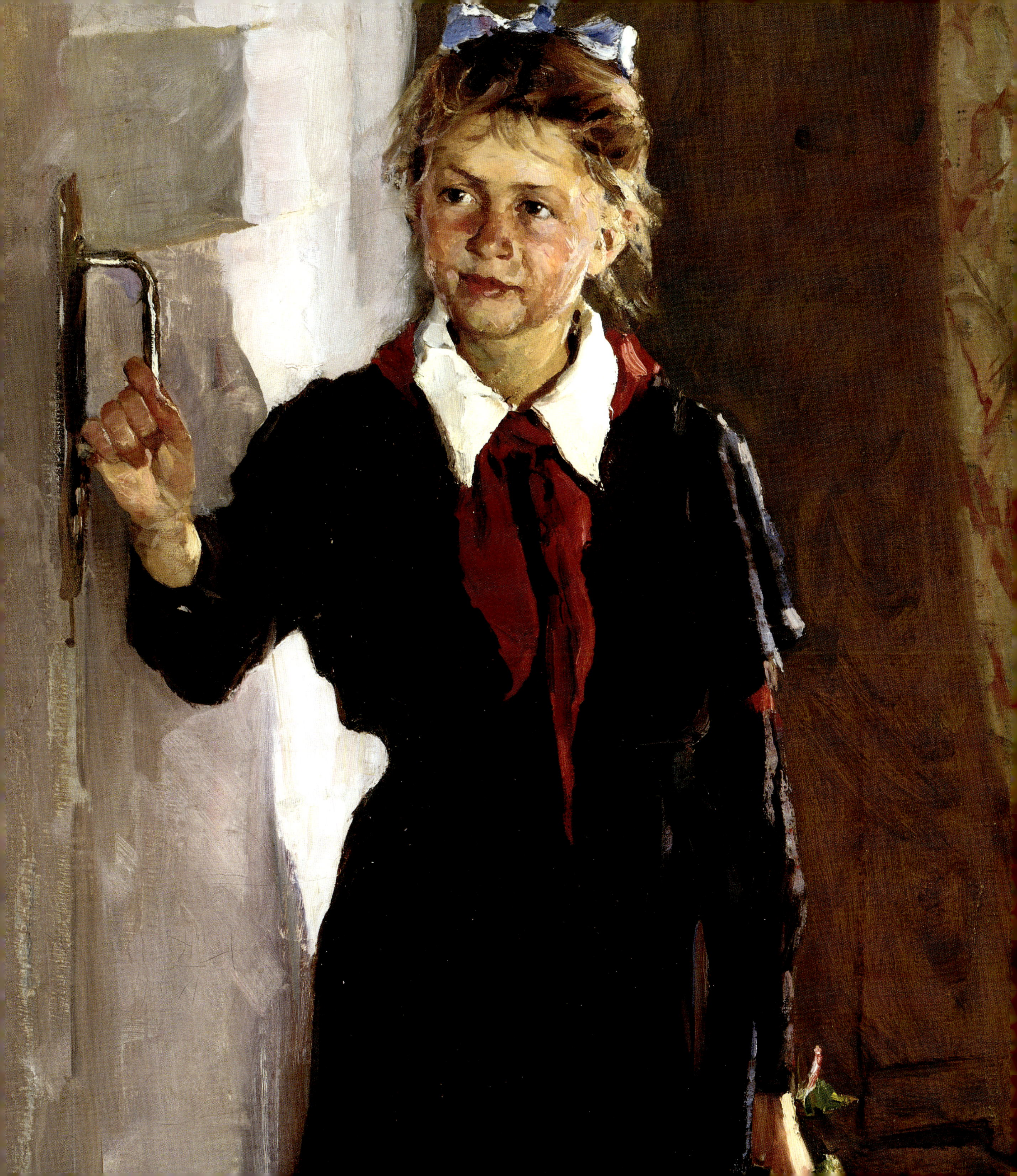

Борис Михайлович Лавренко Елан
Леонова Анатолий Павлович Левити
Олег Леонидович Ломакин Паве
Георгиевич Марков Георги
Степанович Мелихов Азир Мизито
Евгений Мосин Василий Кириллови
Нечитайло Владимир Ильич Некрасо
Анатолий Юрьевич Никич
Кириличевский Николай Ипполитови
Обрынба Николай Васильеви
Овчинников Владимир Петров В.М
Петров-Маслаков Григорий Петругин
Родионов Юрий Станиславови
Подляски Игорь Раздрогин Эри
Ребанэ Семён Аронович Ротницки
Зоя Самойленко Фёдор Шапае
Валентина Шебашева Дмитри
Иванович Шмелёв Константи
Шурупов Вениамин Михайлови
Сибирский Владимир Максимови

Index

INDEX

INDEX

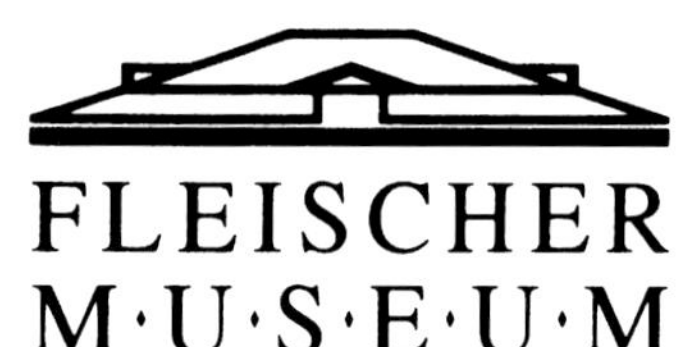
FLEISCHER
M·U·S·E·U·M